Little Queen

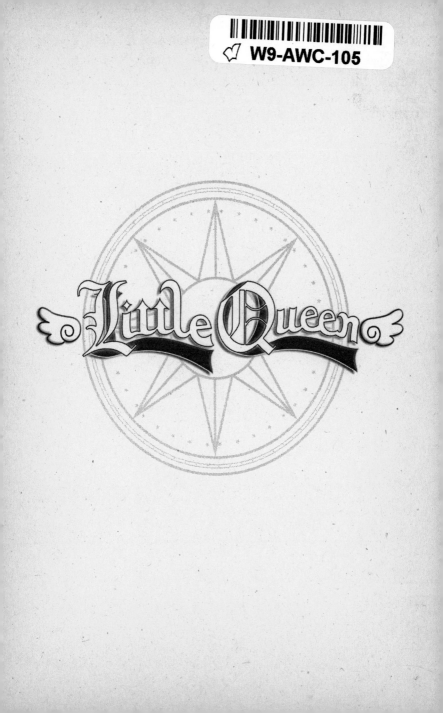

Little Queen Vol. 1
Created by Yeon-Joo Kim

Translation - Jennifer Hahm
English Adaptation - Patrick Neighly
Retouch and Lettering - Jihye "Sophia" Hong
Cover Design - Louis Csontos

Editor - Bryce P. Coleman
Digital Imaging Manager - Chris Buford
Pre-Production Supervisor - Erika Terriquez
Art Director - Anne Marie Horne
Production Manager - Elisabeth Brizzi
Managing Editor - Vy Nguyen
VP of Production - Ron Klamert
Editor-in-Chief - Rob Tokar
Publisher - Mike Kiley
President and C.O.O. - John Parker
C.E.O. and Chief Creative Officer - Stuart Levy

A **TOKYOPOP** Manga

TOKYOPOP Inc.
5900 Wilshire Blvd. Suite 2000
Los Angeles, CA 90036

E-mail: info@TOKYOPOP.com
Come visit us online at www.TOKYOPOP.com

ISBN: 1-59816-639-5

First TOKYOPOP printing: December 2006

10 9 8 7 6 5 4 3 2 1

Printed in the USA

Volume 1
Yeon-Joo Kim

HAMBURG // LONDON // LOS ANGELES // TOKYO

CONTENTS

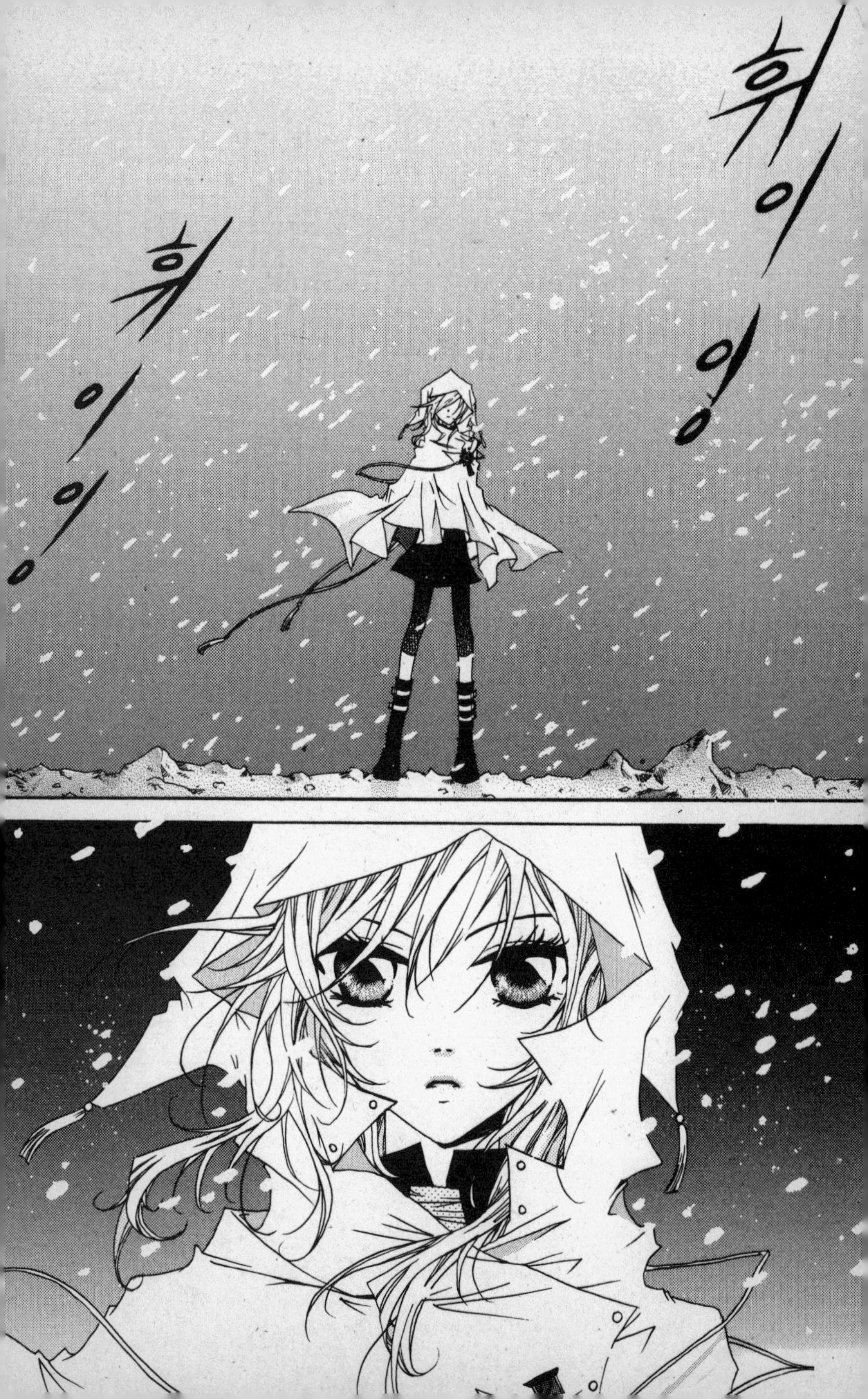
휘이잉
후이잉

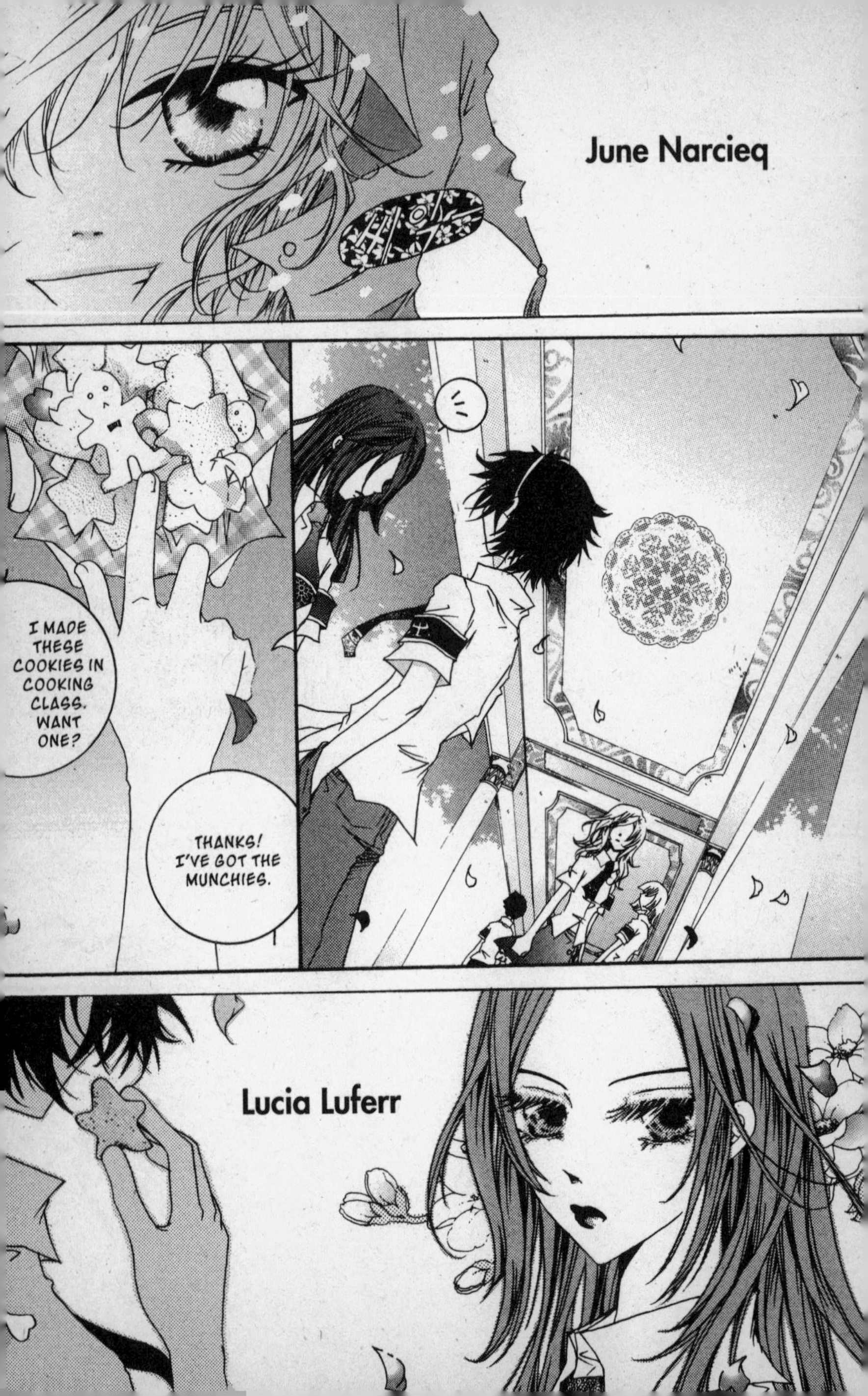
June Narcieq
I MADE THESE COOKIES IN COOKING CLASS. WANT ONE?
THANKS! I'VE GOT THE MUNCHIES.
Lucia Luferr

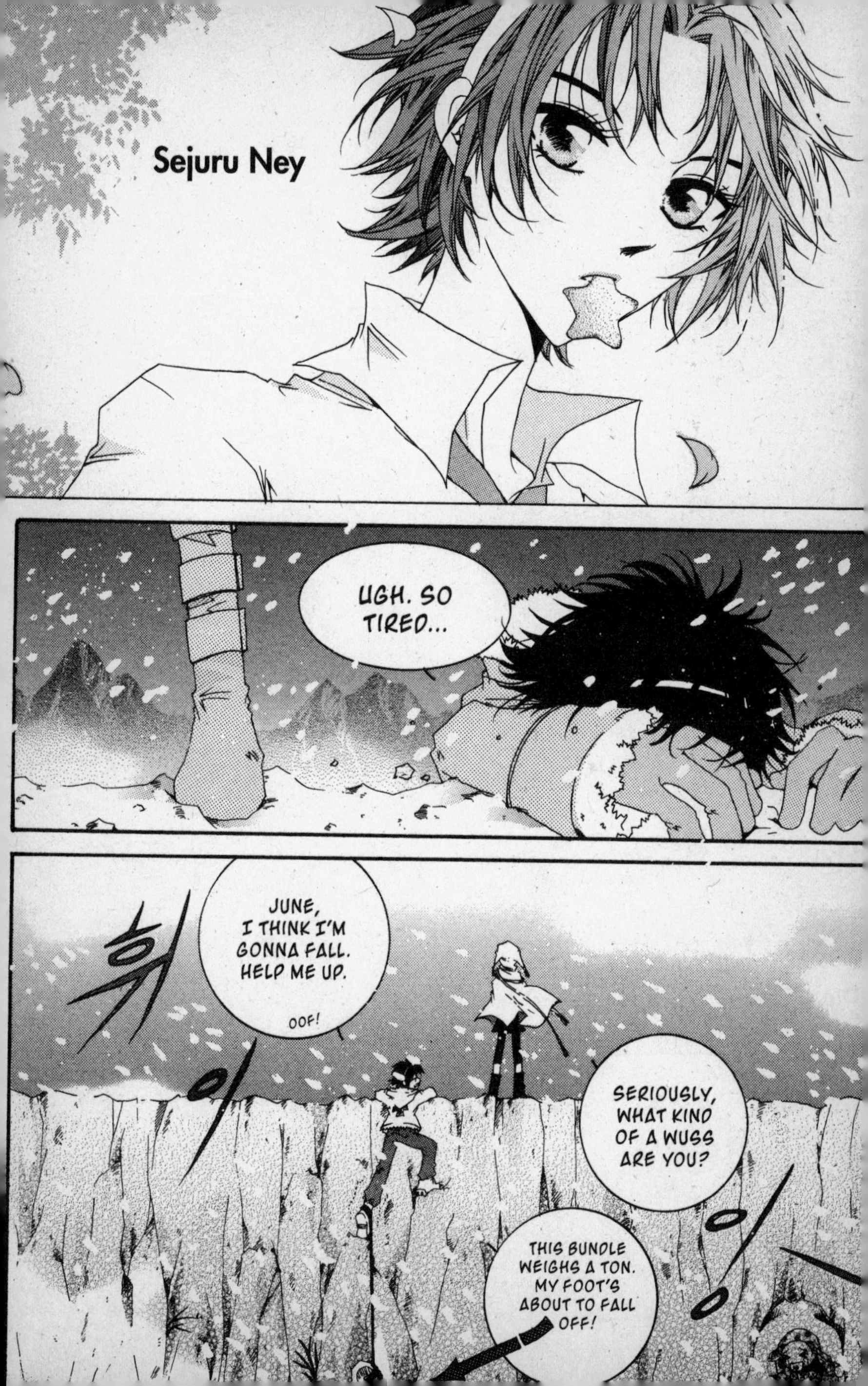
Sejuru Ney
UGH. SO TIRED...
JUNE, I THINK I'M GONNA FALL. HELP ME UP.
OOF!
SERIOUSLY, WHAT KIND OF A WUSS ARE YOU?
THIS BUNDLE WEIGHS A TON. MY FOOT'S ABOUT TO FALL OFF!

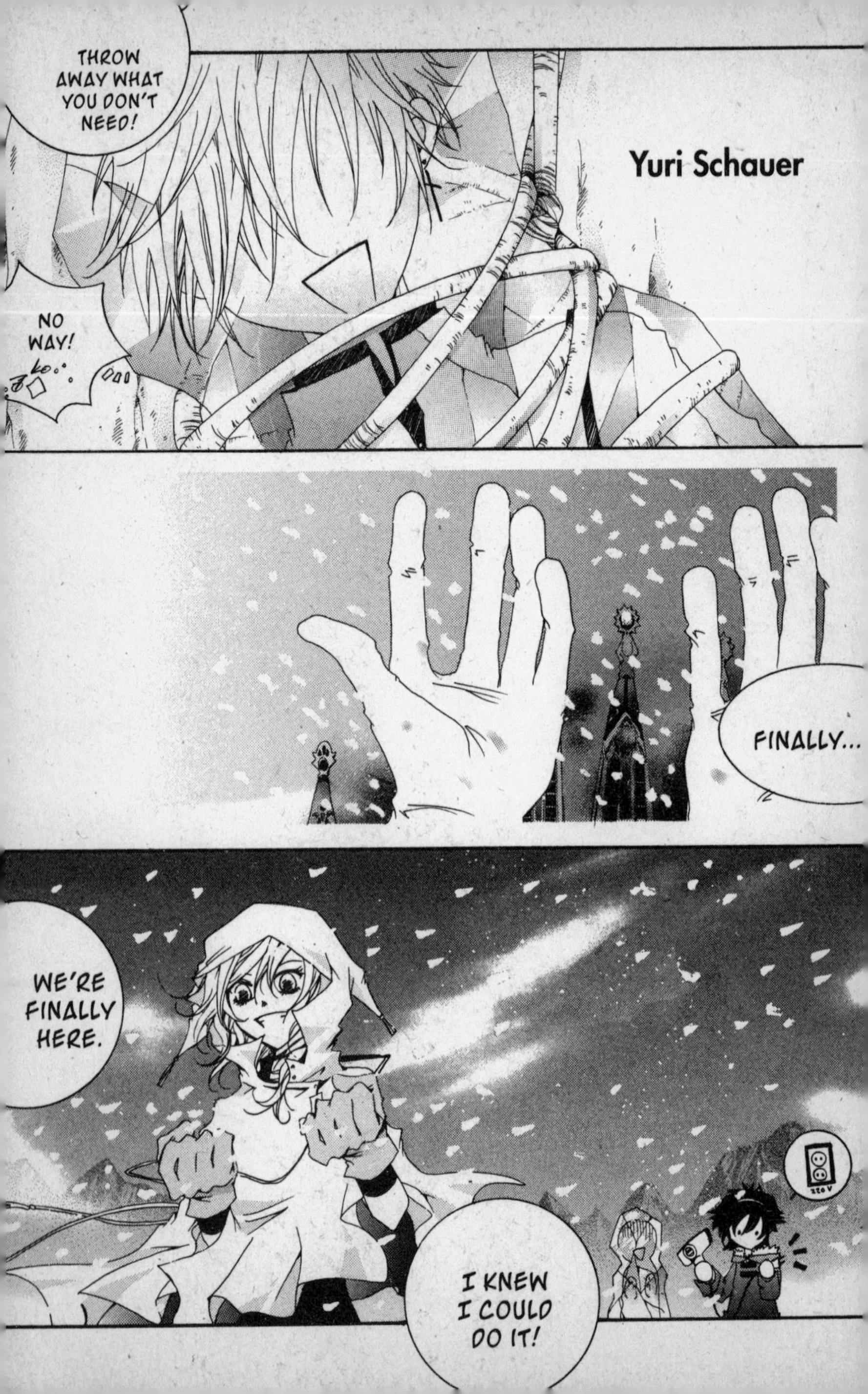
THROW AWAY WHAT YOU DON'T NEED!
Yuri Schauer
NO WAY!
FINALLY...
WE'RE FINALLY HERE.
I KNEW I COULD DO IT!

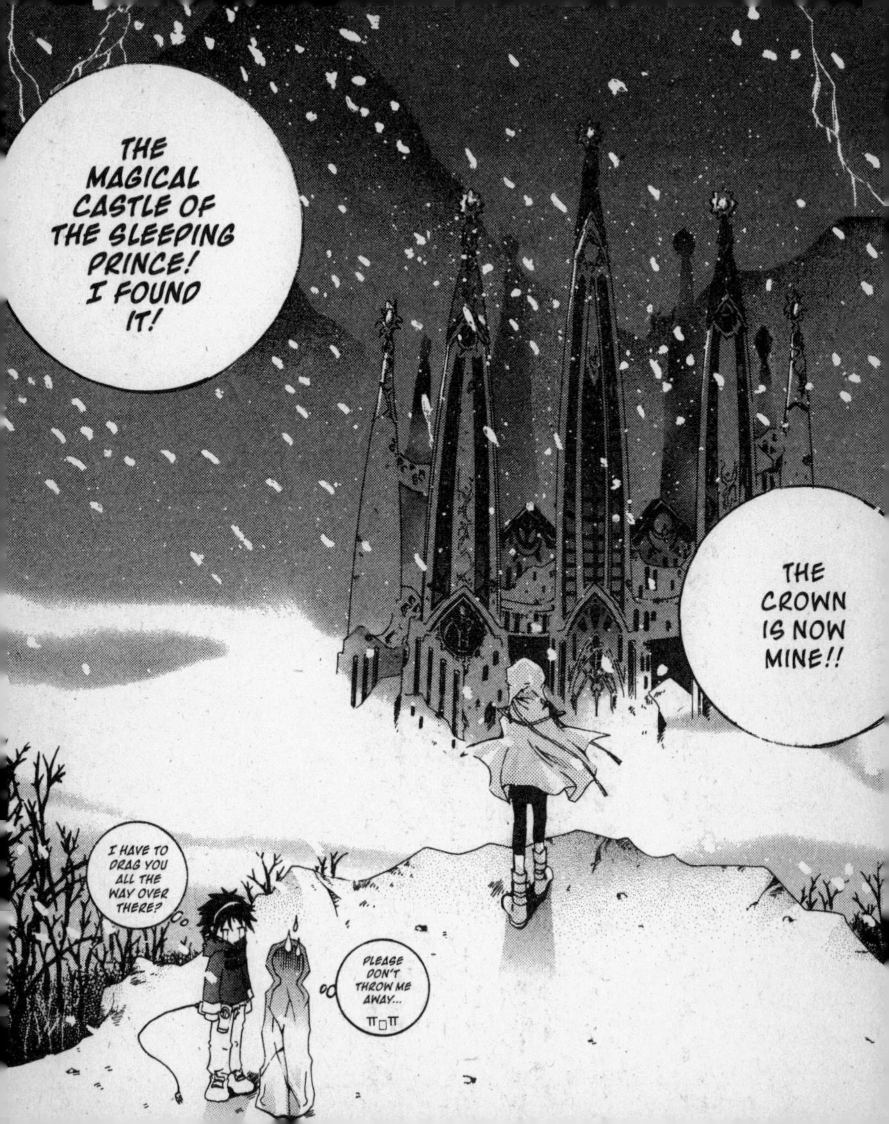
THE CROWN IS NOW MINE!!
THE MAGICAL CASTLE OF THE SLEEPING PRINCE! I FOUND IT!
PLEASE DON'T THROW ME AWAY... ╥□╥
I HAVE TO DRAG YOU ALL THE WAY OVER THERE?

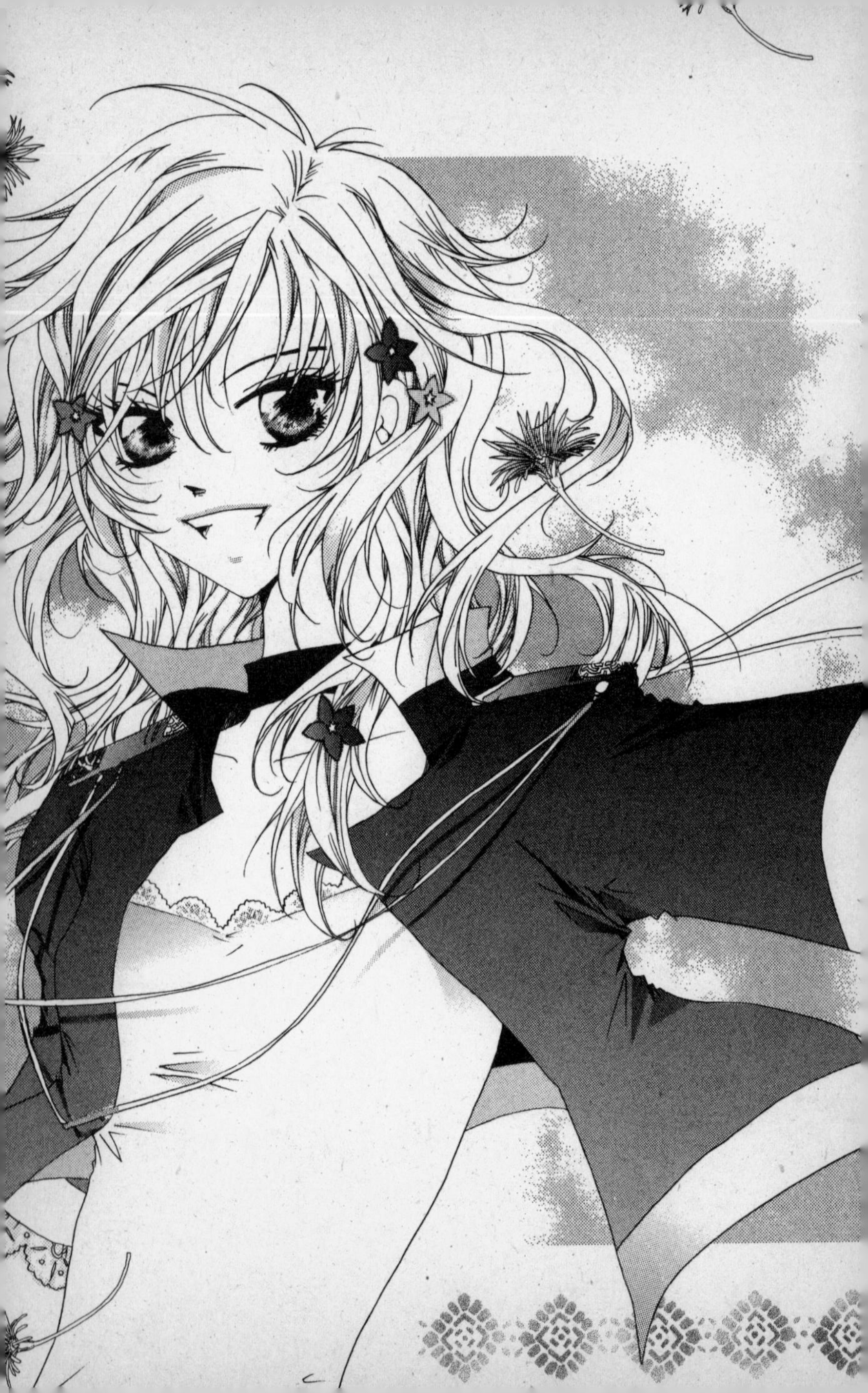

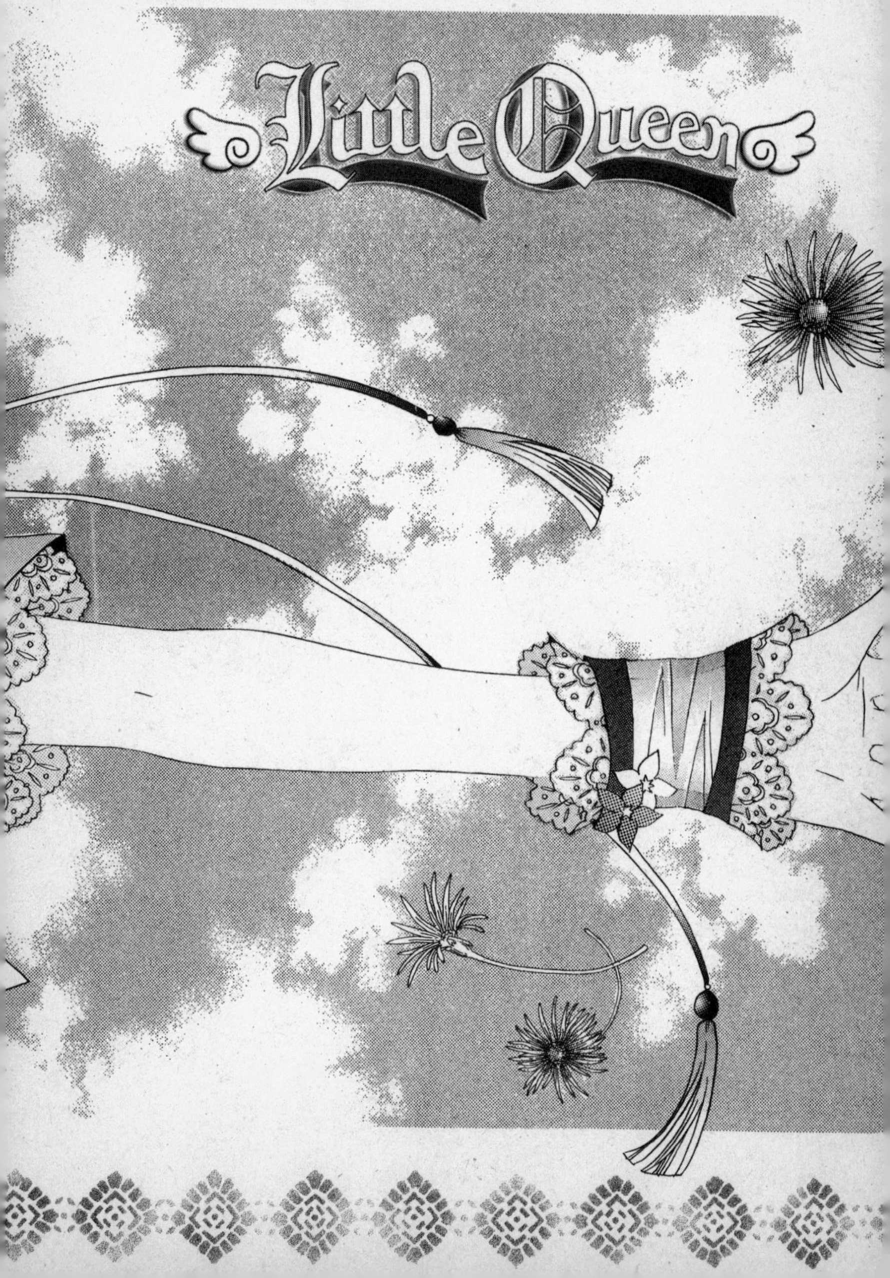
Little Queen

My Dream is Small
That's Why I'm Happy

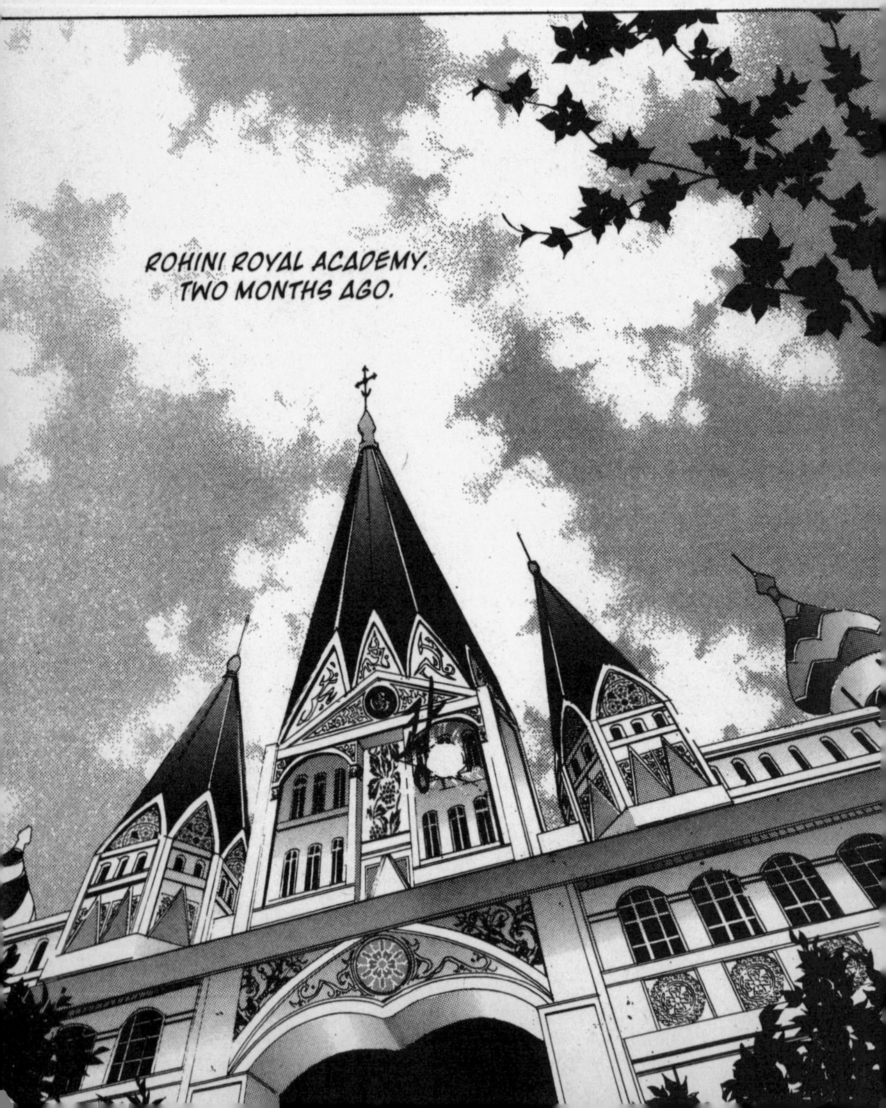
ROHINI ROYAL ACADEMY. TWO MONTHS AGO.

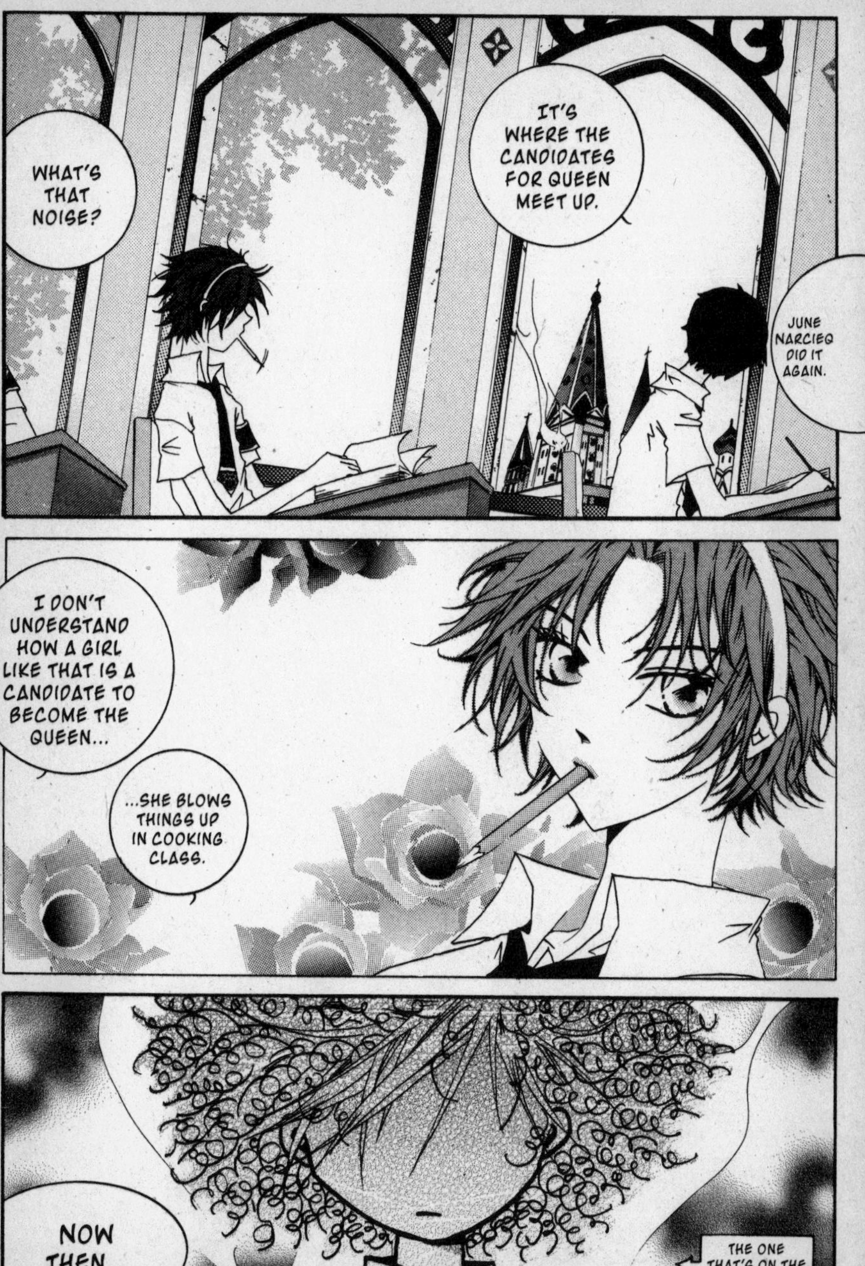
WHAT'S THAT NOISE?
IT'S WHERE THE CANDIDATES FOR QUEEN MEET UP.
JUNE NARCIEQ DID IT AGAIN.
I DON'T UNDERSTAND HOW A GIRL LIKE THAT IS A CANDIDATE TO BECOME THE QUEEN...
...SHE BLOWS THINGS UP IN COOKING CLASS.
NOW THEN...
THE ONE THAT'S ON THE COVER.

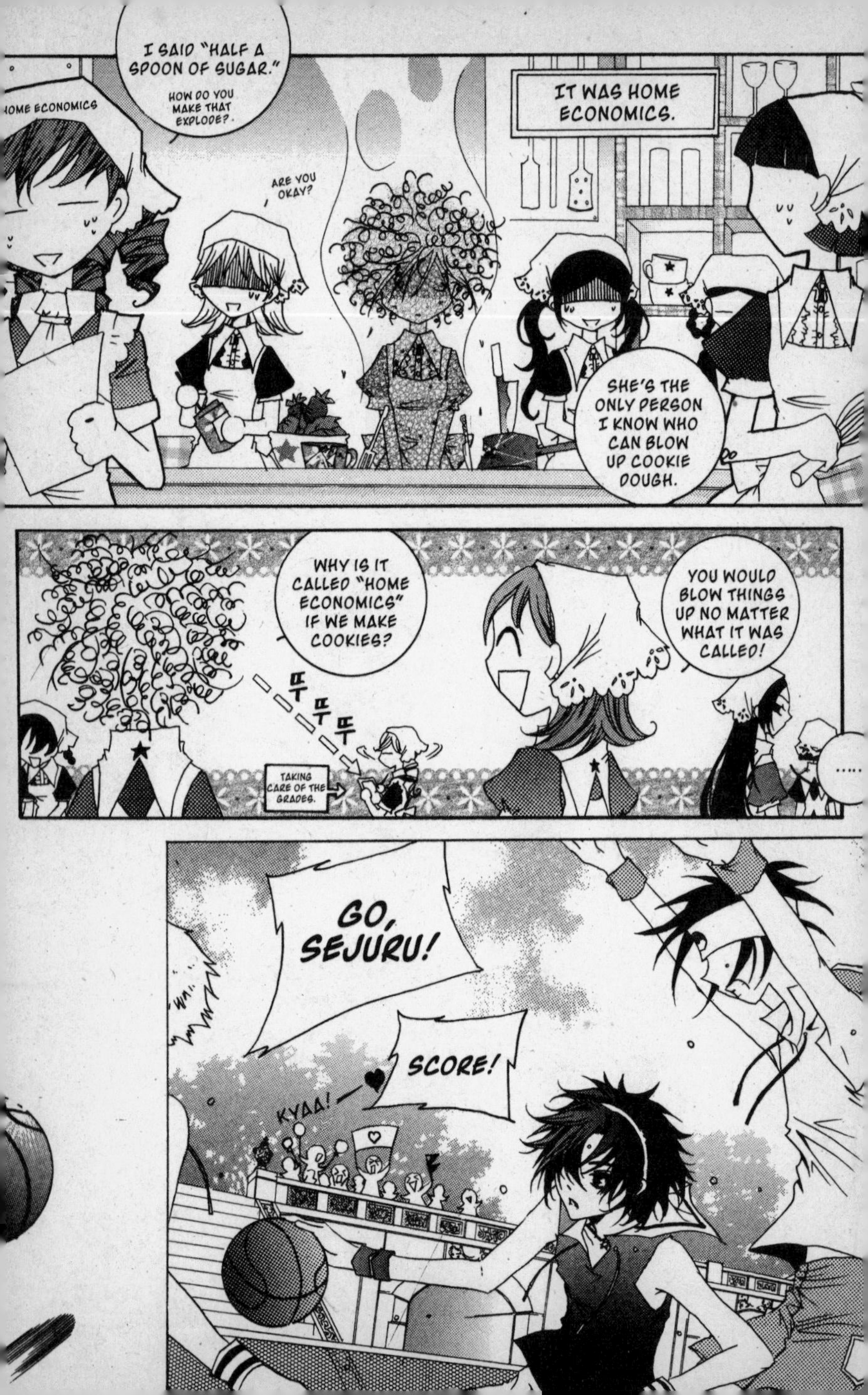
HOME ECONOMICS
I SAID "HALF A SPOON OF SUGAR."
HOW DO YOU MAKE THAT EXPLODE?
ARE YOU OKAY?
IT WAS HOME ECONOMICS.
SHE'S THE ONLY PERSON I KNOW WHO CAN BLOW UP COOKIE DOUGH.
WHY IS IT CALLED "HOME ECONOMICS" IF WE MAKE COOKIES?
뚜 뚜 뚜
TAKING CARE OF THE GRADES.
YOU WOULD BLOW THINGS UP NO MATTER WHAT IT WAS CALLED!
.....
GO, SEJURU!
SCORE!
KYAA!

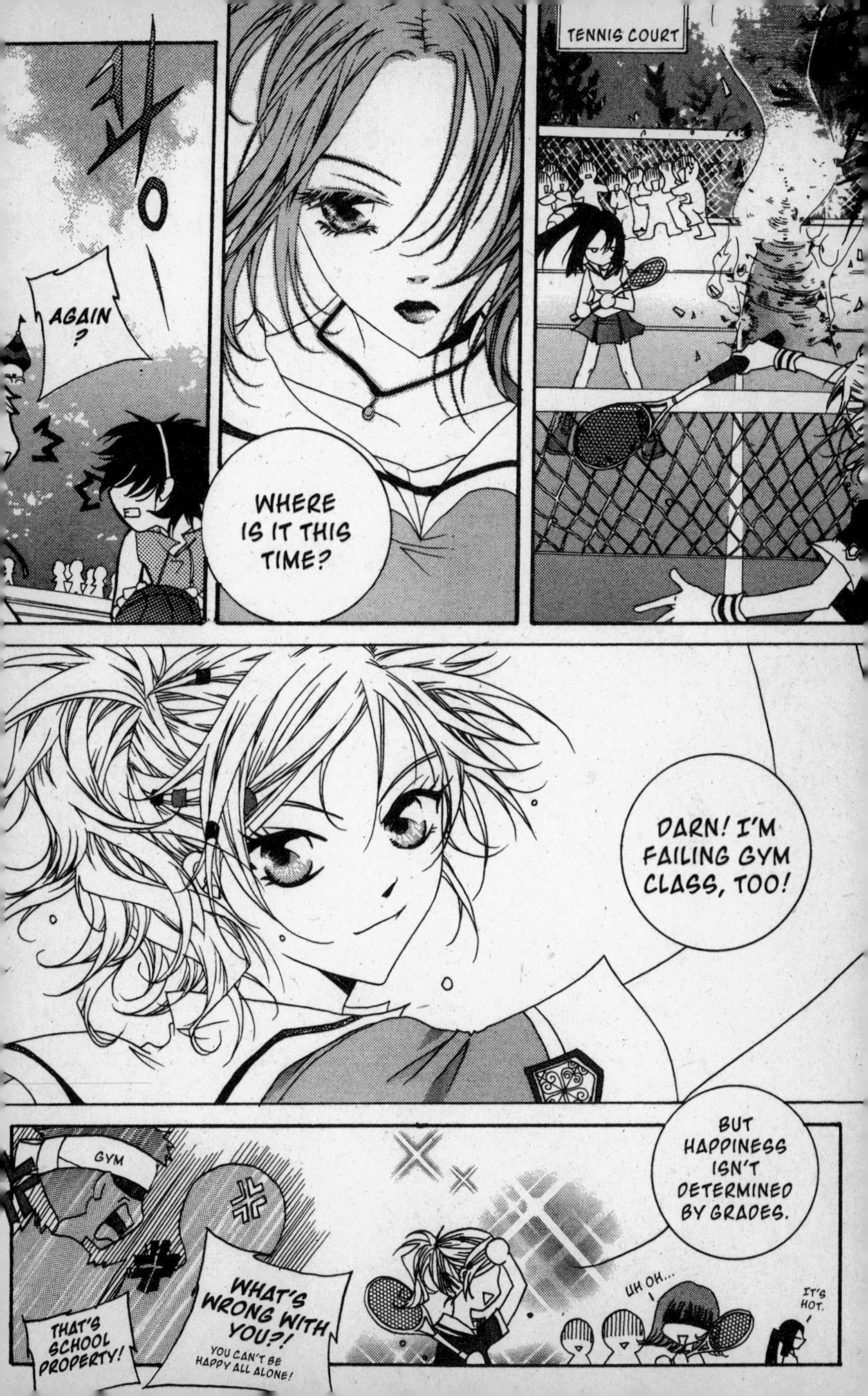
AGAIN?
WHERE IS IT THIS TIME?
TENNIS COURT
DARN! I'M FAILING GYM CLASS, TOO!
BUT HAPPINESS ISN'T DETERMINED BY GRADES.
GYM
THAT'S SCHOOL PROPERTY!
WHAT'S WRONG WITH YOU?!
YOU CAN'T BE HAPPY ALL ALONE!
UH OH...
IT'S HOT.

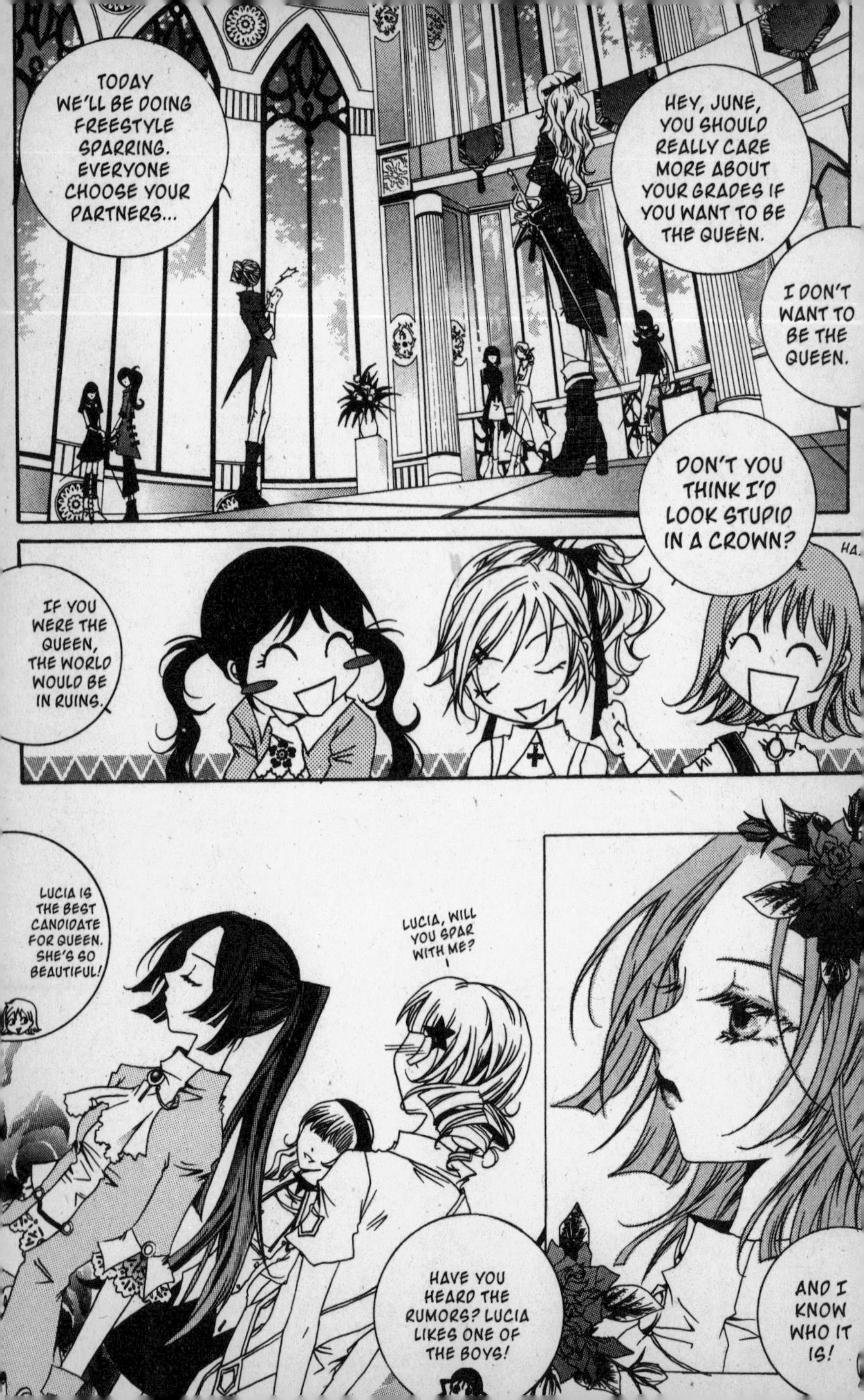
TODAY WE'LL BE DOING FREESTYLE SPARRING. EVERYONE CHOOSE YOUR PARTNERS...
HEY, JUNE, YOU SHOULD REALLY CARE MORE ABOUT YOUR GRADES IF YOU WANT TO BE THE QUEEN.
I DON'T WANT TO BE THE QUEEN.
DON'T YOU THINK I'D LOOK STUPID IN A CROWN?
HA.
IF YOU WERE THE QUEEN, THE WORLD WOULD BE IN RUINS.
LUCIA IS THE BEST CANDIDATE FOR QUEEN. SHE'S SO BEAUTIFUL!
LUCIA, WILL YOU SPAR WITH ME?
HAVE YOU HEARD THE RUMORS? LUCIA LIKES ONE OF THE BOYS!
AND I KNOW WHO IT IS!

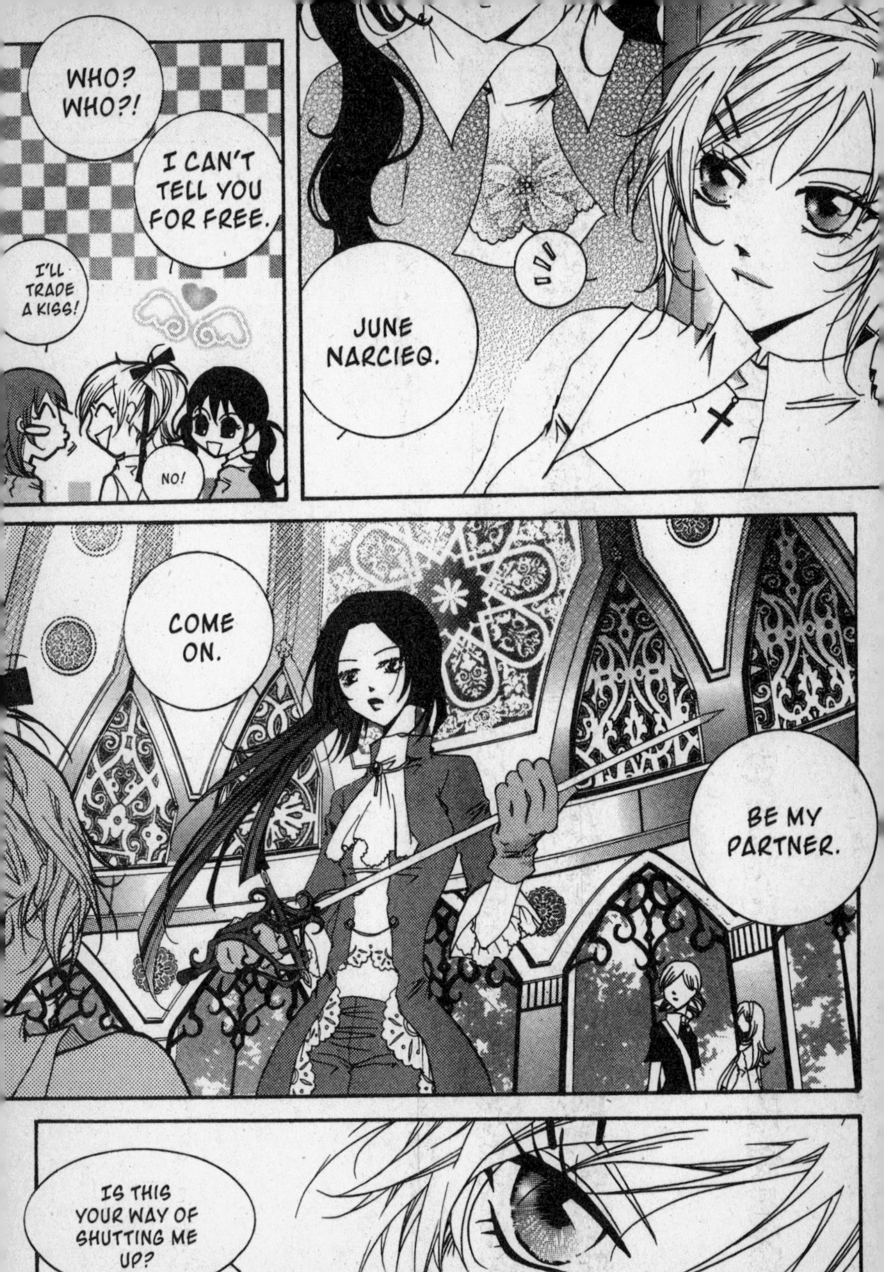
WHO? WHO?!
I CAN'T TELL YOU FOR FREE.
I'LL TRADE A KISS!
NO!
JUNE NARCIEQ.
!!
COME ON.
BE MY PARTNER.
IS THIS YOUR WAY OF SHUTTING ME UP?

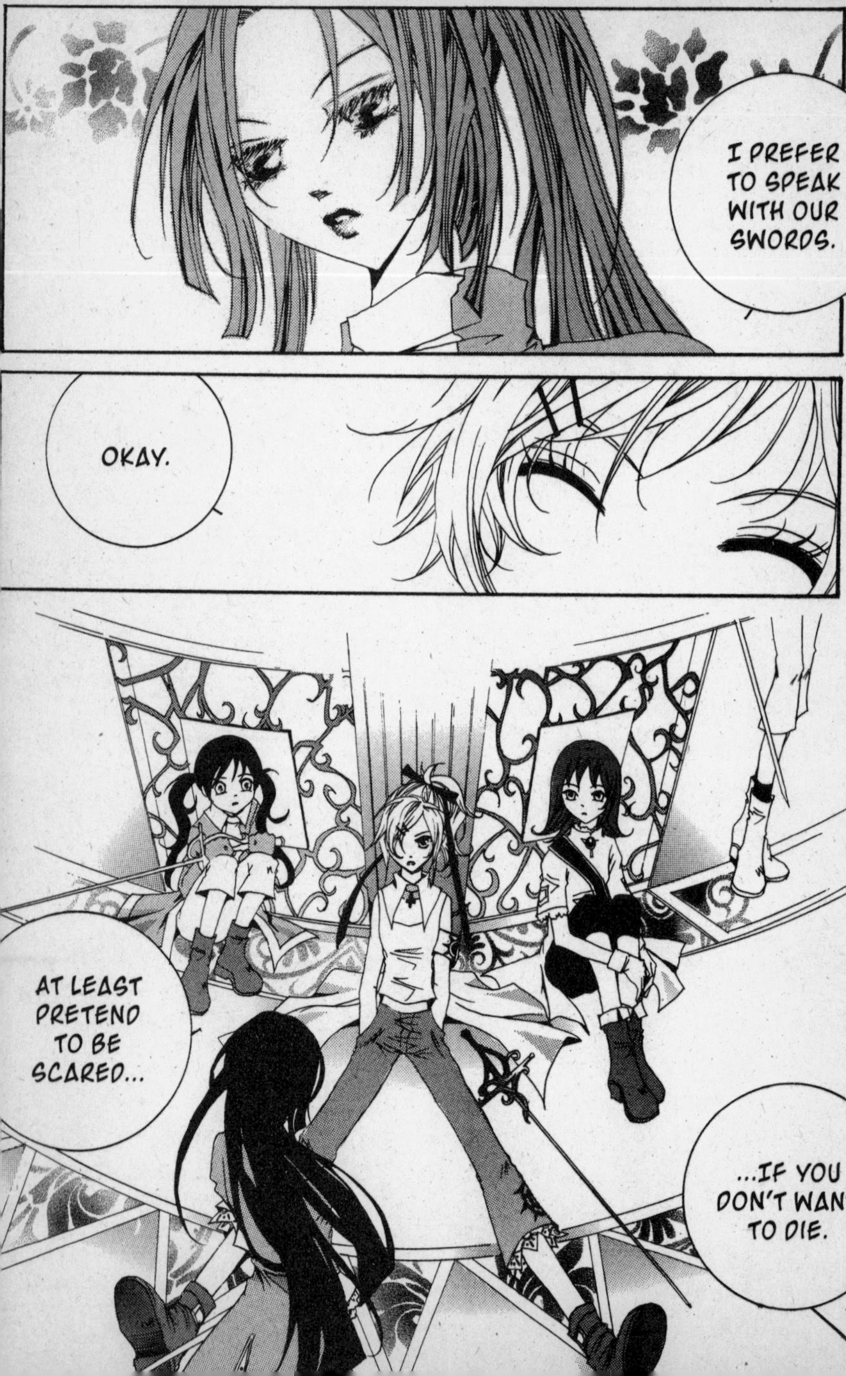
I PREFER TO SPEAK WITH OUR SWORDS.
OKAY.
AT LEAST PRETEND TO BE SCARED...
...IF YOU DON'T WANT TO DIE.

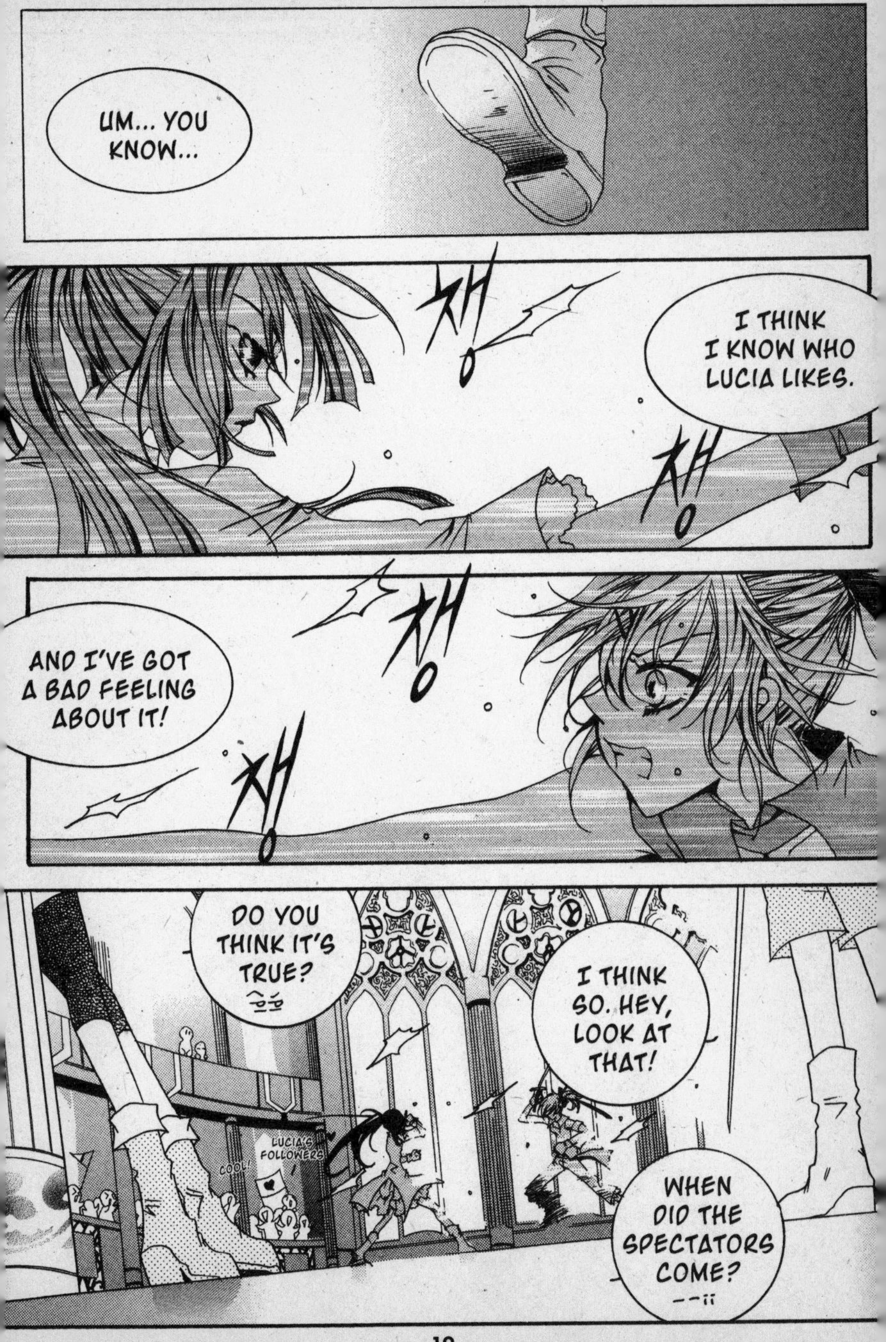
UM... YOU KNOW...
I THINK I KNOW WHO LUCIA LIKES.
AND I'VE GOT A BAD FEELING ABOUT IT!
DO YOU THINK IT'S TRUE?
I THINK SO. HEY, LOOK AT THAT!
LUCIA'S FOLLOWERS
COOL!
WHEN DID THE SPECTATORS COME?

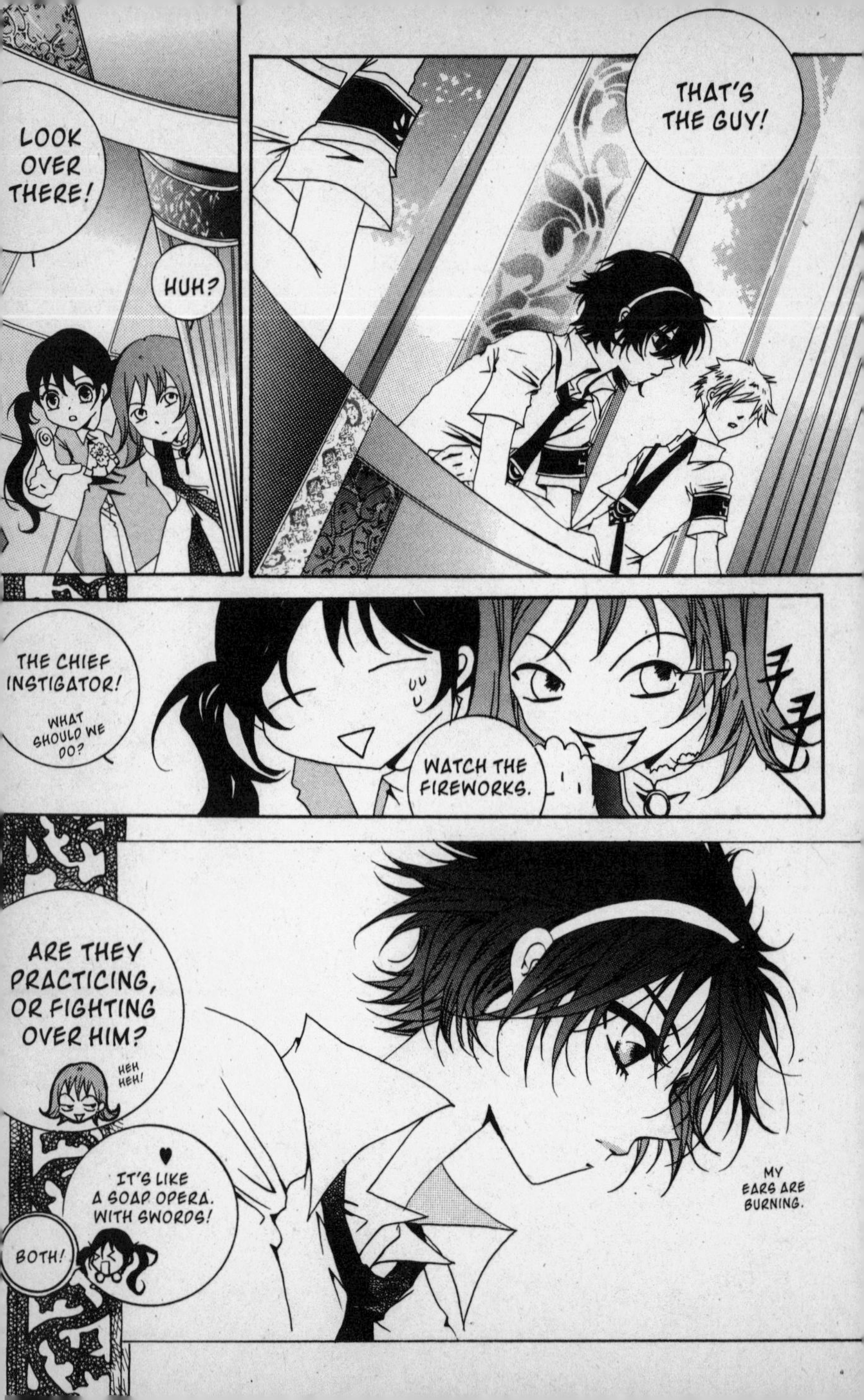
LOOK OVER THERE!
HUH?
THAT'S THE GUY!
THE CHIEF INSTIGATOR!
WHAT SHOULD WE DO?
WATCH THE FIREWORKS.
ARE THEY PRACTICING, OR FIGHTING OVER HIM?
HEH HEH!
IT'S LIKE A SOAP OPERA. WITH SWORDS!
BOTH!
MY EARS ARE BURNING.

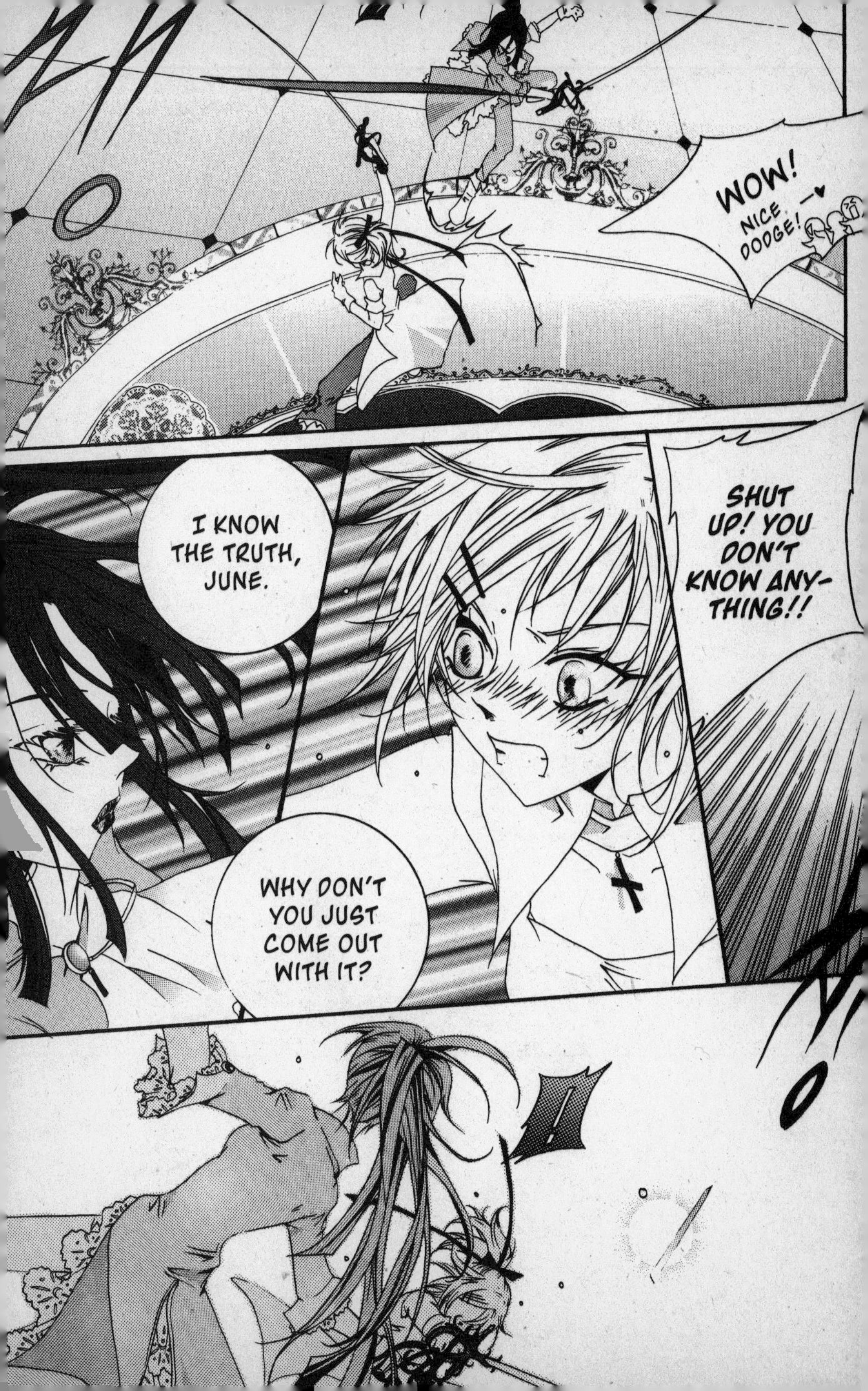
ZA
WOW!
NICE DOOGE!
I KNOW THE TRUTH, JUNE.
SHUT UP! YOU DON'T KNOW ANY-THING!!
WHY DON'T YOU JUST COME OUT WITH IT?
!

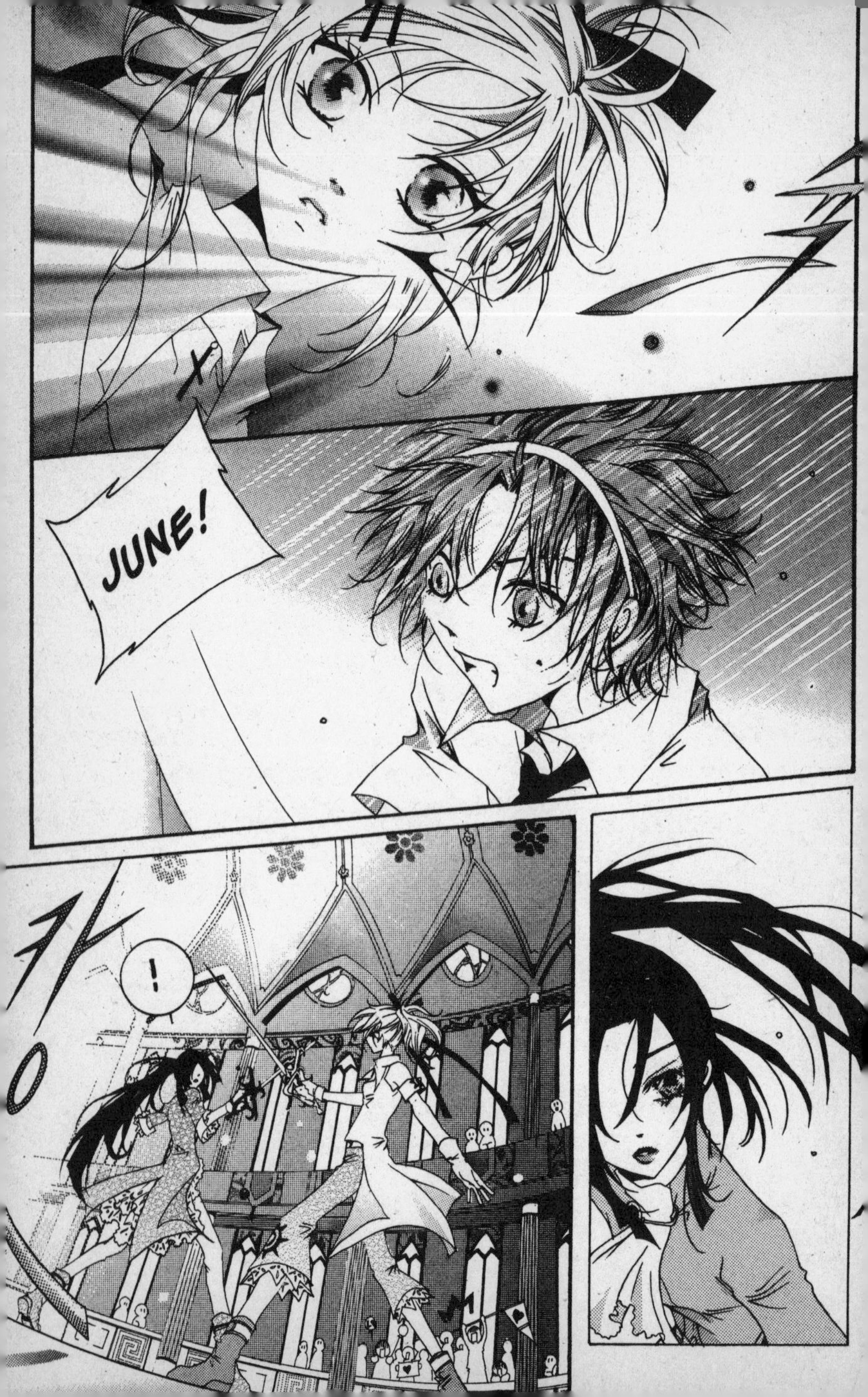
JUNE!
!

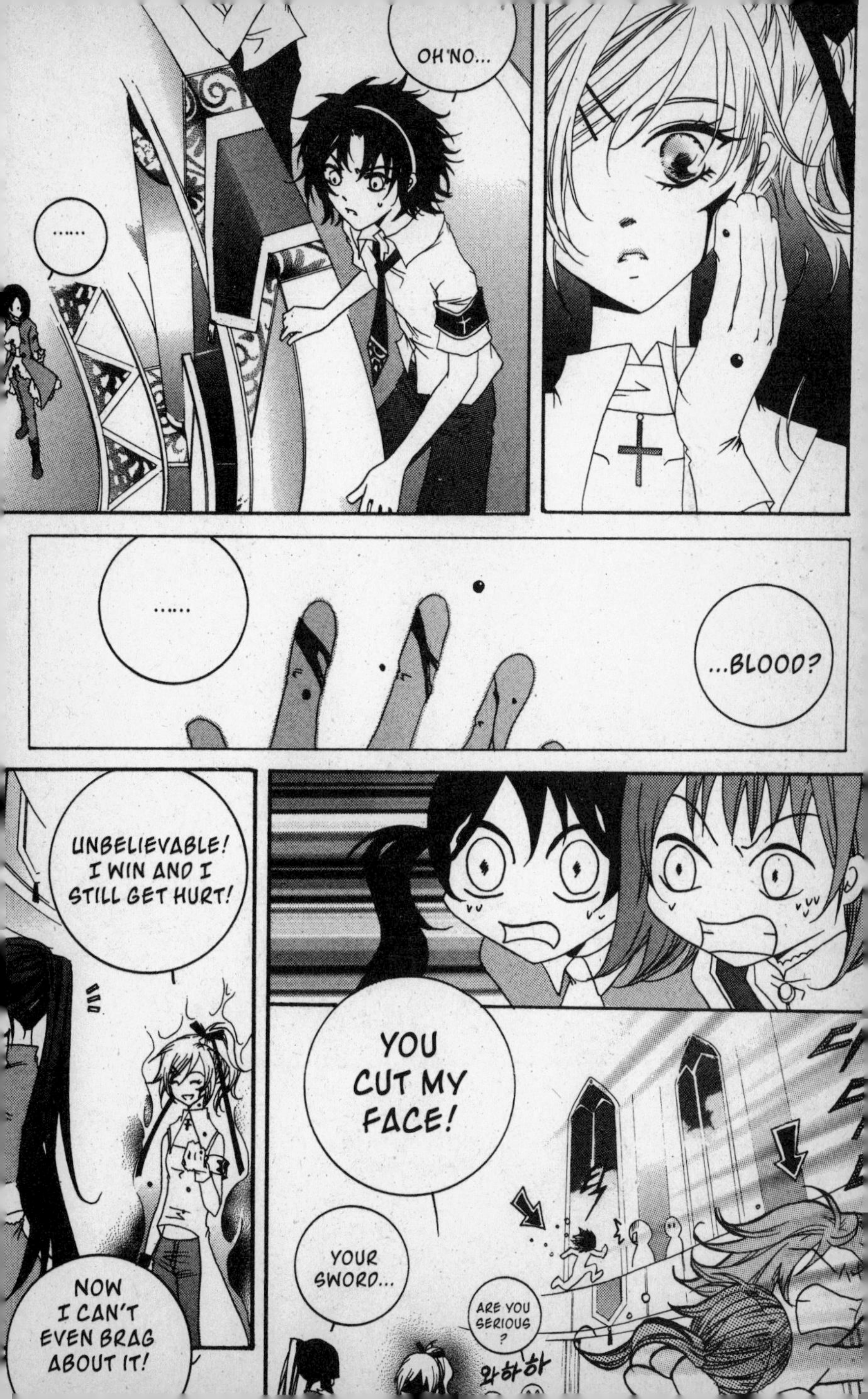
OH'NO...
......
...BLOOD?
......
YOU CUT MY FACE!
YOUR SWORD...
ARE YOU SERIOUS?
와하하
UNBELIEVABLE! I WIN AND I STILL GET HURT!
NOW I CAN'T EVEN BRAG ABOUT IT!

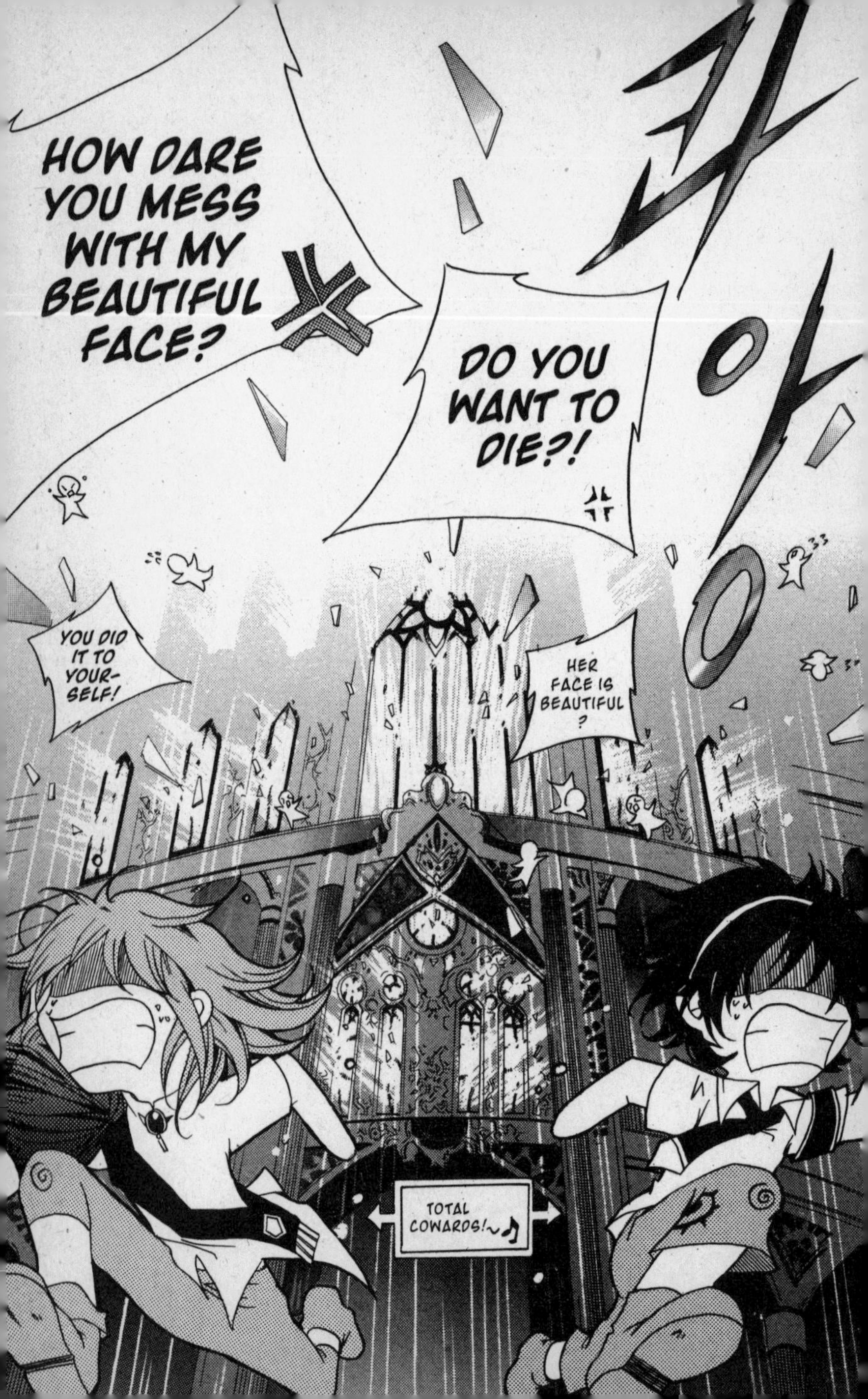
HOW DARE YOU MESS WITH MY BEAUTIFUL FACE?
DO YOU WANT TO DIE?!
HER FACE IS BEAUTIFUL?
YOU DID IT TO YOURSELF!
TOTAL COWARDS!~♪

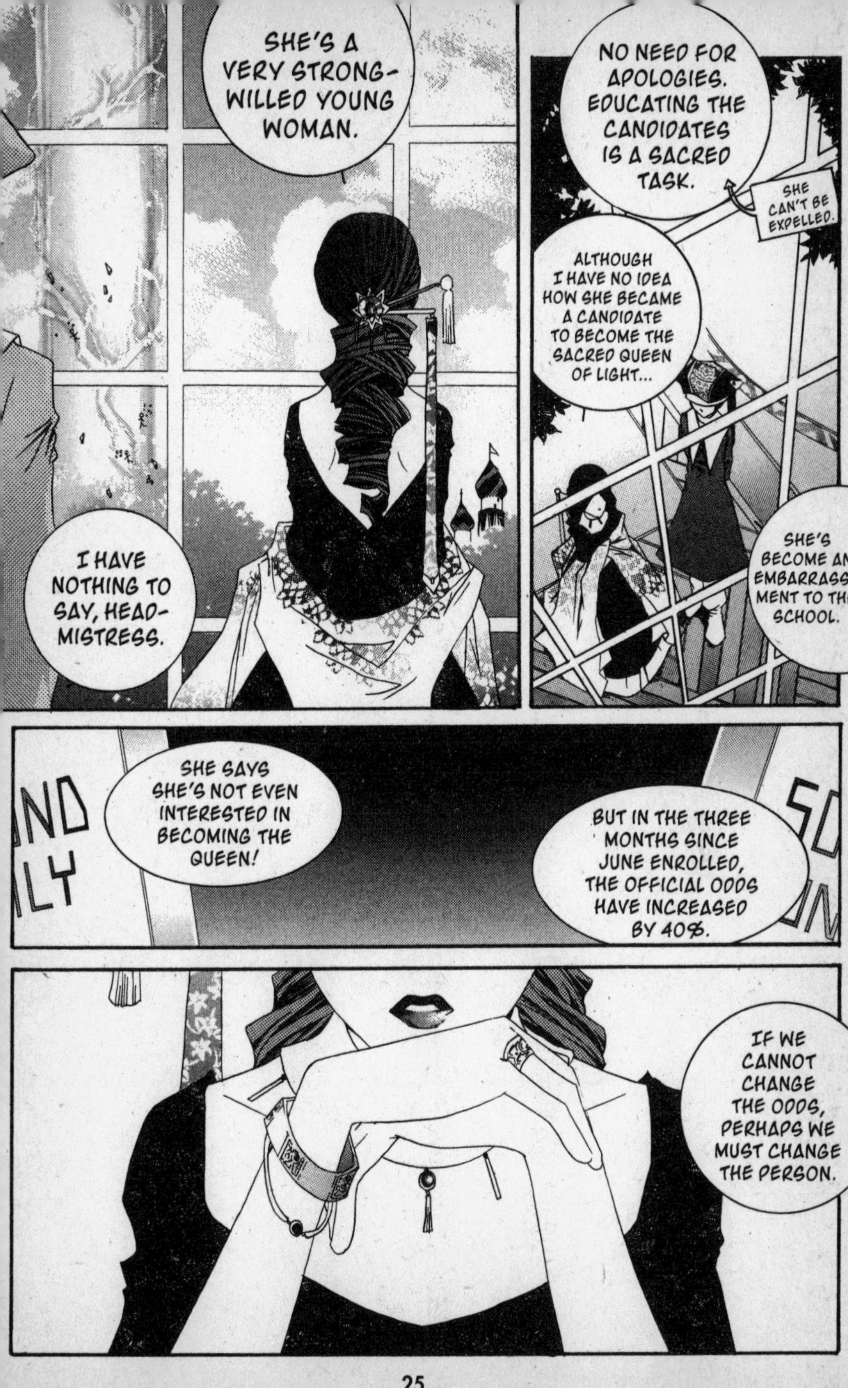
SHE'S A VERY STRONG-WILLED YOUNG WOMAN.
I HAVE NOTHING TO SAY, HEADMISTRESS.
NO NEED FOR APOLOGIES. EDUCATING THE CANDIDATES IS A SACRED TASK.
SHE CAN'T BE EXPELLED.
ALTHOUGH I HAVE NO IDEA HOW SHE BECAME A CANDIDATE TO BECOME THE SACRED QUEEN OF LIGHT...
SHE'S BECOME AN EMBARRASSMENT TO THE SCHOOL.
SHE SAYS SHE'S NOT EVEN INTERESTED IN BECOMING THE QUEEN!
BUT IN THE THREE MONTHS SINCE JUNE ENROLLED, THE OFFICIAL ODDS HAVE INCREASED BY 40%.
IF WE CANNOT CHANGE THE ODDS, PERHAPS WE MUST CHANGE THE PERSON.

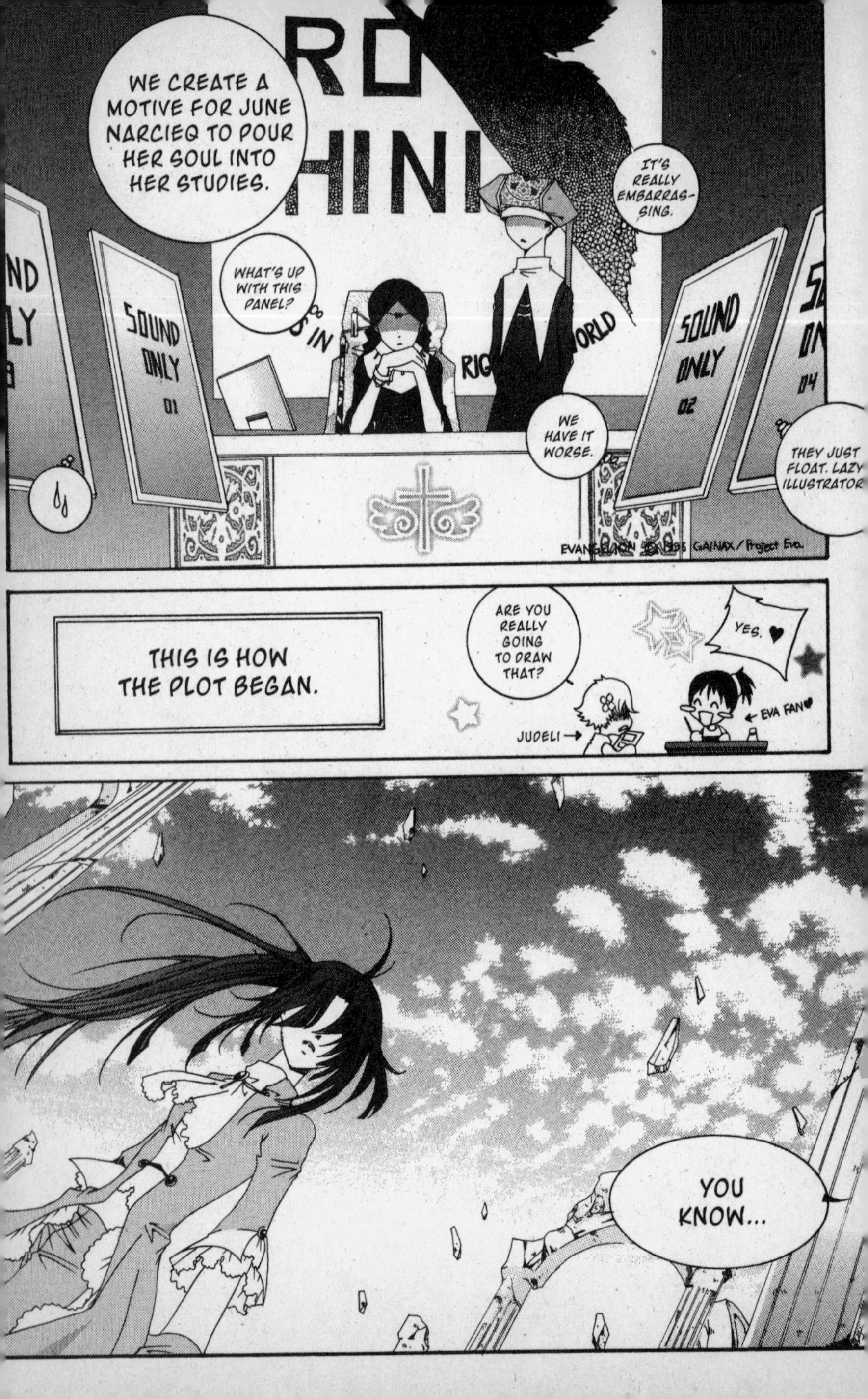

WE CREATE A MOTIVE FOR JUNE NARCIEQ TO POUR HER SOUL INTO HER STUDIES.
IT'S REALLY EMBARRAS-SING.
WHAT'S UP WITH THIS PANEL?
SOUND ONLY 04
SOUND ONLY 02
THEY JUST FLOAT. LAZY ILLUSTRATOR
WE HAVE IT WORSE.
SOUND ONLY 01
EVANGELION © 1995 GAINAX / Project Eva.
ARE YOU REALLY GOING TO DRAW THAT?
YES. ♥
EVA FAN♥
JUDELI
THIS IS HOW THE PLOT BEGAN.
YOU KNOW...

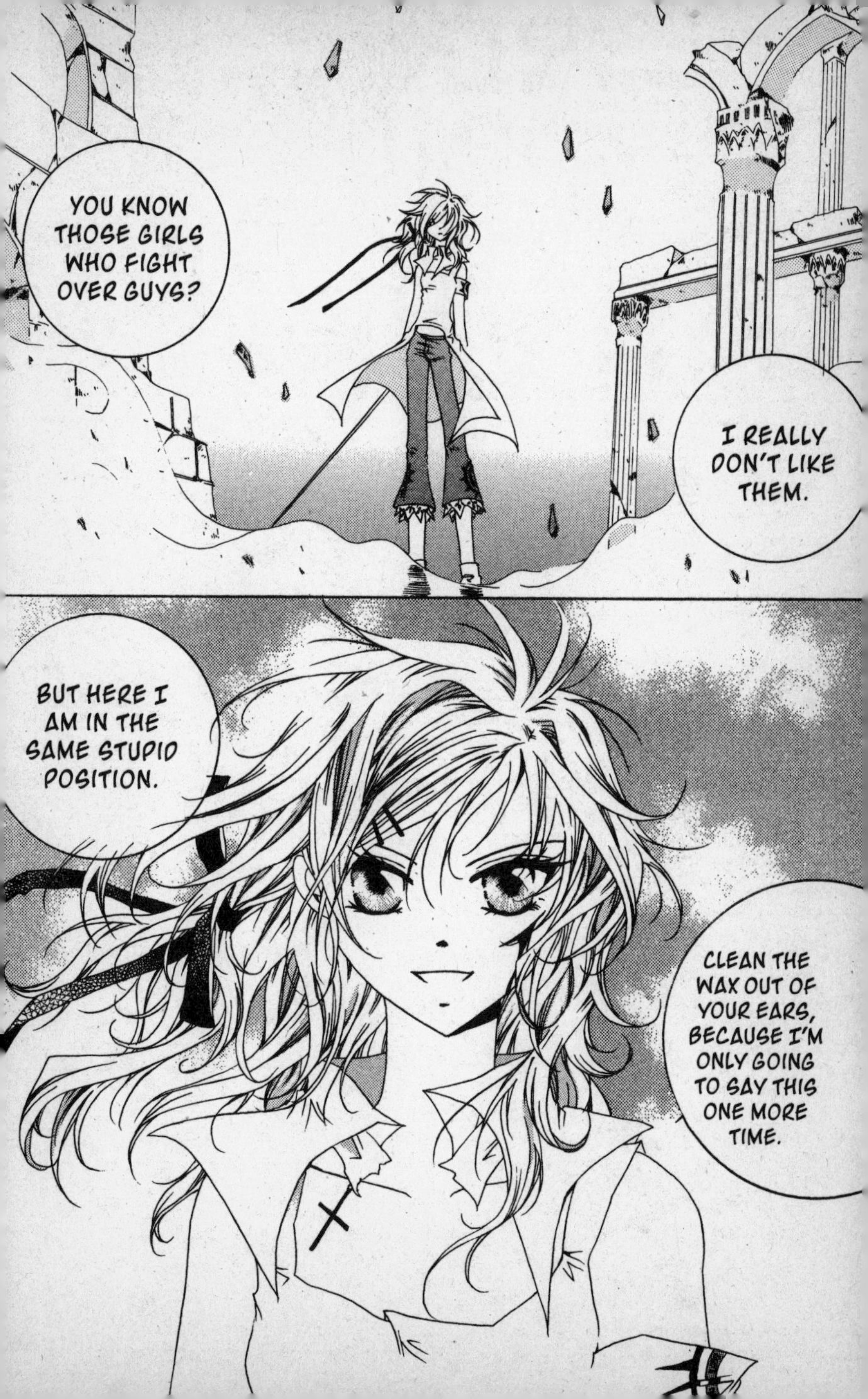
YOU KNOW THOSE GIRLS WHO FIGHT OVER GUYS?
I REALLY DON'T LIKE THEM.
BUT HERE I AM IN THE SAME STUPID POSITION.
CLEAN THE WAX OUT OF YOUR EARS, BECAUSE I'M ONLY GOING TO SAY THIS ONE MORE TIME.

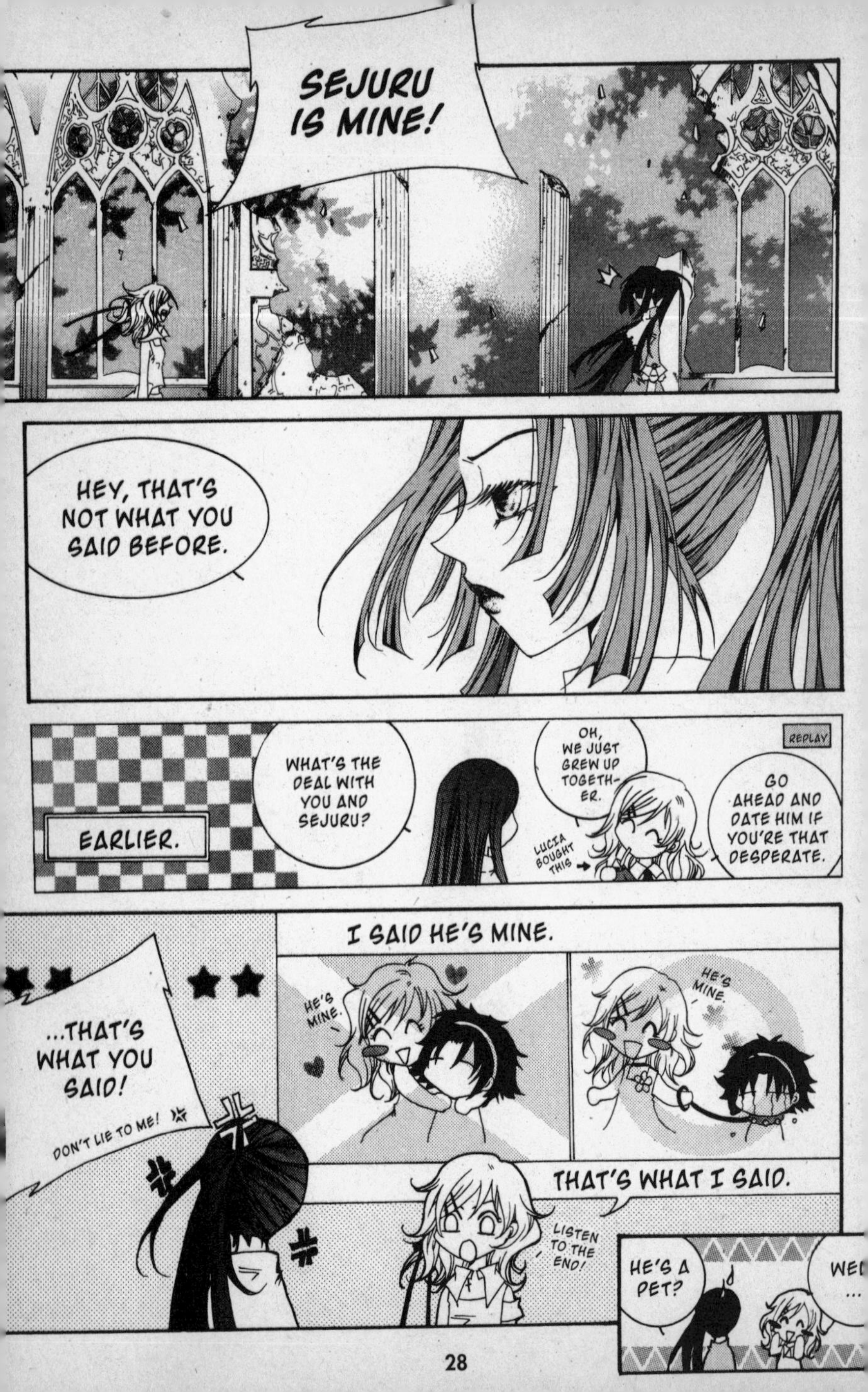
SEJURU IS MINE!
HEY, THAT'S NOT WHAT YOU SAID BEFORE.
EARLIER.
REPLAY
WHAT'S THE DEAL WITH YOU AND SEJURU?
OH, WE JUST GREW UP TOGETH-ER.
LUCIA BOUGHT THIS
GO AHEAD AND DATE HIM IF YOU'RE THAT DESPERATE.
I SAID HE'S MINE.
HE'S MINE.
HE'S MINE.
...THAT'S WHAT YOU SAID!
DON'T LIE TO ME!
THAT'S WHAT I SAID.
LISTEN TO THE END!
HE'S A PET?
WE
...

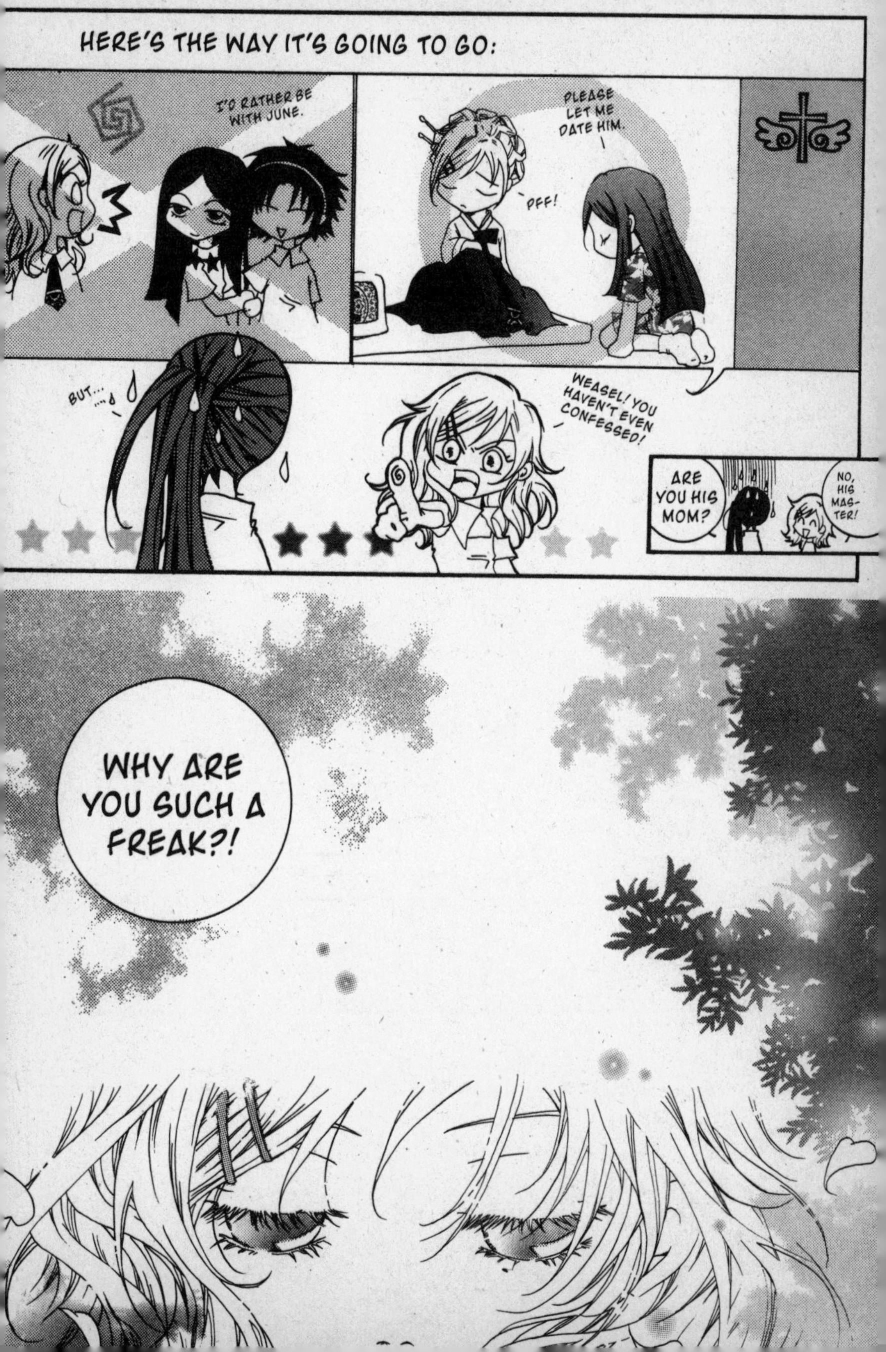
HERE'S THE WAY IT'S GOING TO GO:
PLEASE LET ME DATE HIM.
PFF!
I'D RATHER BE WITH JUNE.
ARE YOU HIS MOM?
NO, HIS MASTER!
WEASEL! YOU HAVEN'T EVEN CONFESSED!
BUT...
WHY ARE YOU SUCH A FREAK?!

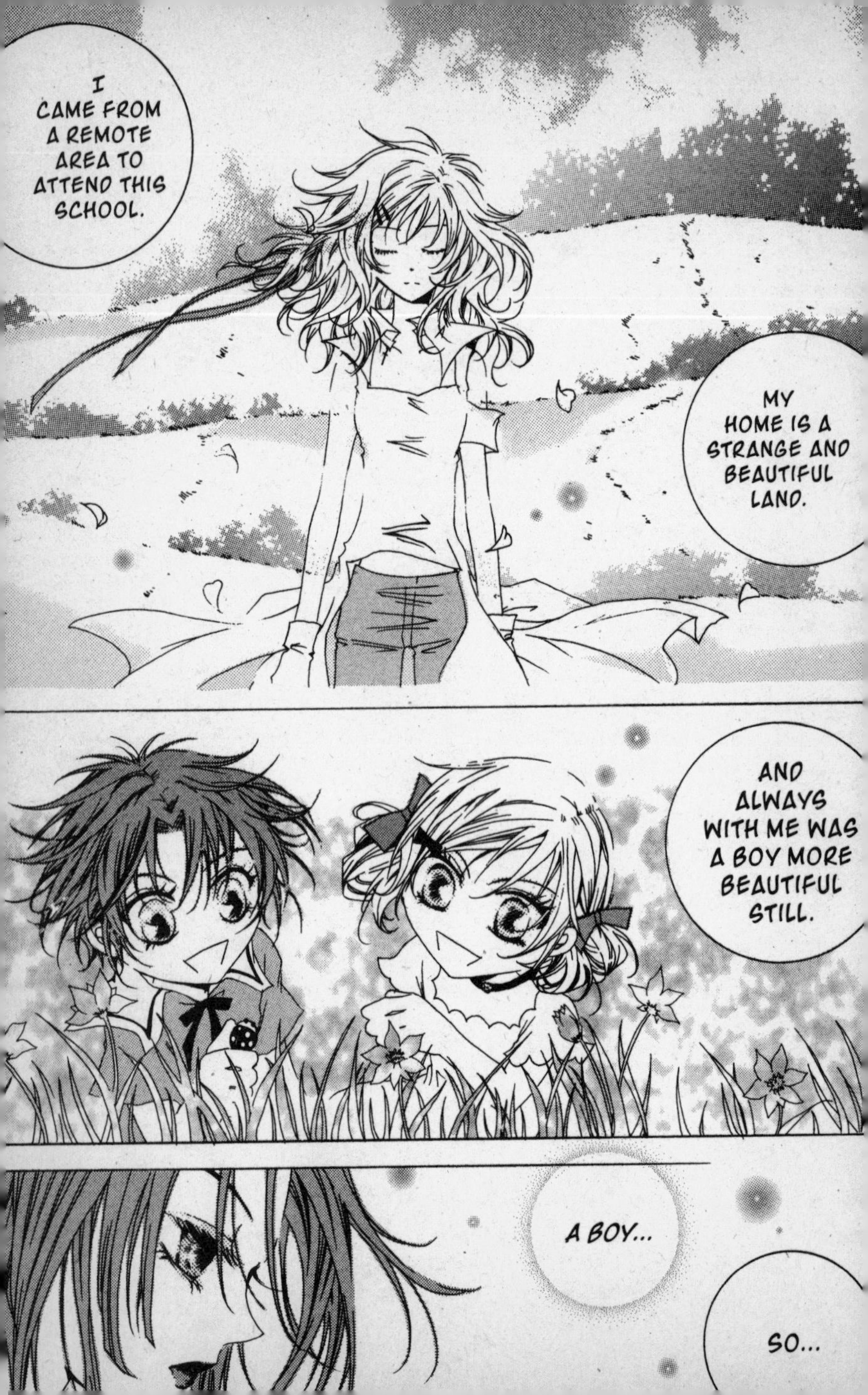
I CAME FROM A REMOTE AREA TO ATTEND THIS SCHOOL.
MY HOME IS A STRANGE AND BEAUTIFUL LAND.
AND ALWAYS WITH ME WAS A BOY MORE BEAUTIFUL STILL.
A BOY...
SO...

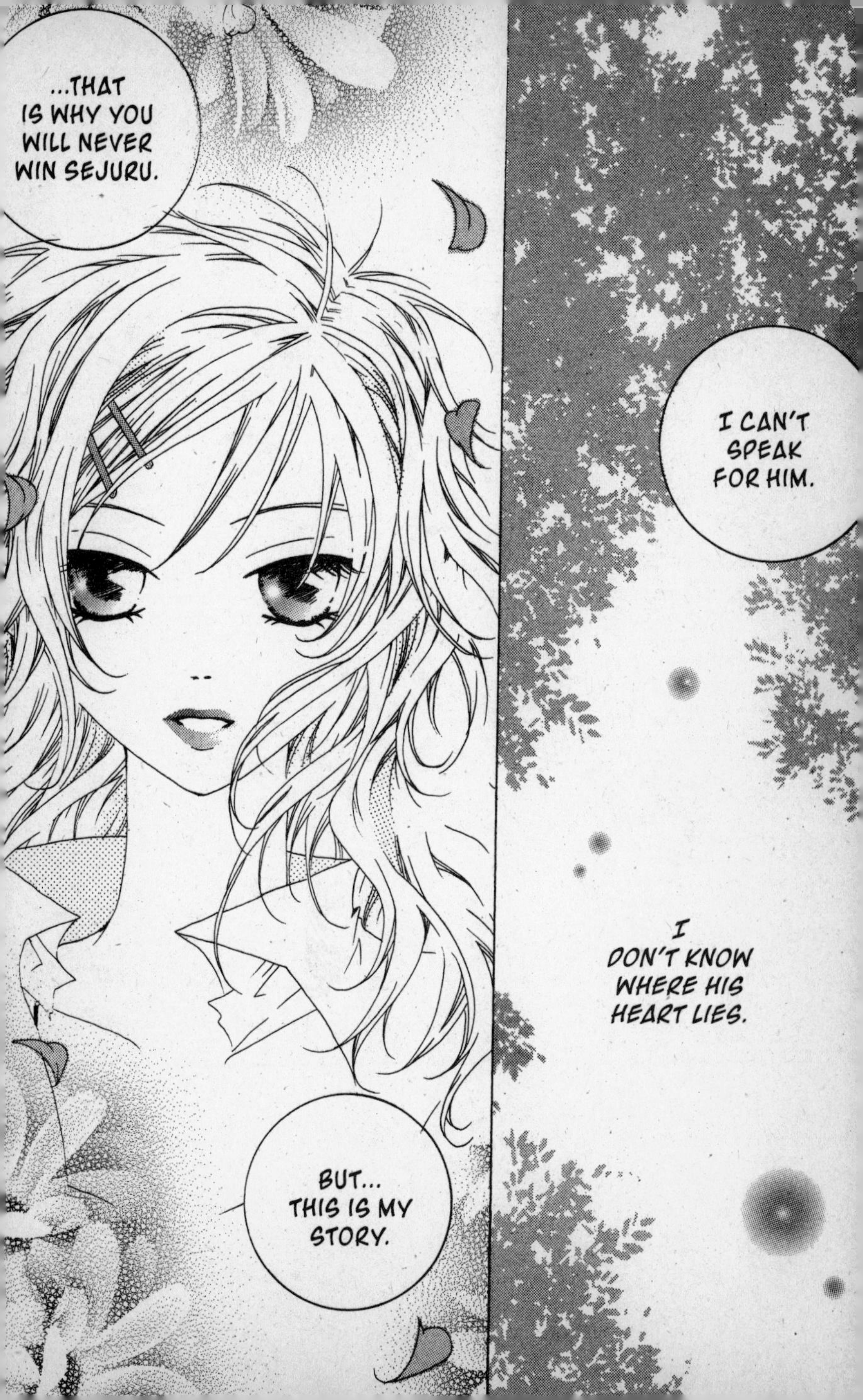
I CAN'T SPEAK FOR HIM.
I DON'T KNOW WHERE HIS HEART LIES.
...THAT IS WHY YOU WILL NEVER WIN SEJURU.
BUT... THIS IS MY STORY.

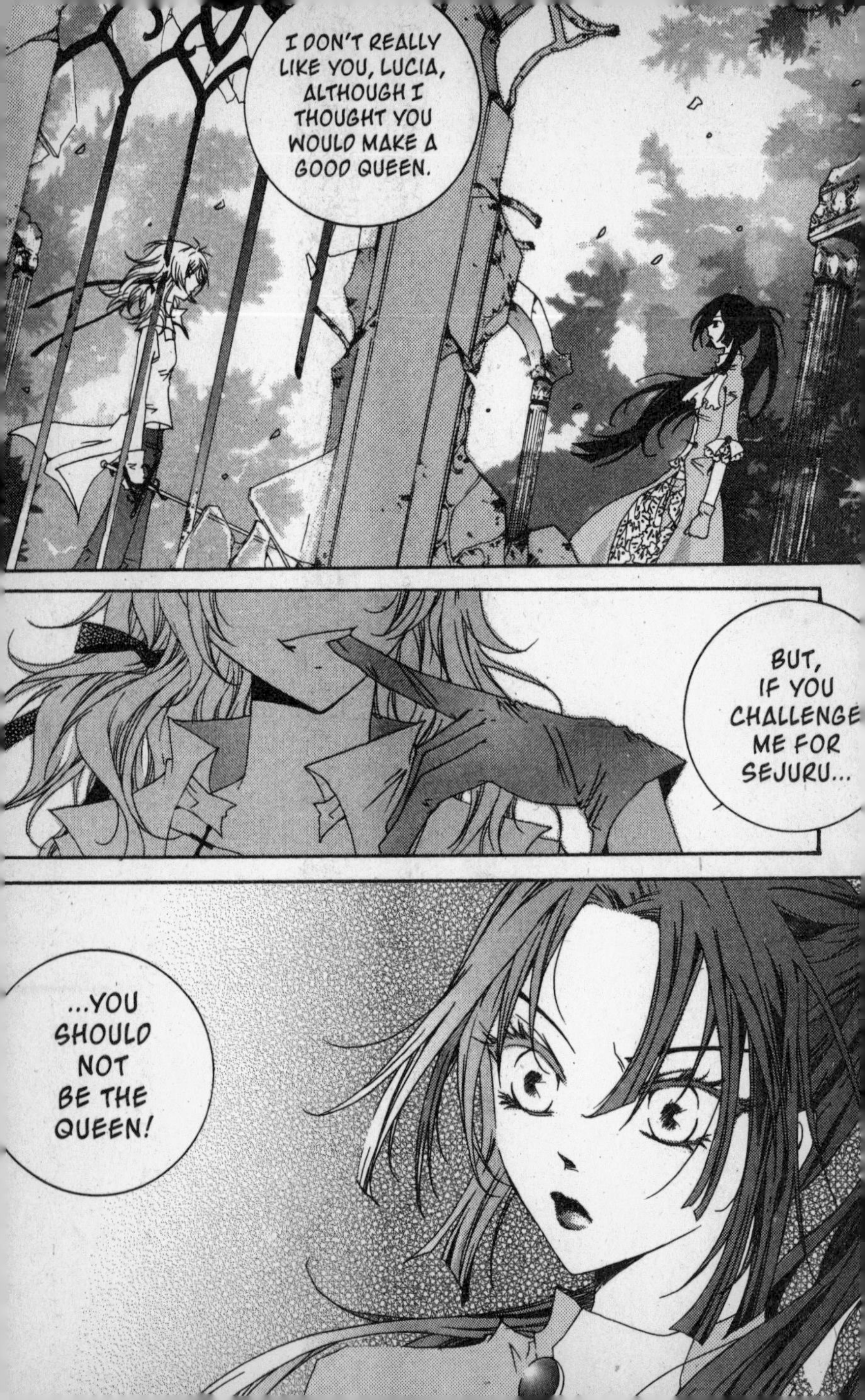
I DON'T REALLY LIKE YOU, LUCIA, ALTHOUGH I THOUGHT YOU WOULD MAKE A GOOD QUEEN.
BUT, IF YOU CHALLENGE ME FOR SEJURU...
...YOU SHOULD NOT BE THE QUEEN!

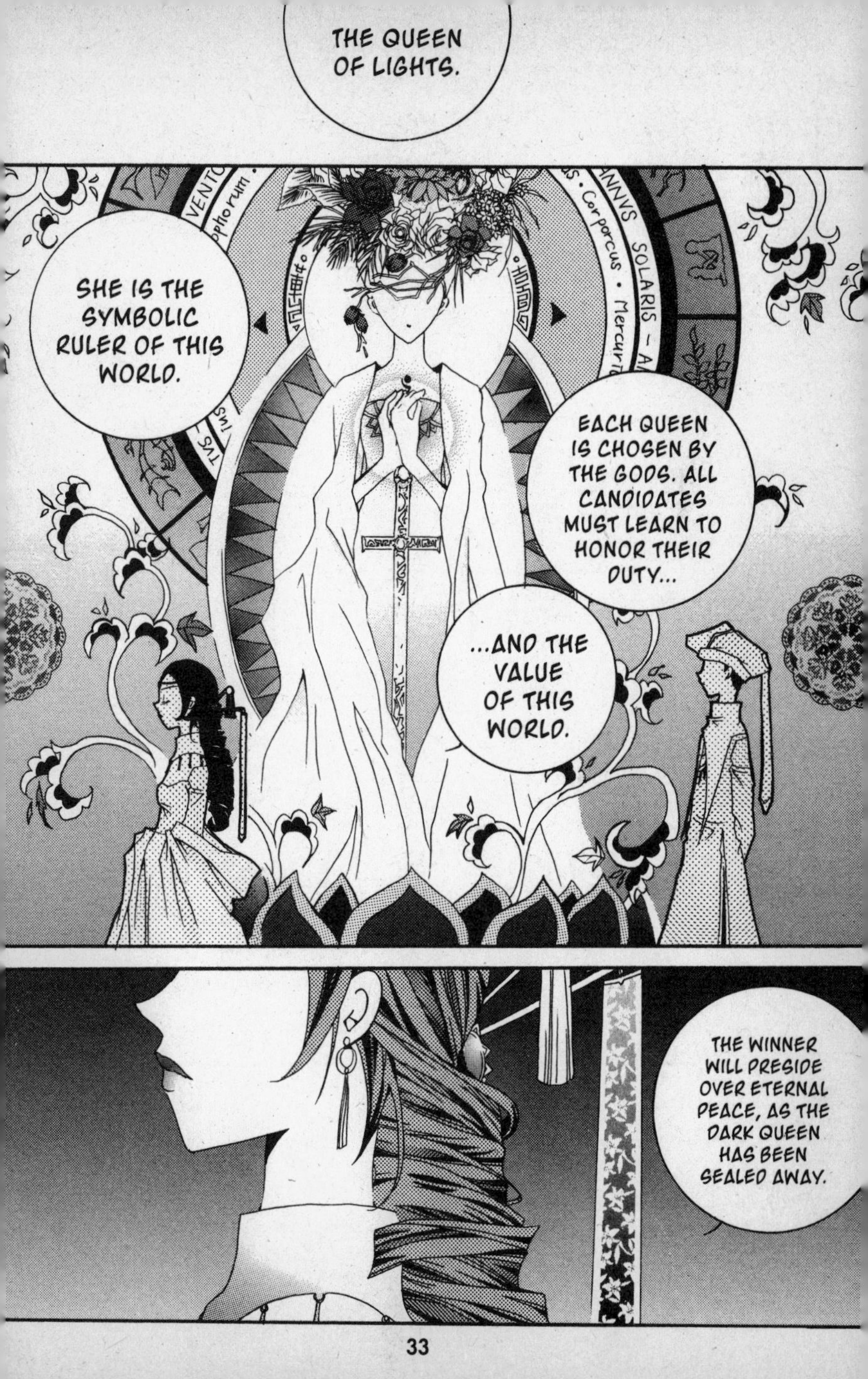
THE QUEEN OF LIGHTS.
SHE IS THE SYMBOLIC RULER OF THIS WORLD.
EACH QUEEN IS CHOSEN BY THE GODS. ALL CANDIDATES MUST LEARN TO HONOR THEIR DUTY...
...AND THE VALUE OF THIS WORLD.
THE WINNER WILL PRESIDE OVER ETERNAL PEACE, AS THE DARK QUEEN HAS BEEN SEALED AWAY.

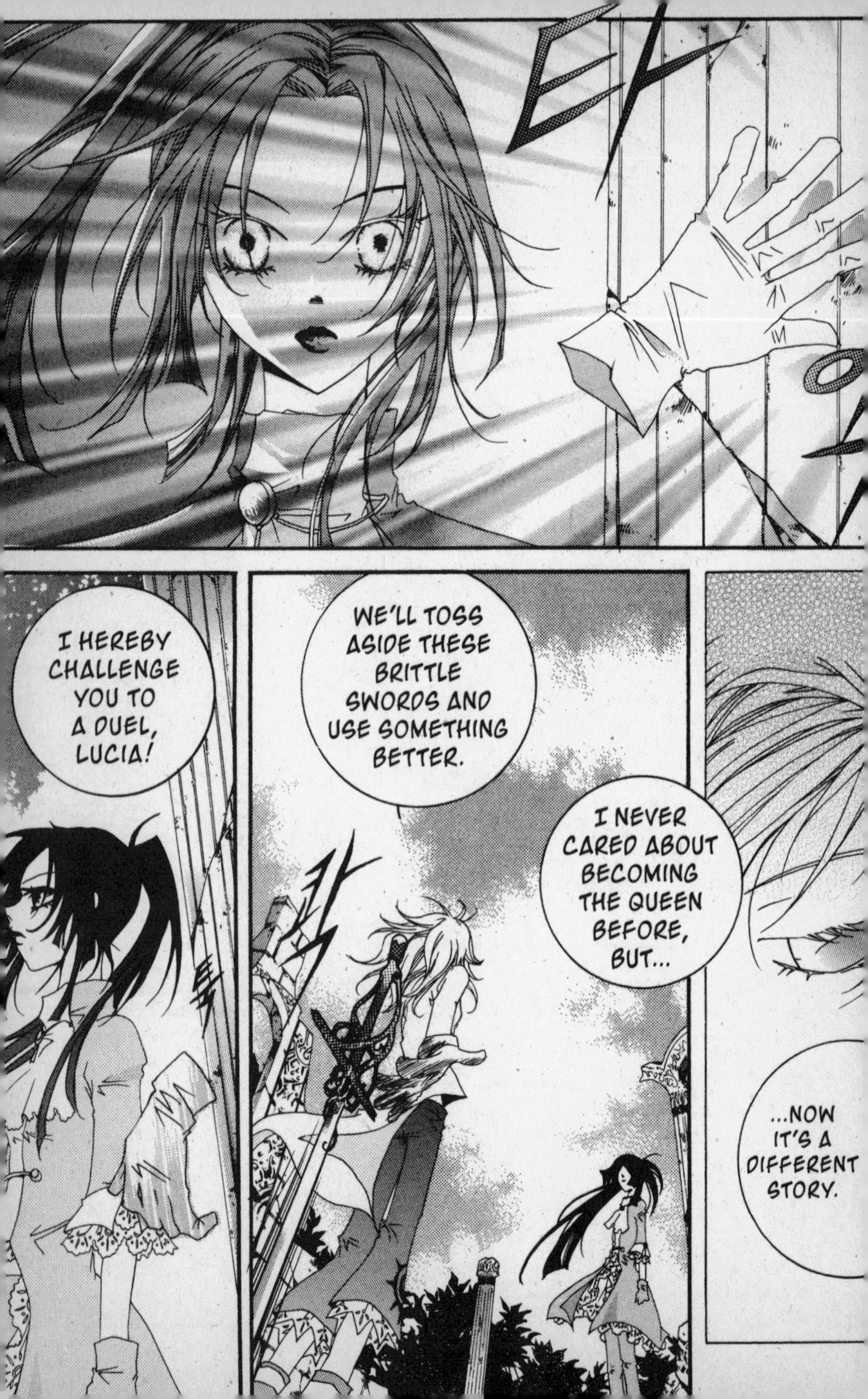
I HEREBY CHALLENGE YOU TO A DUEL, LUCIA!
WE'LL TOSS ASIDE THESE BRITTLE SWORDS AND USE SOMETHING BETTER.
I NEVER CARED ABOUT BECOMING THE QUEEN BEFORE, BUT...
...NOW IT'S A DIFFERENT STORY.

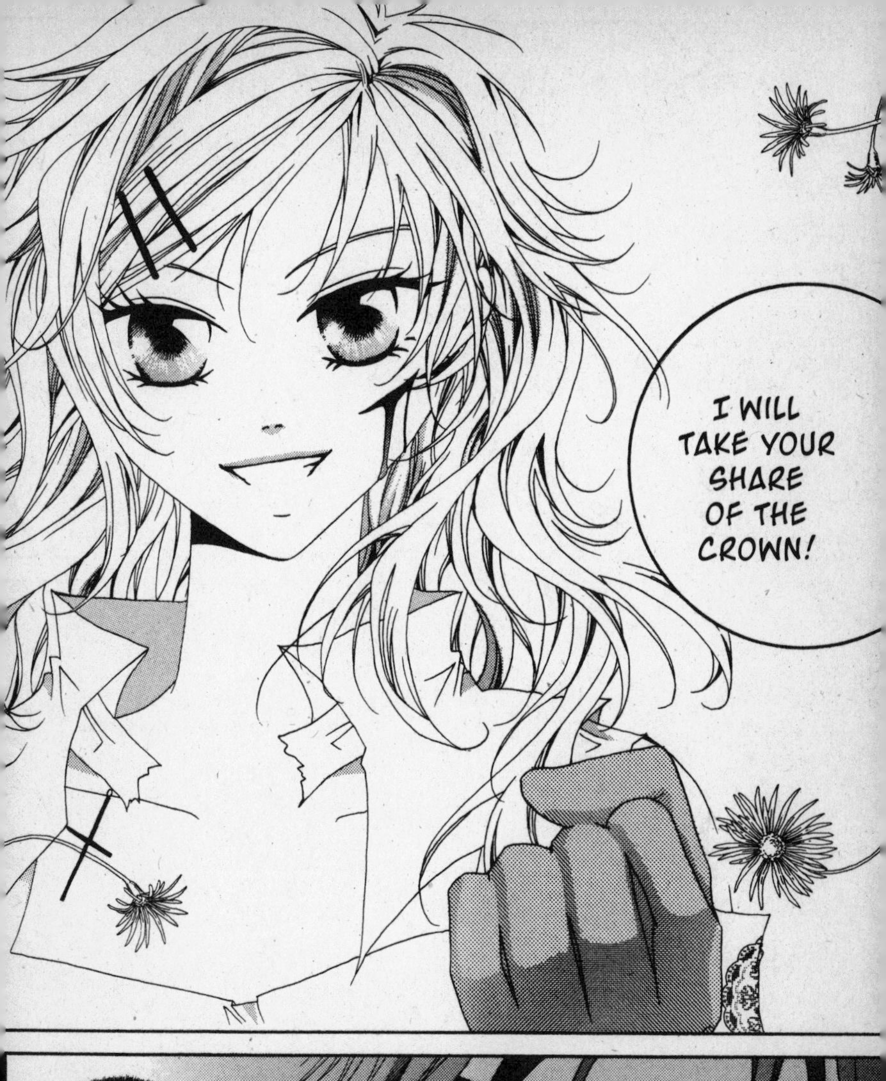
I WILL TAKE YOUR SHARE OF THE CROWN!
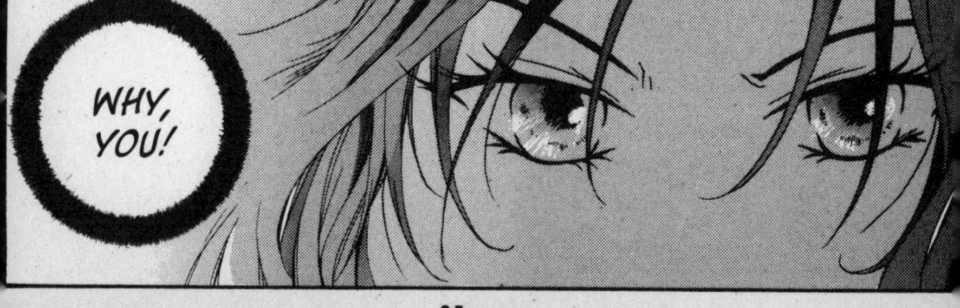
WHY, YOU!

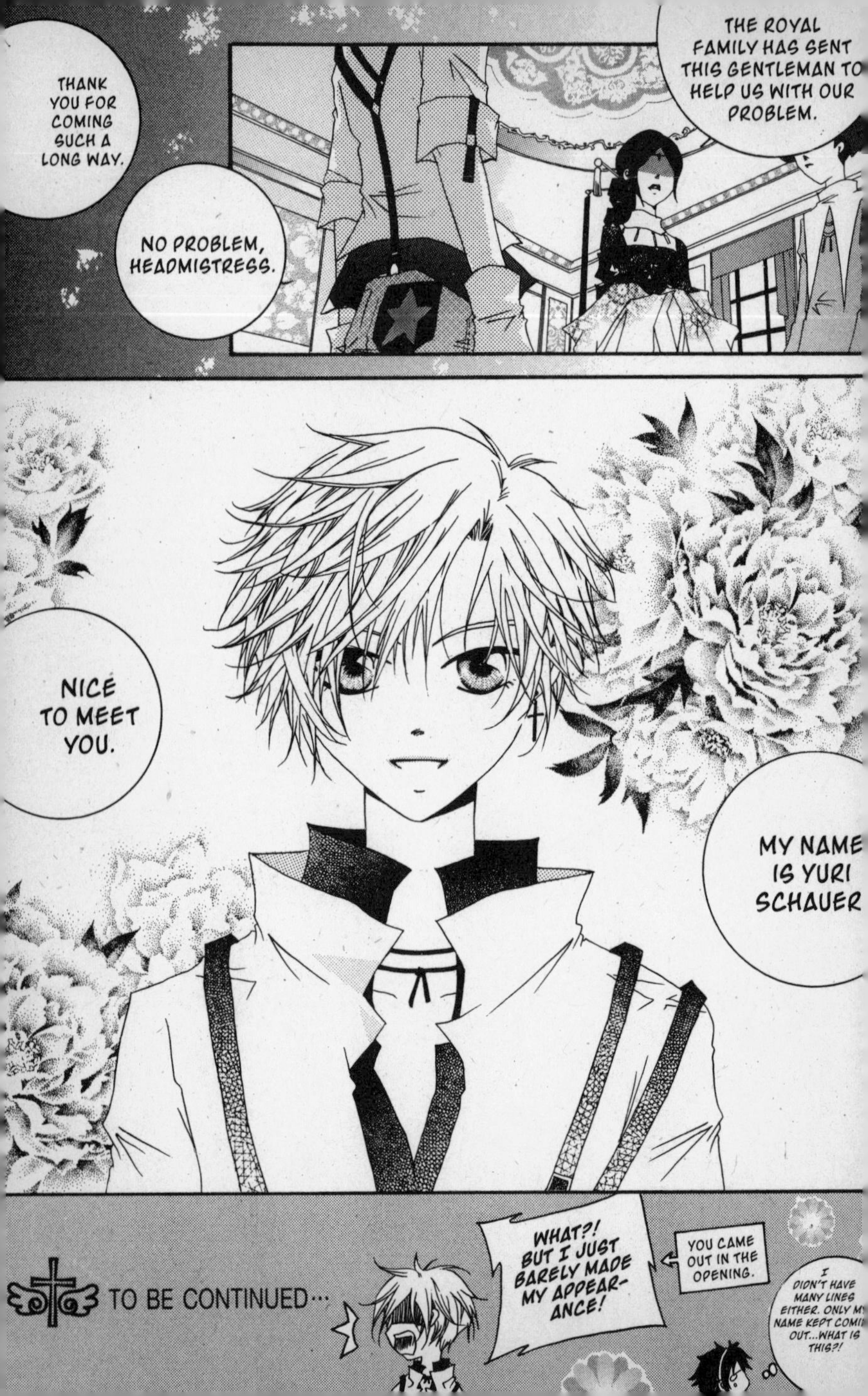
THE ROYAL FAMILY HAS SENT THIS GENTLEMAN TO HELP US WITH OUR PROBLEM.
THANK YOU FOR COMING SUCH A LONG WAY.
NO PROBLEM, HEADMISTRESS.
NICE TO MEET YOU.
MY NAME IS YURI SCHAUER
TO BE CONTINUED…
WHAT?! BUT I JUST BARELY MADE MY APPEAR-ANCE!
YOU CAME OUT IN THE OPENING.
I DIDN'T HAVE MANY LINES EITHER. ONLY M NAME KEPT COMI OUT...WHAT IS THIS?!

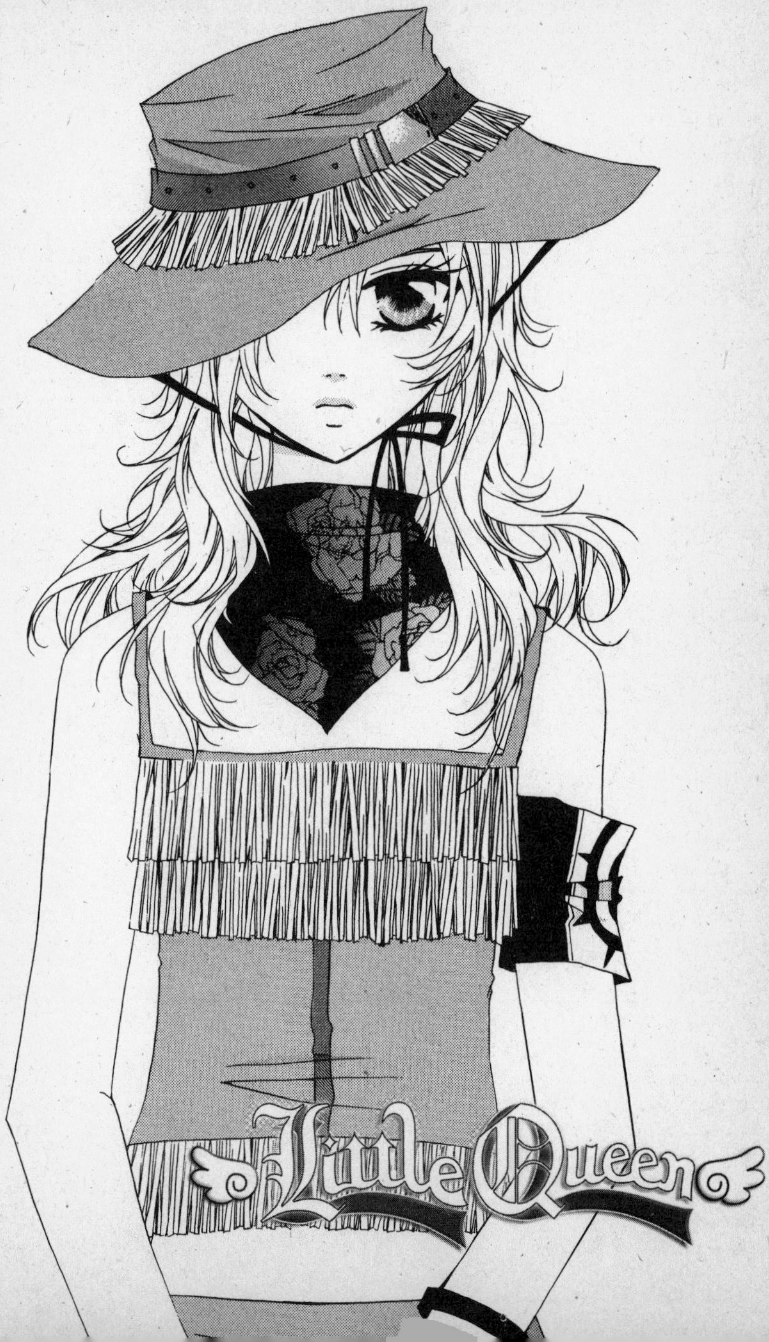
Little Queen

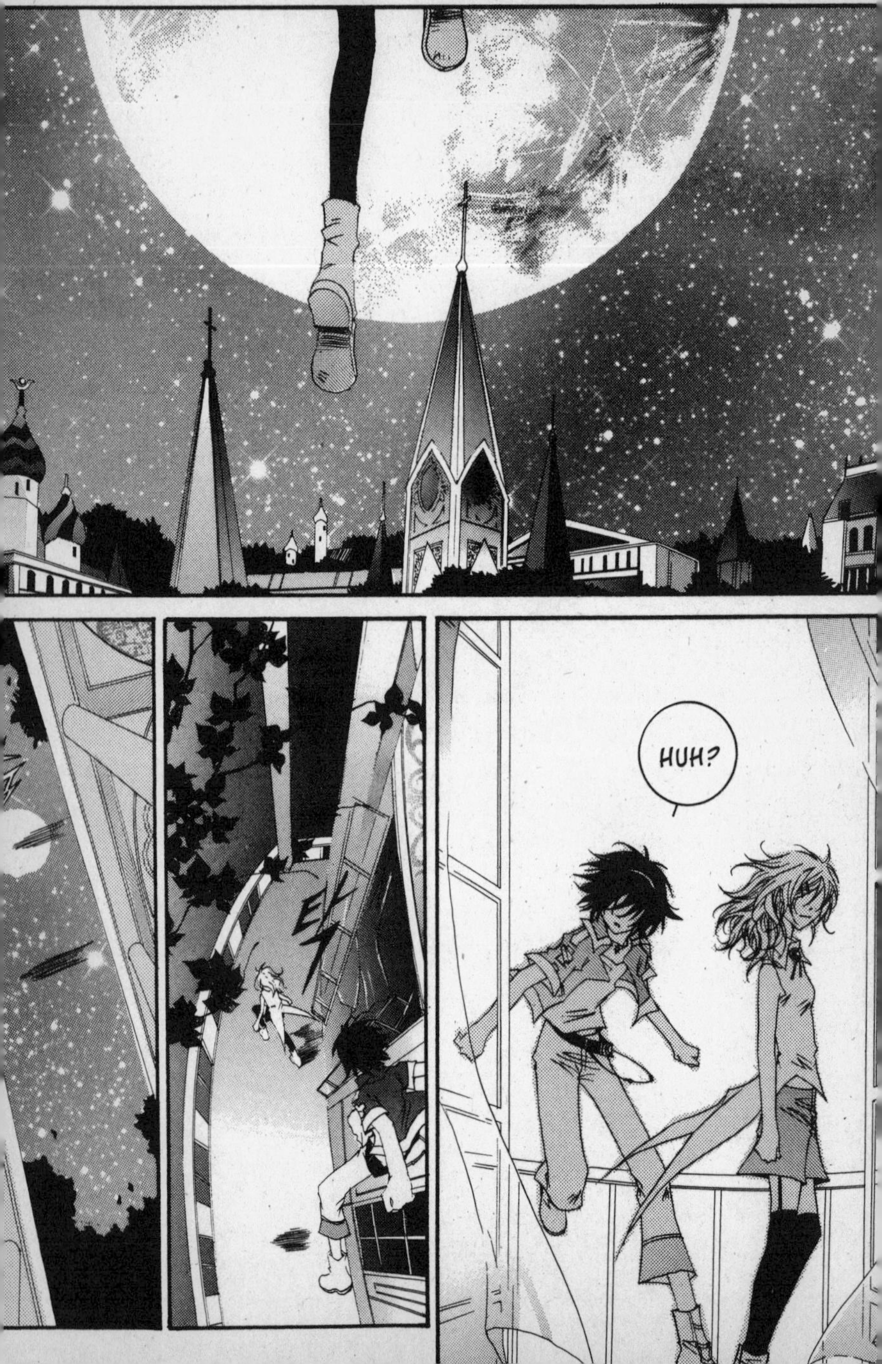
HUH?

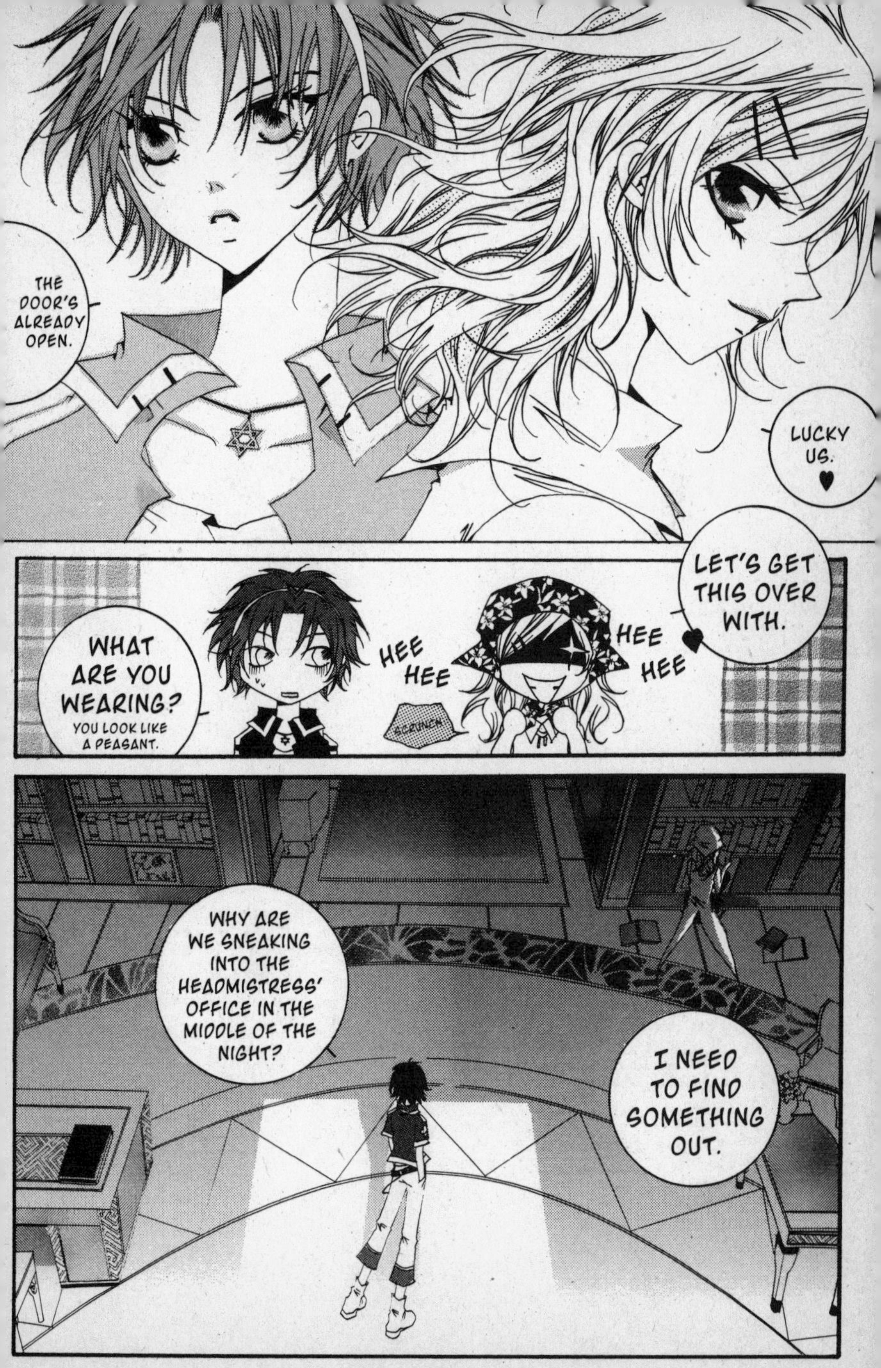
THE DOOR'S ALREADY OPEN.
LUCKY US. ♥
WHAT ARE YOU WEARING? YOU LOOK LIKE A PEASANT.
HEE HEE
CRUNCH
HEE HEE
LET'S GET THIS OVER WITH. ♥
WHY ARE WE SNEAKING INTO THE HEADMISTRESS' OFFICE IN THE MIDDLE OF THE NIGHT?
I NEED TO FIND SOMETHING OUT.

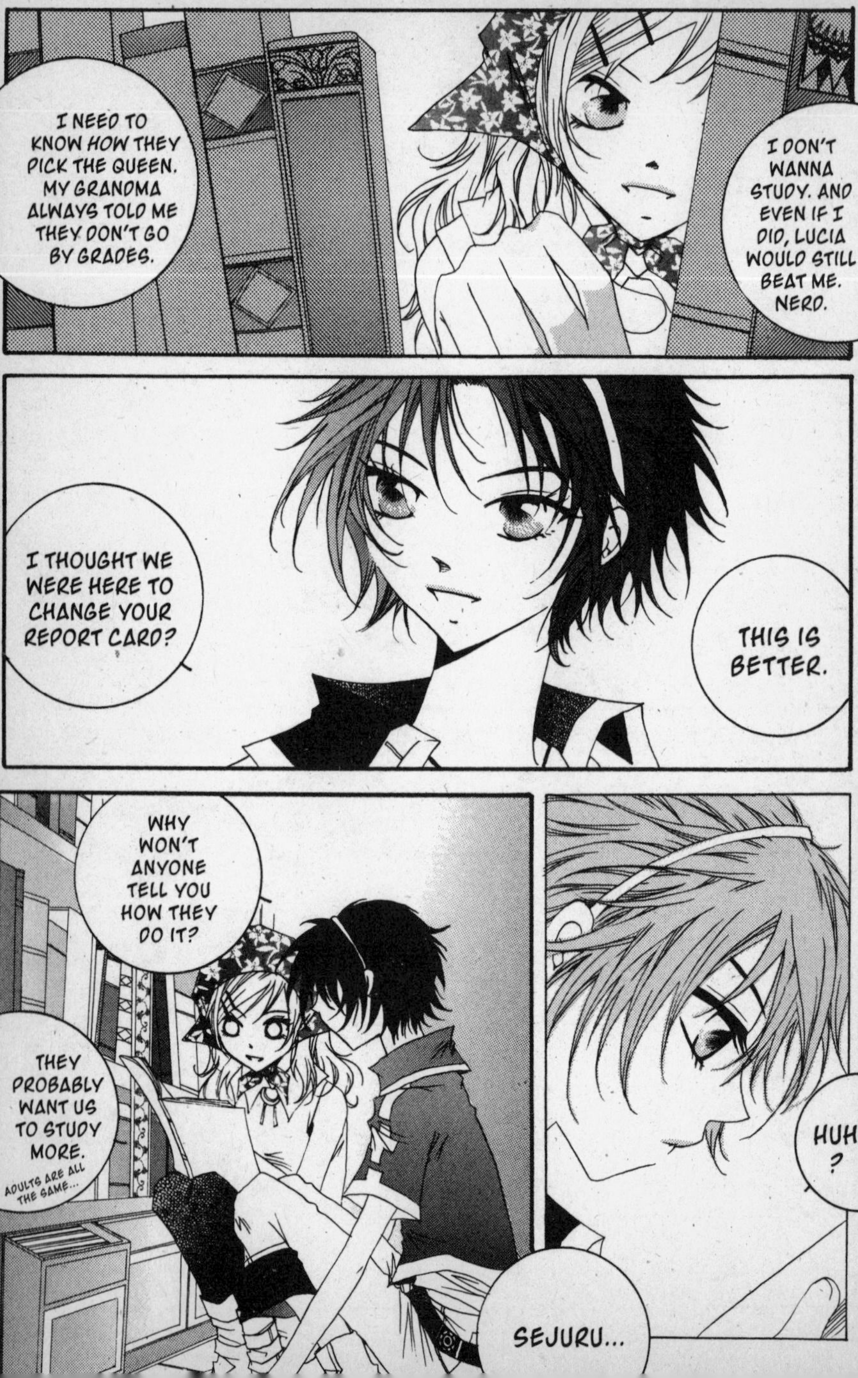
I NEED TO KNOW HOW THEY PICK THE QUEEN. MY GRANDMA ALWAYS TOLD ME THEY DON'T GO BY GRADES.
I DON'T WANNA STUDY. AND EVEN IF I DID, LUCIA WOULD STILL BEAT ME. NERO.
I THOUGHT WE WERE HERE TO CHANGE YOUR REPORT CARD?
THIS IS BETTER.
WHY WON'T ANYONE TELL YOU HOW THEY DO IT?
THEY PROBABLY WANT US TO STUDY MORE.
ADULTS ARE ALL THE SAME...
HUH?
SEJURU...

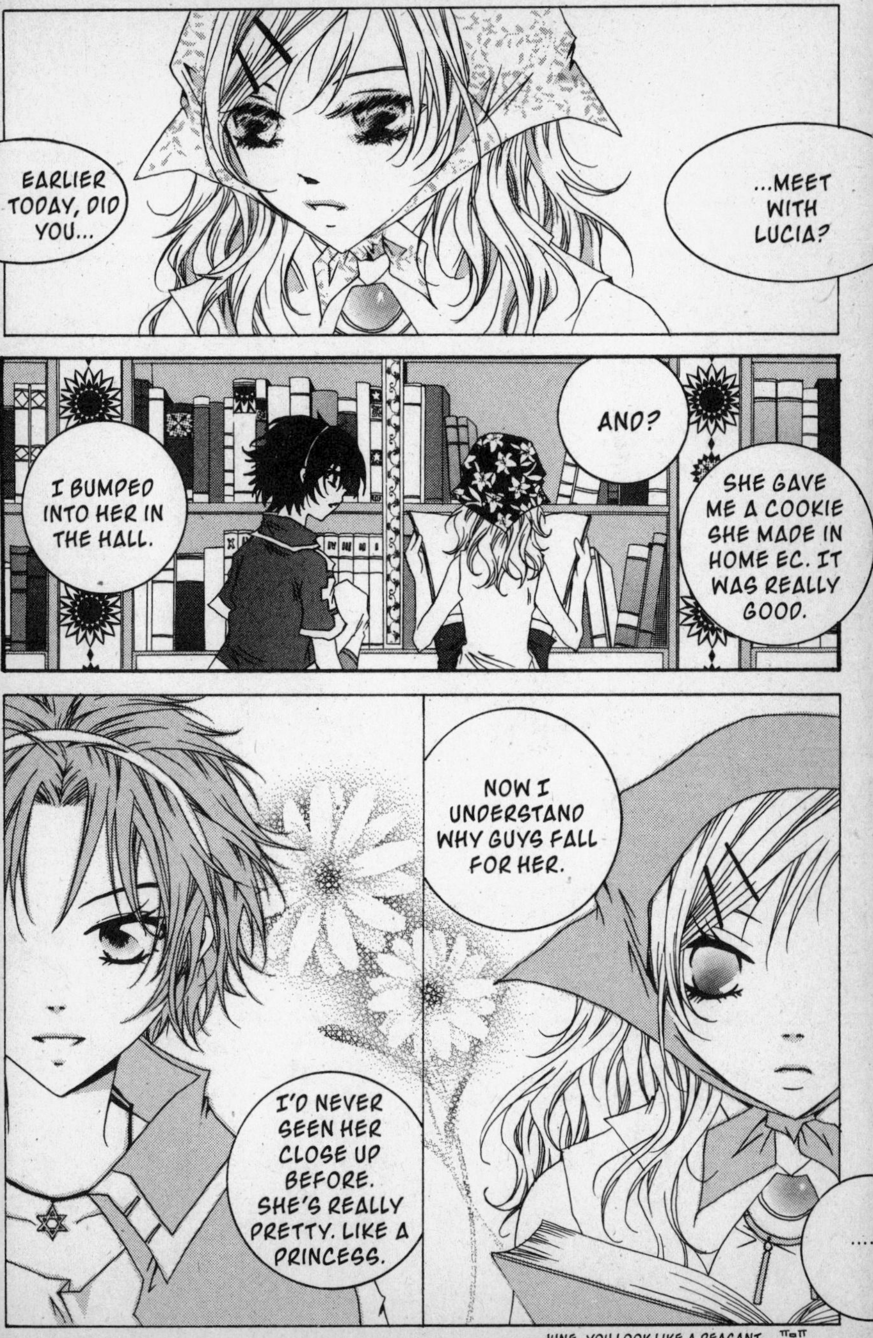
EARLIER TODAY, DID YOU...
...MEET WITH LUCIA?
I BUMPED INTO HER IN THE HALL.
AND?
SHE GAVE ME A COOKIE SHE MADE IN HOME EC. IT WAS REALLY GOOD.
I'D NEVER SEEN HER CLOSE UP BEFORE. SHE'S REALLY PRETTY. LIKE A PRINCESS.
NOW I UNDERSTAND WHY GUYS FALL FOR HER.
....

JUNE, YOU LOOK LIKE A PEASANT. TT_TT

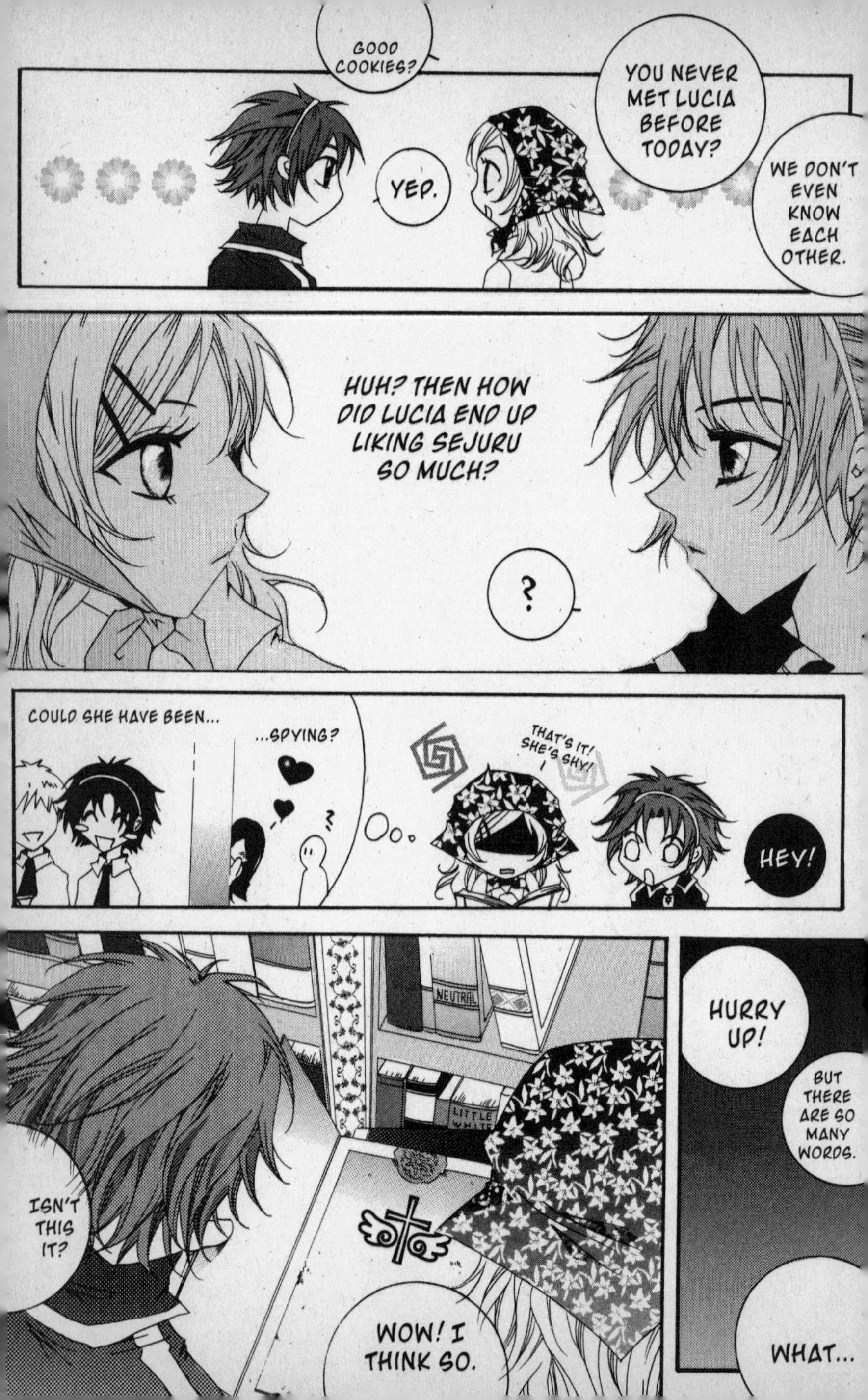
GOOD COOKIES?
YOU NEVER MET LUCIA BEFORE TODAY?
YEP.
WE DON'T EVEN KNOW EACH OTHER.
HUH? THEN HOW DID LUCIA END UP LIKING SEJURU SO MUCH?
?
COULD SHE HAVE BEEN...
...SPYING?
THAT'S IT! SHE'S SHY!
HEY!
HURRY UP!
BUT THERE ARE SO MANY WORDS.
WHAT...
NEUTRAL
ISN'T THIS IT?
WOW! I THINK SO.

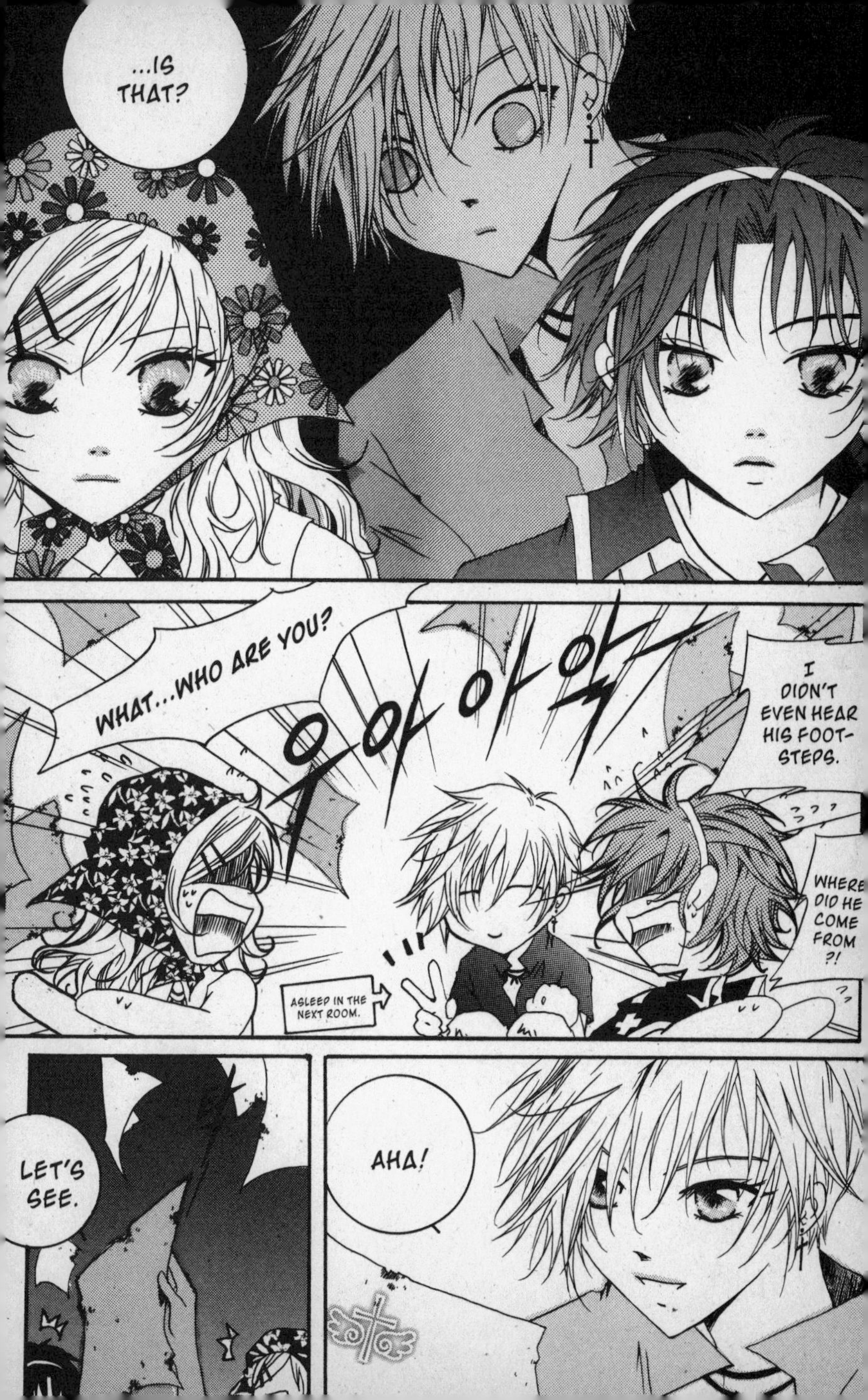
...IS THAT?
WHAT...WHO ARE YOU?
으아아악
I DIDN'T EVEN HEAR HIS FOOT-STEPS.
WHERE DID HE COME FROM ?!
ASLEEP IN THE NEXT ROOM.
LET'S SEE.
AHA!

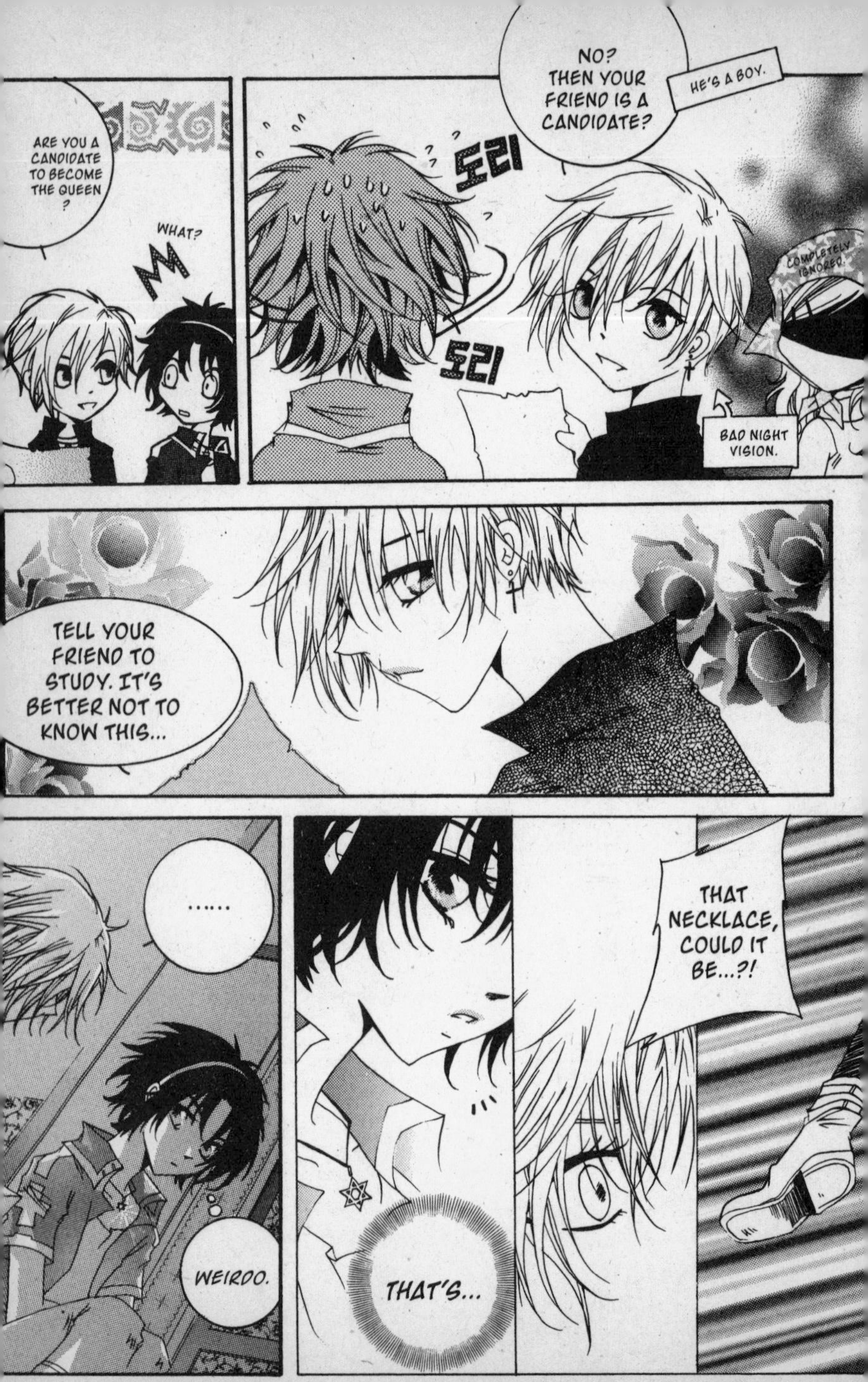
ARE YOU A CANDIDATE TO BECOME THE QUEEN?
WHAT?
도리
도리
NO? THEN YOUR FRIEND IS A CANDIDATE?
HE'S A BOY.
COMPLETELY IGNORED.
BAD NIGHT VISION.
TELL YOUR FRIEND TO STUDY. IT'S BETTER NOT TO KNOW THIS...
......
WEIRDO.
THAT'S...
THAT NECKLACE, COULD IT BE...?!

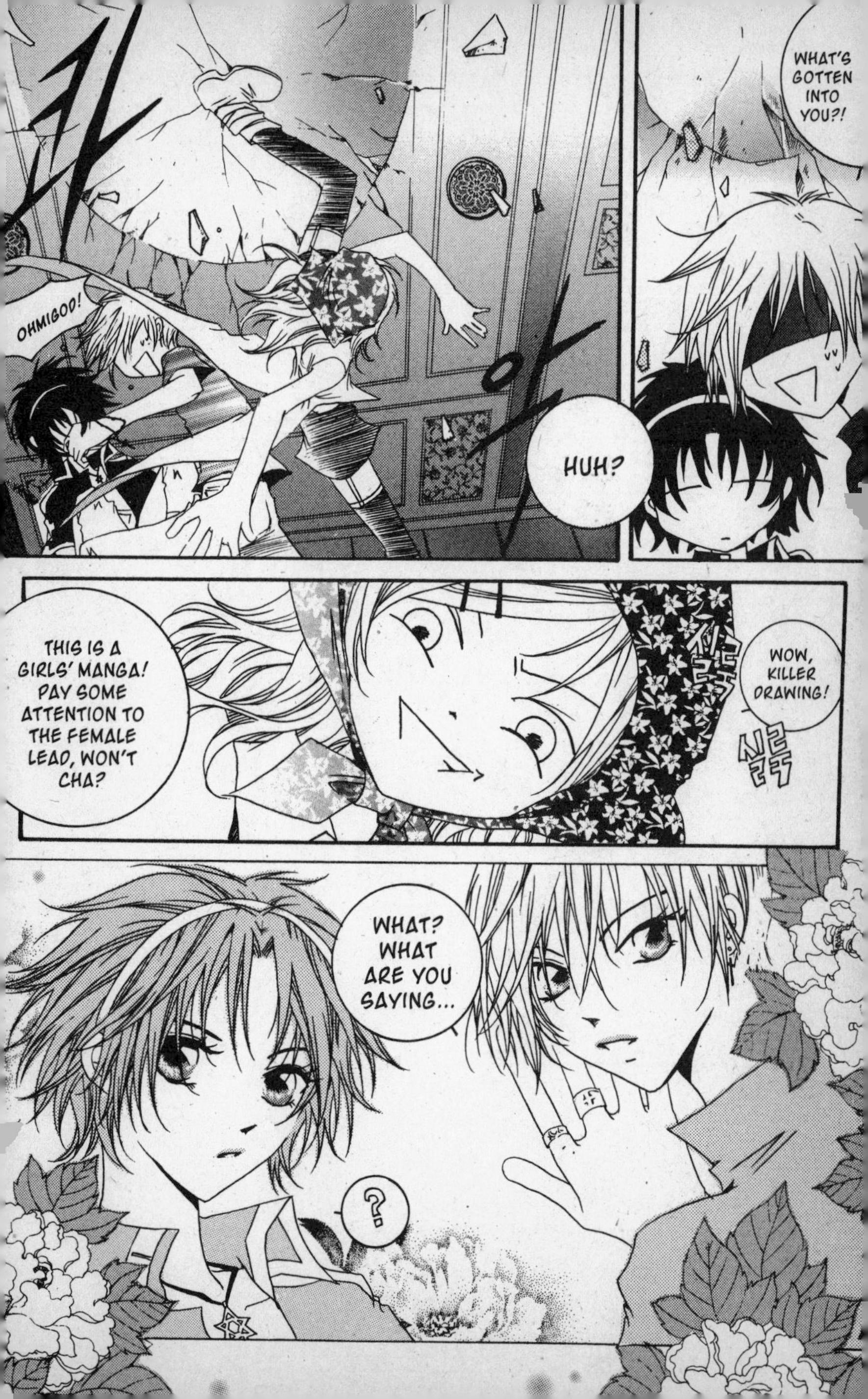
OHMIGOD!
WHAT'S GOTTEN INTO YOU?!
HUH?
THIS IS A GIRLS' MANGA! PAY SOME ATTENTION TO THE FEMALE LEAD, WON'T CHA?
WOW, KILLER DRAWING!
WHAT? WHAT ARE YOU SAYING...
?

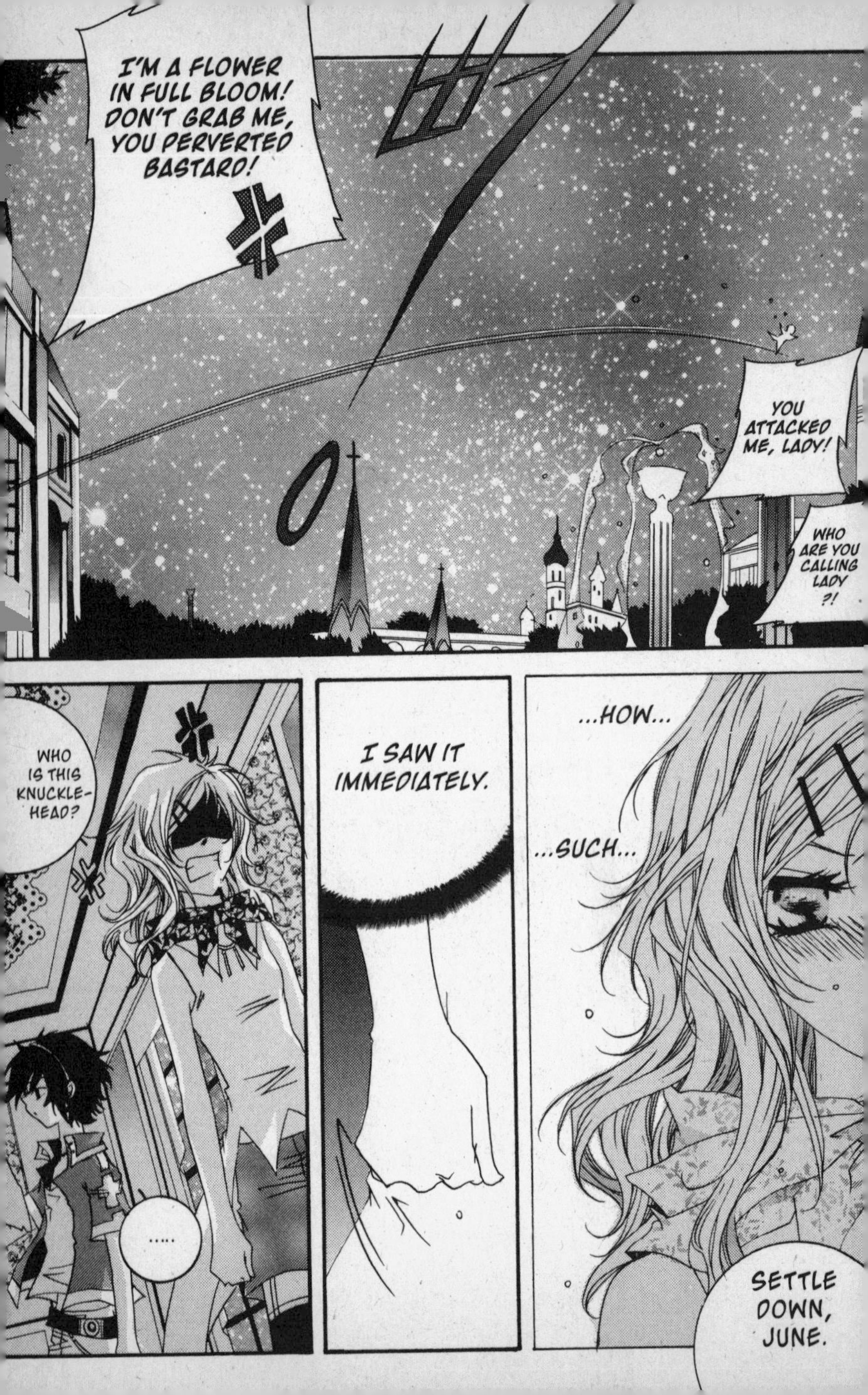
I'M A FLOWER IN FULL BLOOM! DON'T GRAB ME, YOU PERVERTED BASTARD!
YOU ATTACKED ME, LADY!
WHO ARE YOU CALLING LADY ?!
WHO IS THIS KNUCKLE-HEAD?
.....
I SAW IT IMMEDIATELY.
...HOW...
...SUCH...
SETTLE DOWN, JUNE.

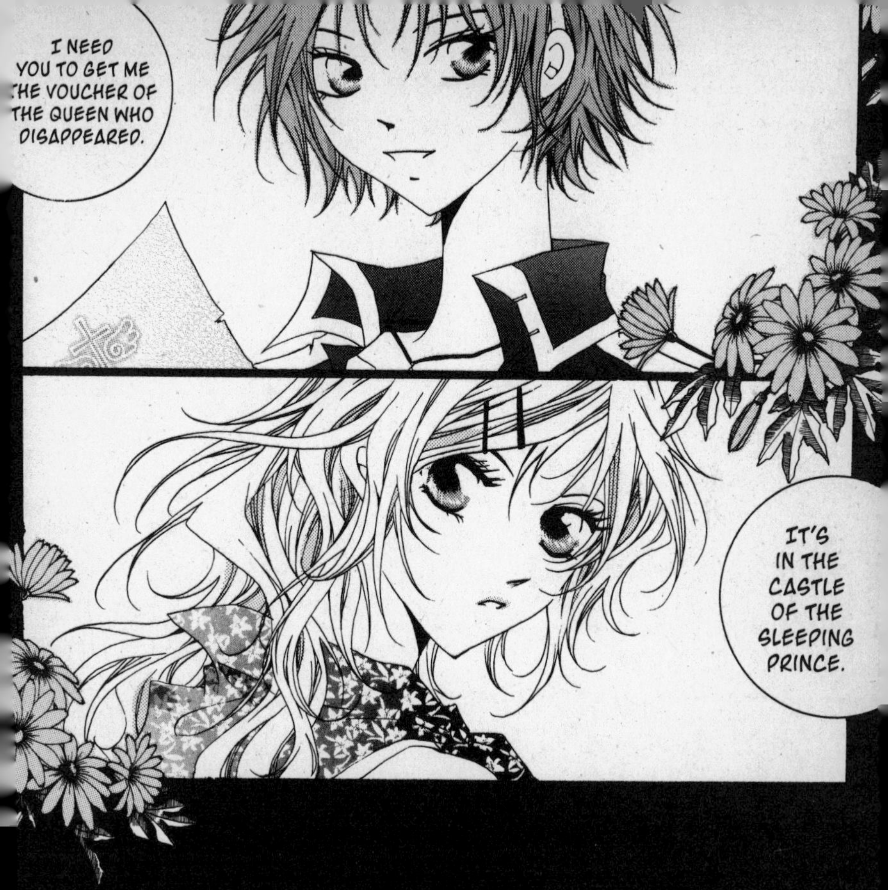
I NEED YOU TO GET ME THE VOUCHER OF THE QUEEN WHO DISAPPEARED.
IT'S IN THE CASTLE OF THE SLEEPING PRINCE.

Hope to Little Girls and Sincerity to Little Boys

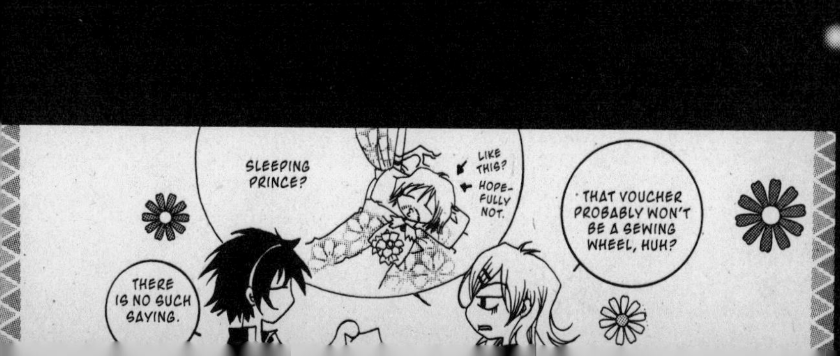
THAT VOUCHER PROBABLY WON'T BE A SEWING WHEEL, HUH?
LIKE THIS?
HOPE-FULLY NOT.
SLEEPING PRINCE?
THERE IS NO SUCH SAYING.

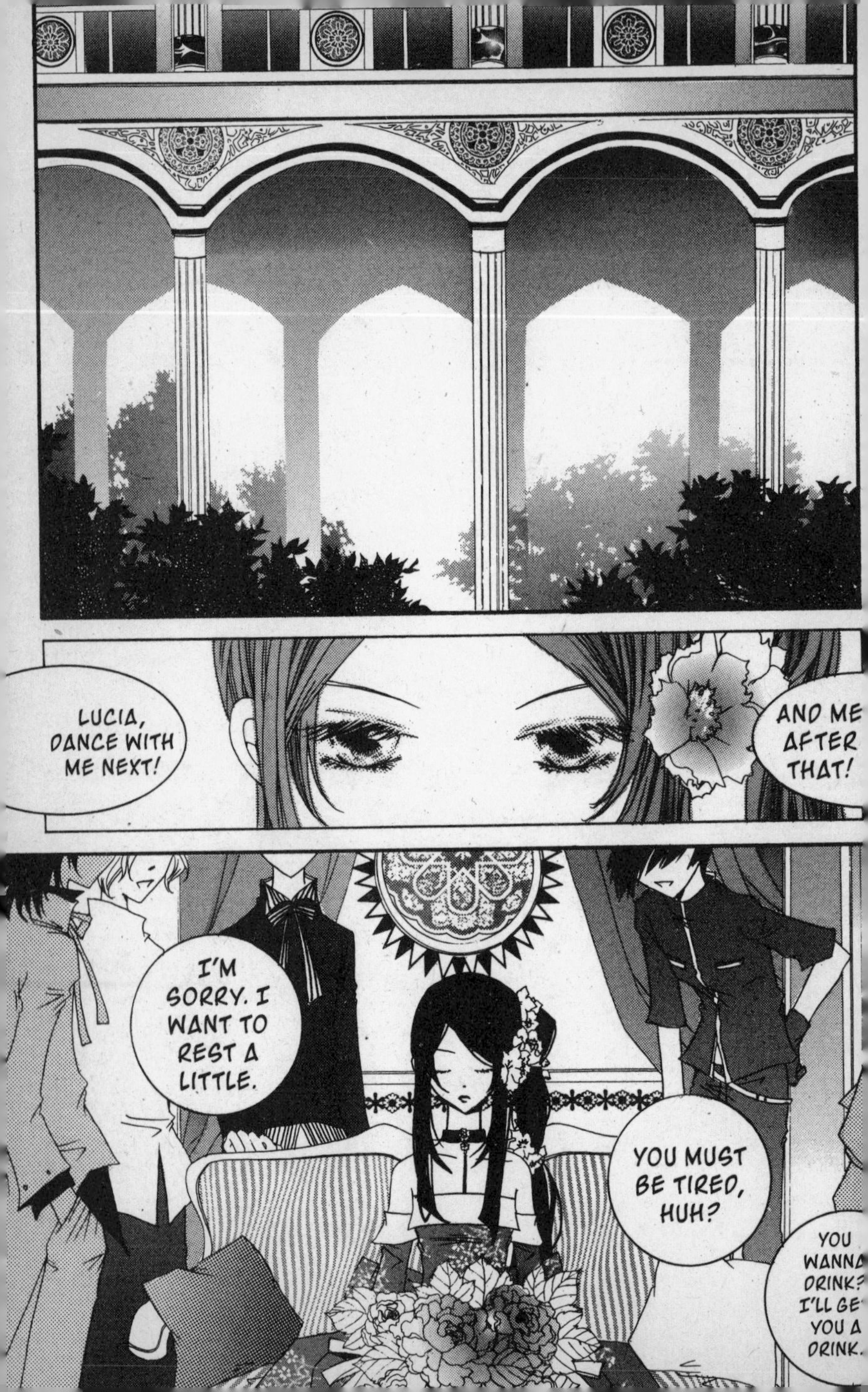
AND ME AFTER THAT!
LUCIA, DANCE WITH ME NEXT!
YOU WANNA DRINK? I'LL GE YOU A DRINK.
YOU MUST BE TIRED, HUH?
I'M SORRY. I WANT TO REST A LITTLE.

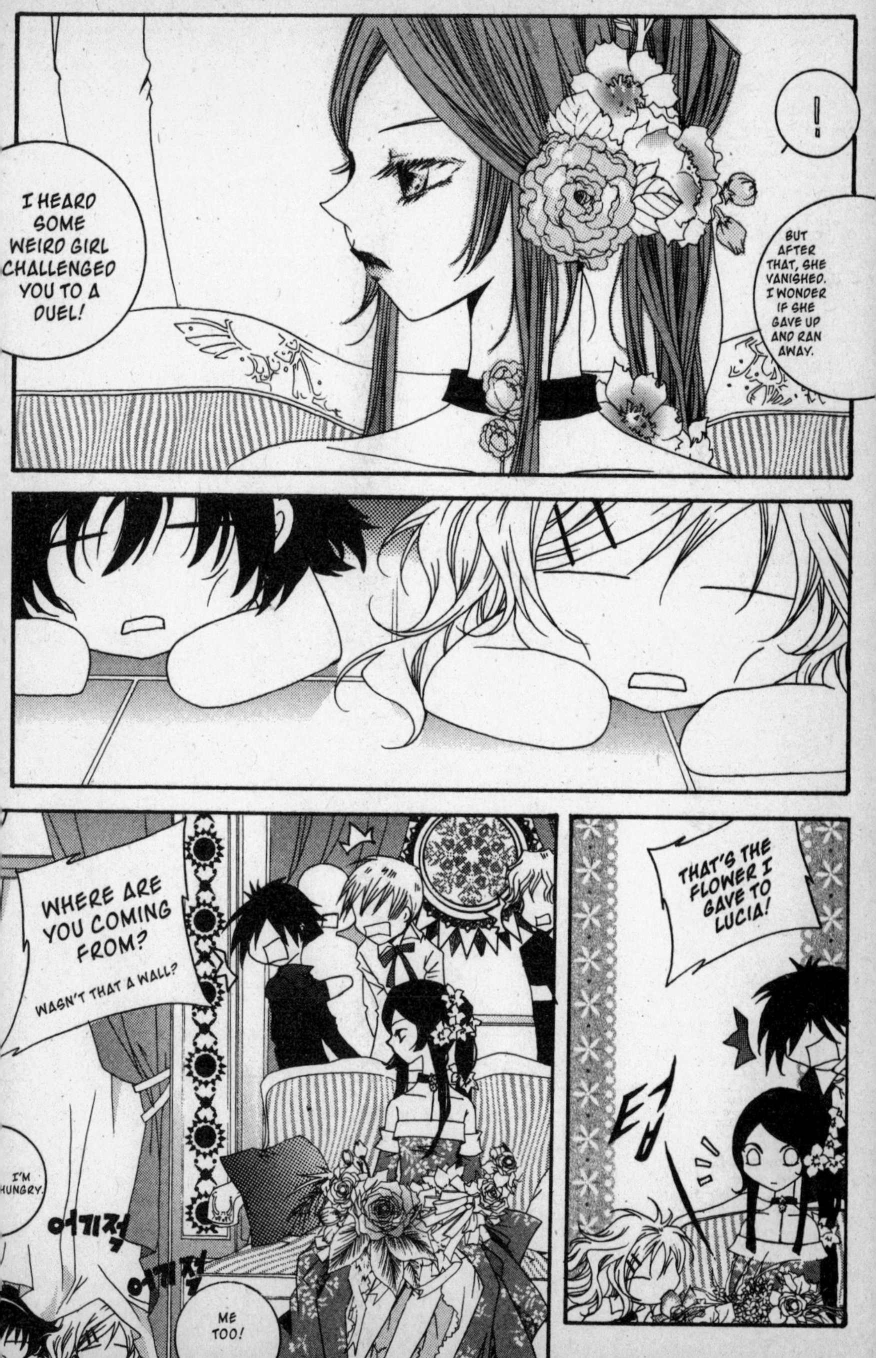
I HEARD SOME WEIRD GIRL CHALLENGED YOU TO A DUEL!
!
BUT AFTER THAT, SHE VANISHED. I WONDER IF SHE GAVE UP AND RAN AWAY.
WHERE ARE YOU COMING FROM?
WASN'T THAT A WALL?
I'M HUNGRY.
어기적
어기적
ME TOO!
THAT'S THE FLOWER I GAVE TO LUCIA!

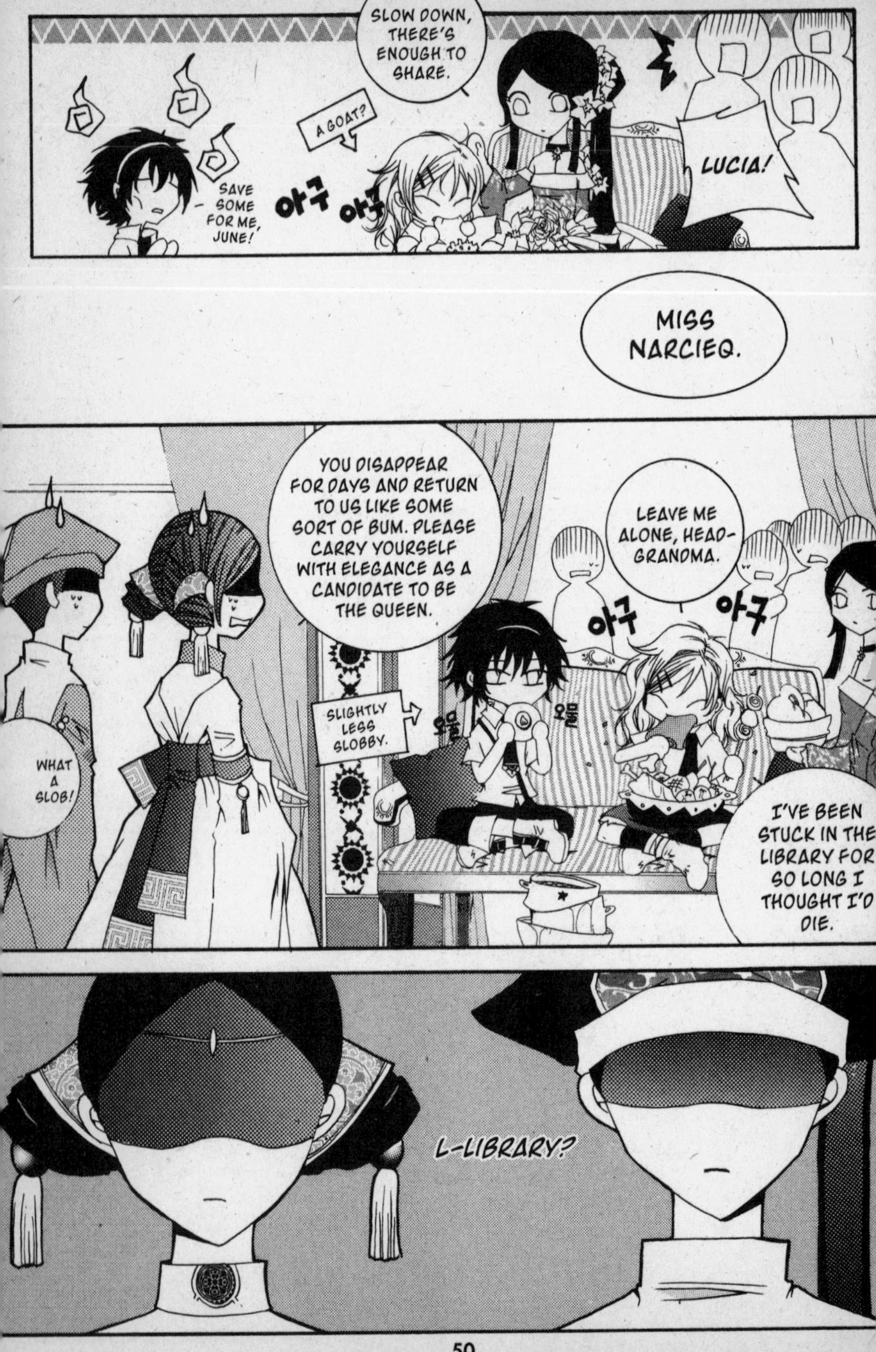
SAVE SOME FOR ME, JUNE!
아구
아구
A GOAT?
SLOW DOWN, THERE'S ENOUGH TO SHARE.
LUCIA!
MISS NARCIEQ.
WHAT A SLOB!
YOU DISAPPEAR FOR DAYS AND RETURN TO US LIKE SOME SORT OF BUM. PLEASE CARRY YOURSELF WITH ELEGANCE AS A CANDIDATE TO BE THE QUEEN.
SLIGHTLY LESS SLOBBY.
오물
오물
LEAVE ME ALONE, HEAD-GRANDMA.
아구
아구
I'VE BEEN STUCK IN THE LIBRARY FOR SO LONG I THOUGHT I'D DIE.
L-LIBRARY?

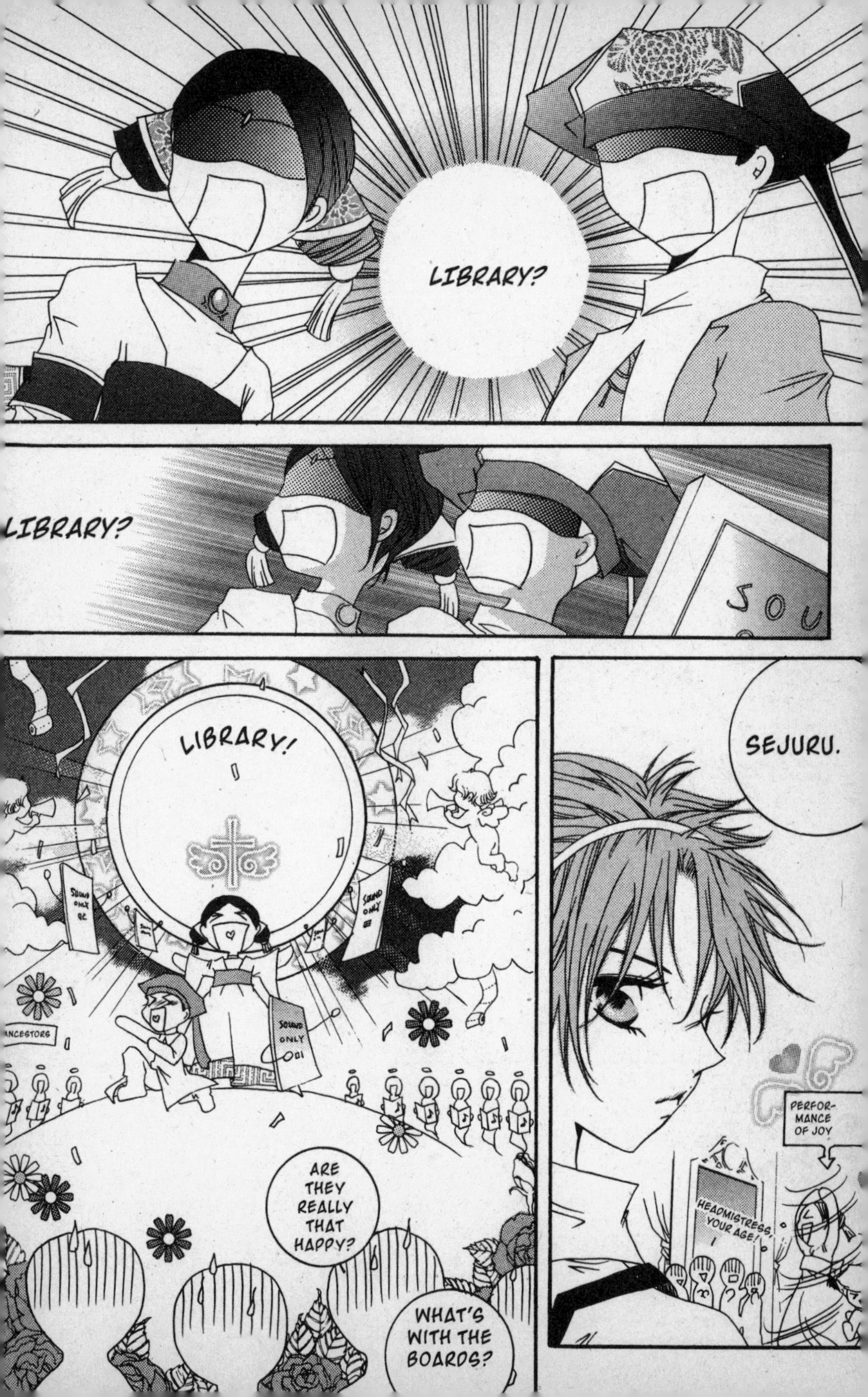
LIBRARY?
LIBRARY?
SOU
SEJURU.
PERFOR-MANCE OF JOY
HEADMISTRESS, YOUR AGE!
LIBRARY!
SOUND ONLY 01
ANCESTORS
ARE THEY REALLY THAT HAPPY?
WHAT'S WITH THE BOARDS?

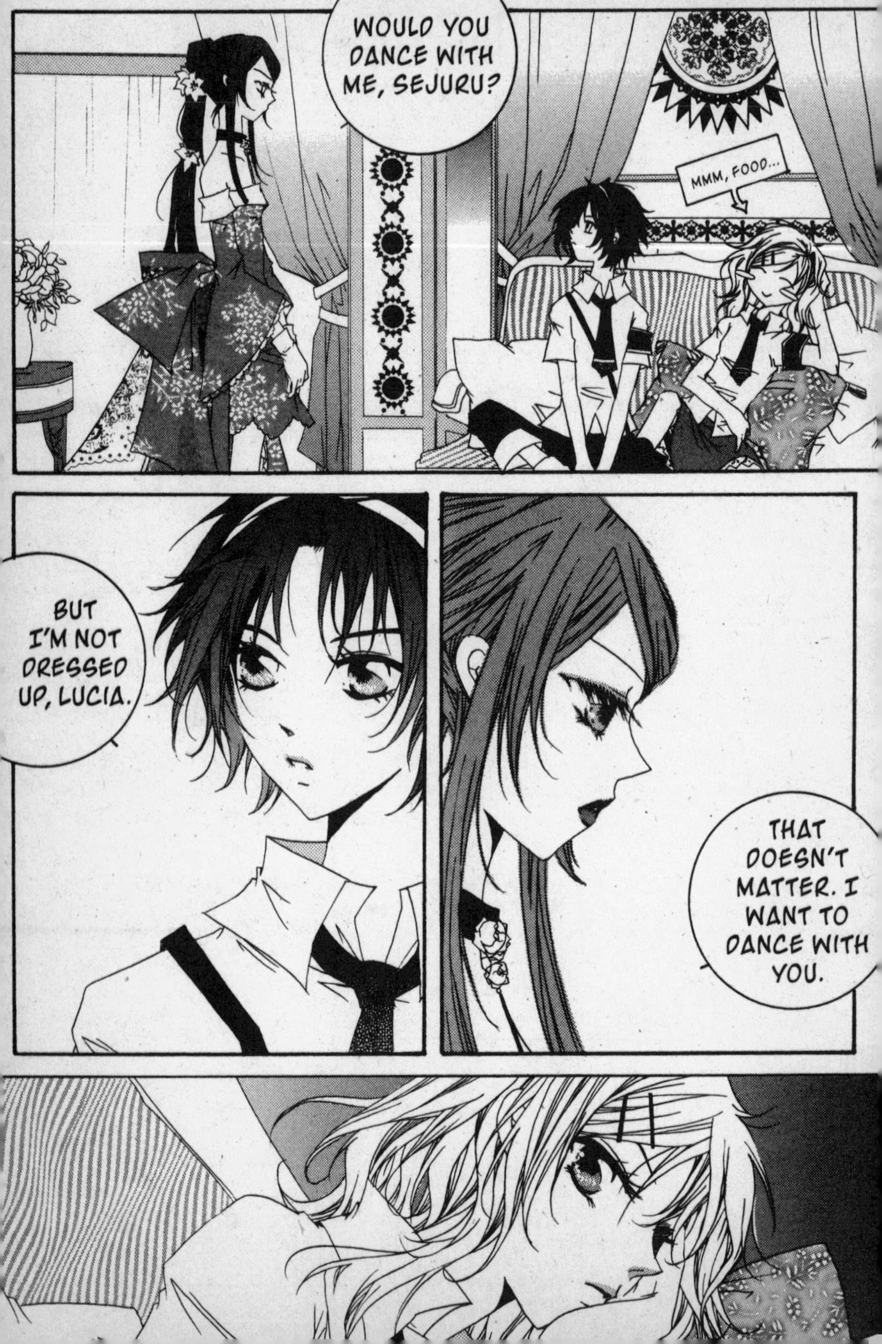
WOULD YOU DANCE WITH ME, SEJURU?
MMM, FOOD...
BUT I'M NOT DRESSED UP, LUCIA.
THAT DOESN'T MATTER. I WANT TO DANCE WITH YOU.

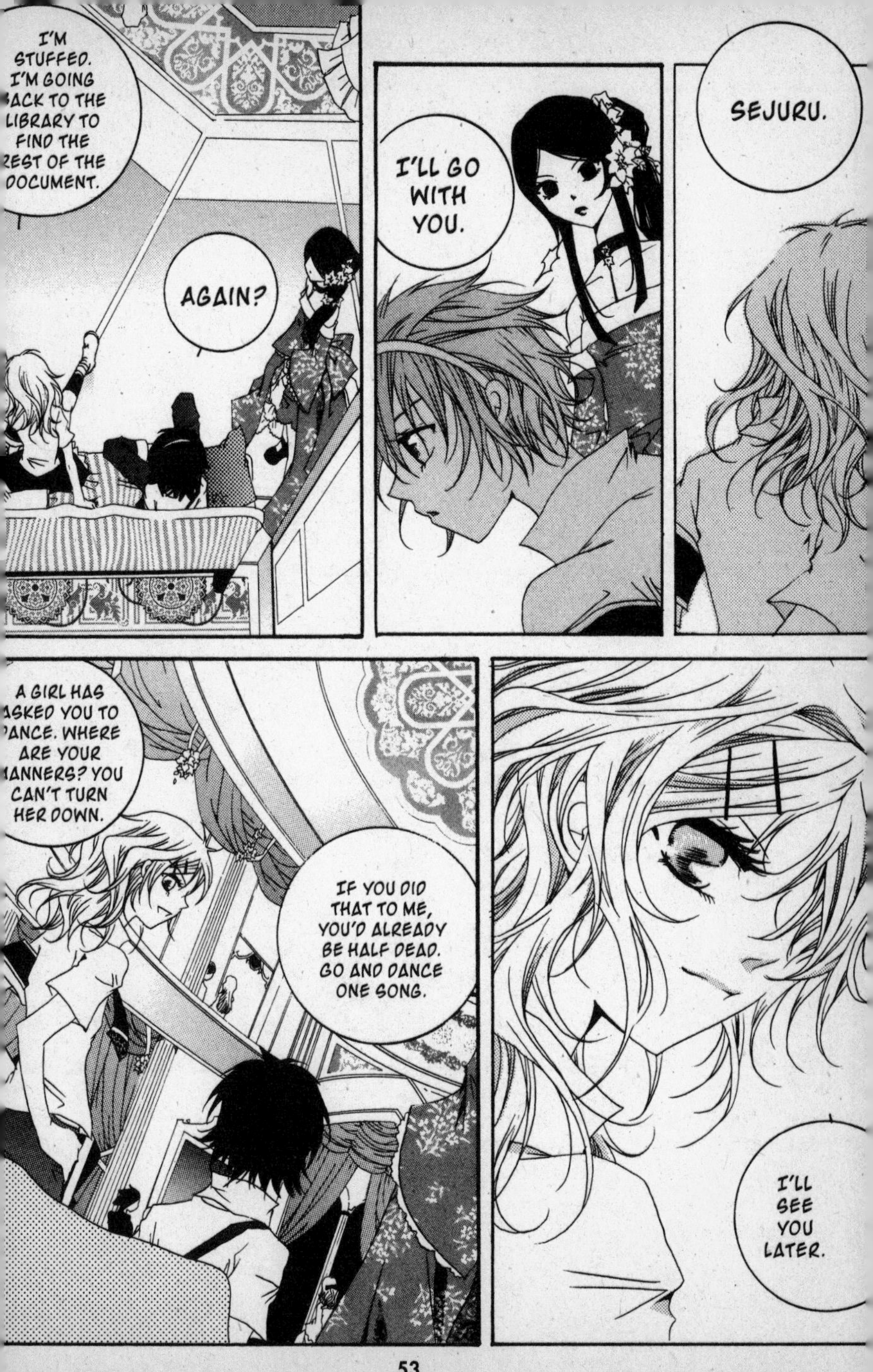
I'M STUFFED. I'M GOING BACK TO THE LIBRARY TO FIND THE REST OF THE DOCUMENT.
AGAIN?
I'LL GO WITH YOU.
SEJURU.
A GIRL HAS ASKED YOU TO DANCE. WHERE ARE YOUR MANNERS? YOU CAN'T TURN HER DOWN.
IF YOU DID THAT TO ME, YOU'D ALREADY BE HALF DEAD. GO AND DANCE ONE SONG.
I'LL SEE YOU LATER.

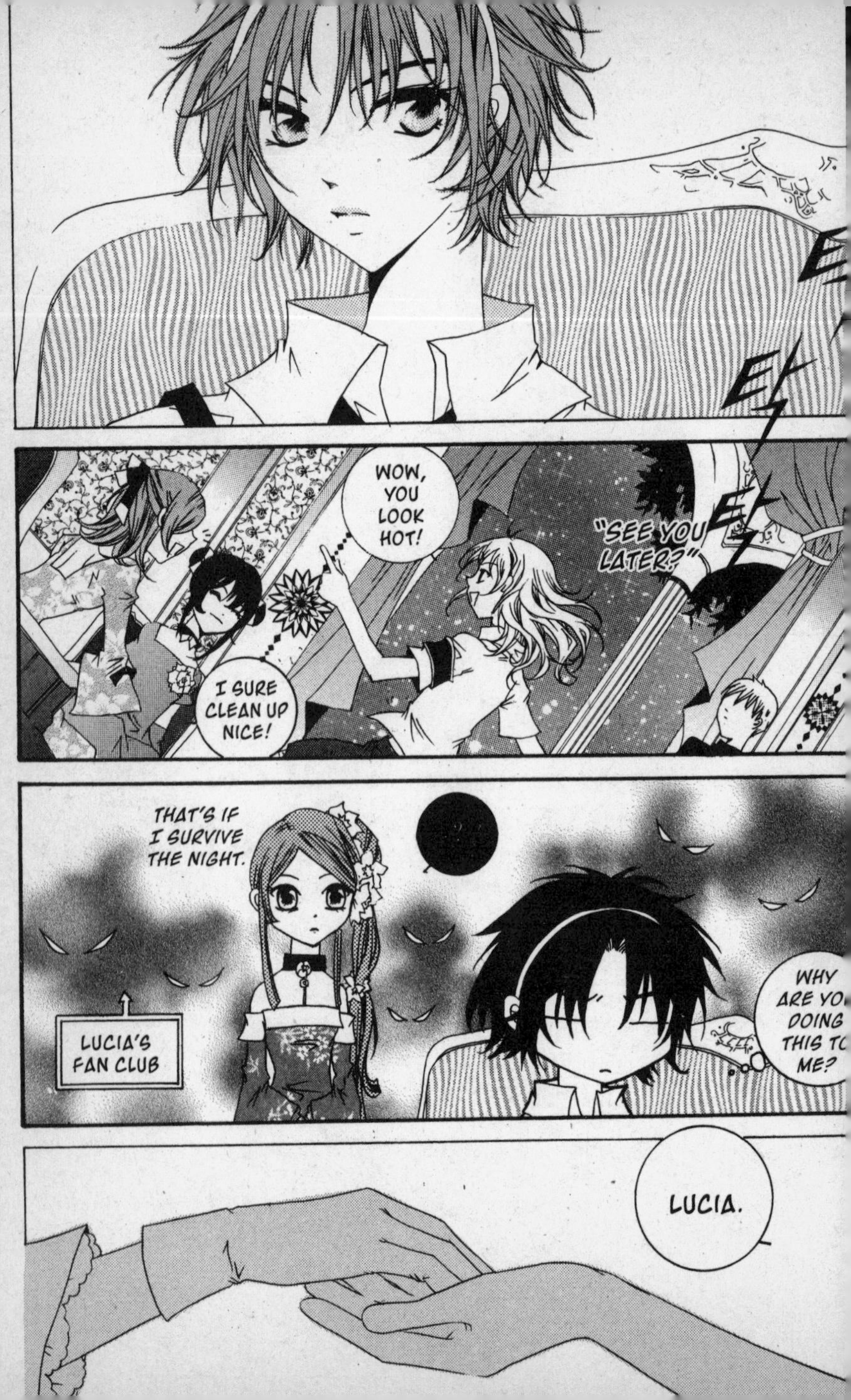
EEEE
"SEE YOU LATER?"
WOW, YOU LOOK HOT!
I SURE CLEAN UP NICE!
THAT'S IF I SURVIVE THE NIGHT.
LUCIA'S FAN CLUB
WHY ARE YO DOING THIS TO ME?
LUCIA.

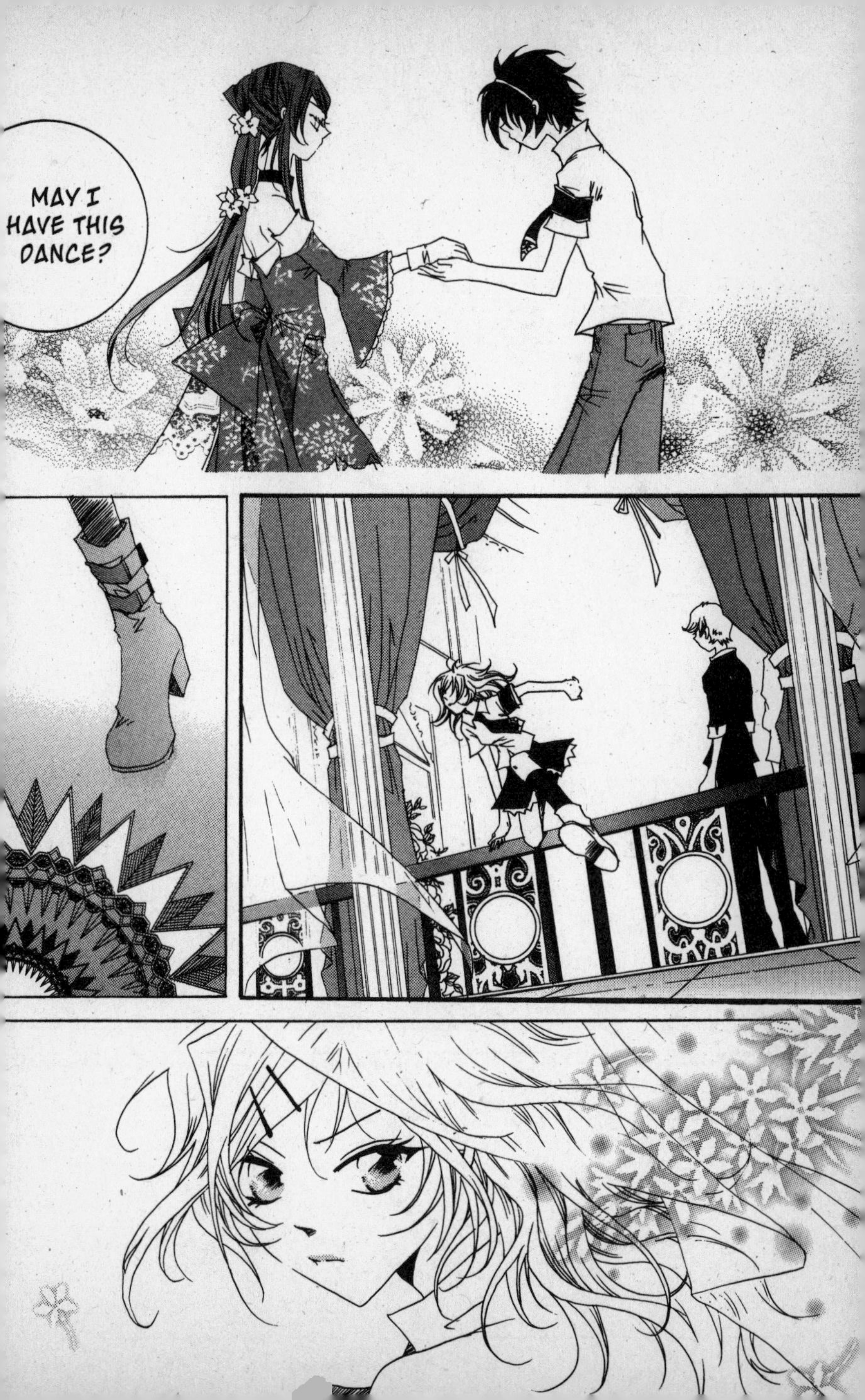
MAY I HAVE THIS DANCE?

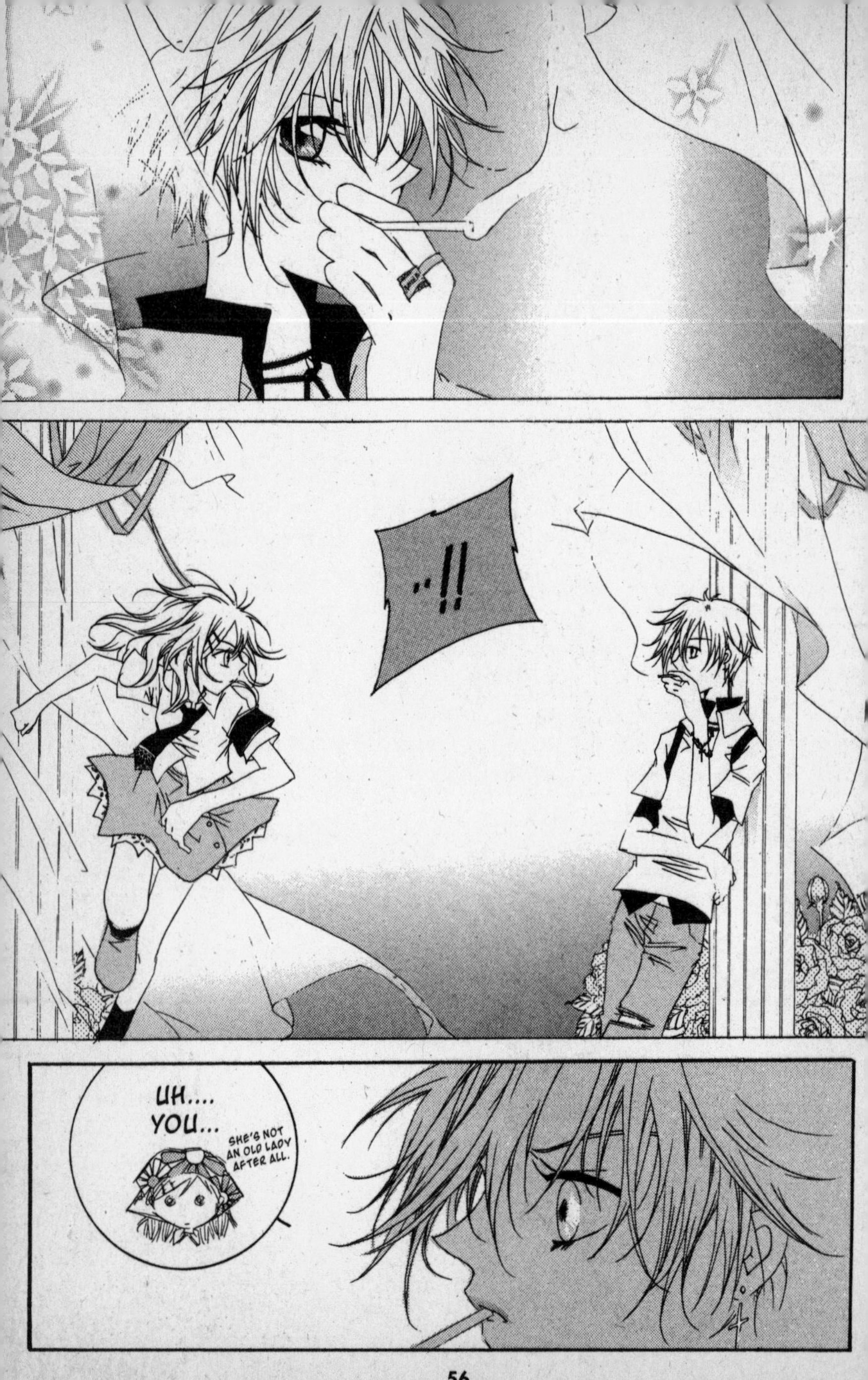
..!!
UH.... YOU...
SHE'S NOT AN OLD LADY AFTER ALL.

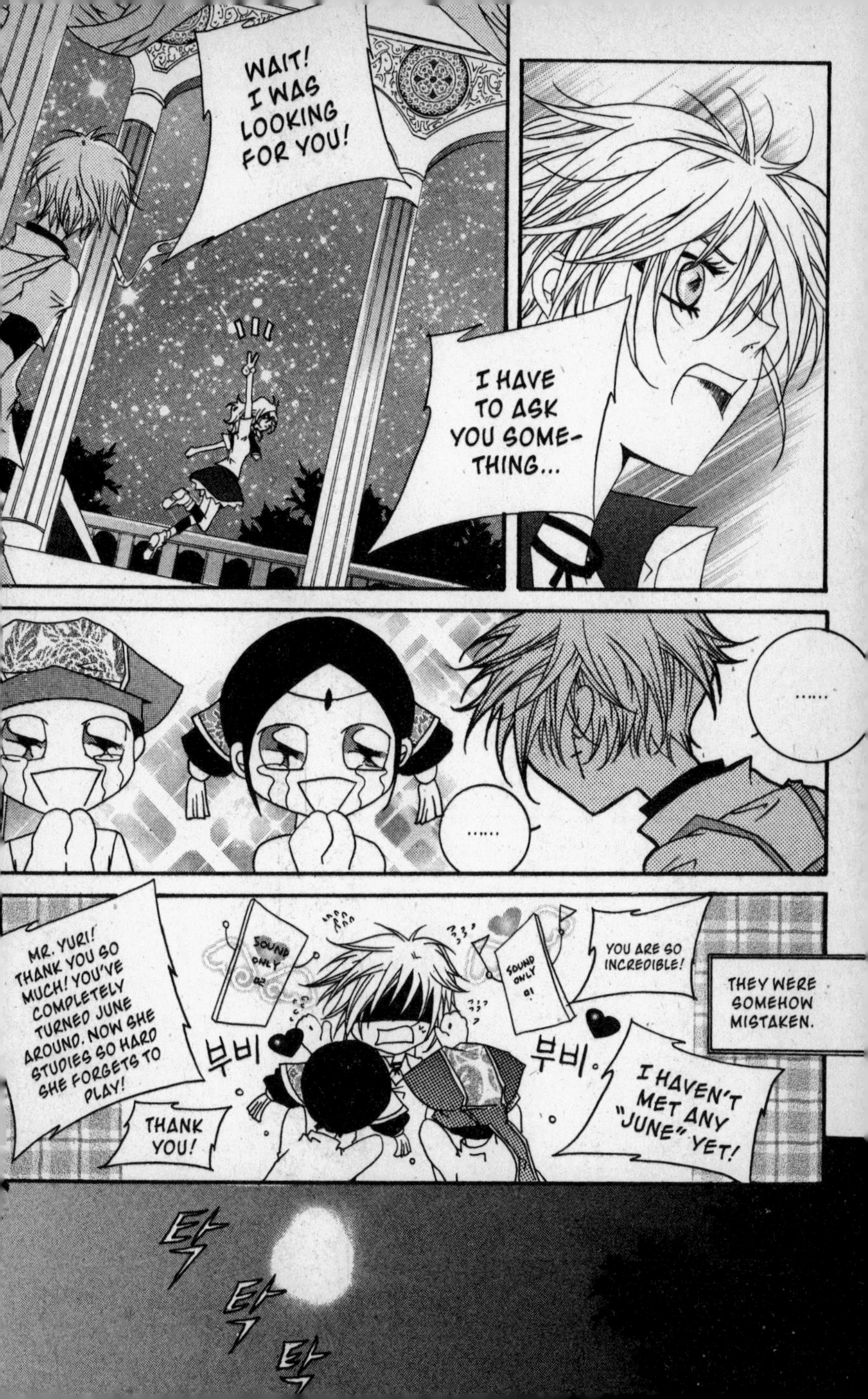
WAIT! I WAS LOOKING FOR YOU!
I HAVE TO ASK YOU SOME-THING...
......
......
MR. YURI! THANK YOU SO MUCH! YOU'VE COMPLETELY TURNED JUNE AROUND. NOW SHE STUDIES SO HARD SHE FORGETS TO PLAY!
THANK YOU!
SOUND ONLY 02
부비
SOUND ONLY 01
부비
YOU ARE SO INCREDIBLE!
I HAVEN'T MET ANY "JUNE" YET!
THEY WERE SOMEHOW MISTAKEN.
탁
탁
탁

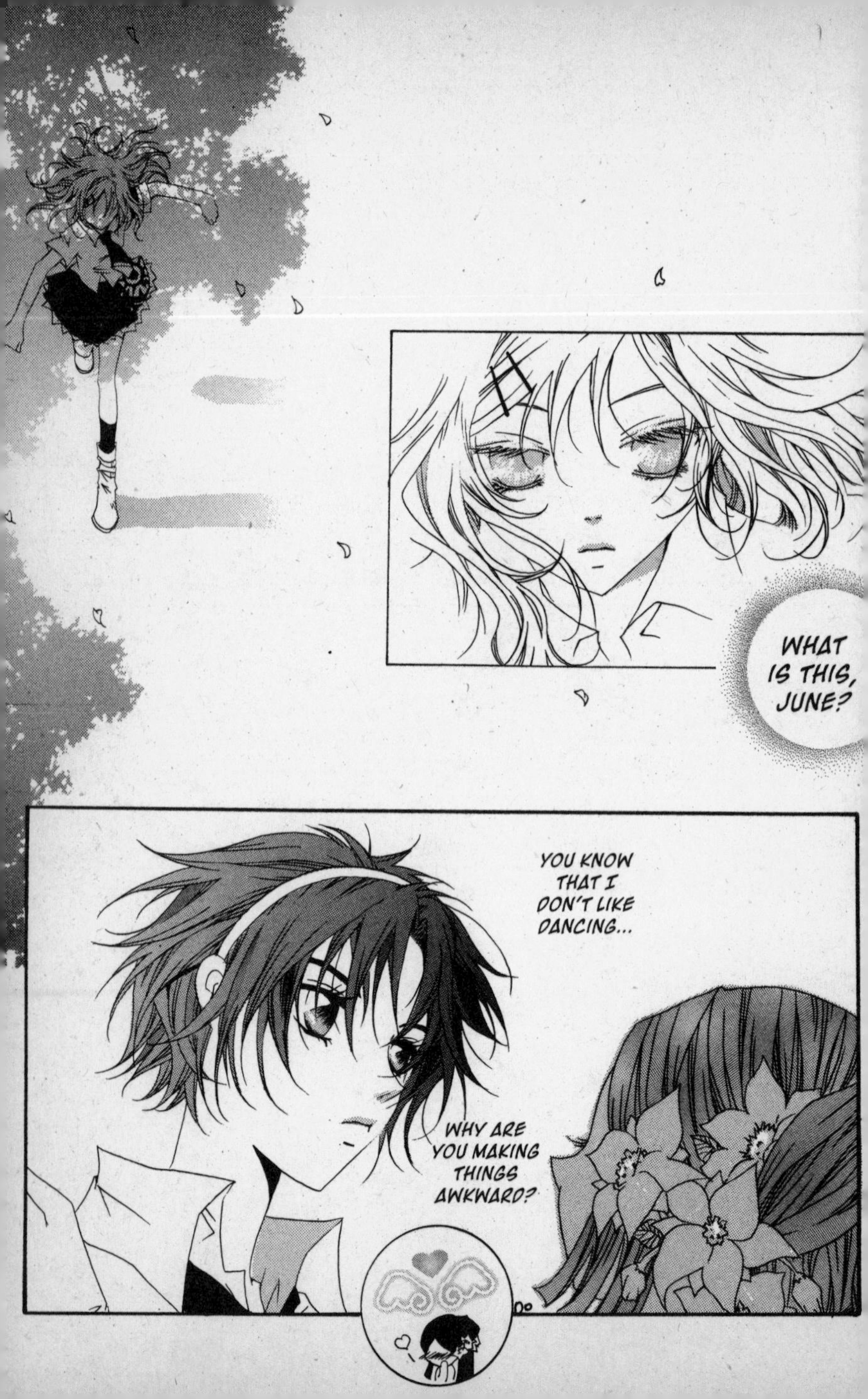
WHAT IS THIS, JUNE?
YOU KNOW THAT I DON'T LIKE DANCING...
WHY ARE YOU MAKING THINGS AWKWARD?

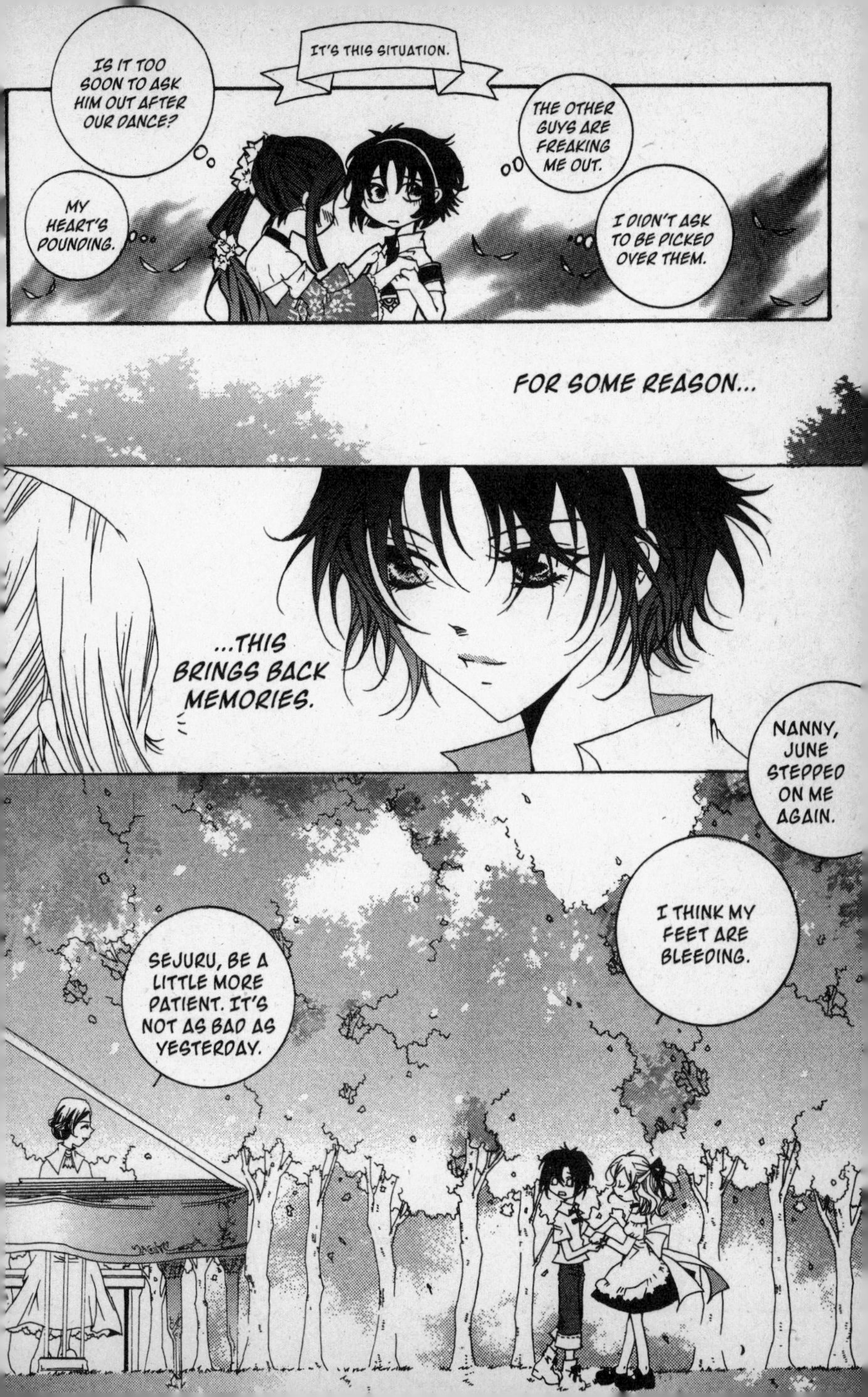

IT'S THIS SITUATION.
THE OTHER GUYS ARE FREAKING ME OUT.
I DIDN'T ASK TO BE PICKED OVER THEM.
IS IT TOO SOON TO ASK HIM OUT AFTER OUR DANCE?
MY HEART'S POUNDING.
FOR SOME REASON...
...THIS BRINGS BACK MEMORIES.
NANNY, JUNE STEPPED ON ME AGAIN.
I THINK MY FEET ARE BLEEDING.
SEJURU, BE A LITTLE MORE PATIENT. IT'S NOT AS BAD AS YESTERDAY.

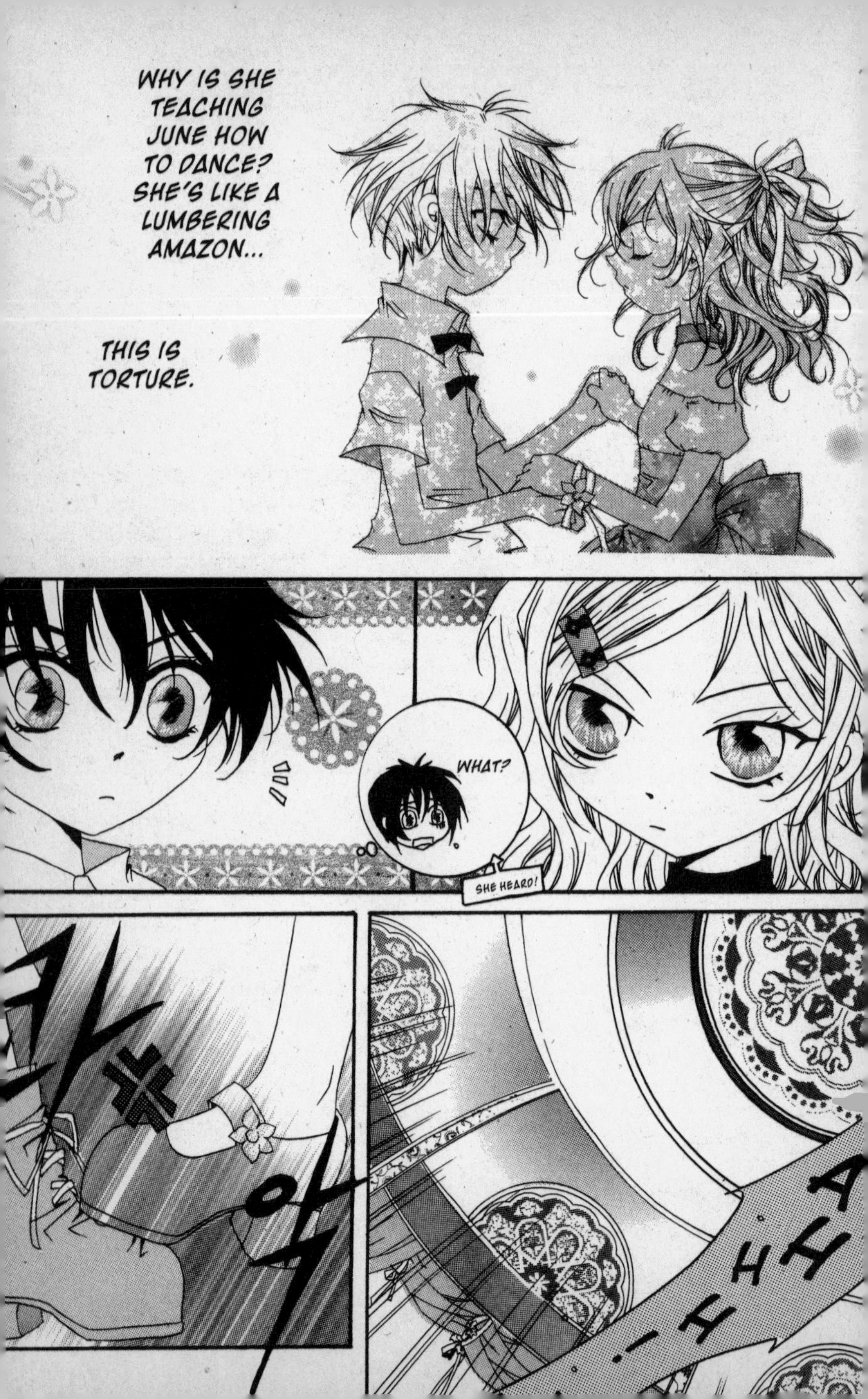
WHY IS SHE TEACHING JUNE HOW TO DANCE? SHE'S LIKE A LUMBERING AMAZON...
THIS IS TORTURE.
WHAT?
SHE HEARD!
AHHH--!!

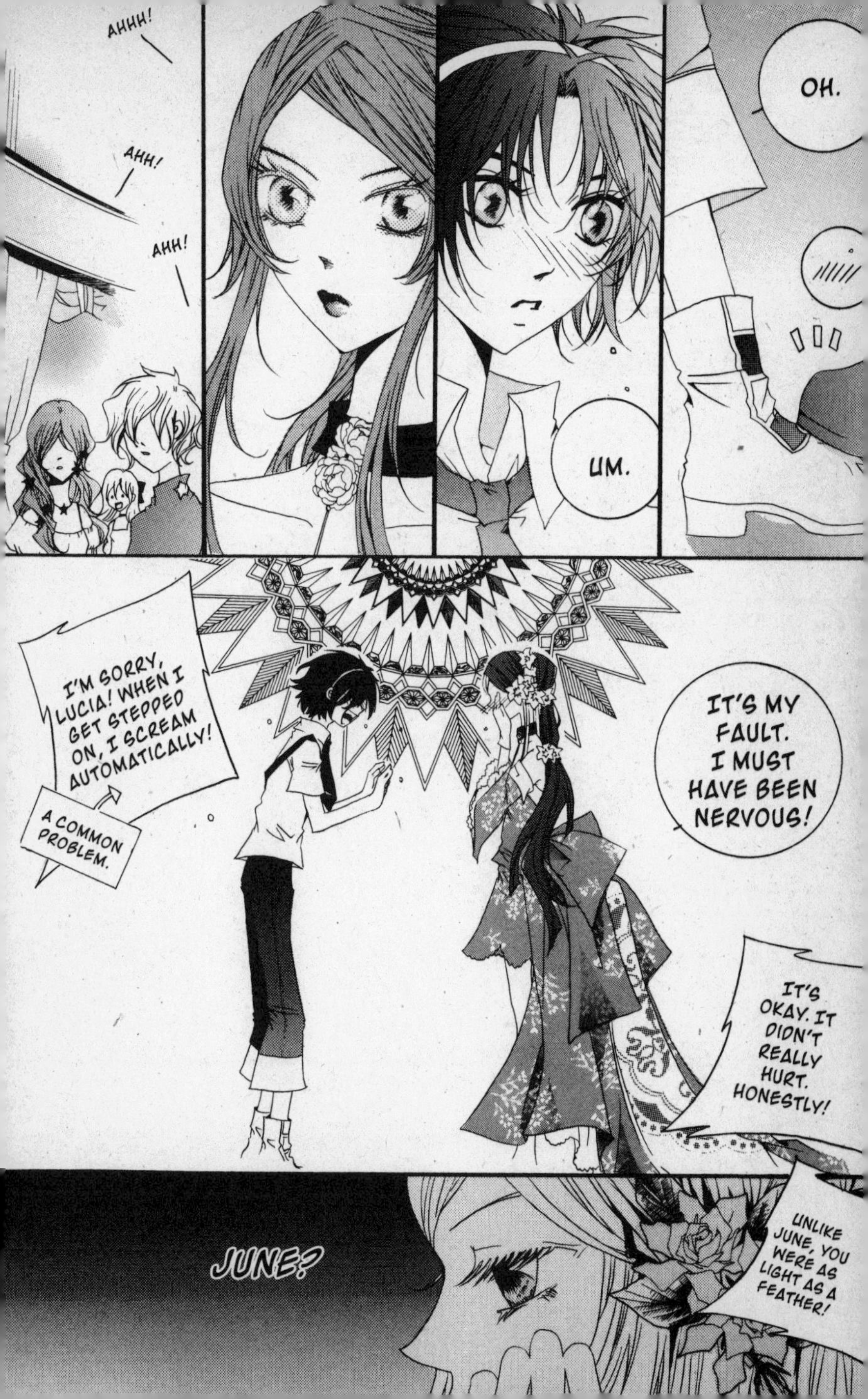
OH.
UM.
AHHH!
AHH!
AHH!
IT'S MY FAULT. I MUST HAVE BEEN NERVOUS!
I'M SORRY, LUCIA! WHEN I GET STEPPED ON, I SCREAM AUTOMATICALLY!
A COMMON PROBLEM.
IT'S OKAY. IT DIDN'T REALLY HURT. HONESTLY!
UNLIKE JUNE, YOU WERE AS LIGHT AS A FEATHER!
JUNE?

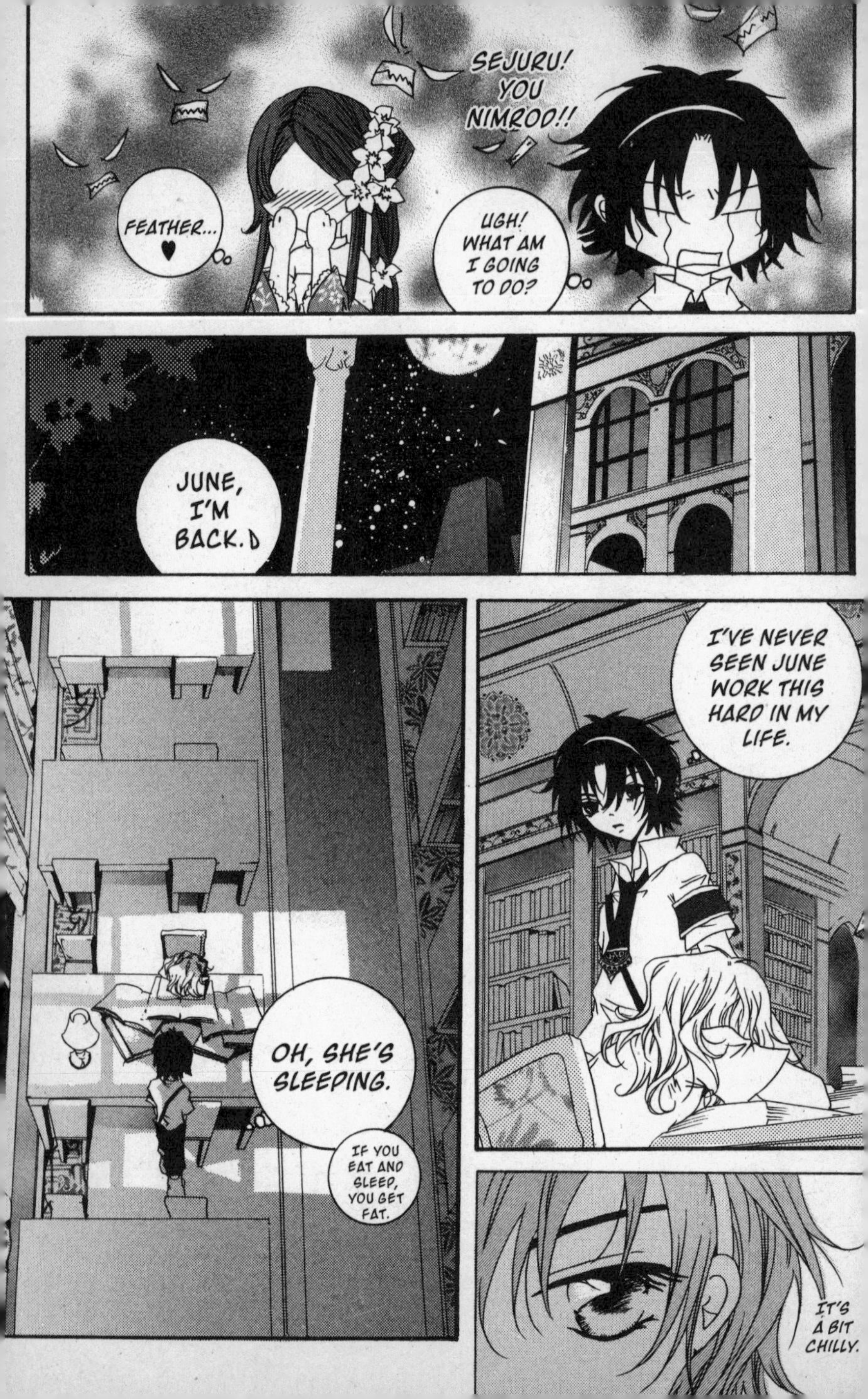
SEJURU! YOU NIMROD!!
UGH! WHAT AM I GOING TO DO?
FEATHER... ♥
JUNE, I'M BACK. D
I'VE NEVER SEEN JUNE WORK THIS HARD IN MY LIFE.
IT'S A BIT CHILLY.
OH, SHE'S SLEEPING.
IF YOU EAT AND SLEEP, YOU GET FAT.

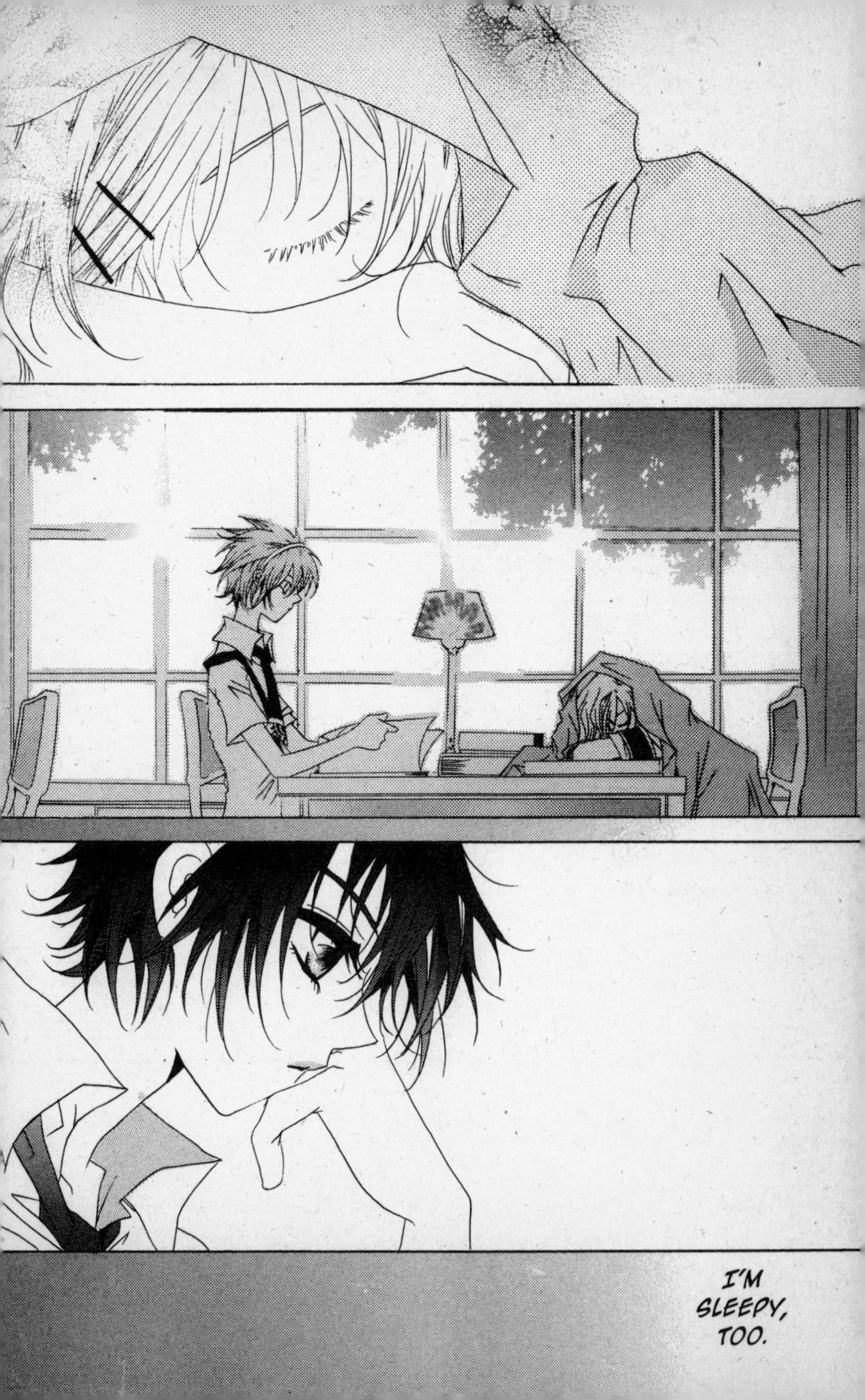
I'M SLEEPY, TOO.

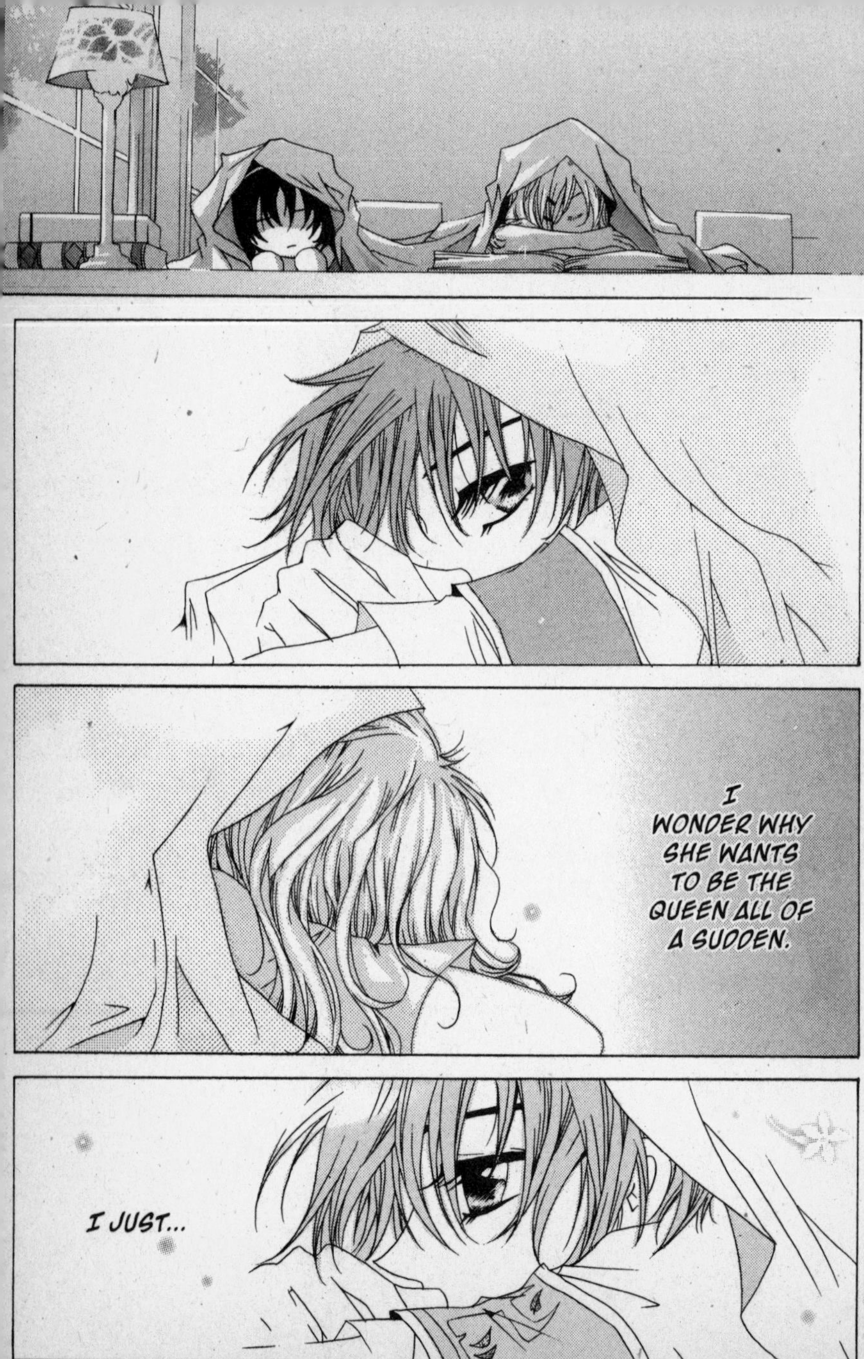
I WONDER WHY SHE WANTS TO BE THE QUEEN ALL OF A SUDDEN.
I JUST...

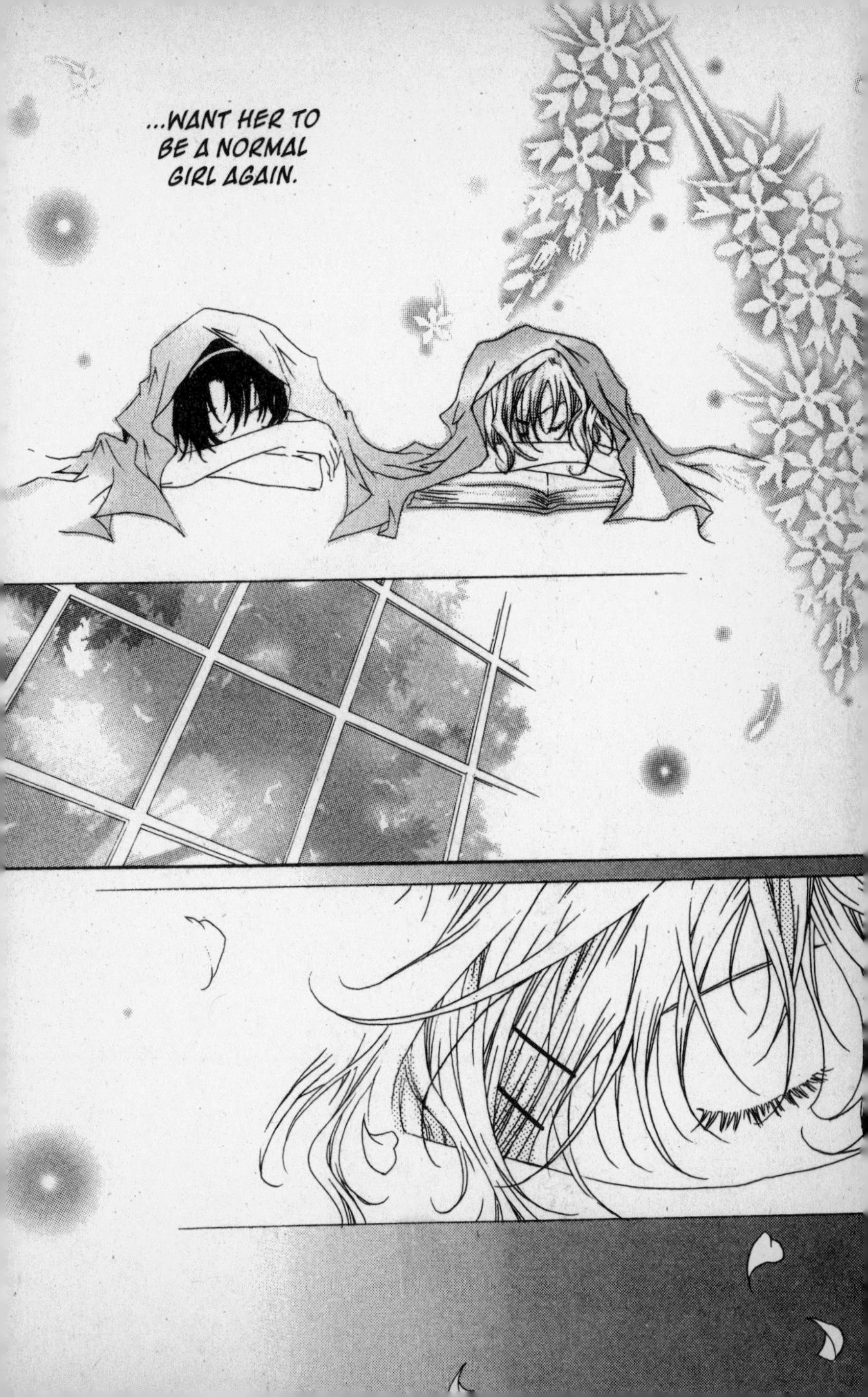
...WANT HER TO
BE A NORMAL
GIRL AGAIN.

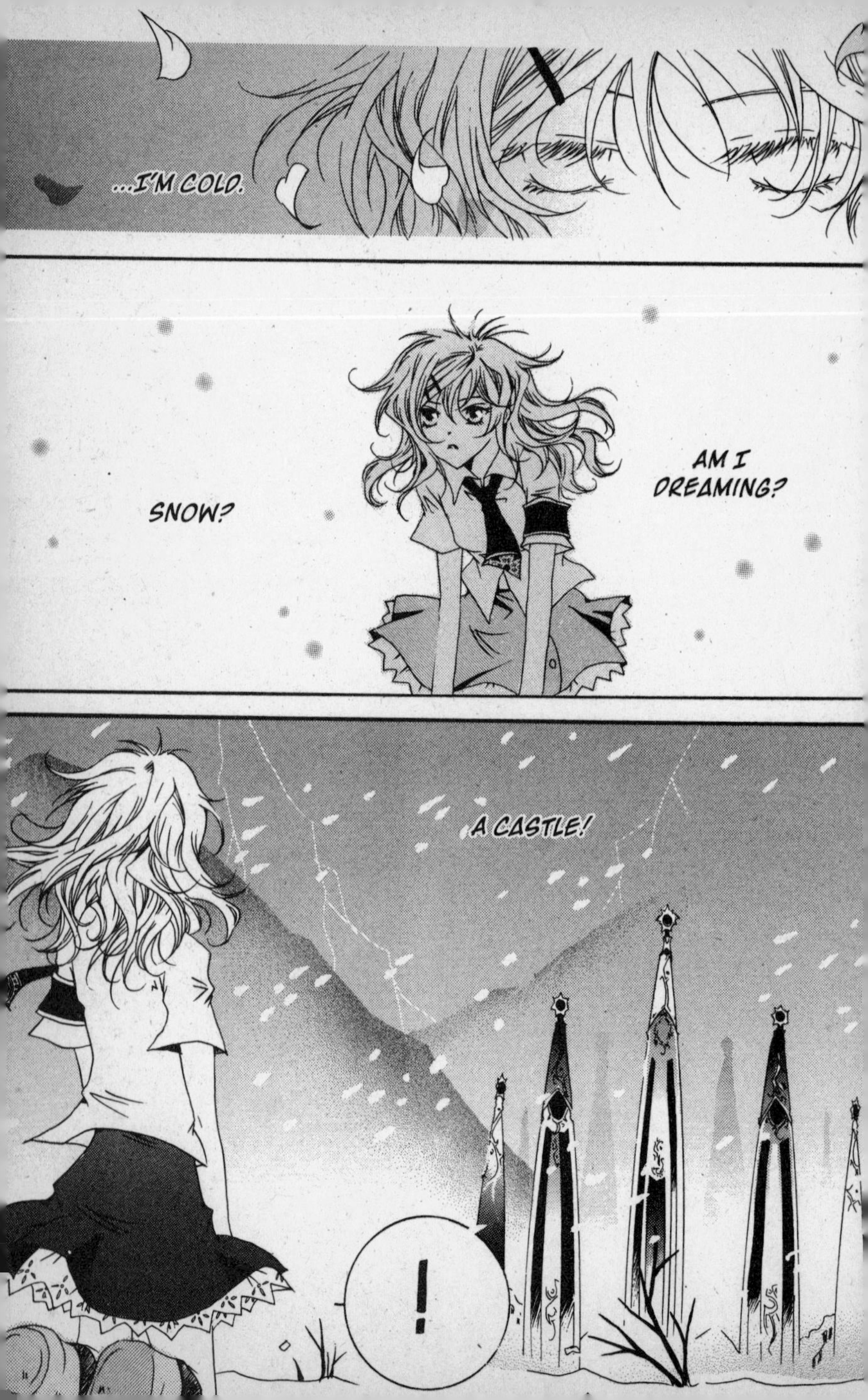
...I'M COLD.
AM I DREAMING?
SNOW?
A CASTLE!
!

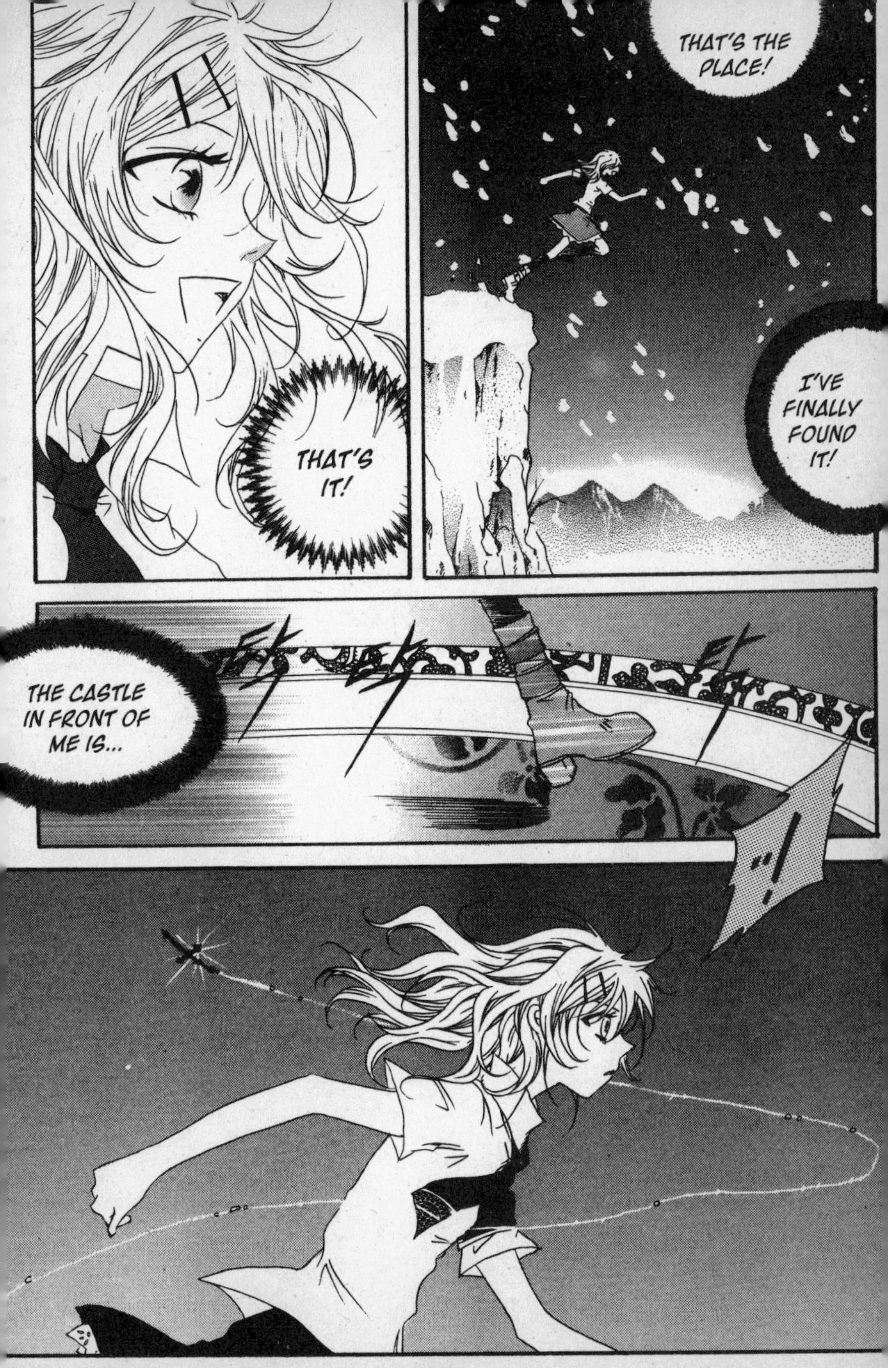
THAT'S THE PLACE!
I'VE FINALLY FOUND IT!
THAT'S IT!
THE CASTLE IN FRONT OF ME IS...

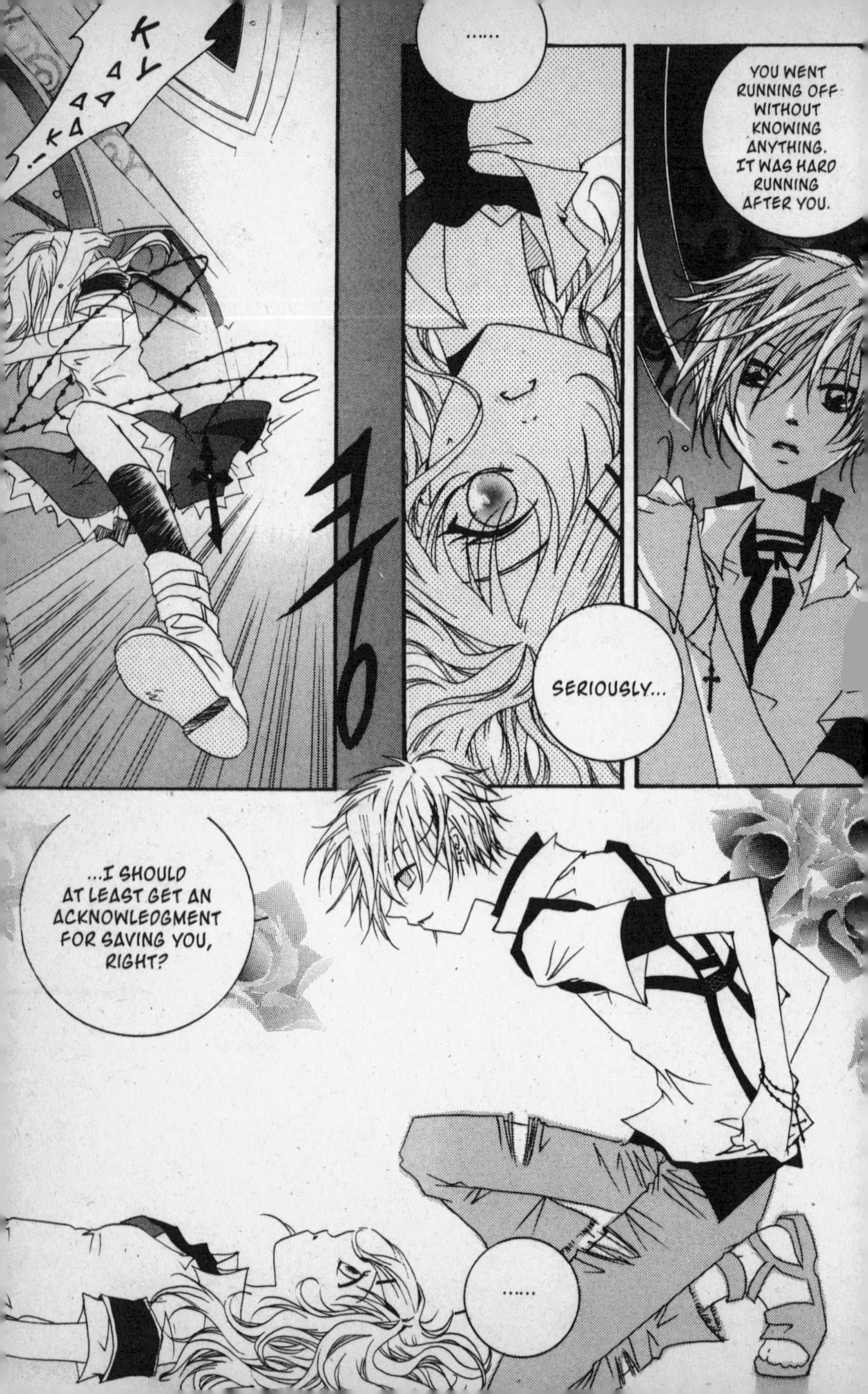
YOU WENT RUNNING OFF WITHOUT KNOWING ANYTHING. IT WAS HARD RUNNING AFTER YOU.
SERIOUSLY...
......
...I SHOULD AT LEAST GET AN ACKNOWLEDGMENT FOR SAVING YOU, RIGHT?
......

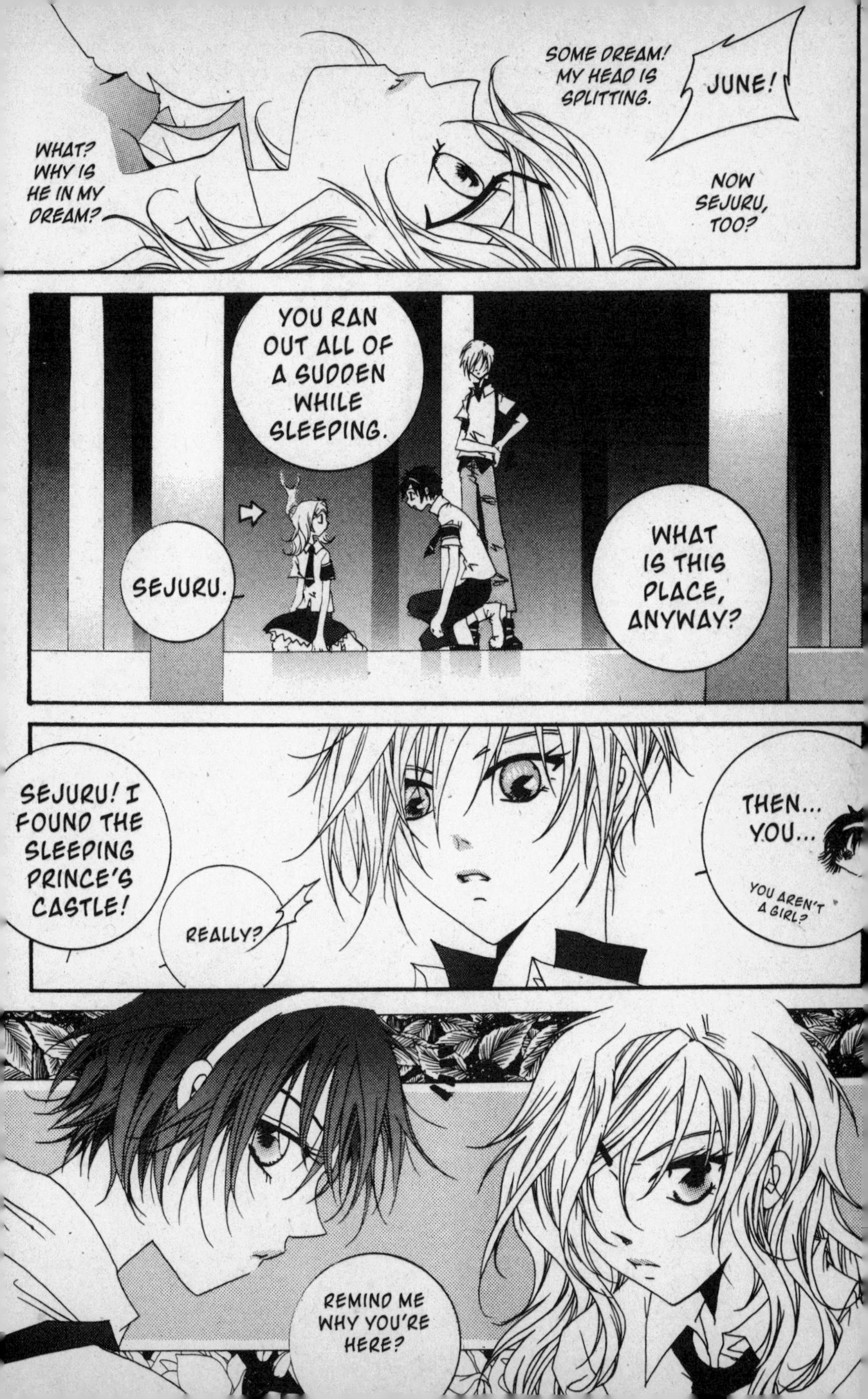
JUNE!
SOME DREAM! MY HEAD IS SPLITTING.
NOW SEJURU, TOO?
WHAT? WHY IS HE IN MY DREAM?
WHAT IS THIS PLACE, ANYWAY?
YOU RAN OUT ALL OF A SUDDEN WHILE SLEEPING.
SEJURU.
THEN... YOU...
YOU AREN'T A GIRL?
SEJURU! I FOUND THE SLEEPING PRINCE'S CASTLE!
REALLY?
REMIND ME WHY YOU'RE HERE?

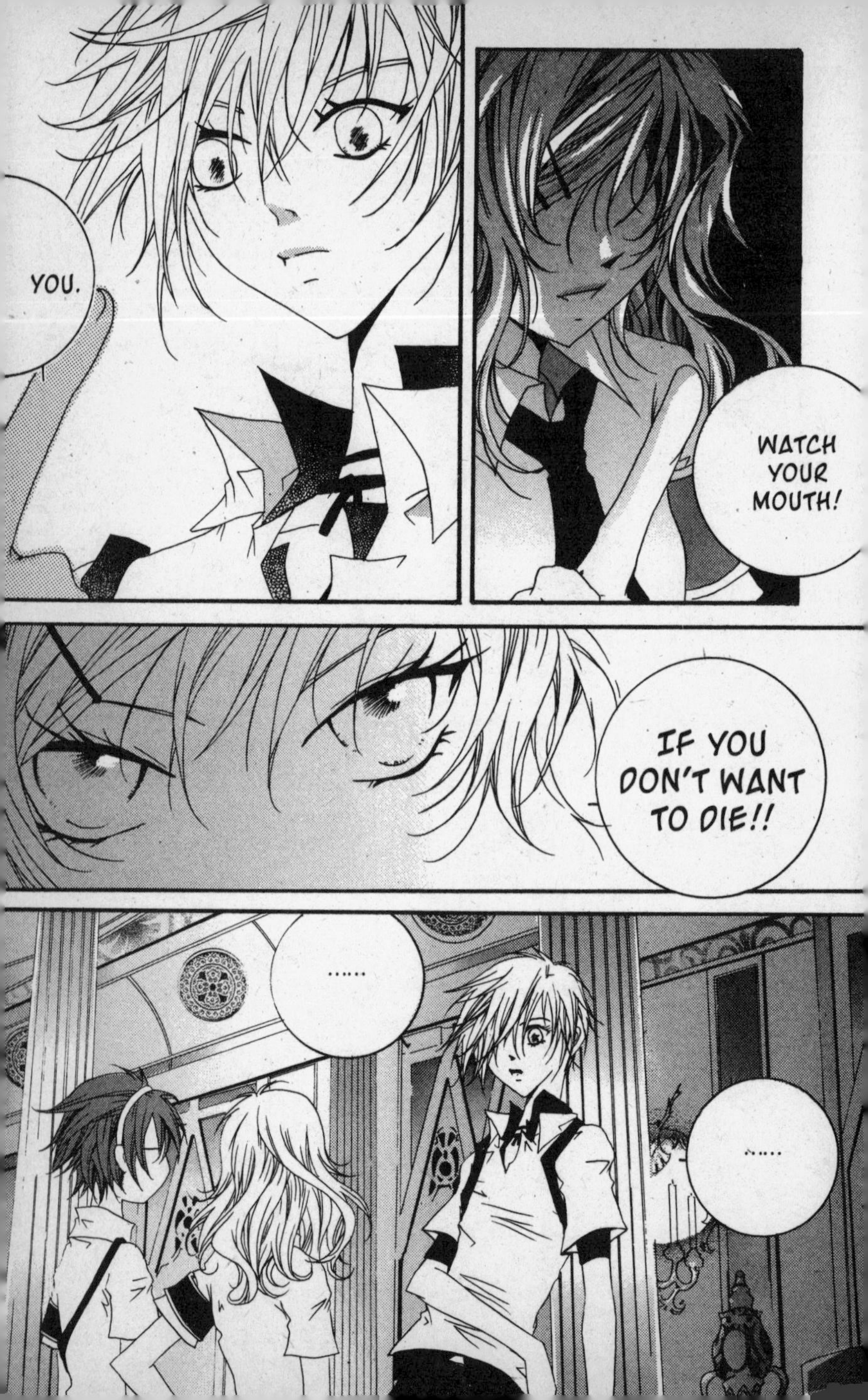
YOU.
WATCH YOUR MOUTH!
IF YOU DON'T WANT TO DIE!!
......
.....

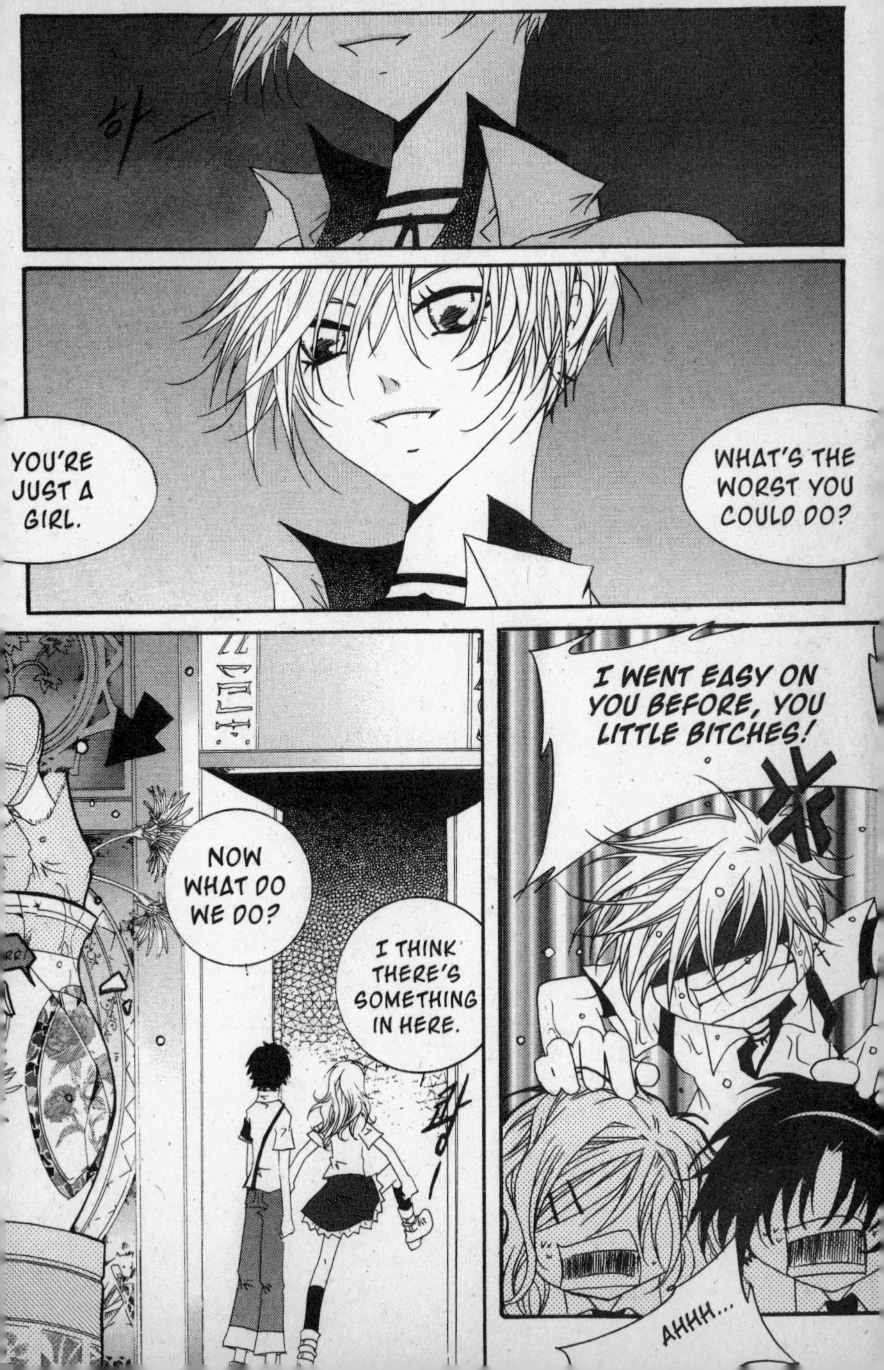
WHAT'S THE WORST YOU COULD DO?
YOU'RE JUST A GIRL.
I WENT EASY ON YOU BEFORE, YOU LITTLE BITCHES!
AHHH...
NOW WHAT DO WE DO?
I THINK THERE'S SOMETHING IN HERE.

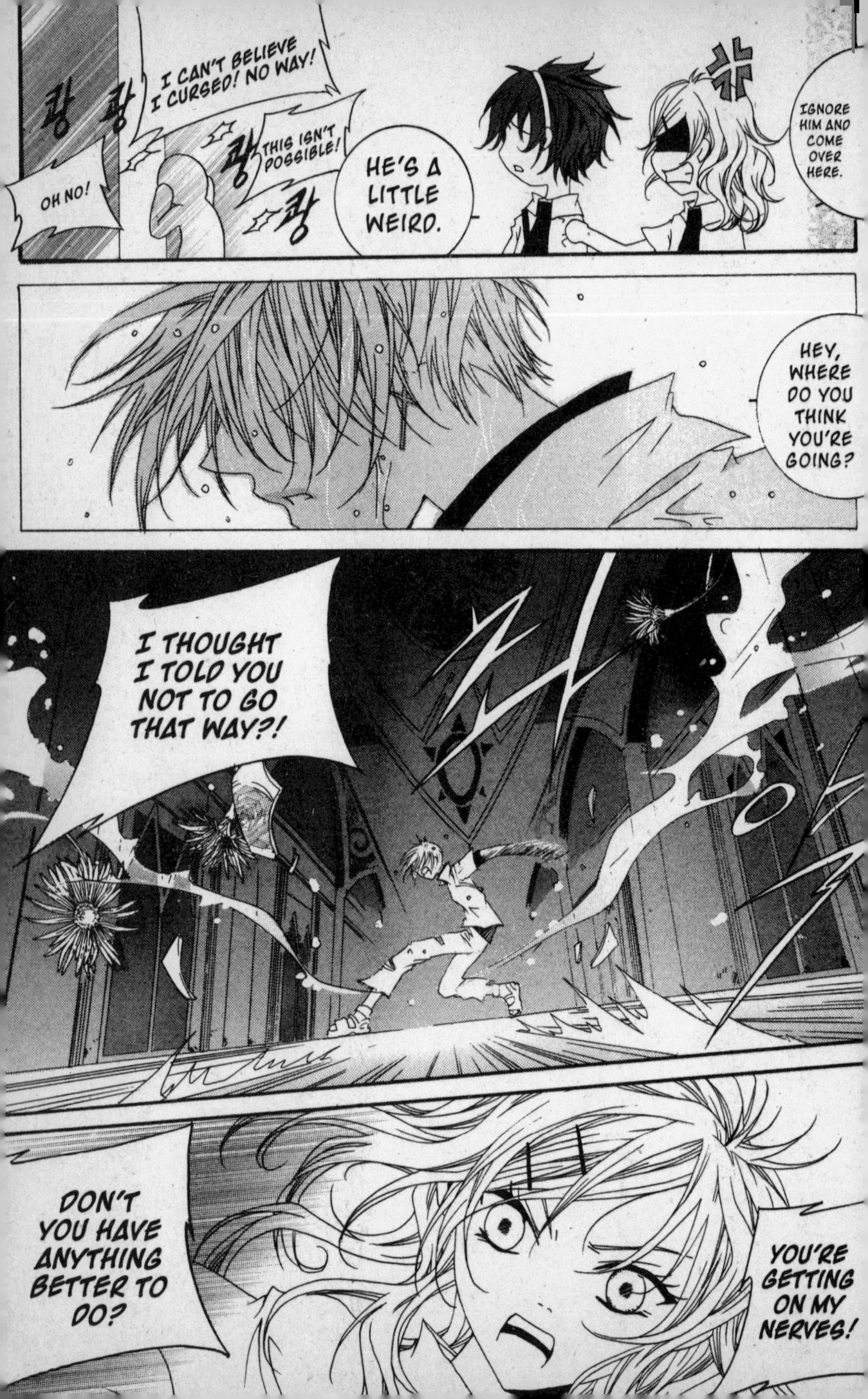

쾅 쾅
I CAN'T BELIEVE I CURSED! NO WAY!
OH NO!
쾅
THIS ISN'T POSSIBLE!
쾅
HE'S A LITTLE WEIRD.
IGNORE HIM AND COME OVER HERE.
HEY, WHERE DO YOU THINK YOU'RE GOING?
I THOUGHT I TOLD YOU NOT TO GO THAT WAY?!
DON'T YOU HAVE ANYTHING BETTER TO DO?
YOU'RE GETTING ON MY NERVES!

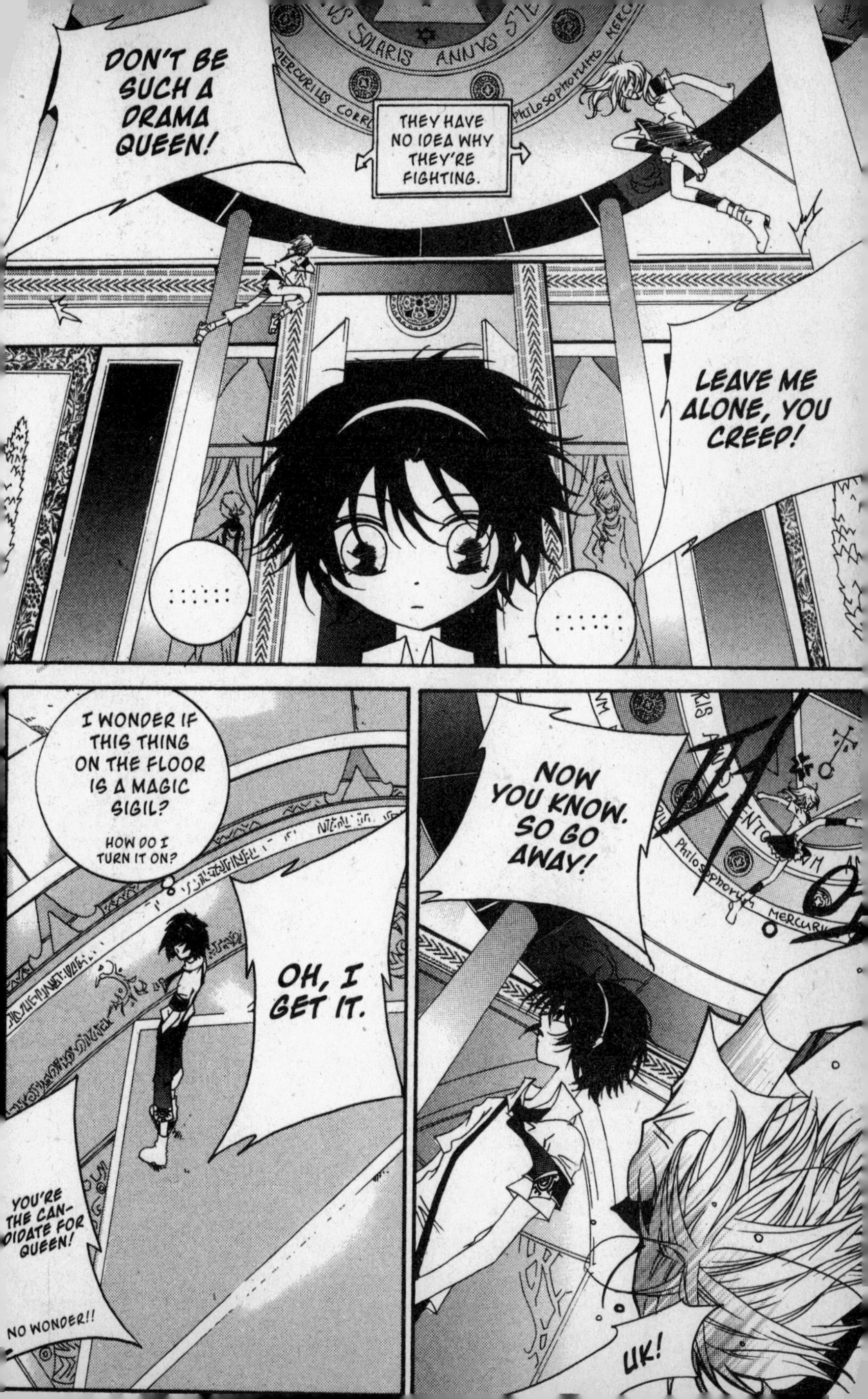
DON'T BE SUCH A DRAMA QUEEN!
THEY HAVE NO IDEA WHY THEY'RE FIGHTING.
LEAVE ME ALONE, YOU CREEP!
......
......
I WONDER IF THIS THING ON THE FLOOR IS A MAGIC SIGIL?
HOW DO I TURN IT ON?
OH, I GET IT.
YOU'RE THE CAN-DIDATE FOR QUEEN!
NO WONDER!!
NOW YOU KNOW. SO GO AWAY!
UK!

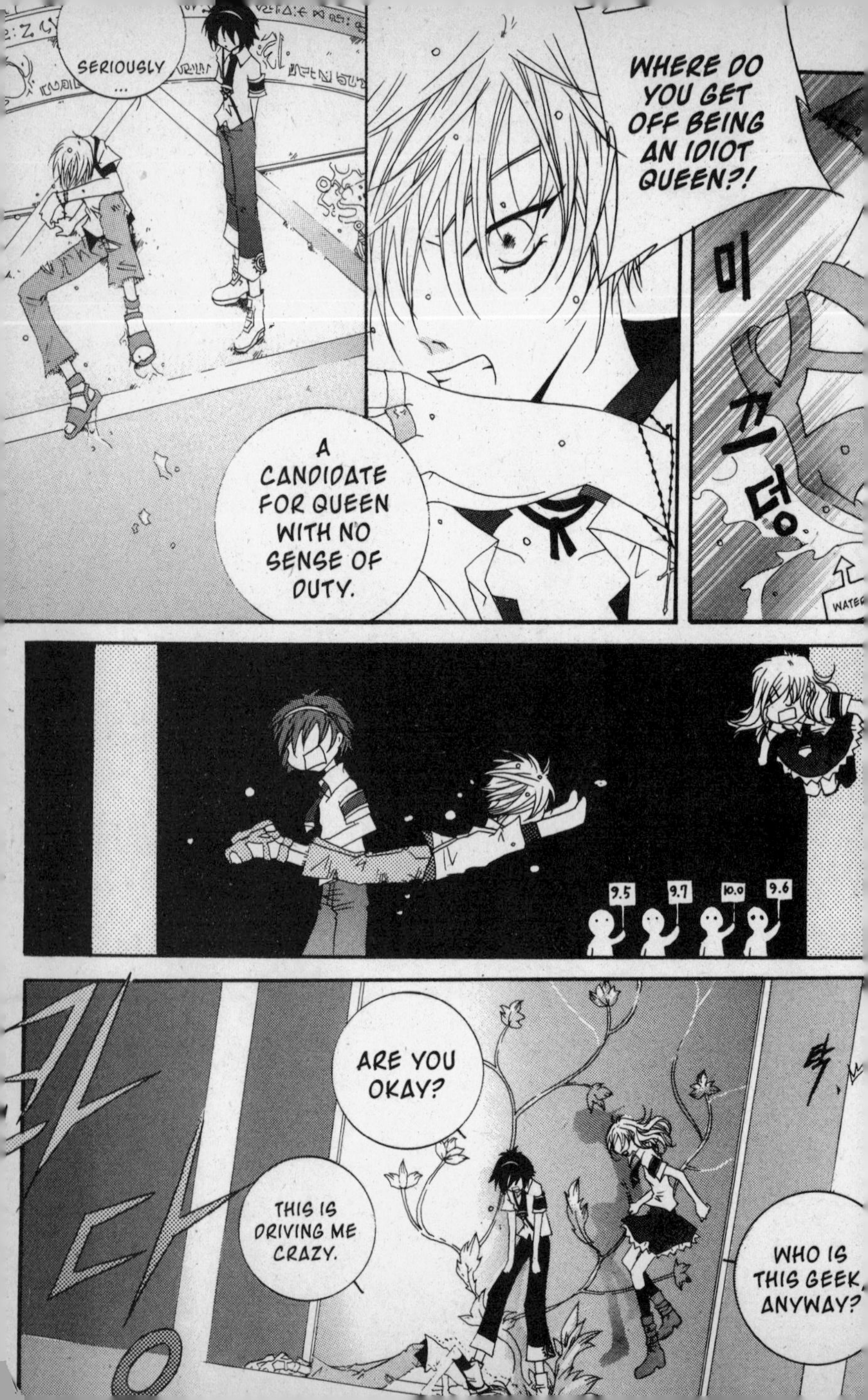
SERIOUSLY ...
WHERE DO YOU GET OFF BEING AN IDIOT QUEEN?!
A CANDIDATE FOR QUEEN WITH NO SENSE OF DUTY.
미끄덩
9.5
9.7
10.0
9.6
ARE YOU OKAY?
THIS IS DRIVING ME CRAZY.
WHO IS THIS GEEK ANYWAY?

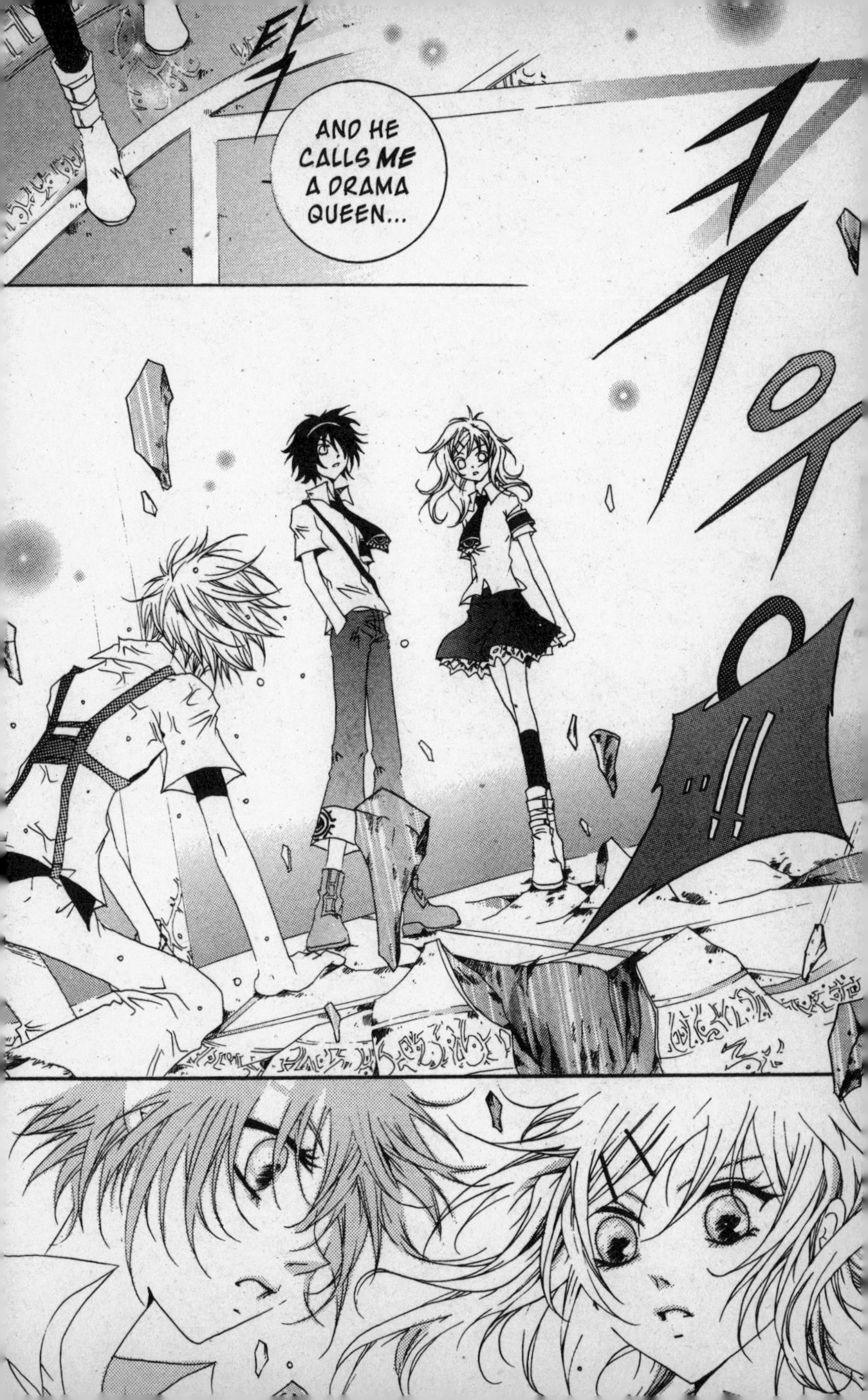
AND HE CALLS ME A DRAMA QUEEN...

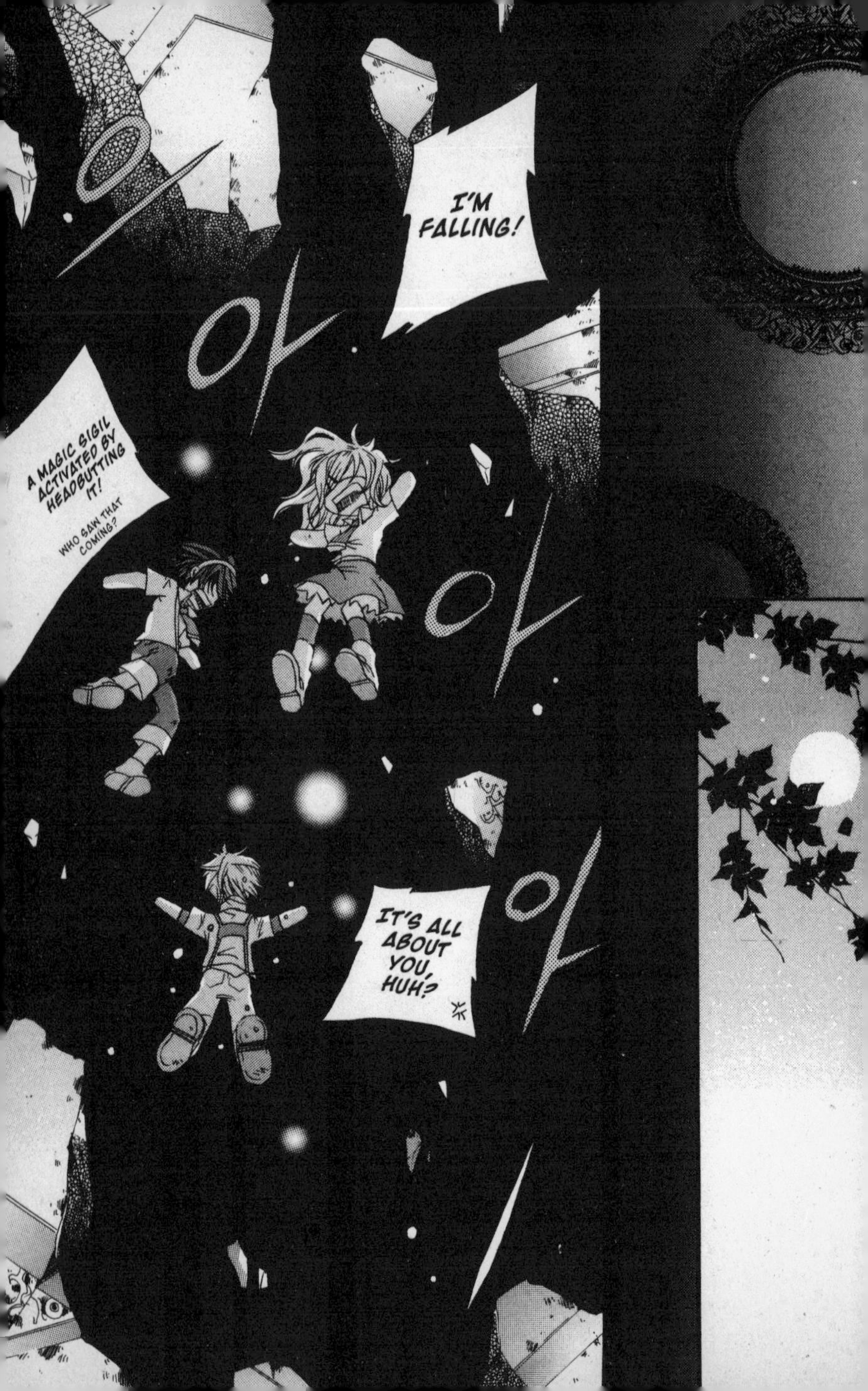
I'M FALLING!
A MAGIC SIGIL ACTIVATED BY HEADBUTTING IT!
WHO SAW THAT COMING?
IT'S ALL ABOUT YOU, HUH?

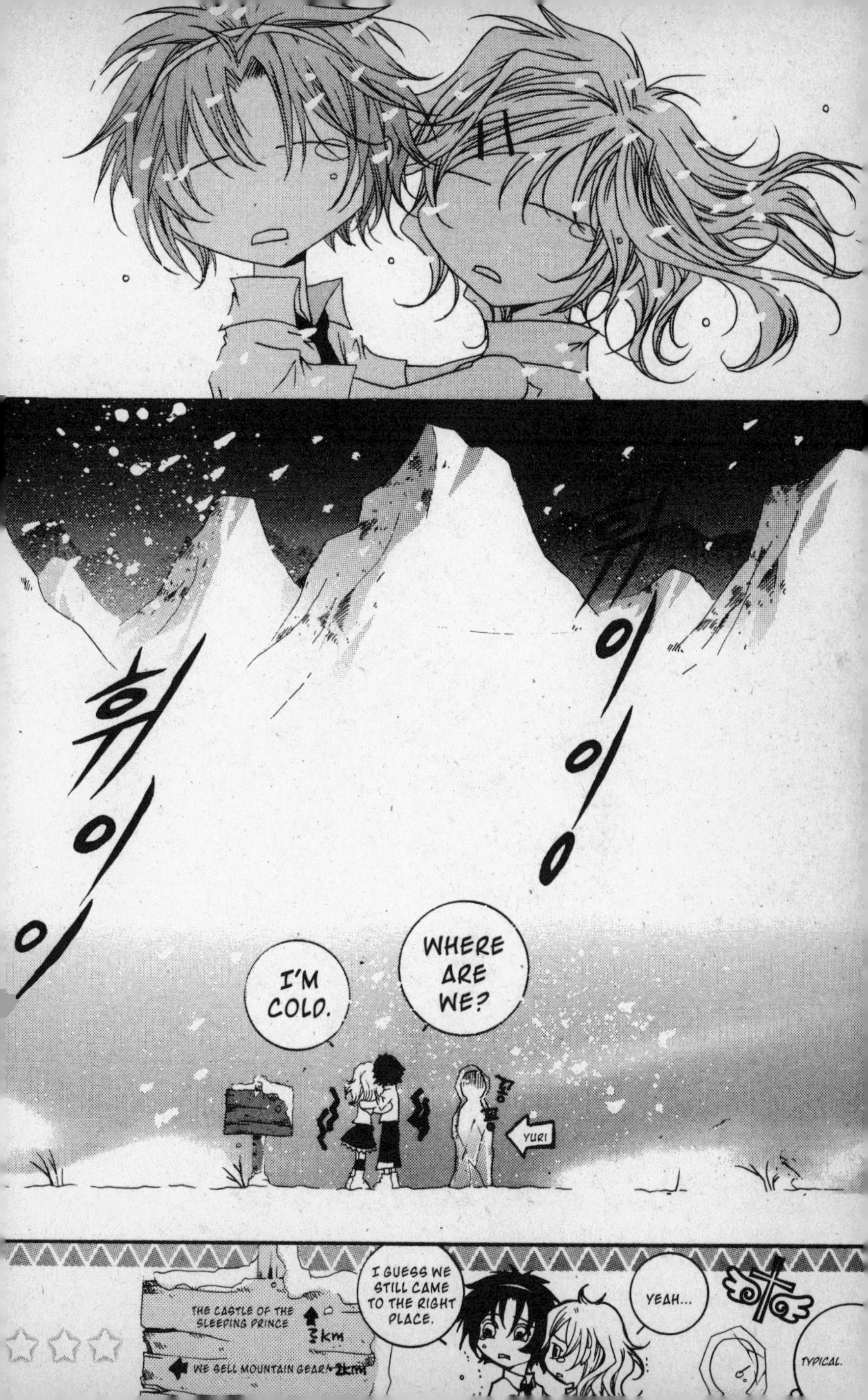
휴이이이
이이이이
I'M COLD.
WHERE ARE WE?
YURI
THE CASTLE OF THE SLEEPING PRINCE
3km
WE SELL MOUNTAIN GEAR! 2km
I GUESS WE STILL CAME TO THE RIGHT PLACE.
YEAH...
TYPICAL.

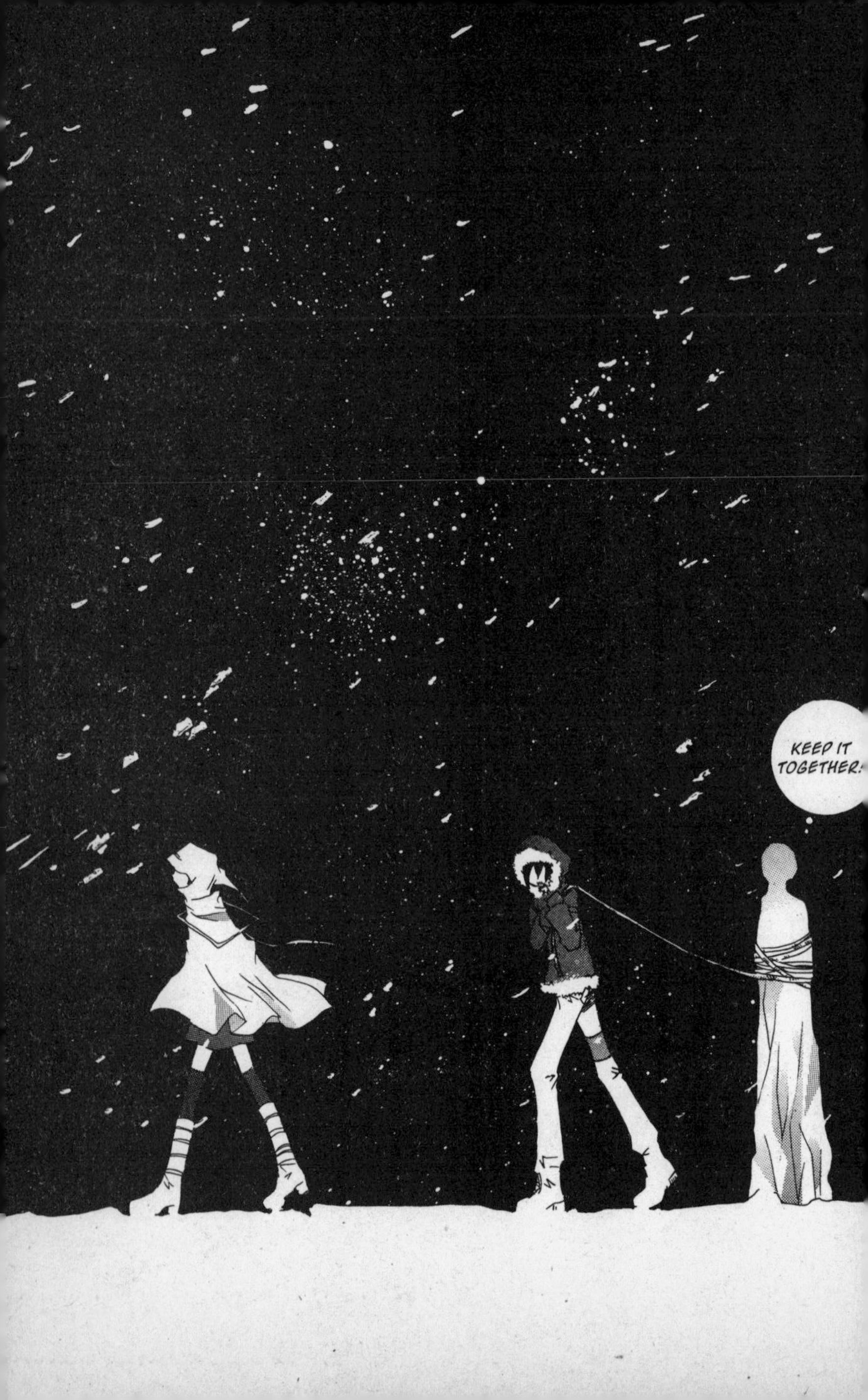
KEEP IT TOGETHER.

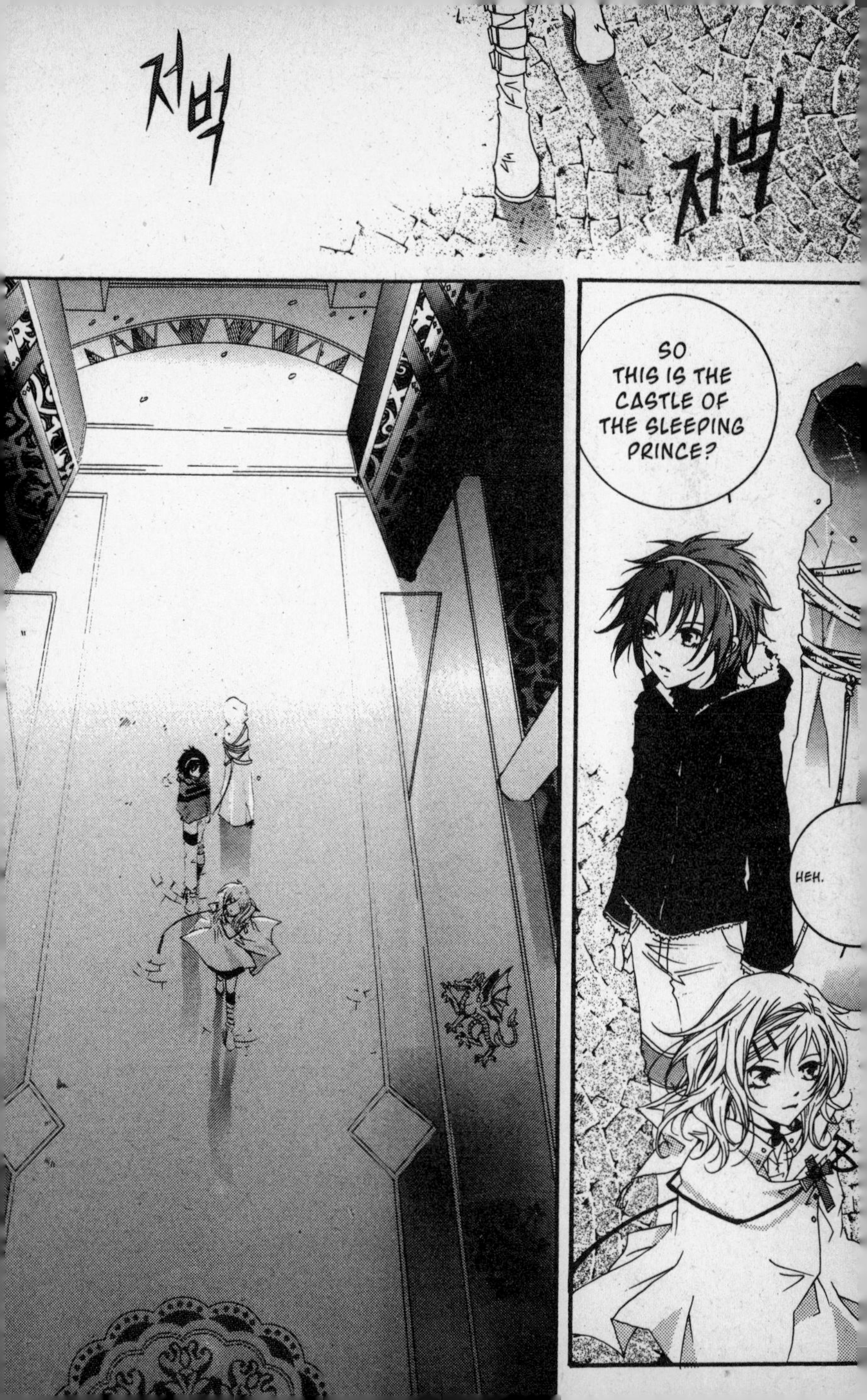
저벅
저벅
SO THIS IS THE CASTLE OF THE SLEEPING PRINCE?
HEH.

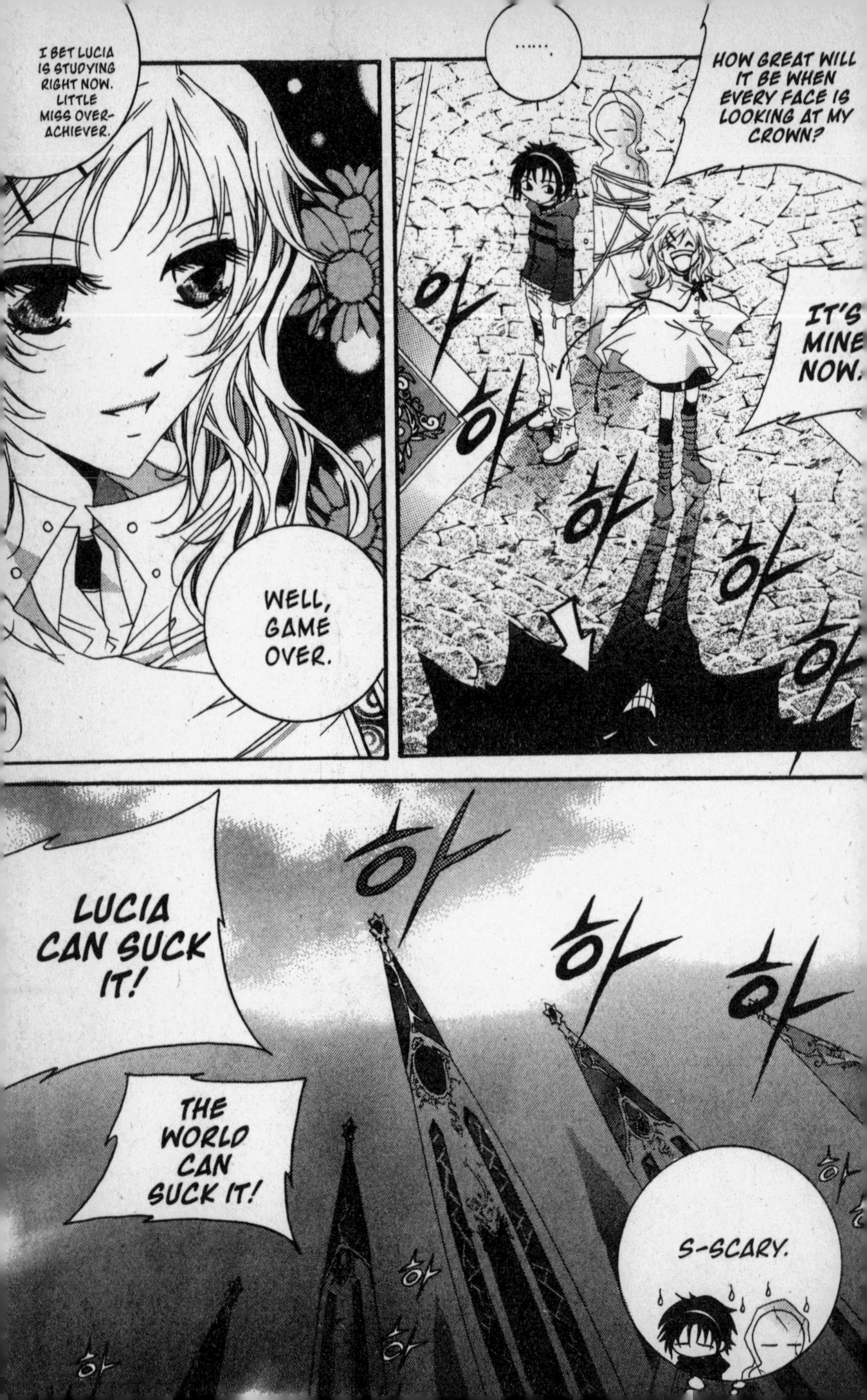
I BET LUCIA IS STUDYING RIGHT NOW. LITTLE MISS OVER-ACHIEVER.
WELL, GAME OVER.
......
HOW GREAT WILL IT BE WHEN EVERY FACE IS LOOKING AT MY CROWN?
IT'S MINE NOW.
하 하 하 하 하
LUCIA CAN SUCK IT!
THE WORLD CAN SUCK IT!
하 하 하
S-SCARY.

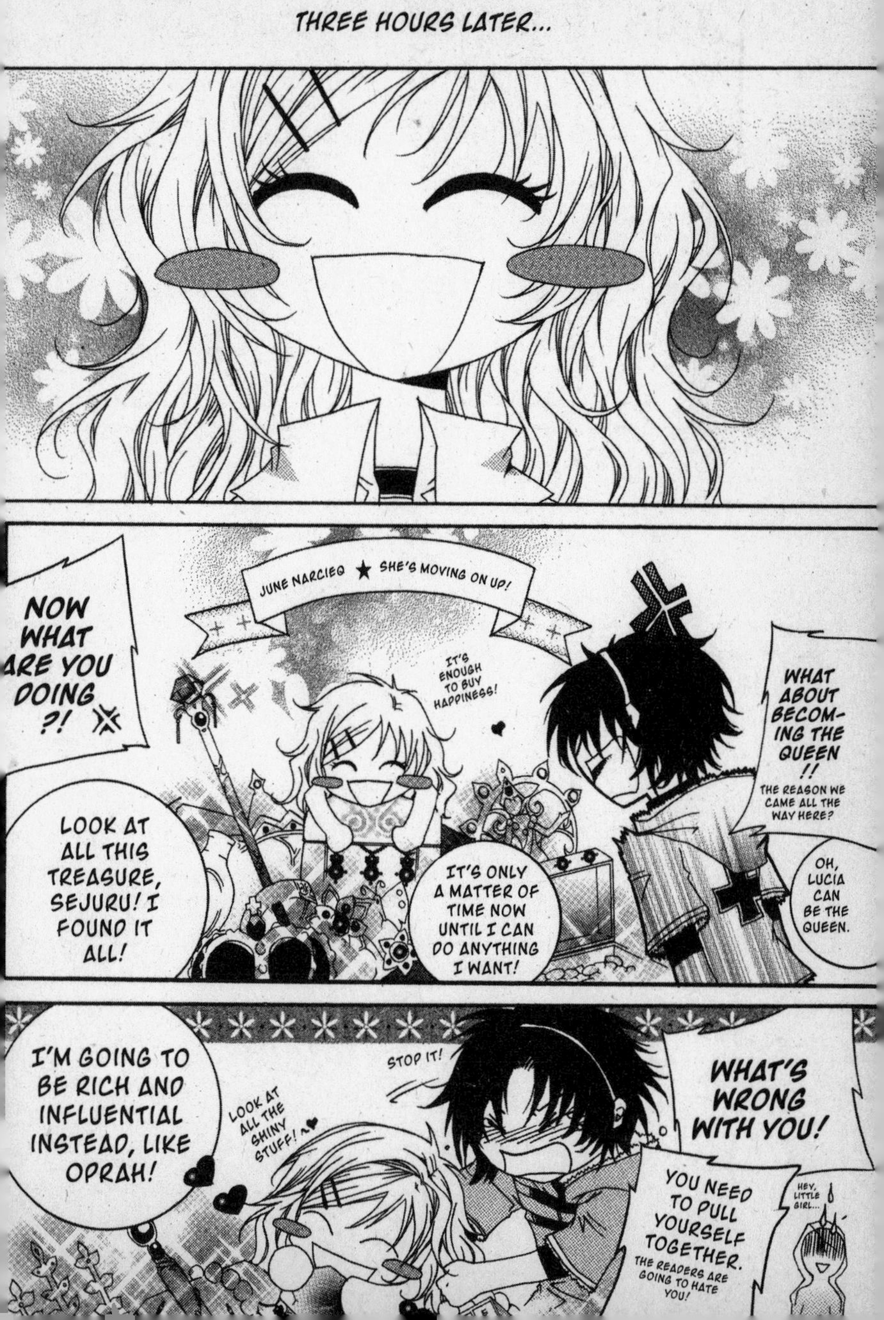
THREE HOURS LATER...
JUNE NARCIEQ ★ SHE'S MOVING ON UP!
NOW WHAT ARE YOU DOING ?!
IT'S ENOUGH TO BUY HAPPINESS!
LOOK AT ALL THIS TREASURE, SEJURU! I FOUND IT ALL!
IT'S ONLY A MATTER OF TIME NOW UNTIL I CAN DO ANYTHING I WANT!
WHAT ABOUT BECOMING THE QUEEN !!
THE REASON WE CAME ALL THE WAY HERE?
OH, LUCIA CAN BE THE QUEEN.
I'M GOING TO BE RICH AND INFLUENTIAL INSTEAD, LIKE OPRAH!
LOOK AT ALL THE SHINY STUFF!
STOP IT!
WHAT'S WRONG WITH YOU!
YOU NEED TO PULL YOURSELF TOGETHER.
THE READERS ARE GOING TO HATE YOU!
HEY, LITTLE GIRL...

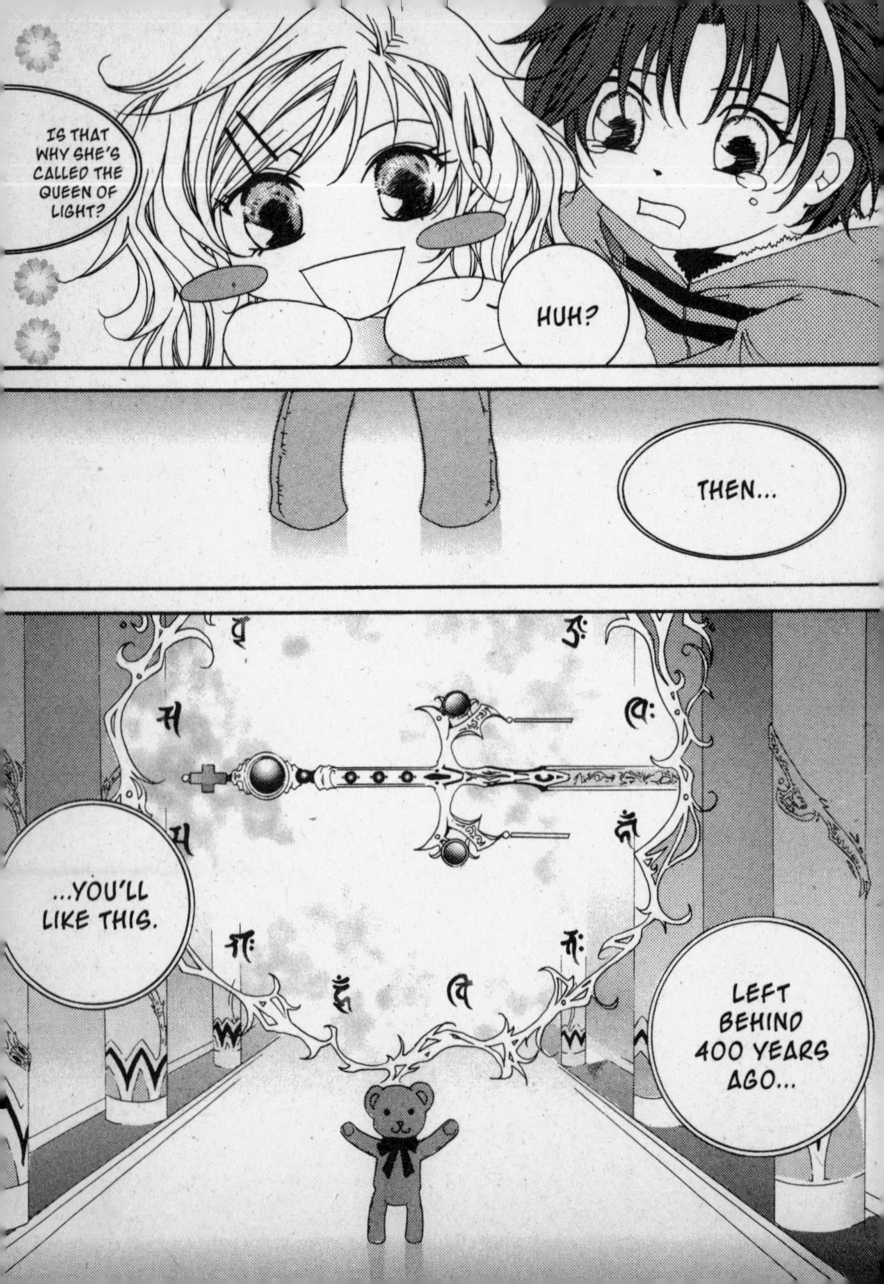
IS THAT WHY SHE'S CALLED THE QUEEN OF LIGHT?
HUH?
THEN...
...YOU'LL LIKE THIS.
LEFT BEHIND 400 YEARS AGO...

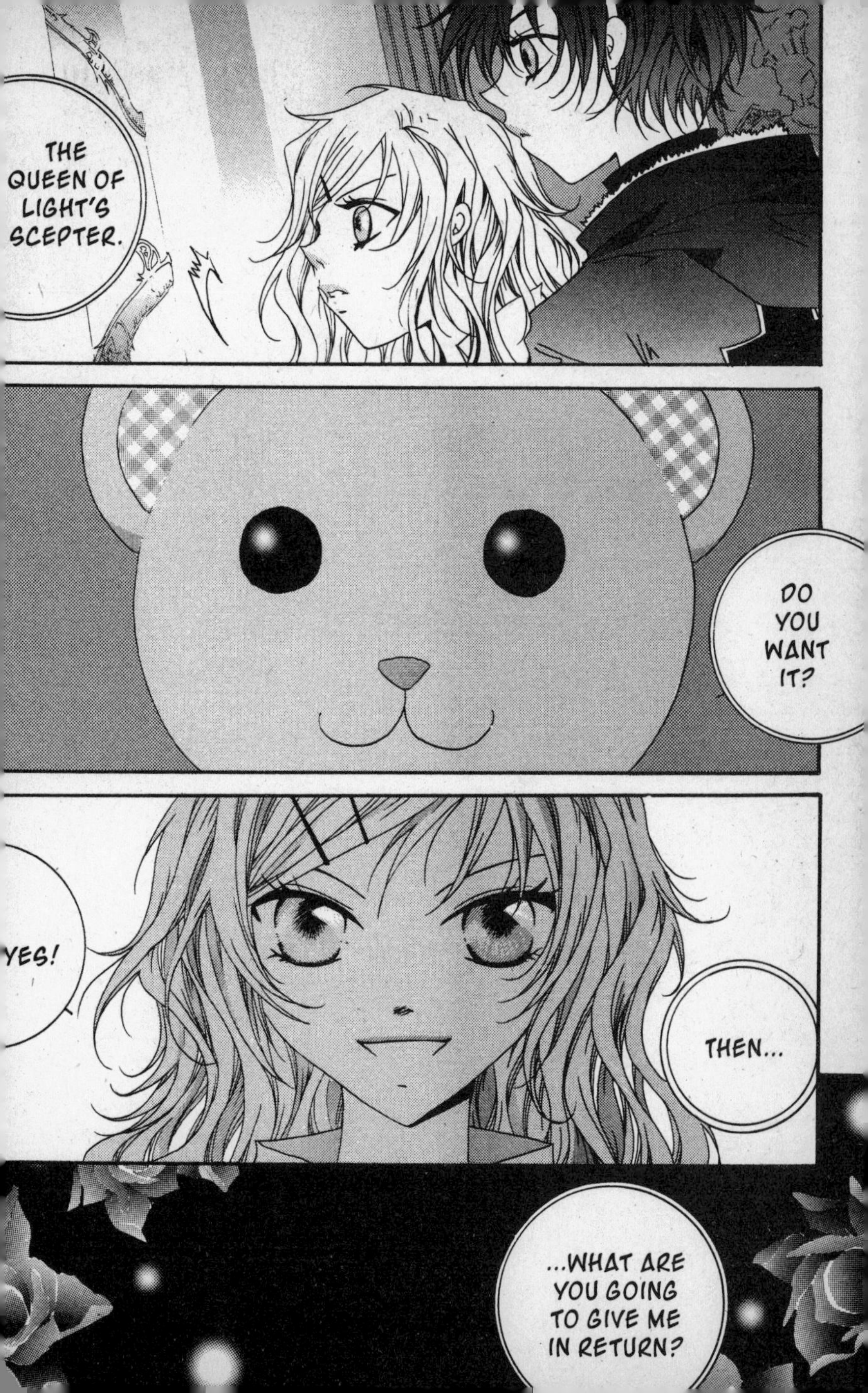
THE QUEEN OF LIGHT'S SCEPTER.
DO YOU WANT IT?
THEN...
YES!
...WHAT ARE YOU GOING TO GIVE ME IN RETURN?

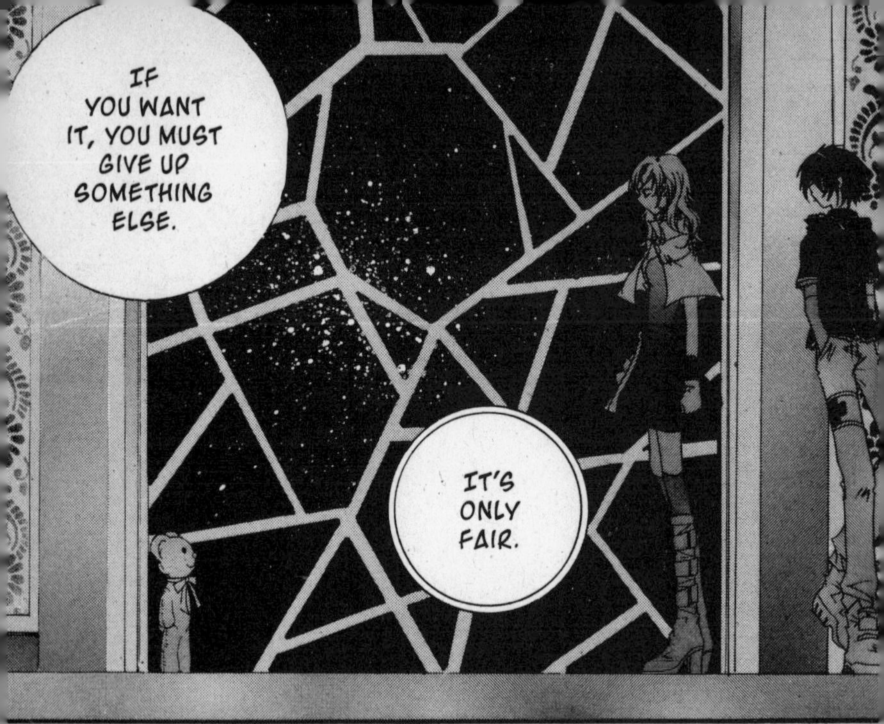
IF YOU WANT IT, YOU MUST GIVE UP SOMETHING ELSE.
IT'S ONLY FAIR.

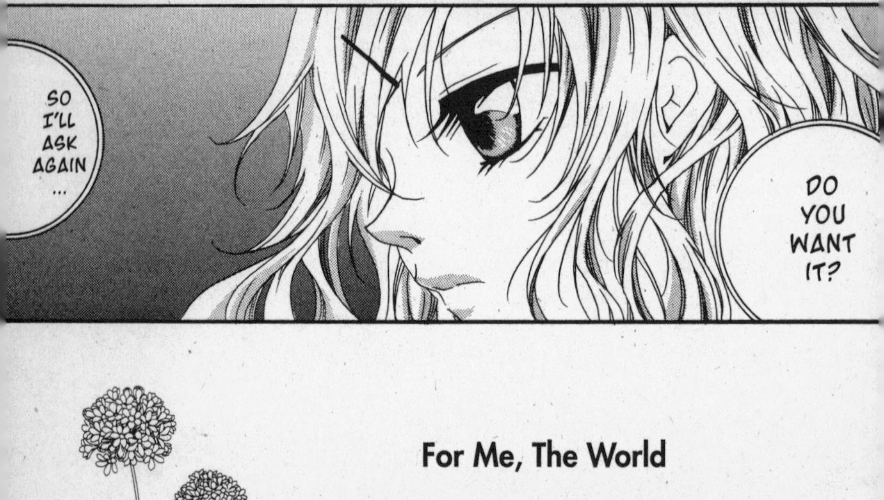
SO I'LL ASK AGAIN ...
DO YOU WANT IT?

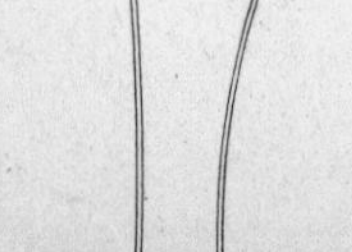

For Me, The World

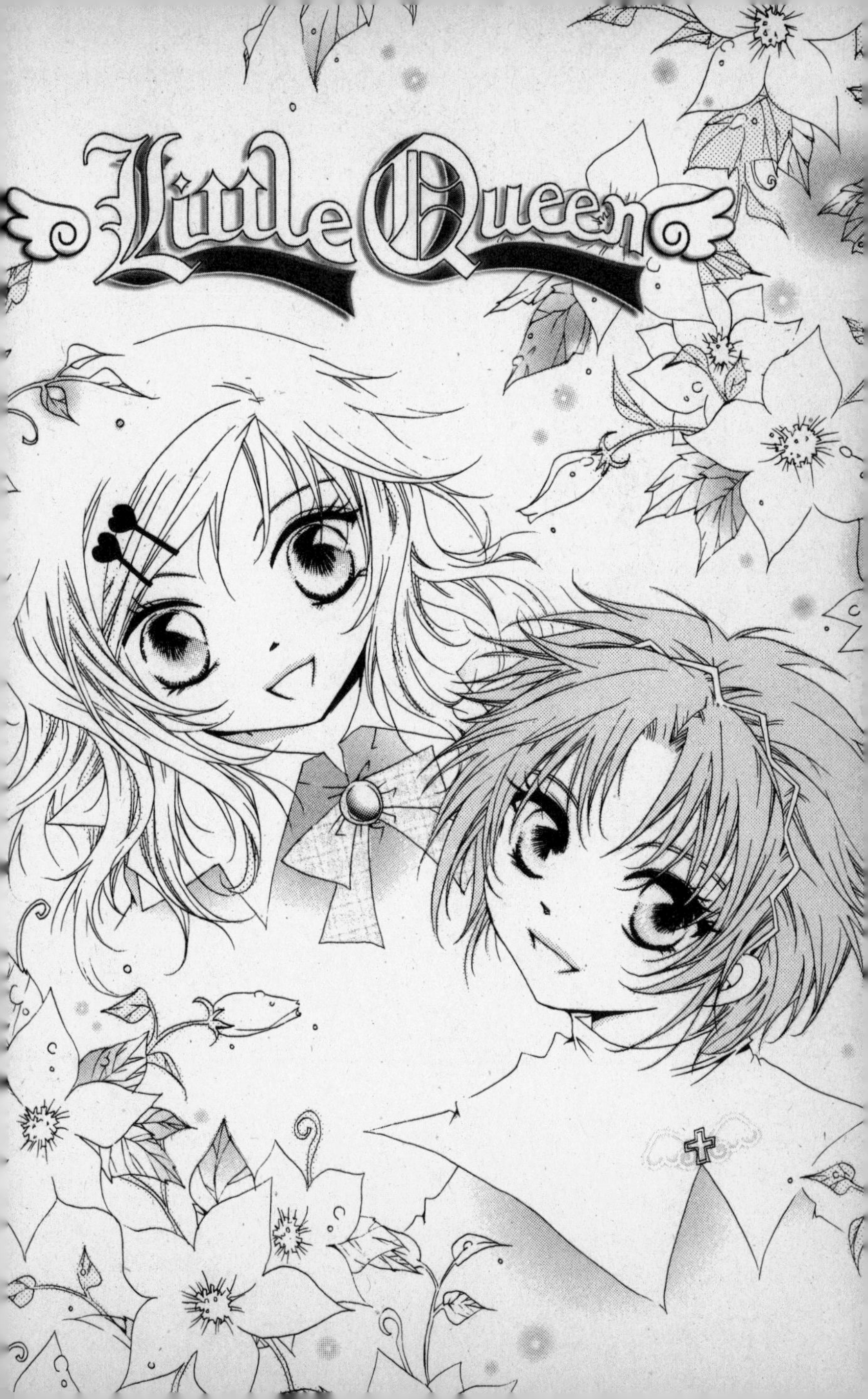
Little Queen

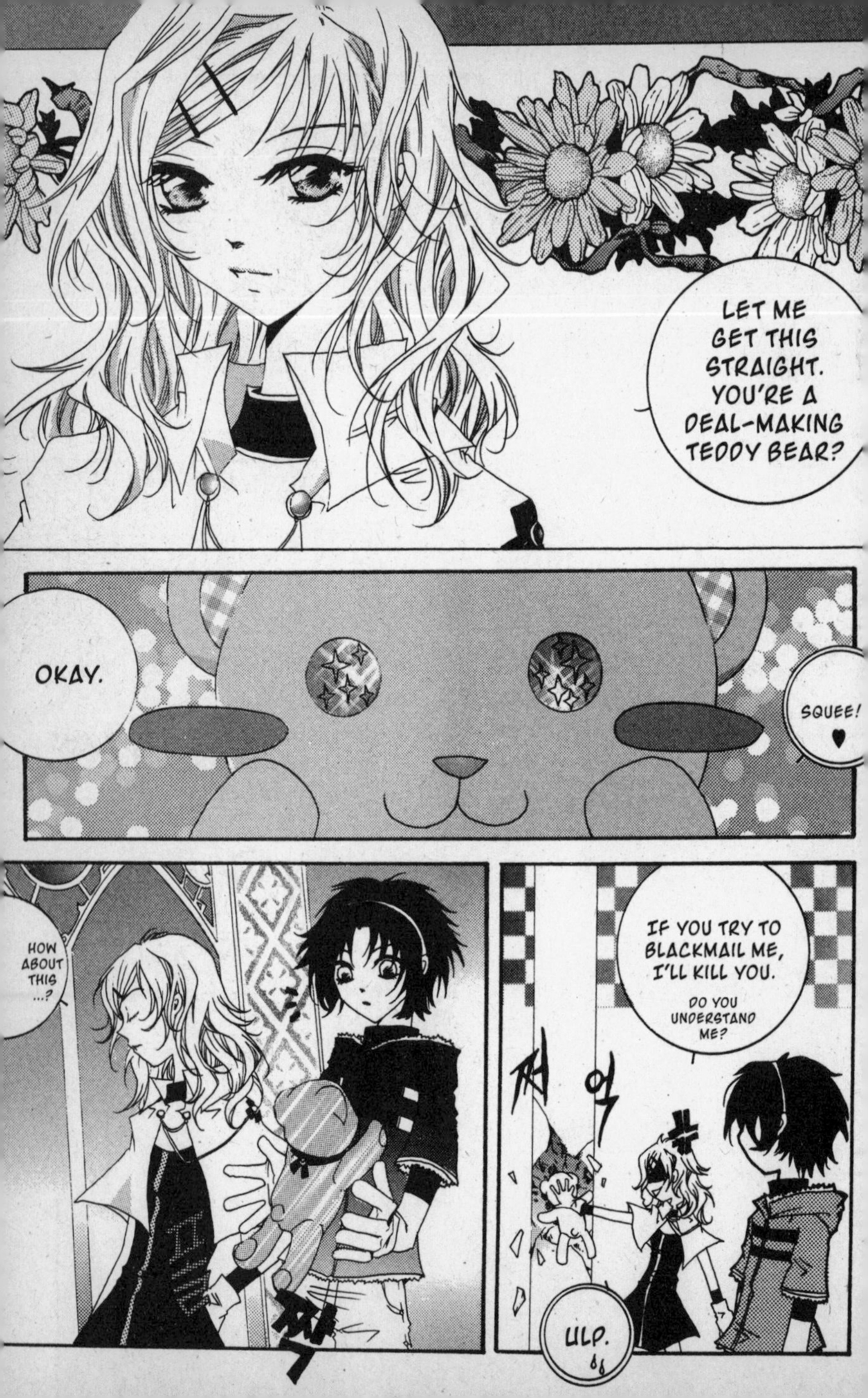
LET ME GET THIS STRAIGHT. YOU'RE A DEAL-MAKING TEDDY BEAR?
OKAY.
SQUEE! ♥
HOW ABOUT THIS ...?
IF YOU TRY TO BLACKMAIL ME, I'LL KILL YOU.
DO YOU UNDERSTAND ME?
ULP.

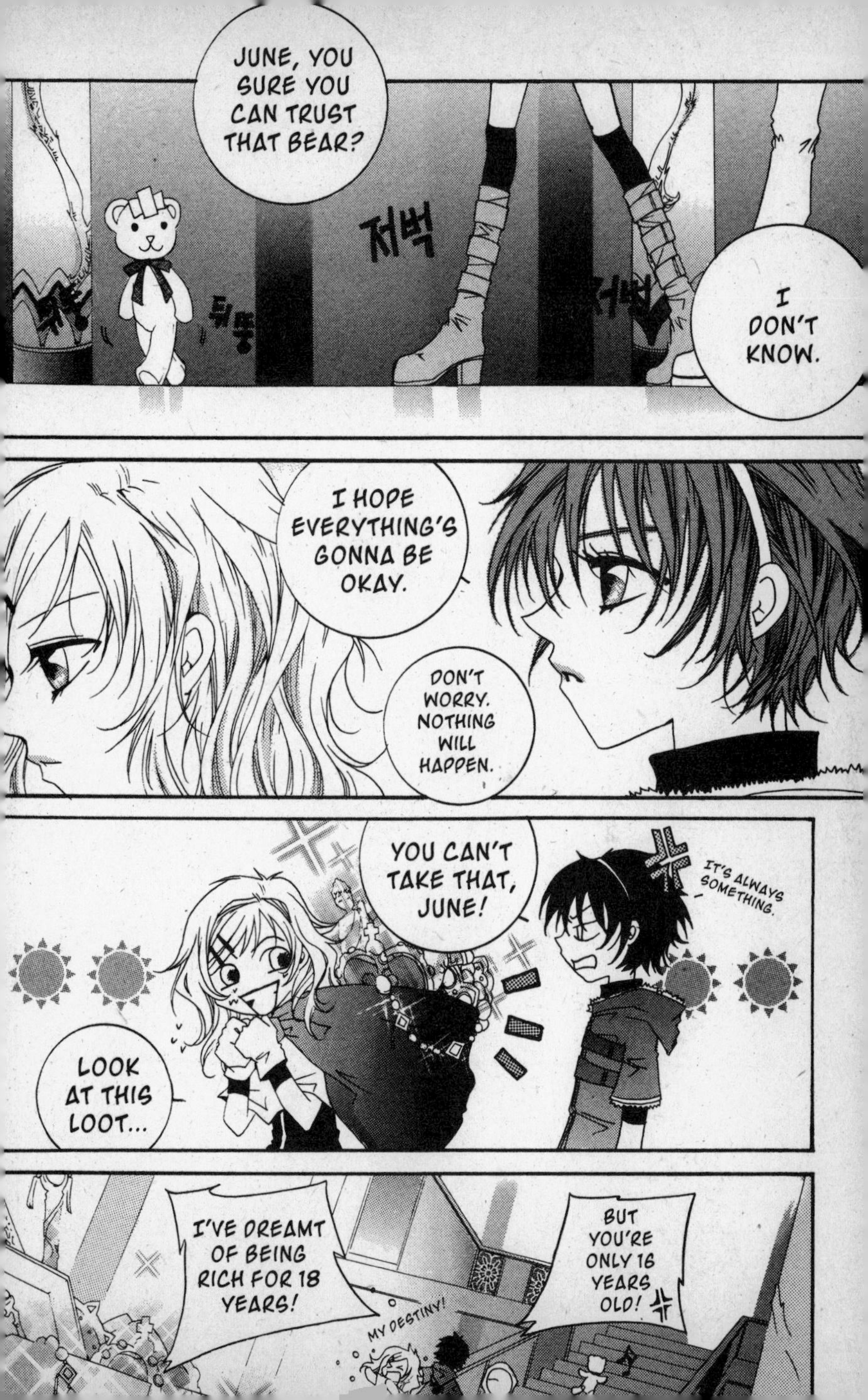
JUNE, YOU SURE YOU CAN TRUST THAT BEAR?
뒤뚱
저벅
I DON'T KNOW.
I HOPE EVERYTHING'S GONNA BE OKAY.
DON'T WORRY. NOTHING WILL HAPPEN.
LOOK AT THIS LOOT...
YOU CAN'T TAKE THAT, JUNE!
IT'S ALWAYS SOMETHING.
I'VE DREAMT OF BEING RICH FOR 18 YEARS!
MY DESTINY!
BUT YOU'RE ONLY 16 YEARS OLD!

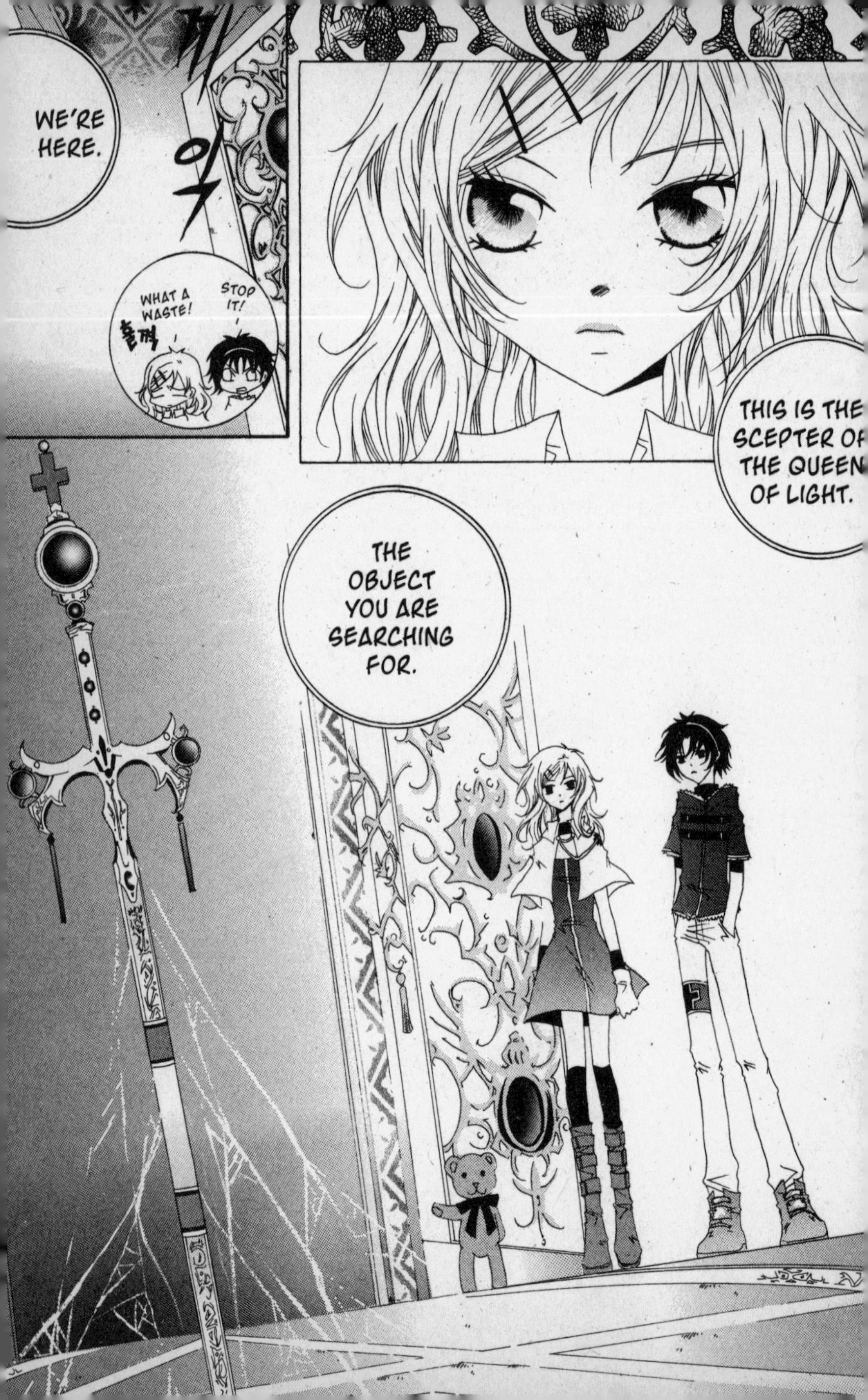
WE'RE HERE.
WHAT A WASTE!
STOP IT!
THIS IS THE SCEPTER OF THE QUEEN OF LIGHT.
THE OBJECT YOU ARE SEARCHING FOR.

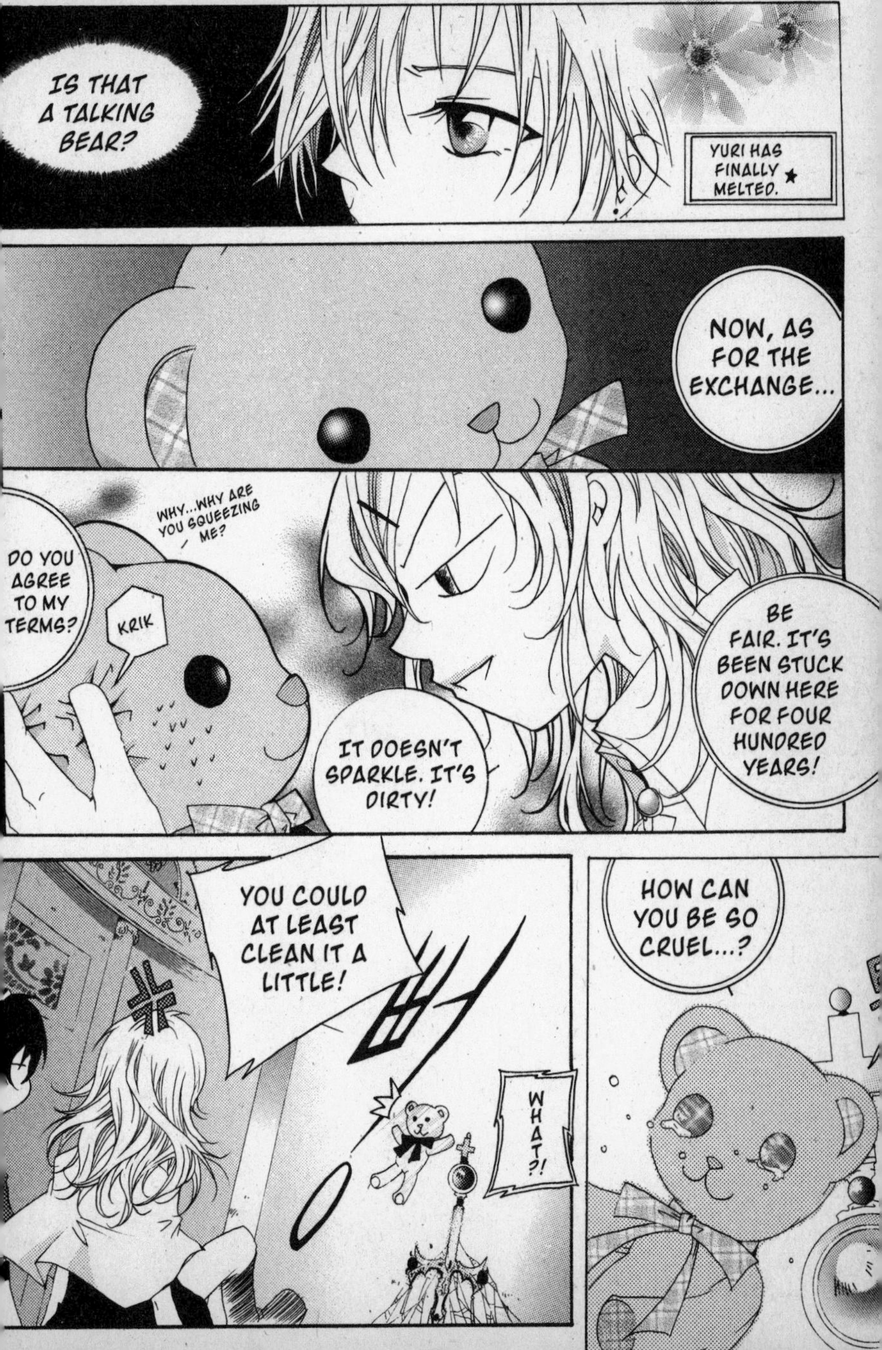
IS THAT A TALKING BEAR?
YURI HAS FINALLY MELTED. ★
NOW, AS FOR THE EXCHANGE...
DO YOU AGREE TO MY TERMS?
KRIK
WHY...WHY ARE YOU SQUEEZING ME?
IT DOESN'T SPARKLE. IT'S DIRTY!
BE FAIR. IT'S BEEN STUCK DOWN HERE FOR FOUR HUNDRED YEARS!
YOU COULD AT LEAST CLEAN IT A LITTLE!
WHAT?!
HOW CAN YOU BE SO CRUEL...?

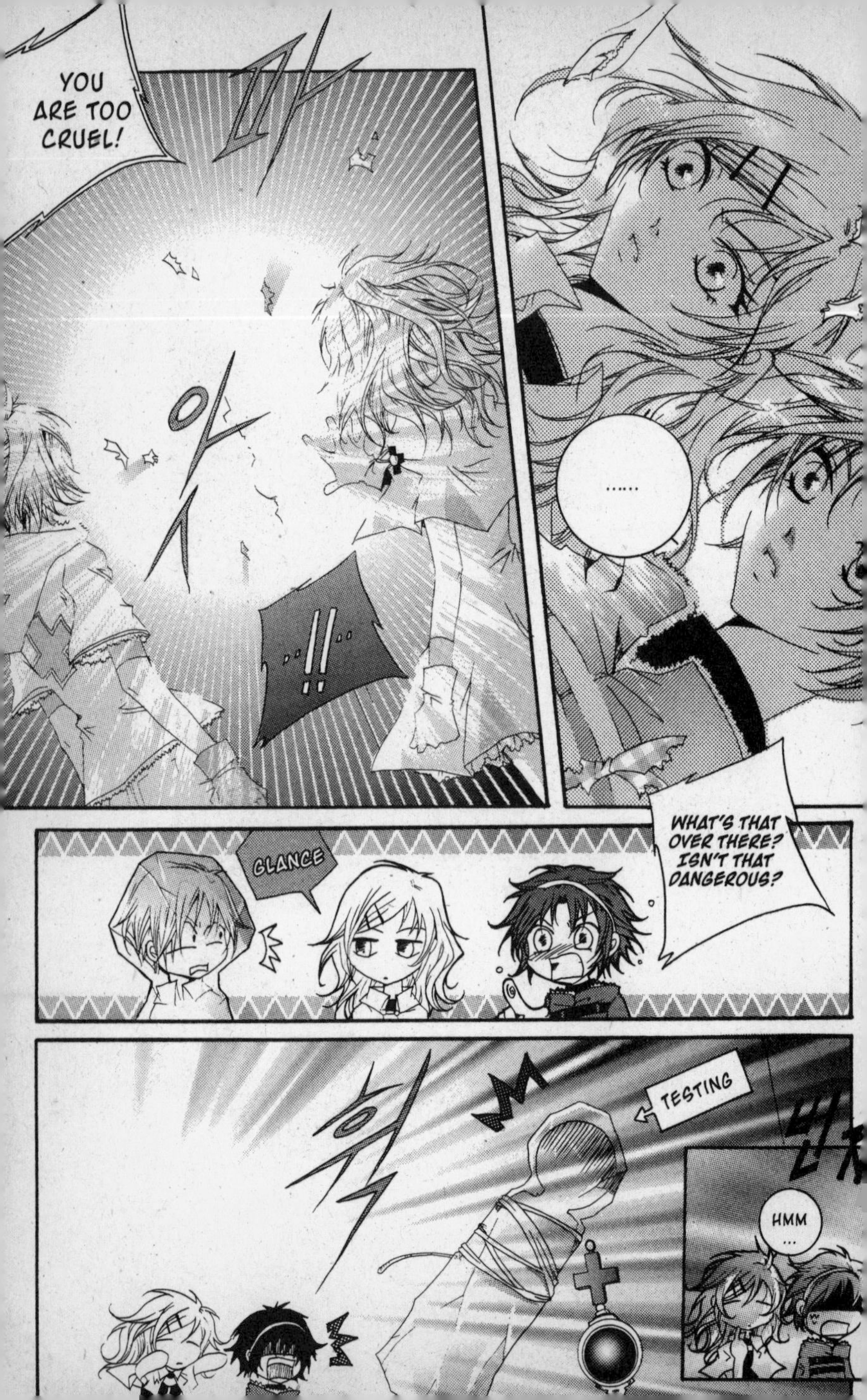

......
YOU ARE TOO CRUEL!
..!!..
WHAT'S THAT OVER THERE? ISN'T THAT DANGEROUS?
GLANCE
HMM ...
TESTING

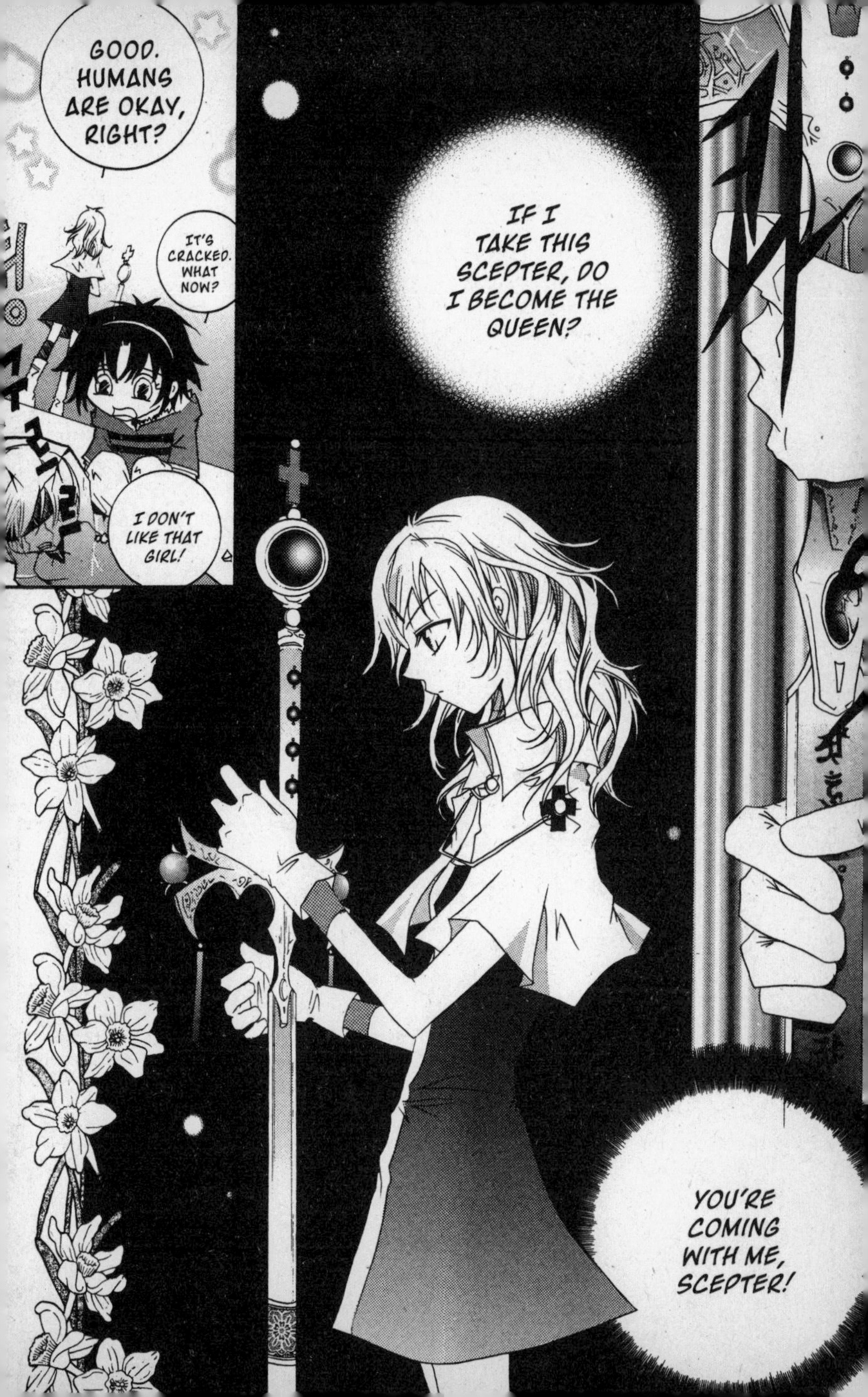
IF I TAKE THIS SCEPTER, DO I BECOME THE QUEEN?
YOU'RE COMING WITH ME, SCEPTER!
GOOD. HUMANS ARE OKAY, RIGHT?
IT'S CRACKED. WHAT NOW?
I DON'T LIKE THAT GIRL!

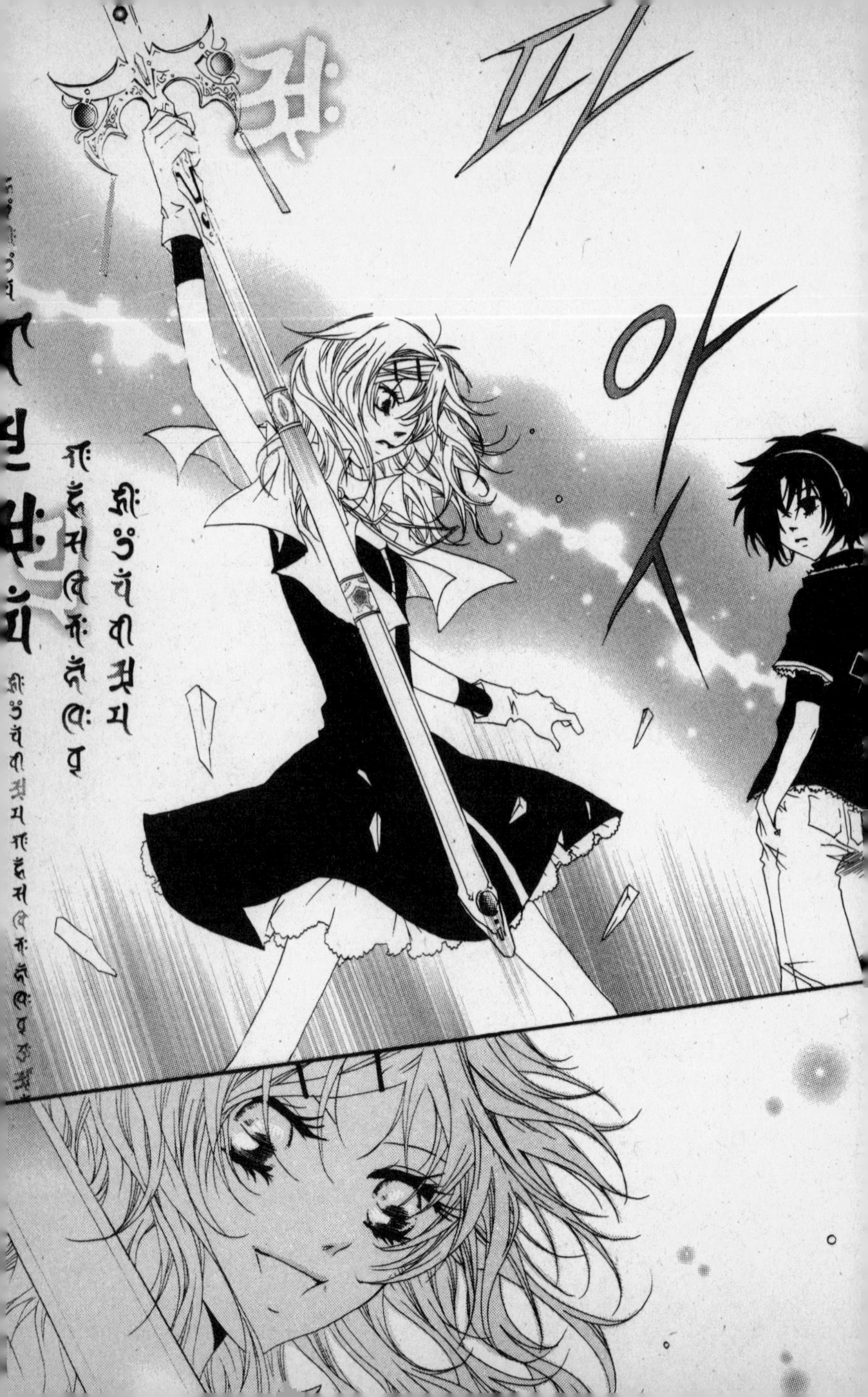
파앗

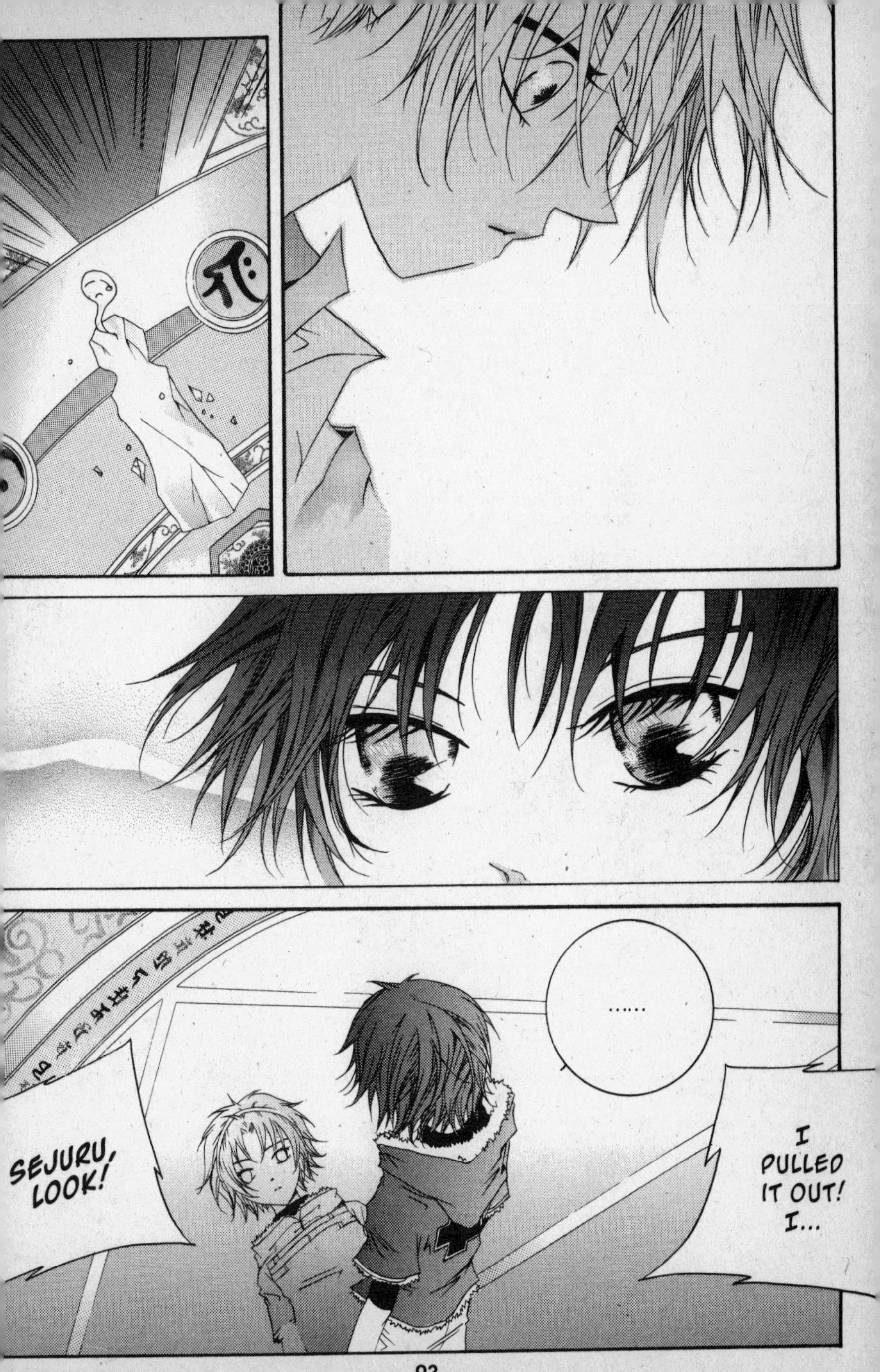
......
I PULLED IT OUT! I...
SEJURU, LOOK!

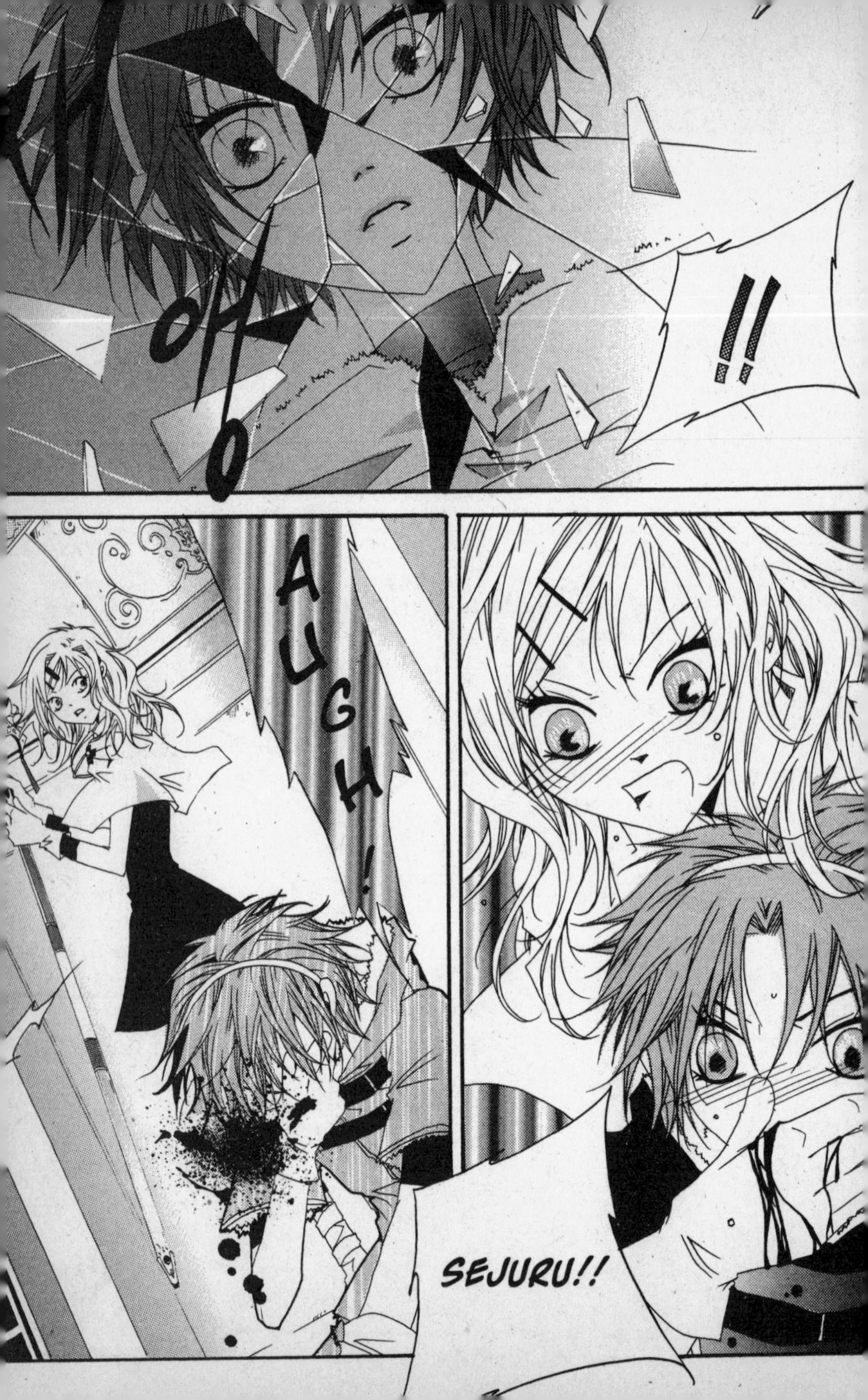
!!
SEJURU!!
AUGH!

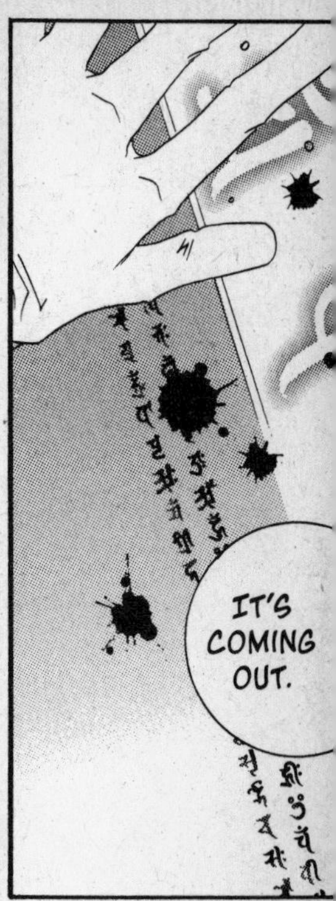
IT'S COMING OUT.
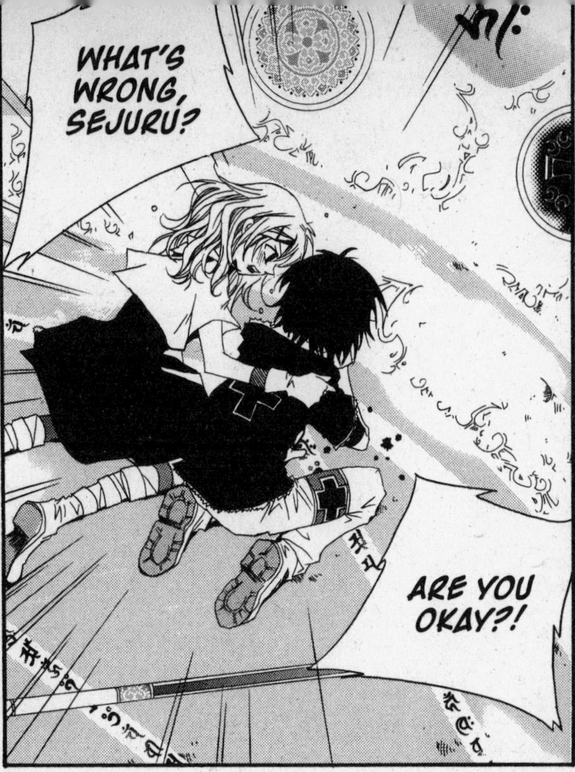
WHAT'S WRONG, SEJURU?
ARE YOU OKAY?!
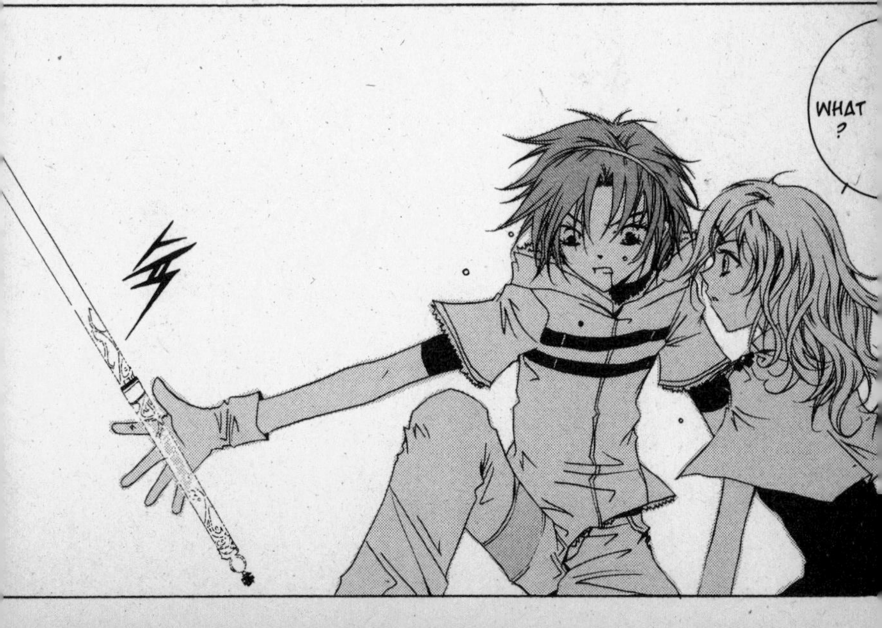
WHAT ?

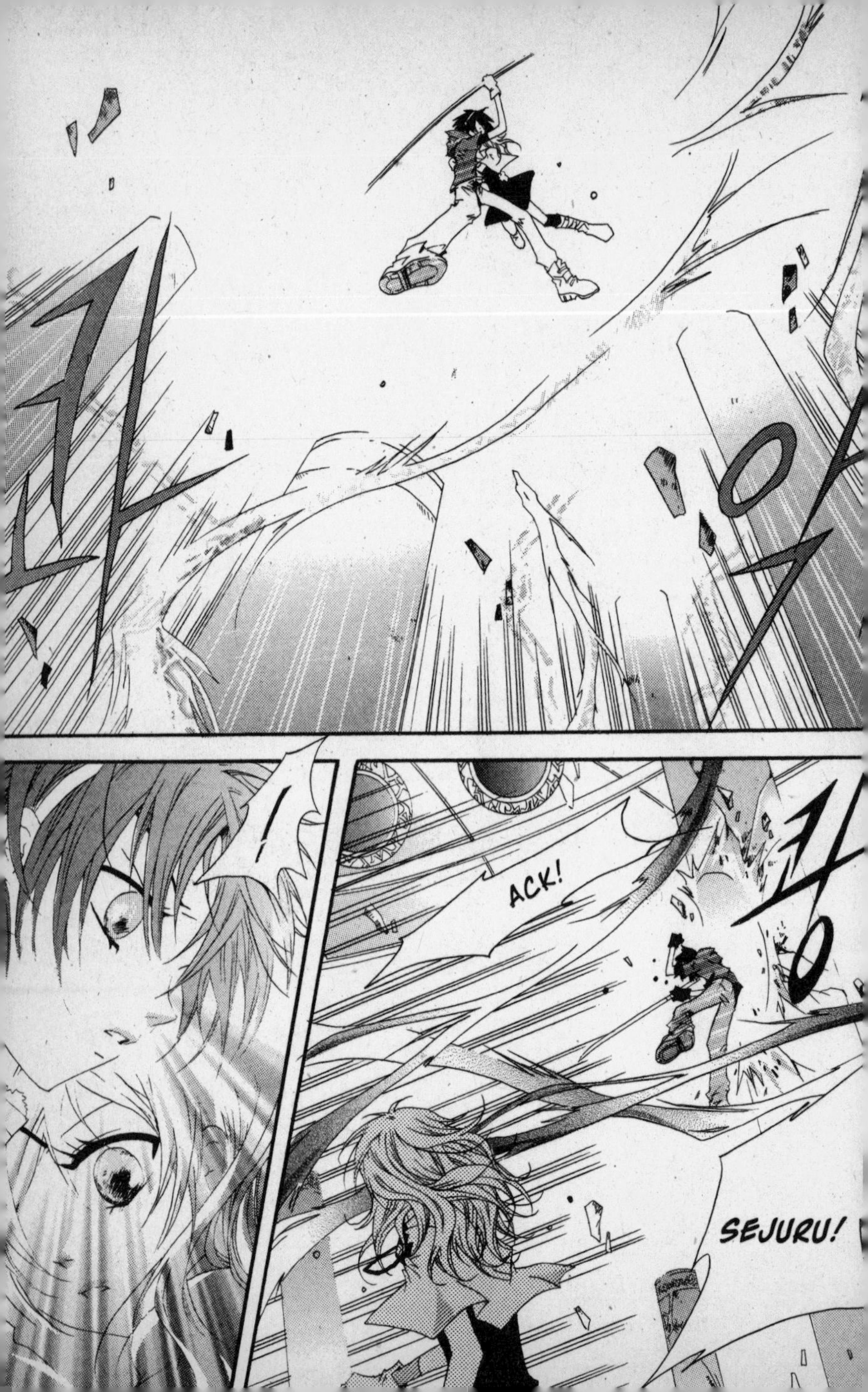
ACK!
SEJURU!

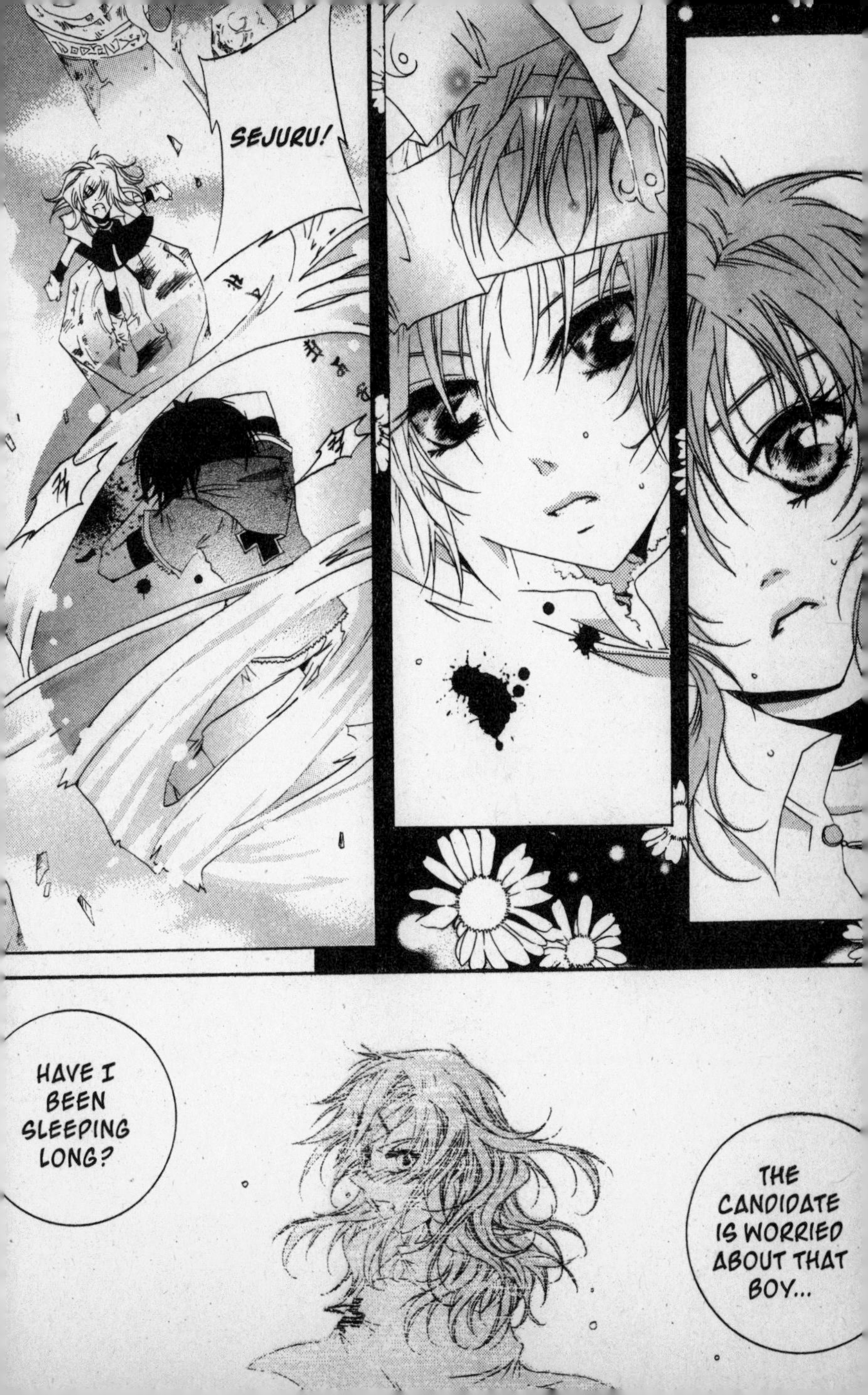
SEJURU!
THE CANDIDATE IS WORRIED ABOUT THAT BOY...
HAVE I BEEN SLEEPING LONG?

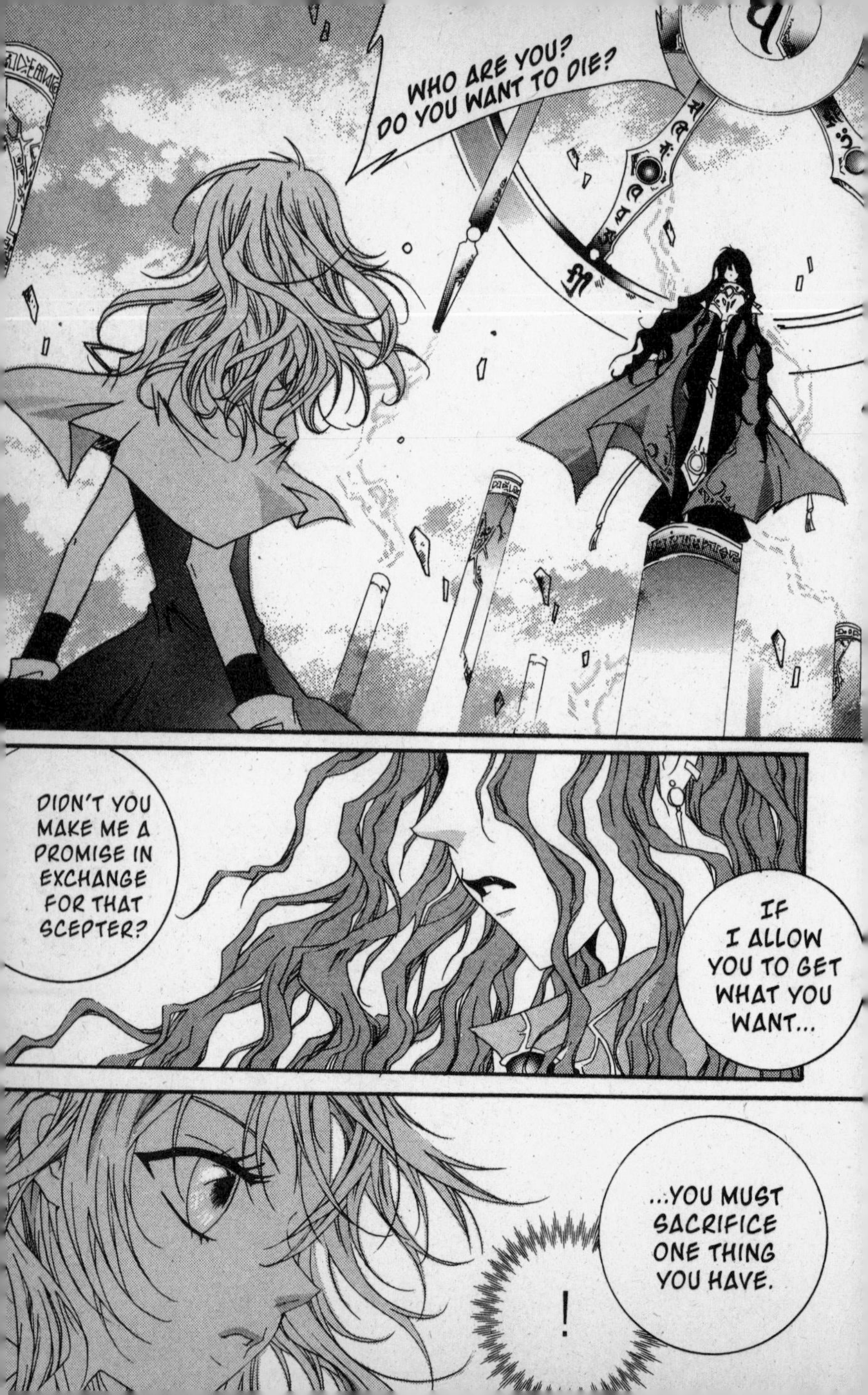
WHO ARE YOU? DO YOU WANT TO DIE?
DIDN'T YOU MAKE ME A PROMISE IN EXCHANGE FOR THAT SCEPTER?
IF I ALLOW YOU TO GET WHAT YOU WANT...
...YOU MUST SACRIFICE ONE THING YOU HAVE.
!

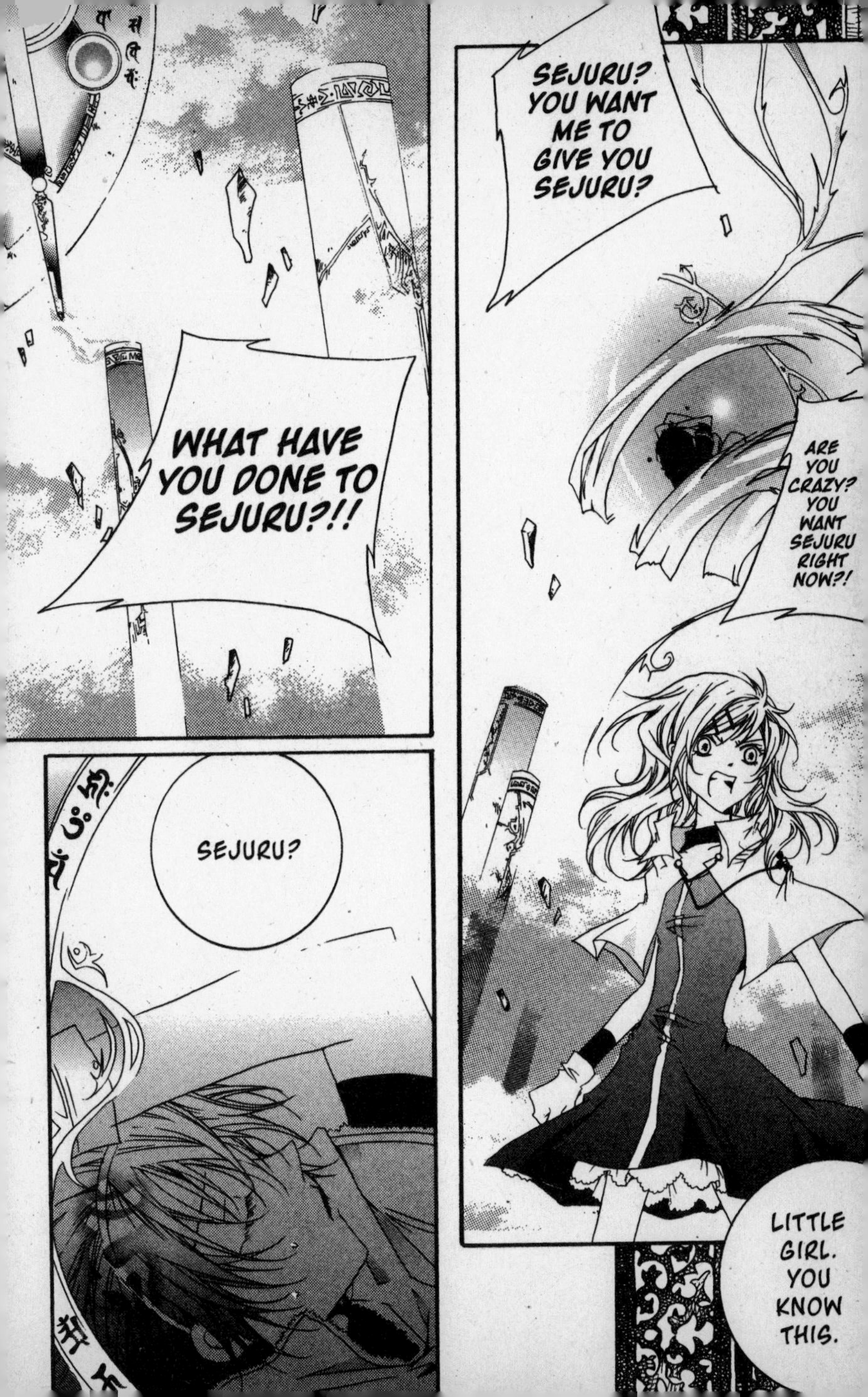
WHAT HAVE YOU DONE TO SEJURU?!!
SEJURU?
SEJURU? YOU WANT ME TO GIVE YOU SEJURU?
ARE YOU CRAZY? YOU WANT SEJURU RIGHT NOW?!
LITTLE GIRL. YOU KNOW THIS.

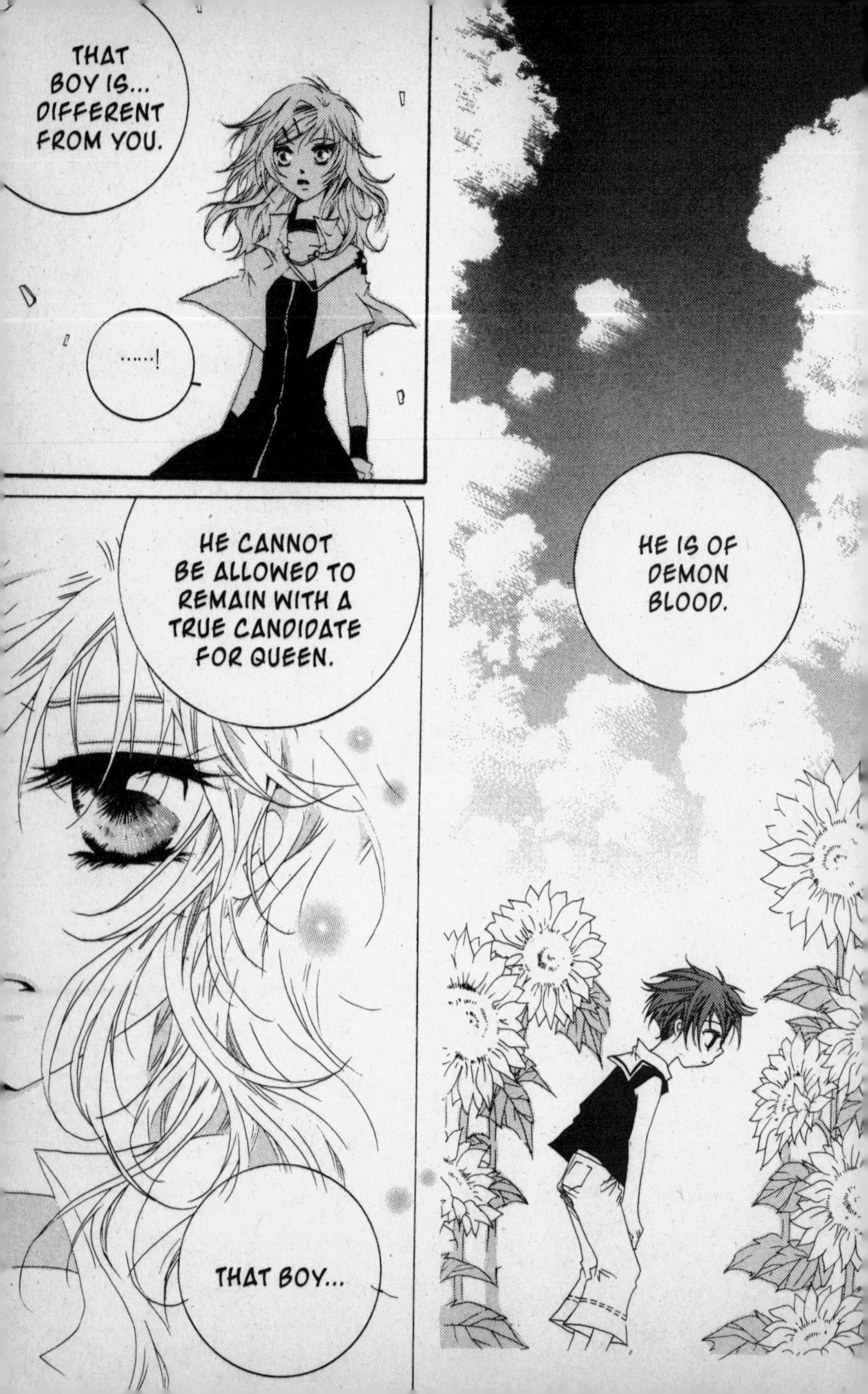
HE IS OF DEMON BLOOD.
THAT BOY IS... DIFFERENT FROM YOU.
......!
HE CANNOT BE ALLOWED TO REMAIN WITH A TRUE CANDIDATE FOR QUEEN.
THAT BOY...

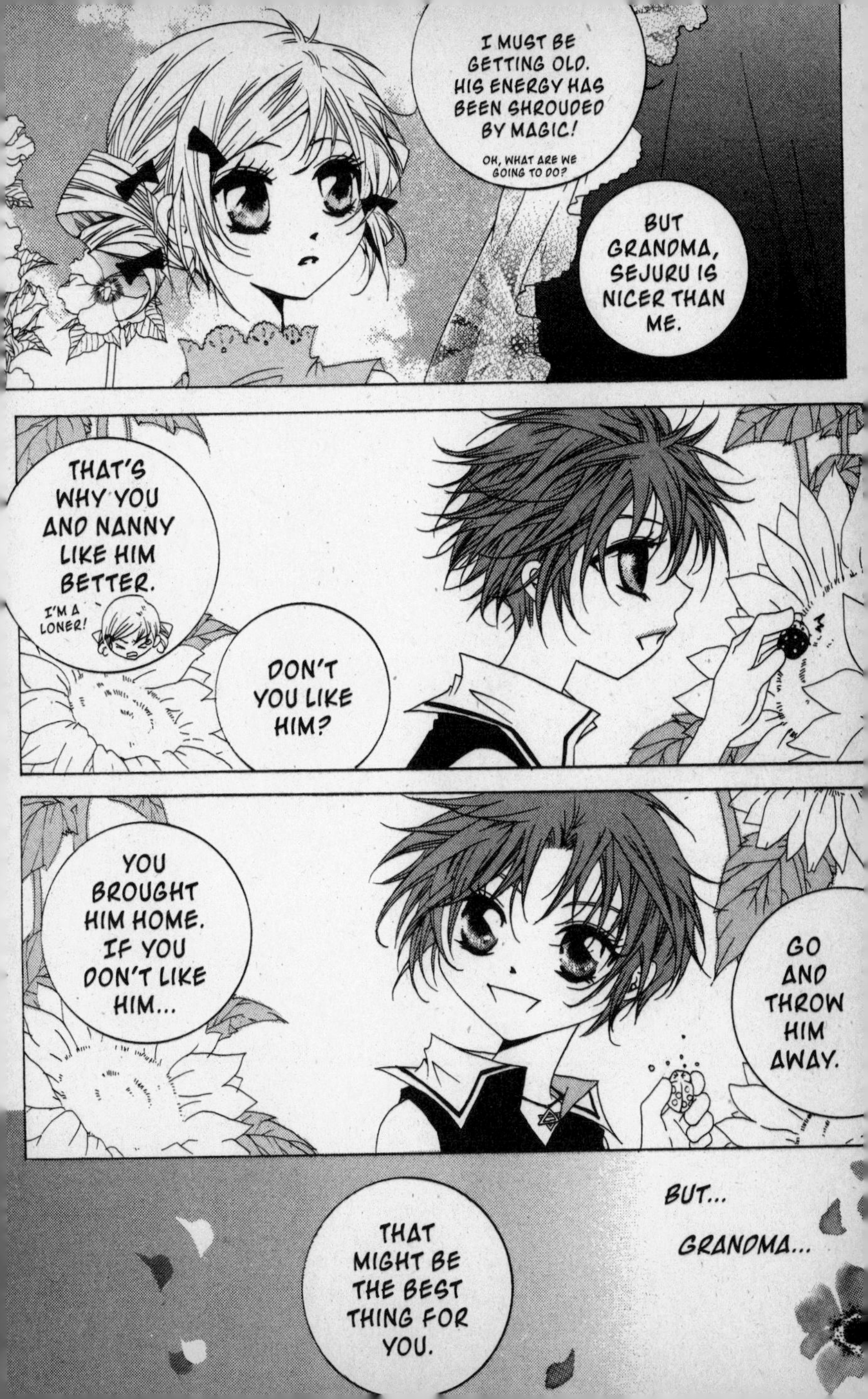
I MUST BE GETTING OLD. HIS ENERGY HAS BEEN SHROUDED BY MAGIC!
OH, WHAT ARE WE GOING TO DO?
BUT GRANDMA, SEJURU IS NICER THAN ME.
THAT'S WHY YOU AND NANNY LIKE HIM BETTER.
I'M A LONER!
DON'T YOU LIKE HIM?
YOU BROUGHT HIM HOME. IF YOU DON'T LIKE HIM...
GO AND THROW HIM AWAY.
THAT MIGHT BE THE BEST THING FOR YOU.
BUT...
GRANDMA...

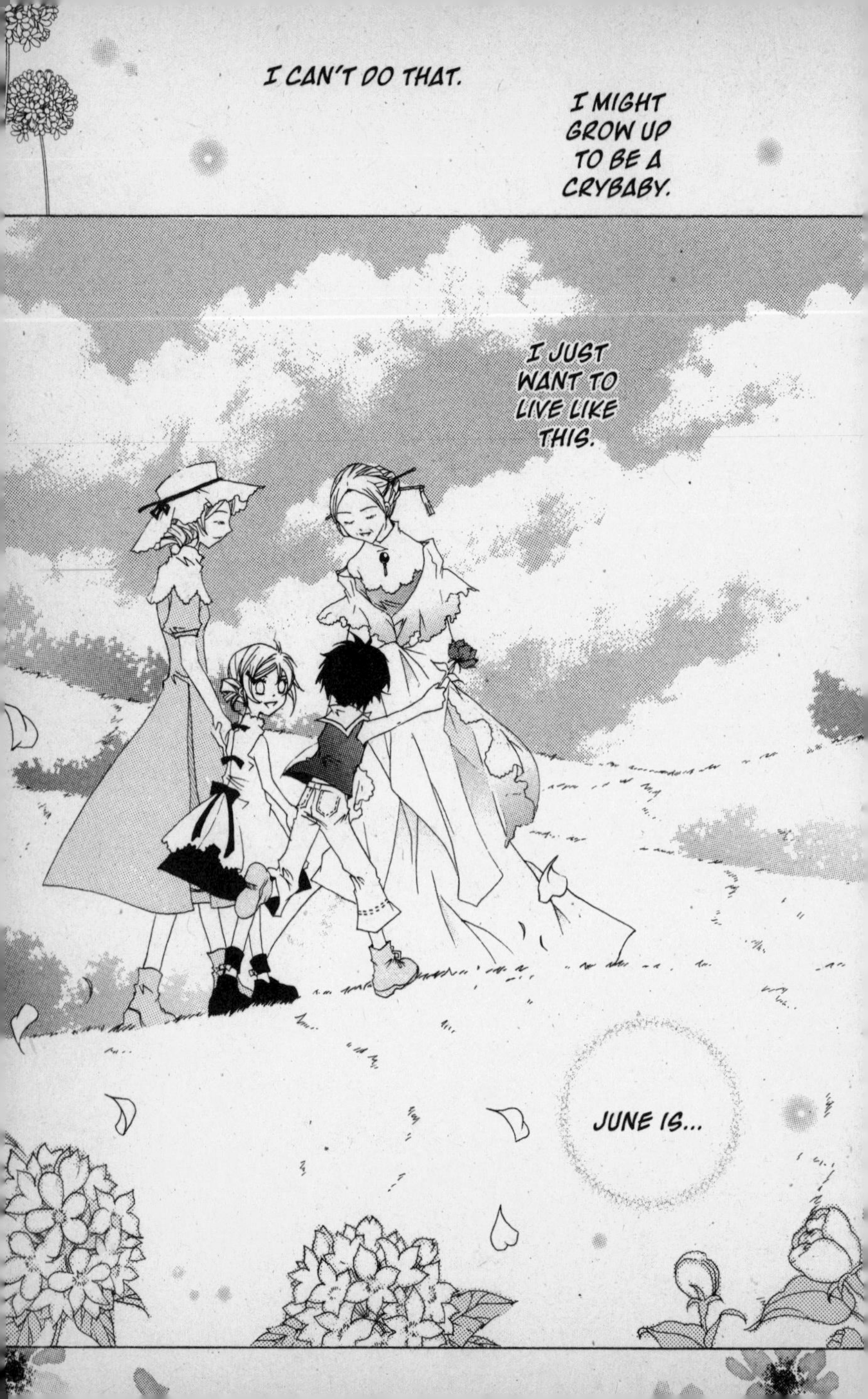
I CAN'T DO THAT.
I MIGHT GROW UP TO BE A CRYBABY.
I JUST WANT TO LIVE LIKE THIS.
JUNE IS...

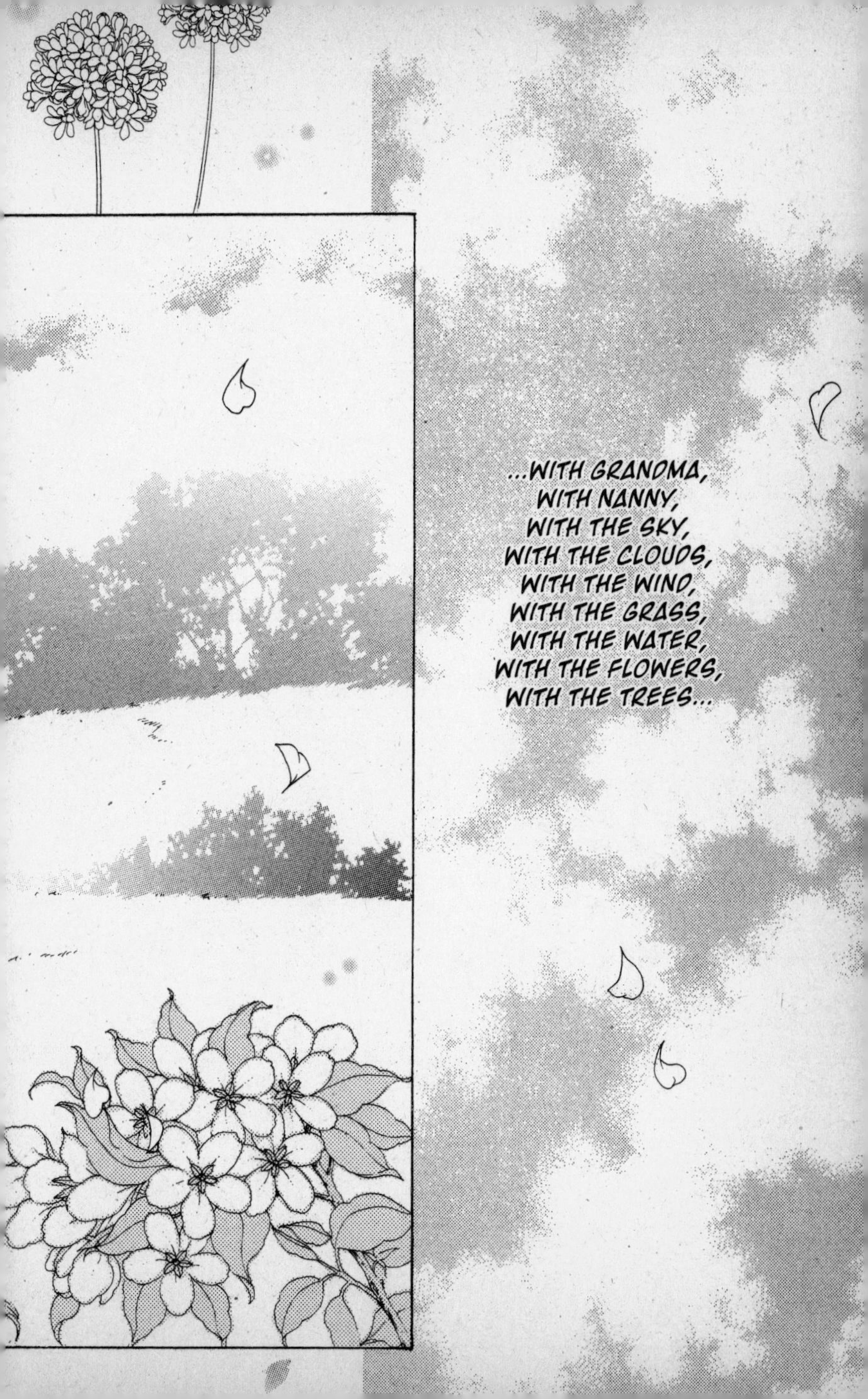
...WITH GRANDMA,
WITH NANNY,
WITH THE SKY,
WITH THE CLOUDS,
WITH THE WIND,
WITH THE GRASS,
WITH THE WATER,
WITH THE FLOWERS,
WITH THE TREES...

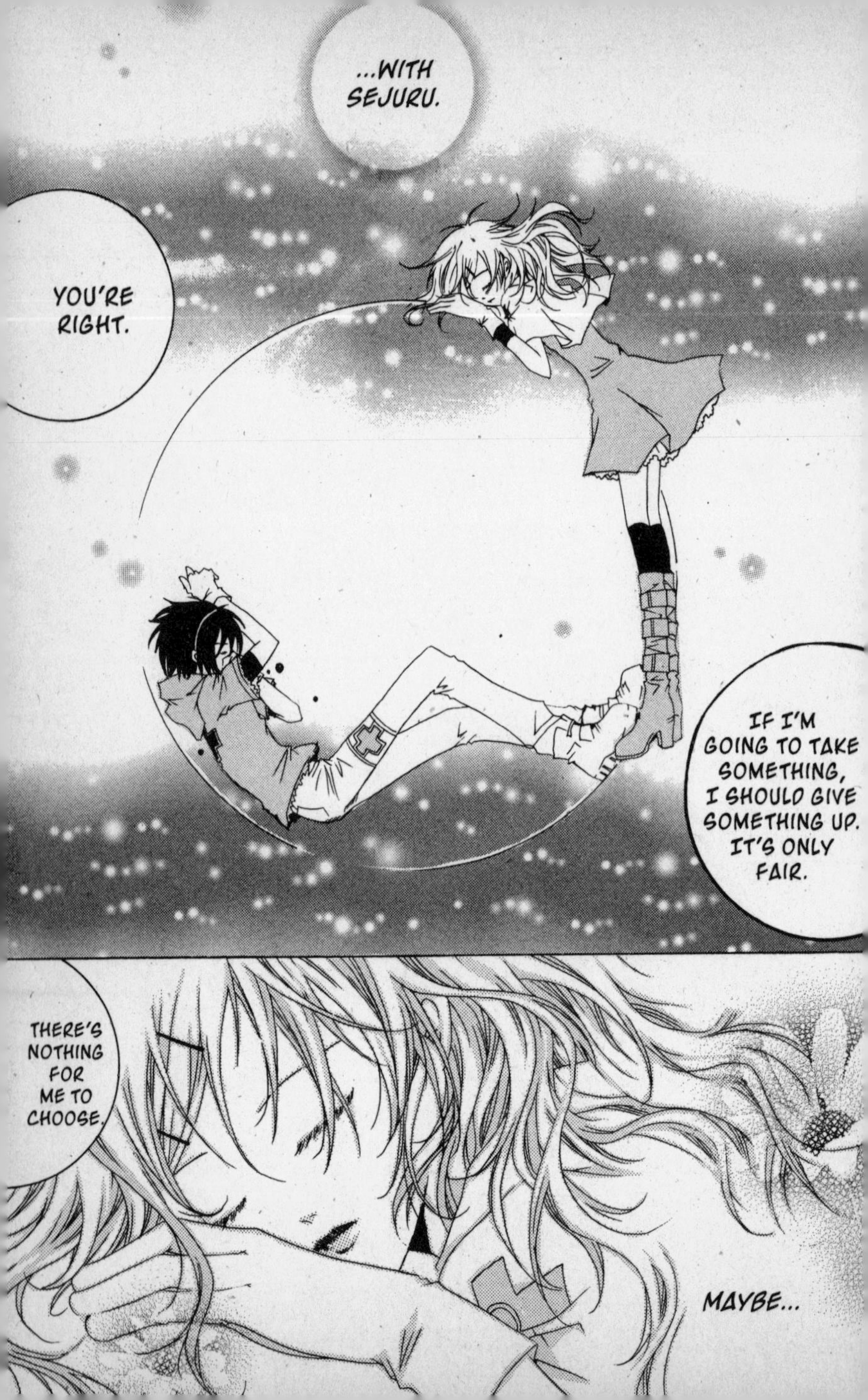
...WITH SEJURU.
YOU'RE RIGHT.
IF I'M GOING TO TAKE SOMETHING, I SHOULD GIVE SOMETHING UP. IT'S ONLY FAIR.
THERE'S NOTHING FOR ME TO CHOOSE.
MAYBE...

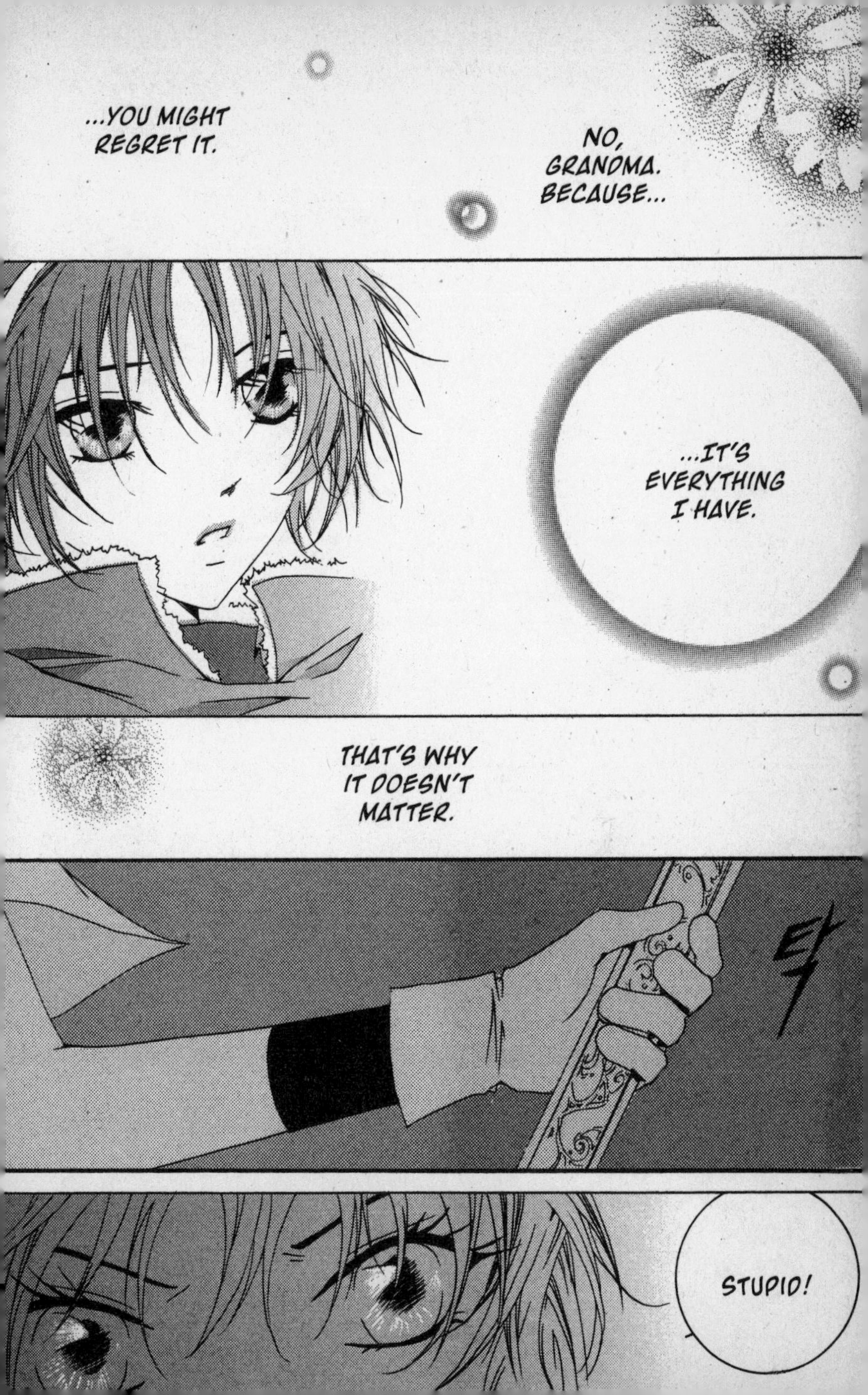
...YOU MIGHT REGRET IT.
NO, GRANDMA. BECAUSE...
...IT'S EVERYTHING I HAVE.
THAT'S WHY IT DOESN'T MATTER.
STUPID!

YOU SAID YOU WANTED TO BE THE QUEEN!
GOODBYE.
ARE YOU REALLY GOING TO MAKE A FOOL OUT OF ME?
JUNE! ARE YOU GIVING UP THE QUEEN'S SCEPTER?
HOW CAN YOU JUST GIVE IT UP WITHOUT EVEN FIGHTING FOR IT!
STOP! DAMMIT!!
IT'S FAREWELL AS SOON AS WE MEET.

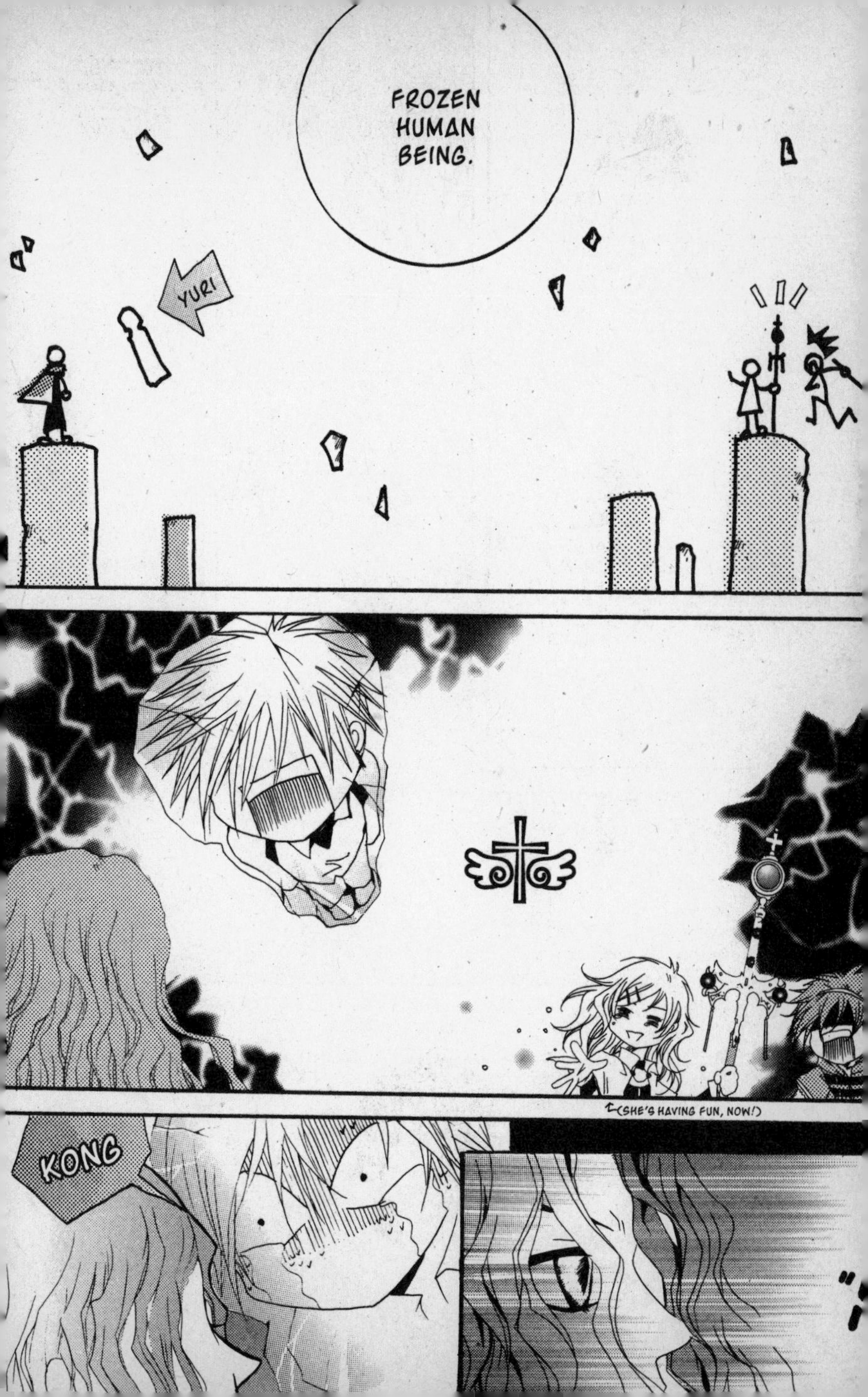
FROZEN HUMAN BEING.
YURI
(SHE'S HAVING FUN, NOW!)
KONG

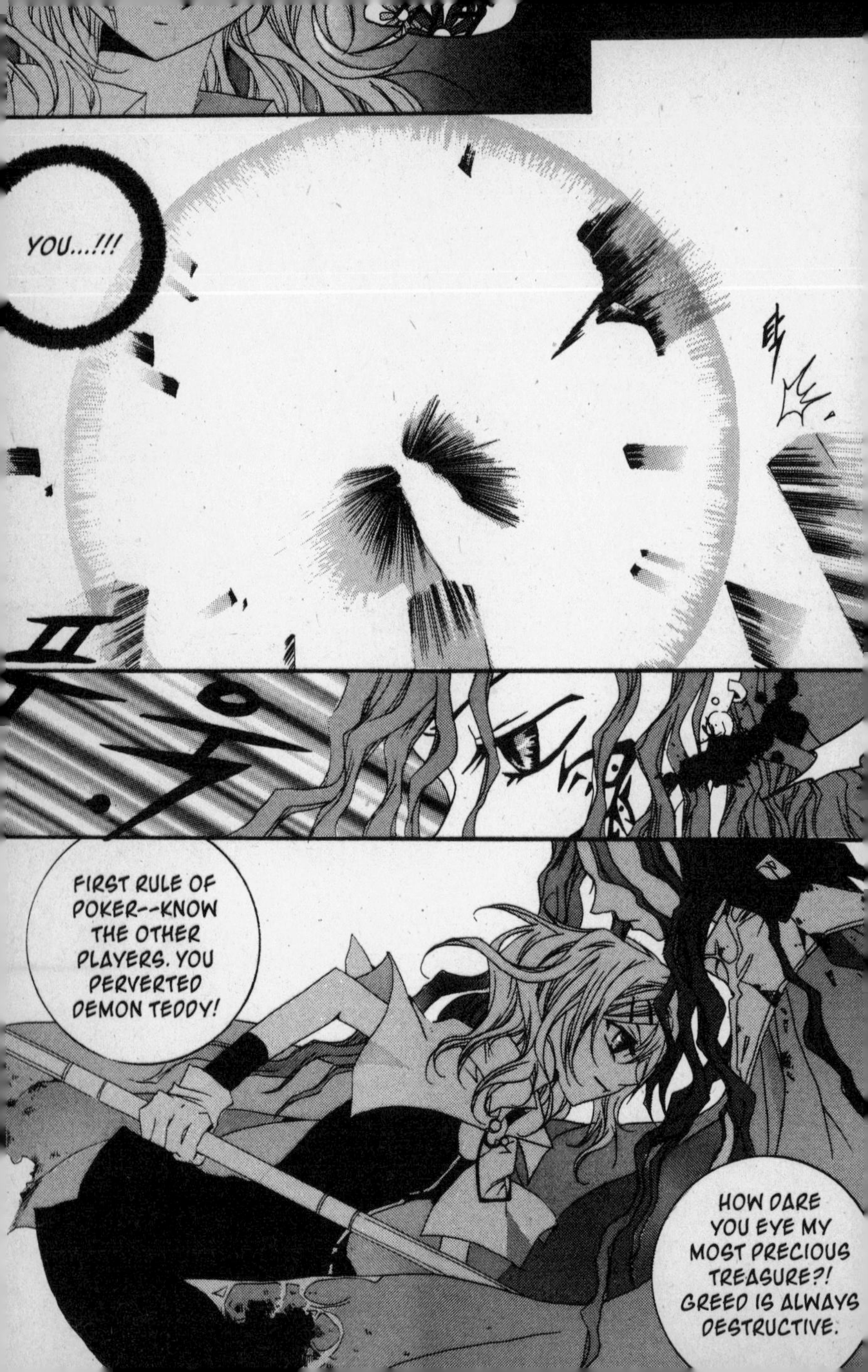
YOU...!!!
FIRST RULE OF POKER--KNOW THE OTHER PLAYERS. YOU PERVERTED DEMON TEDDY!
HOW DARE YOU EYE MY MOST PRECIOUS TREASURE?! GREED IS ALWAYS DESTRUCTIVE.

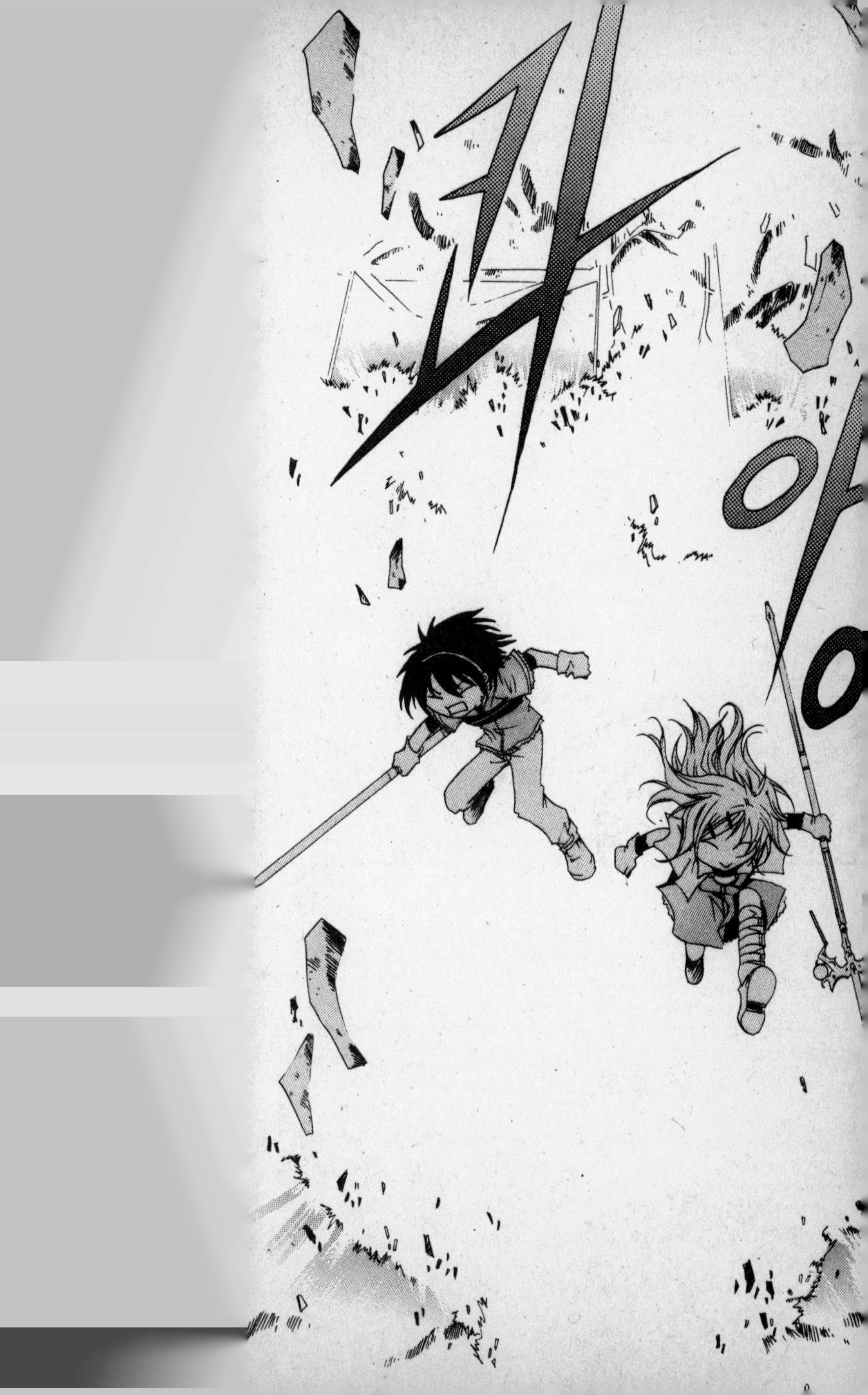

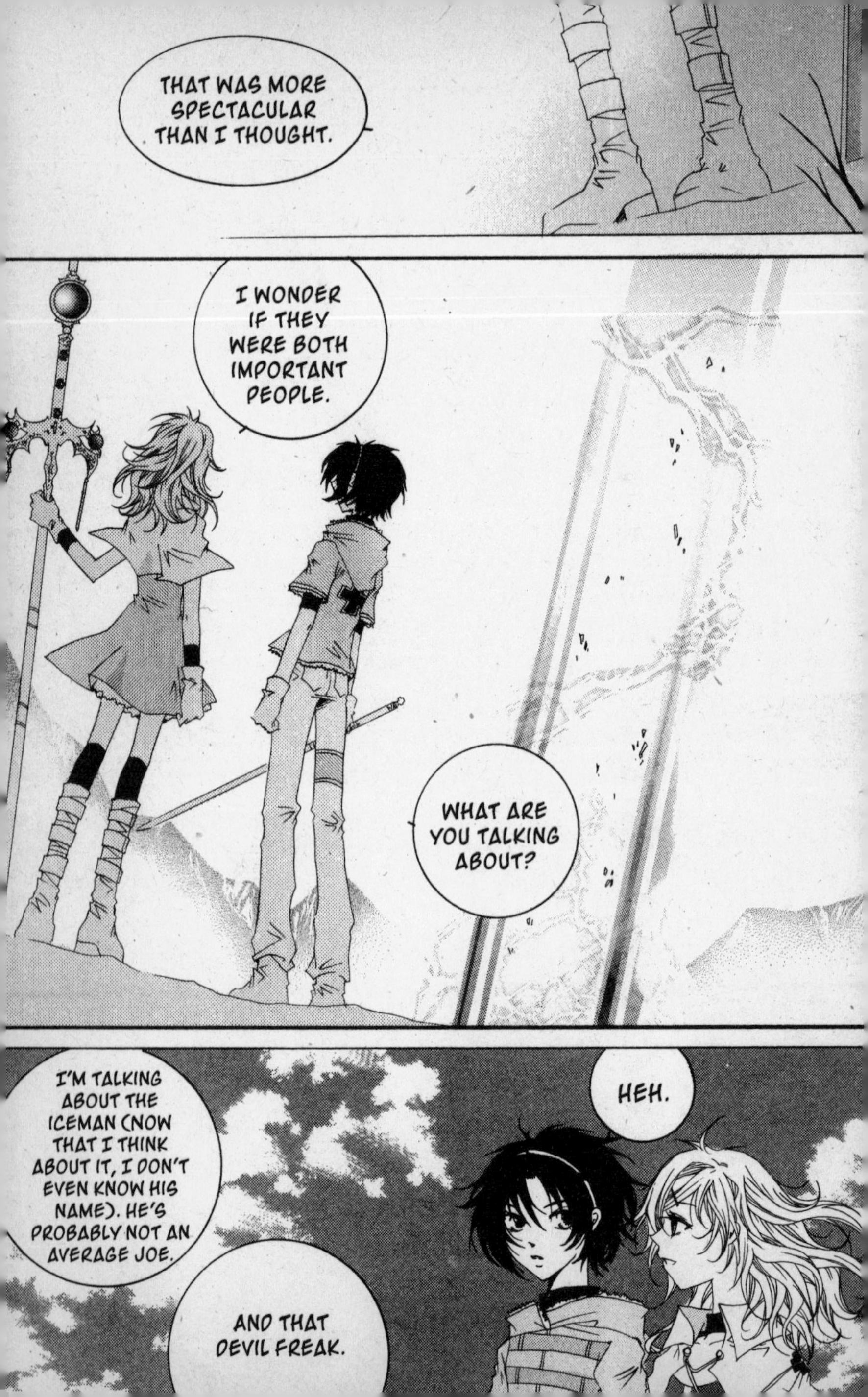
THAT WAS MORE SPECTACULAR THAN I THOUGHT.
I WONDER IF THEY WERE BOTH IMPORTANT PEOPLE.
WHAT ARE YOU TALKING ABOUT?
I'M TALKING ABOUT THE ICEMAN (NOW THAT I THINK ABOUT IT, I DON'T EVEN KNOW HIS NAME). HE'S PROBABLY NOT AN AVERAGE JOE.
AND THAT DEVIL FREAK.
HEH.

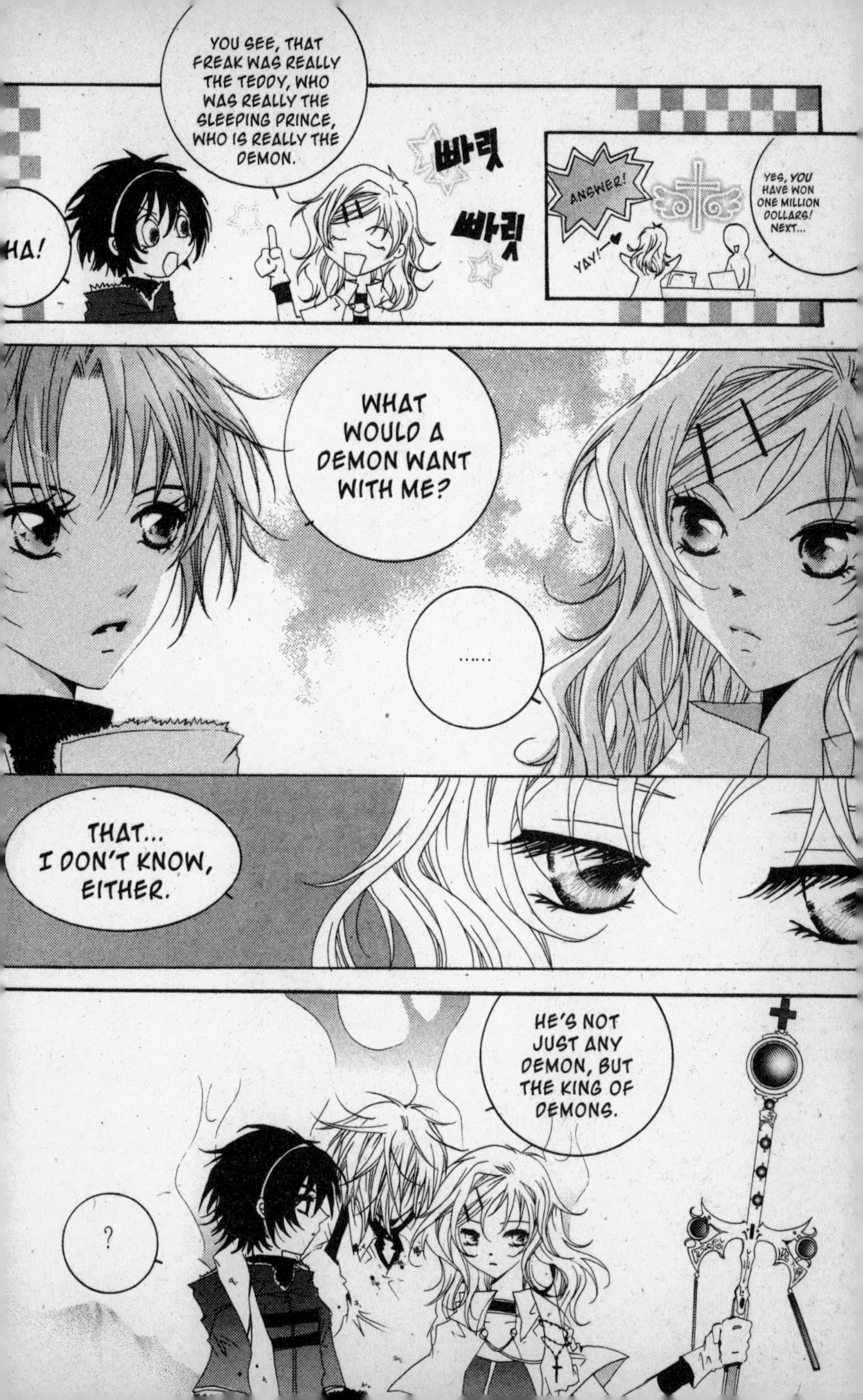
HA!
YOU SEE, THAT FREAK WAS REALLY THE TEDDY, WHO WAS REALLY THE SLEEPING PRINCE, WHO IS REALLY THE DEMON.
빠릿
빠릿
ANSWER!
YAY!—♥
YES, YOU HAVE WON ONE MILLION DOLLARS! NEXT...
WHAT WOULD A DEMON WANT WITH ME?
......
THAT... I DON'T KNOW, EITHER.
HE'S NOT JUST ANY DEMON, BUT THE KING OF DEMONS.
?

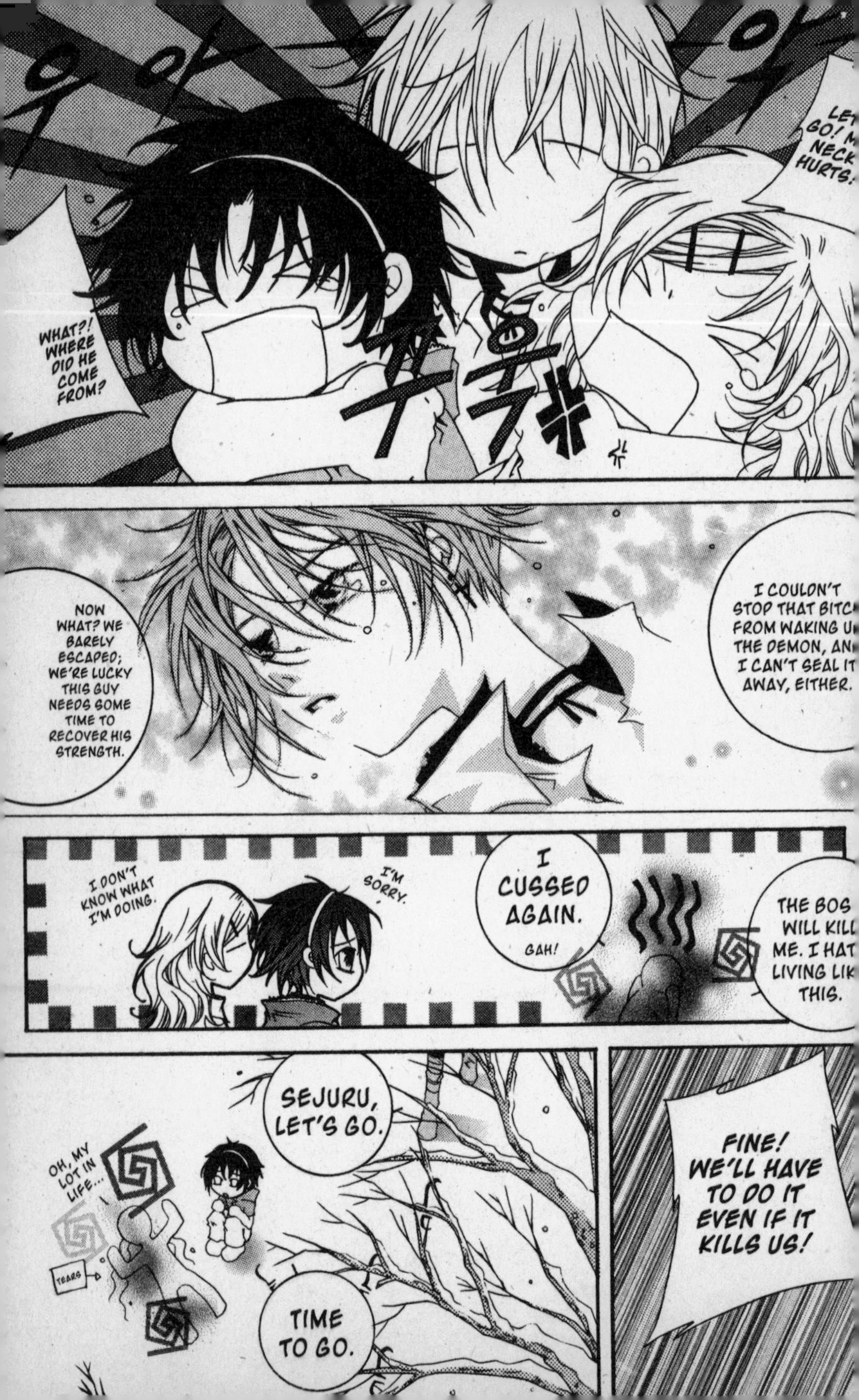
LET GO! M NECK HURTS!
WHAT?! WHERE DID HE COME FROM?
I COULDN'T STOP THAT BITC FROM WAKING U THE DEMON, AN I CAN'T SEAL IT AWAY, EITHER.
NOW WHAT? WE BARELY ESCAPED; WE'RE LUCKY THIS GUY NEEDS SOME TIME TO RECOVER HIS STRENGTH.
THE BOS WILL KILL ME. I HAT LIVING LIK THIS.
I CUSSED AGAIN.
GAH!
I'M SORRY.
I DON'T KNOW WHAT I'M DOING.
FINE! WE'LL HAVE TO DO IT EVEN IF IT KILLS US!
SEJURU, LET'S GO.
OH, MY LOT IN LIFE...
TEARS
TIME TO GO.

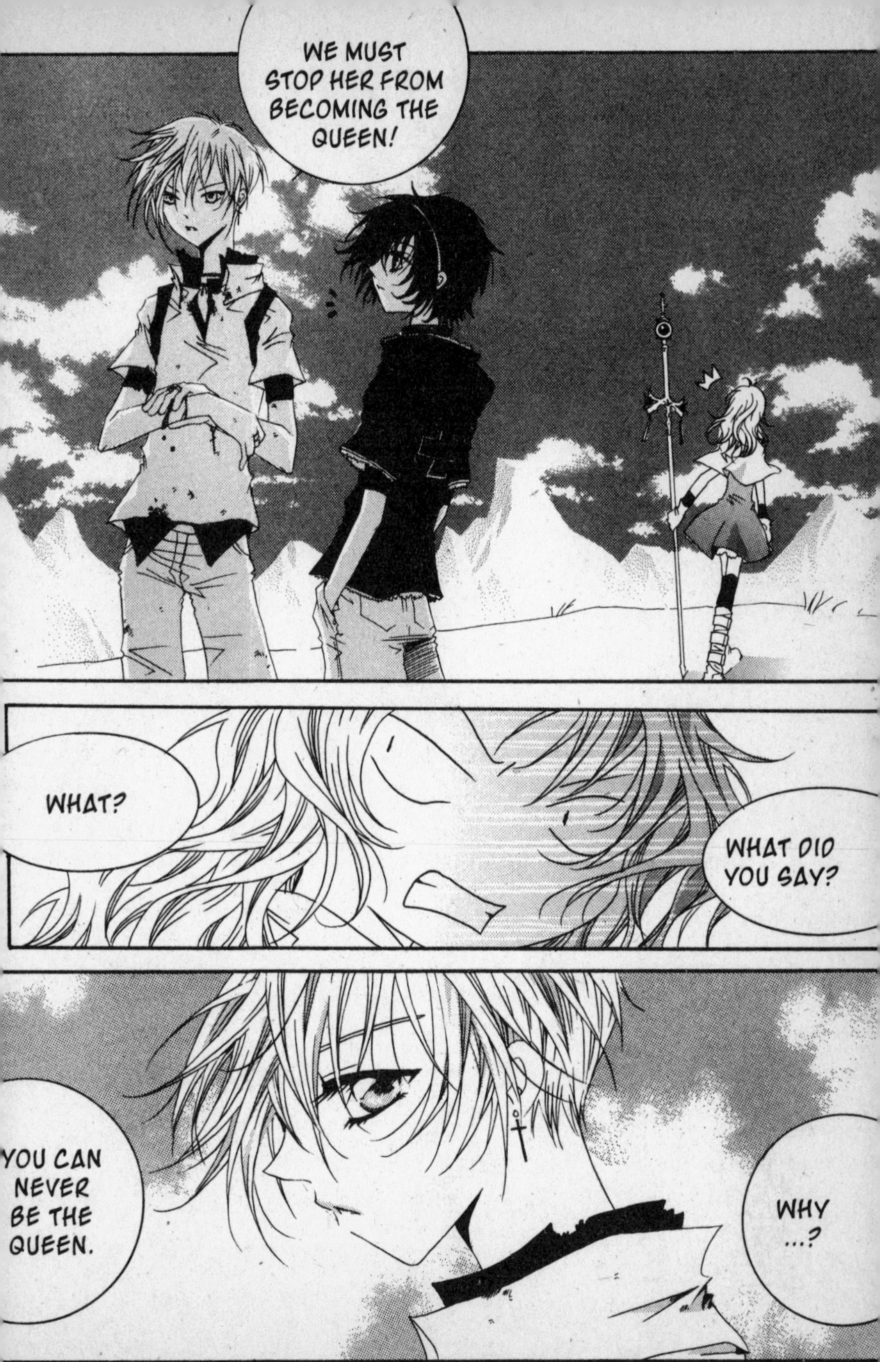
WE MUST STOP HER FROM BECOMING THE QUEEN!
WHAT?
WHAT DID YOU SAY?
YOU CAN NEVER BE THE QUEEN.
WHY ...?

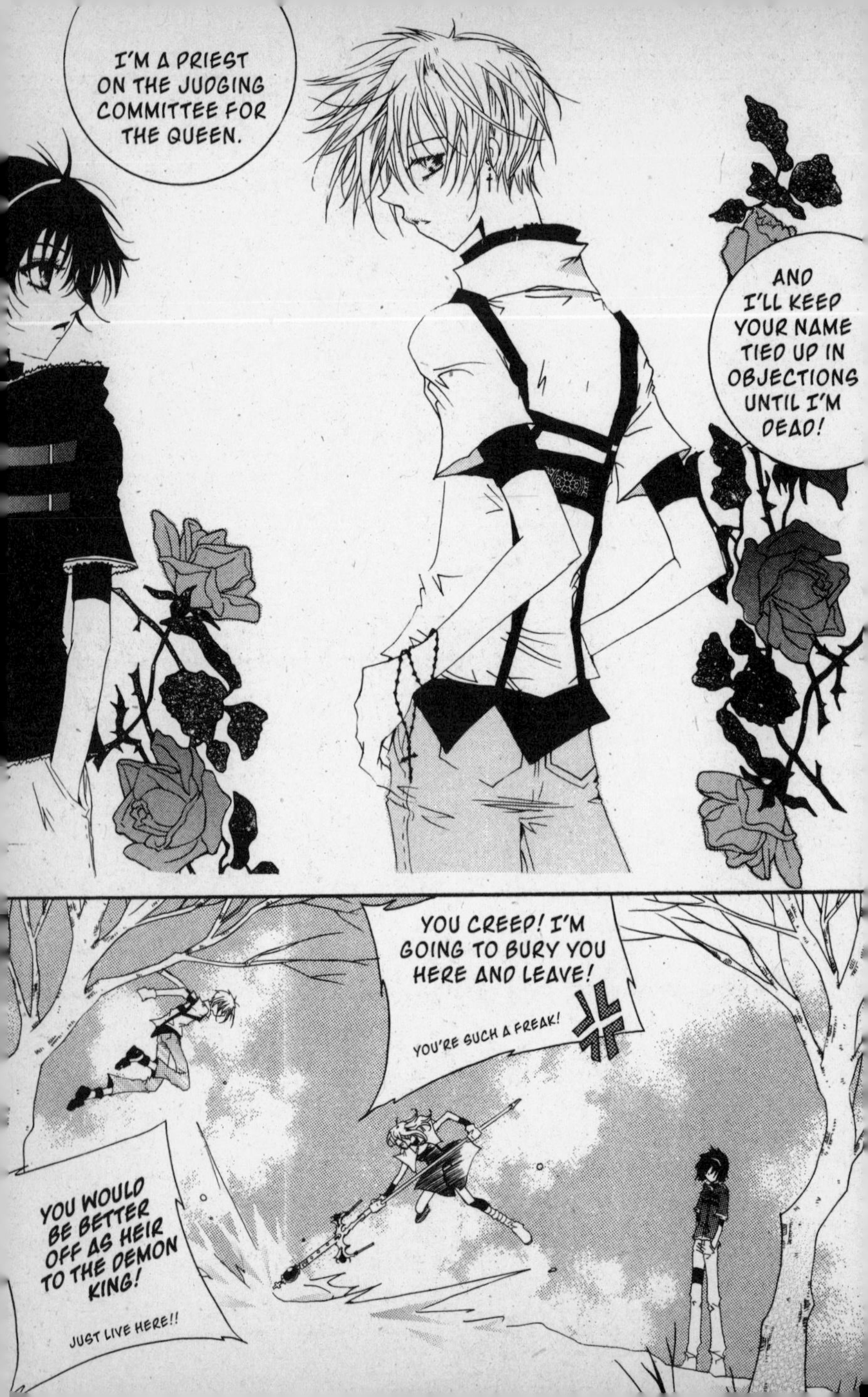
I'M A PRIEST ON THE JUDGING COMMITTEE FOR THE QUEEN.
AND I'LL KEEP YOUR NAME TIED UP IN OBJECTIONS UNTIL I'M DEAD!
YOU CREEP! I'M GOING TO BURY YOU HERE AND LEAVE!
YOU'RE SUCH A FREAK!
YOU WOULD BE BETTER OFF AS HEIR TO THE DEMON KING!
JUST LIVE HERE!!

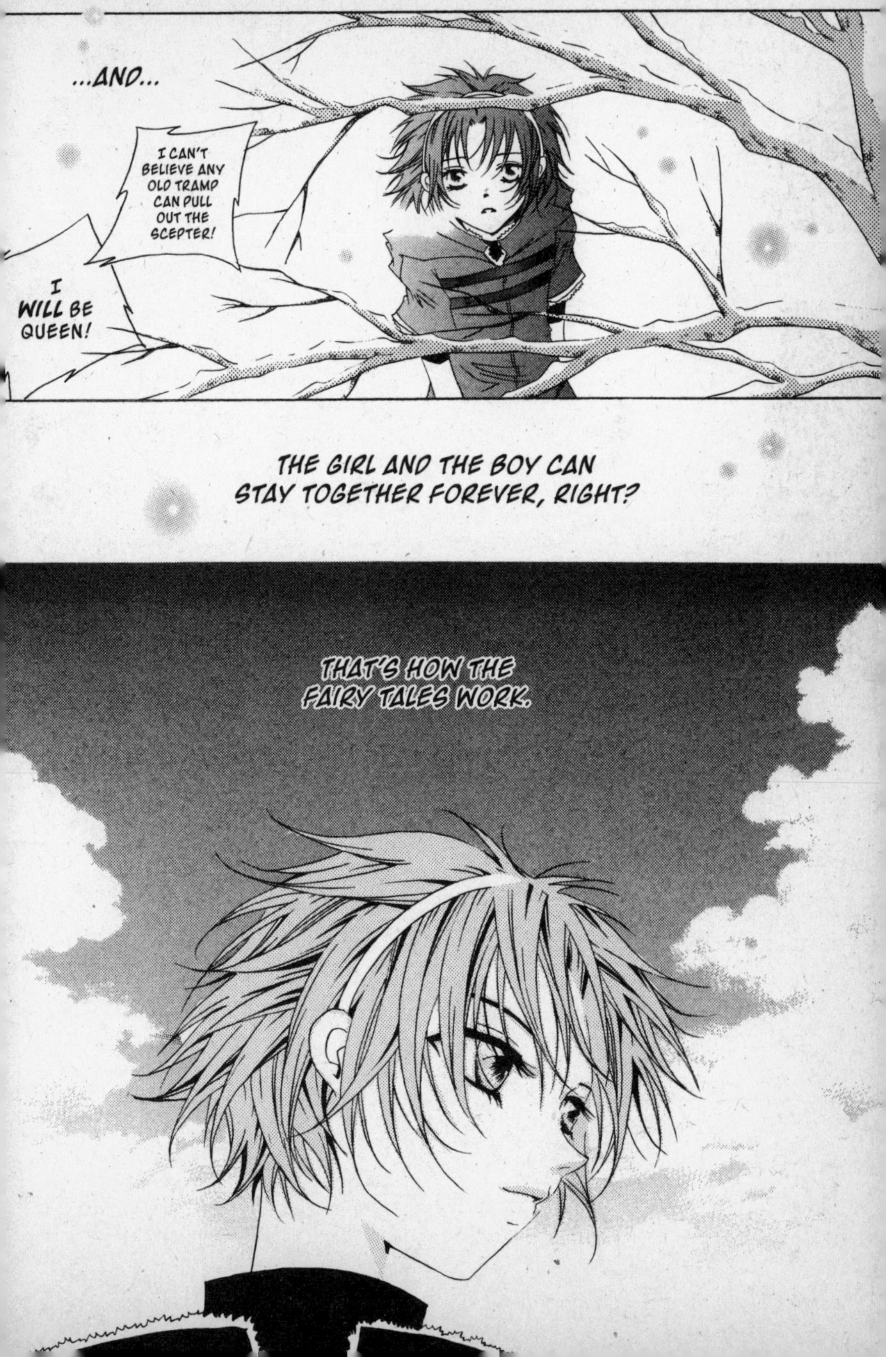
...AND...
I CAN'T BELIEVE ANY OLD TRAMP CAN PULL OUT THE SCEPTER!
I WILL BE QUEEN!
THE GIRL AND THE BOY CAN STAY TOGETHER FOREVER, RIGHT?
THAT'S HOW THE FAIRY TALES WORK.

BY EACH OTHER'S SIDE...

WOULD WE DREAM THE SAME DREAMS?

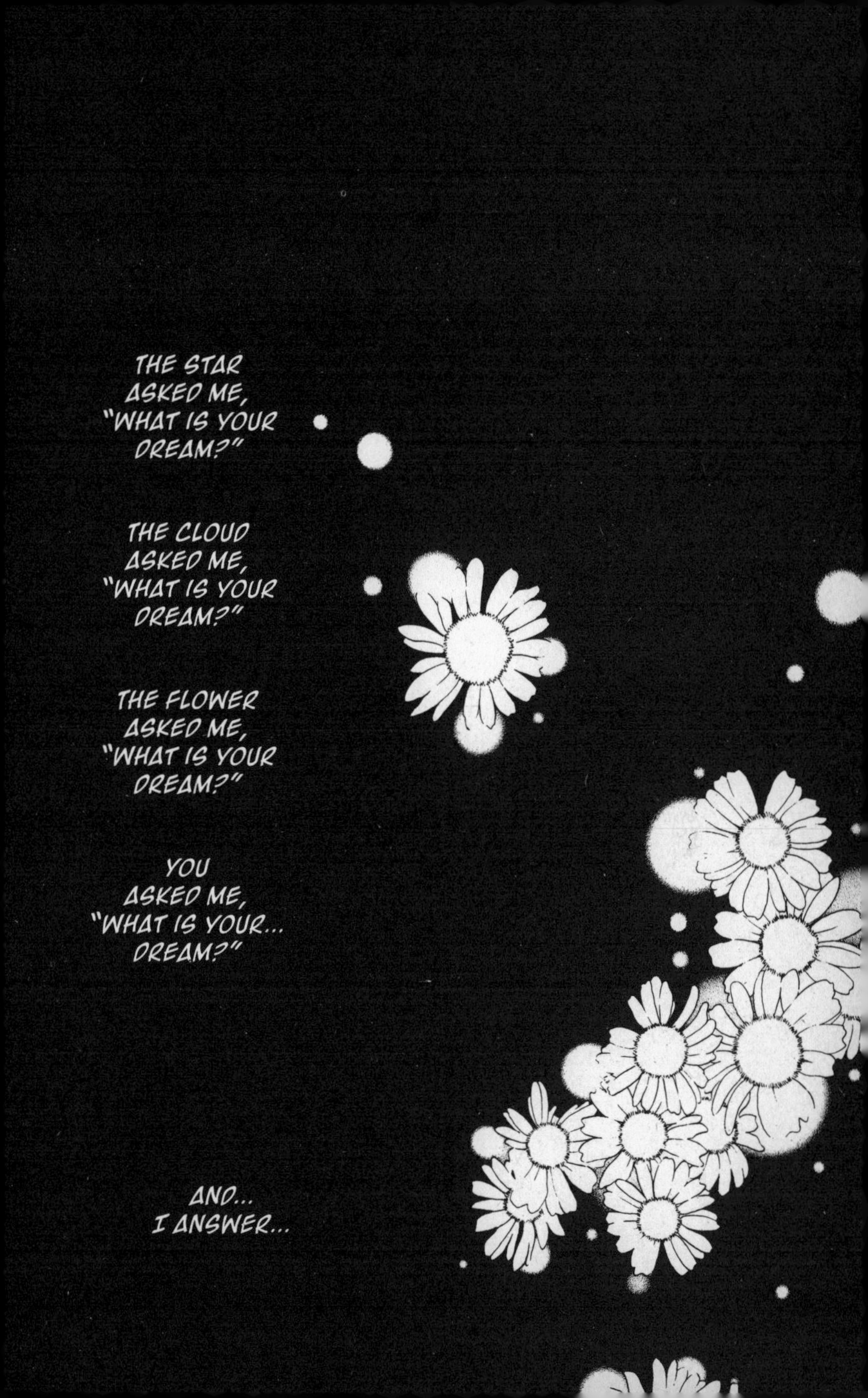
THE STAR ASKED ME, "WHAT IS YOUR DREAM?"
THE CLOUD ASKED ME, "WHAT IS YOUR DREAM?"
THE FLOWER ASKED ME, "WHAT IS YOUR DREAM?"
YOU ASKED ME, "WHAT IS YOUR... DREAM?"
AND... I ANSWER...

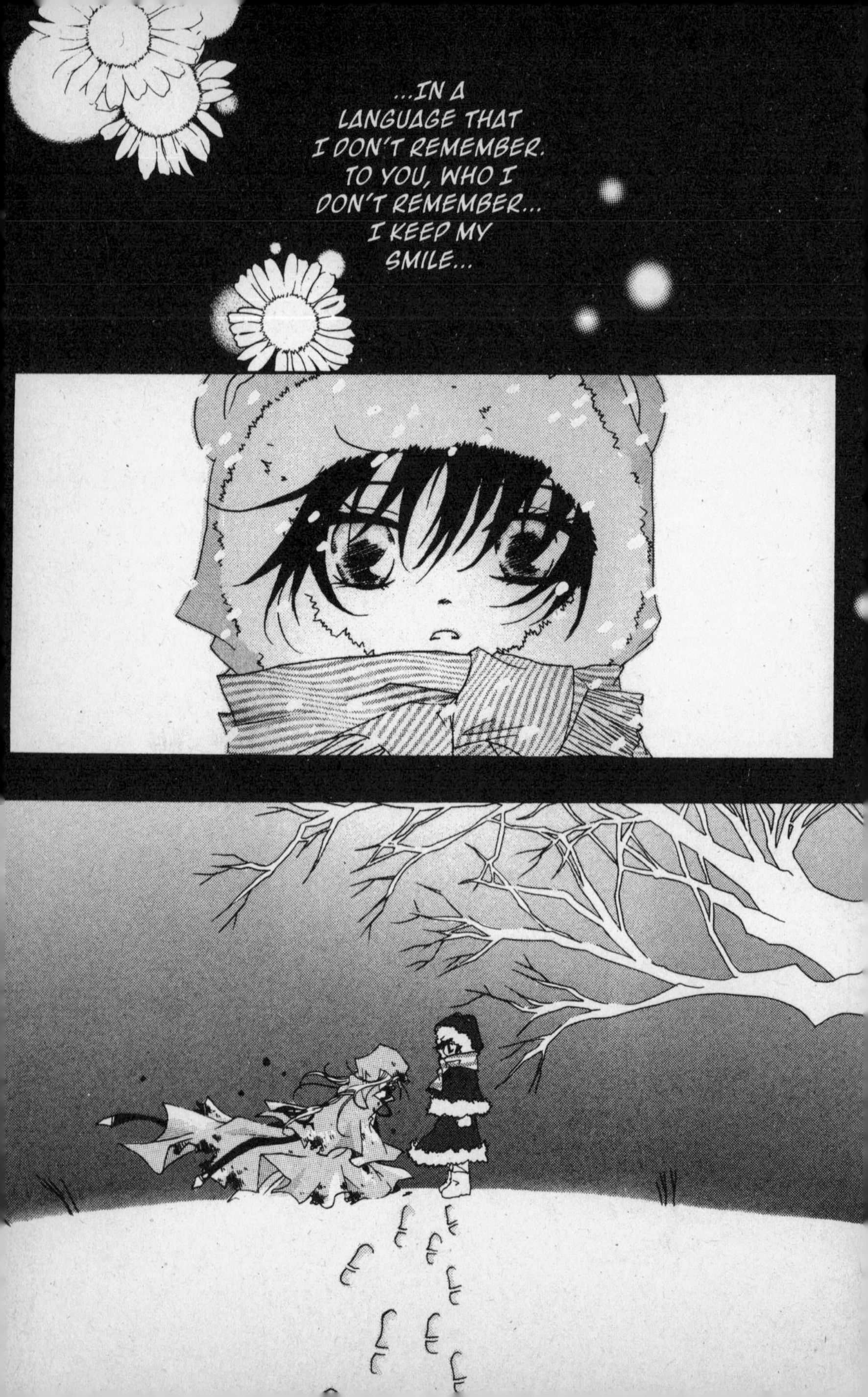
...IN A LANGUAGE THAT I DON'T REMEMBER. TO YOU, WHO I DON'T REMEMBER... I KEEP MY SMILE...

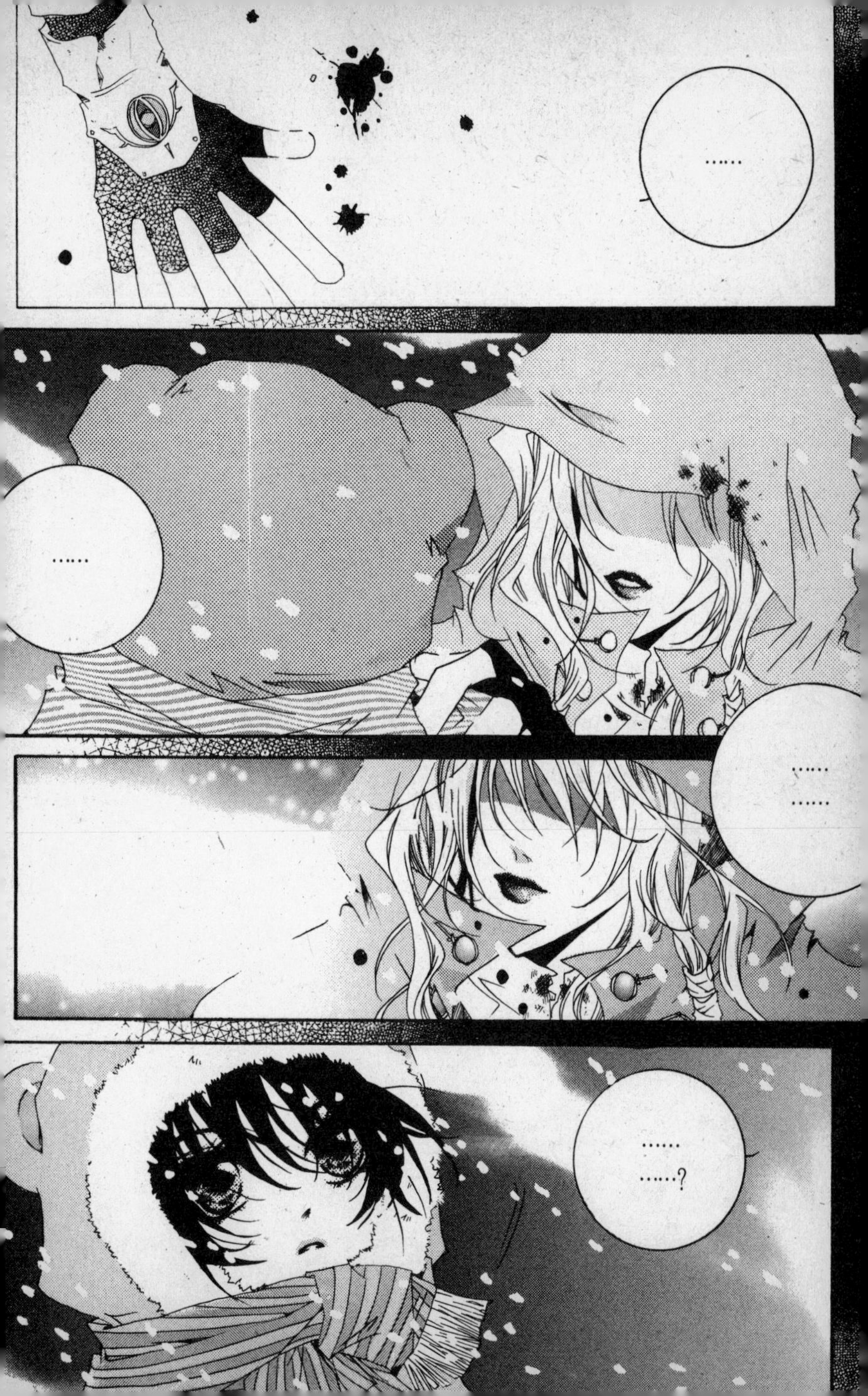
......
......
....
....?

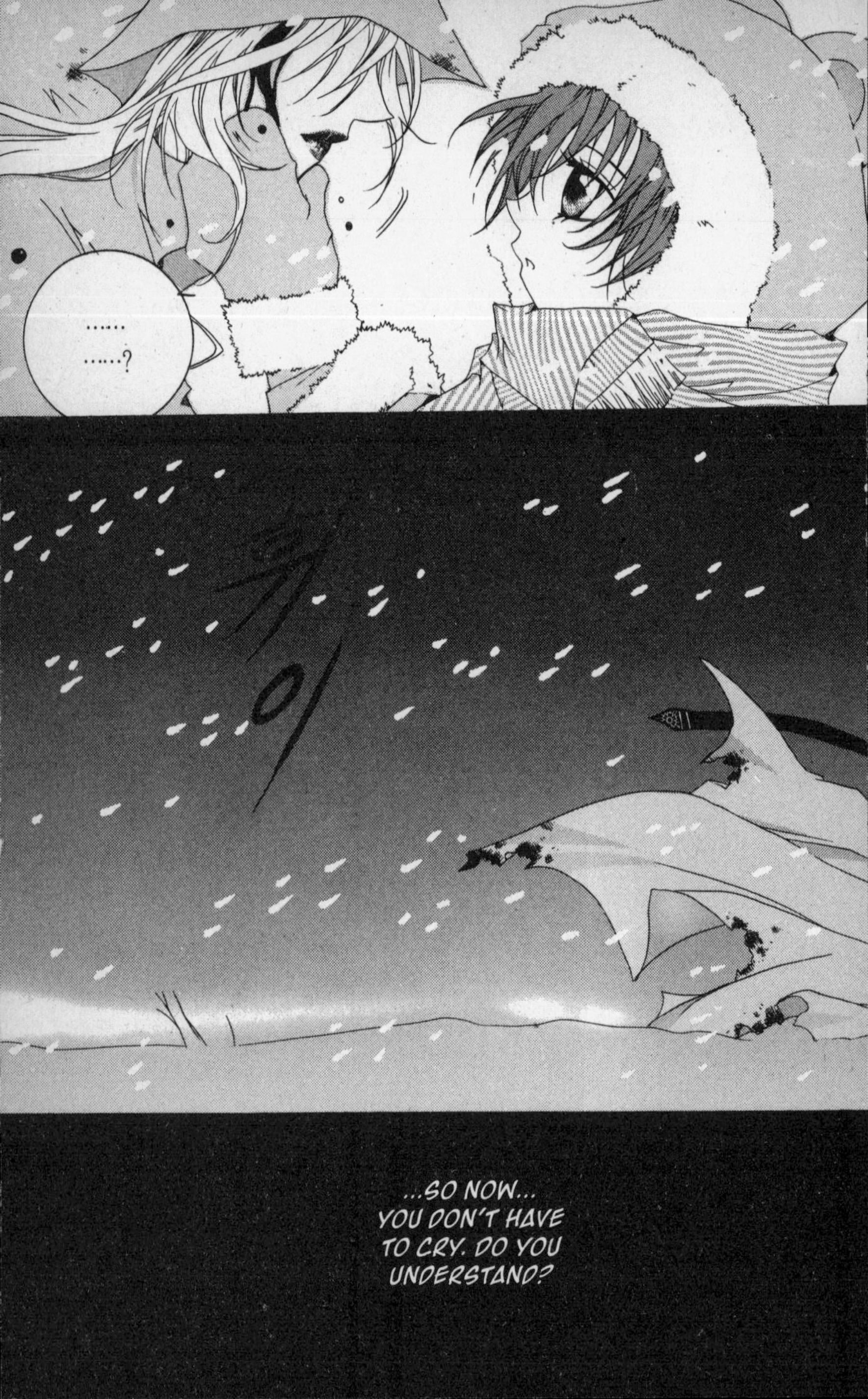
......
......?
...SO NOW... YOU DON'T HAVE TO CRY. DO YOU UNDERSTAND?

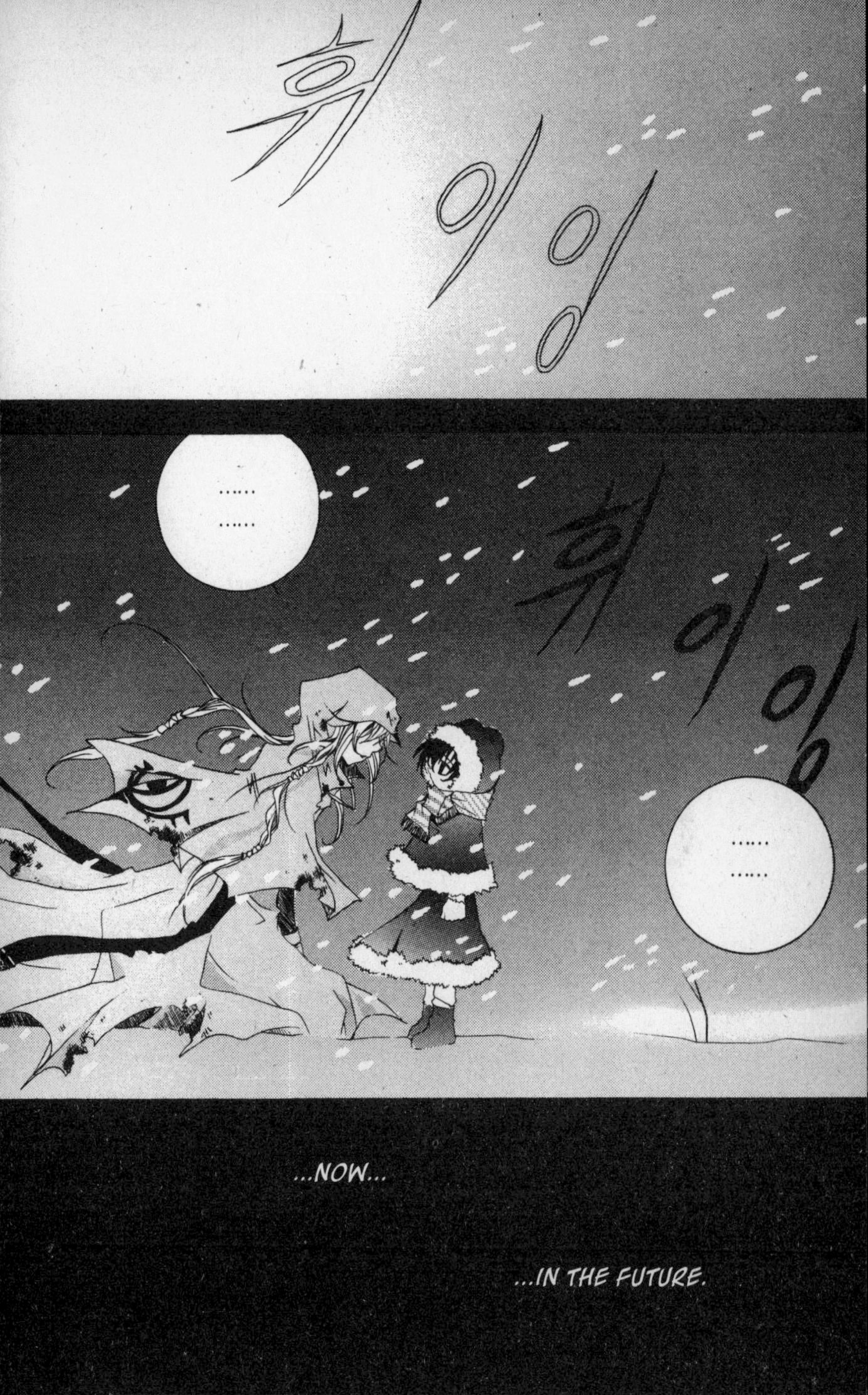
휘이이잉
......
......
휘이이잉
......
......
...NOW...
...IN THE FUTURE.

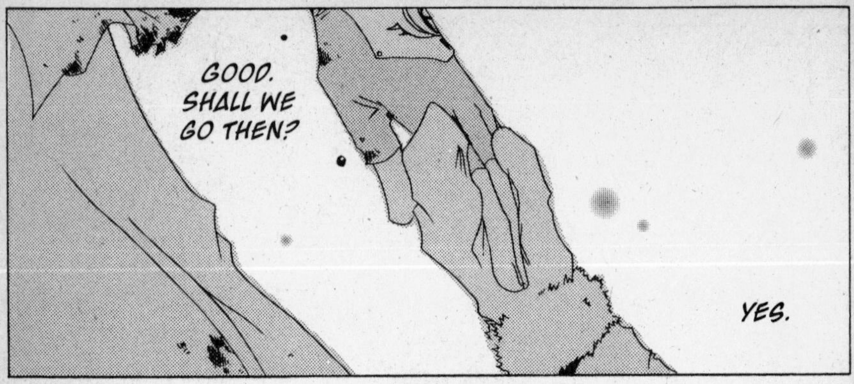
GOOD. SHALL WE GO THEN?
YES.

God Bless You

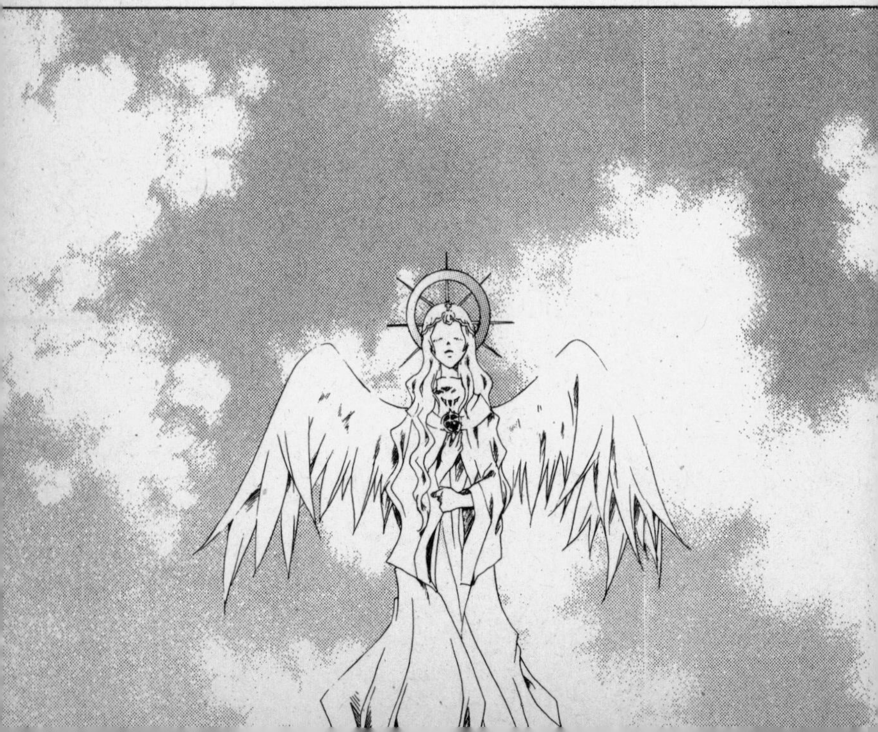

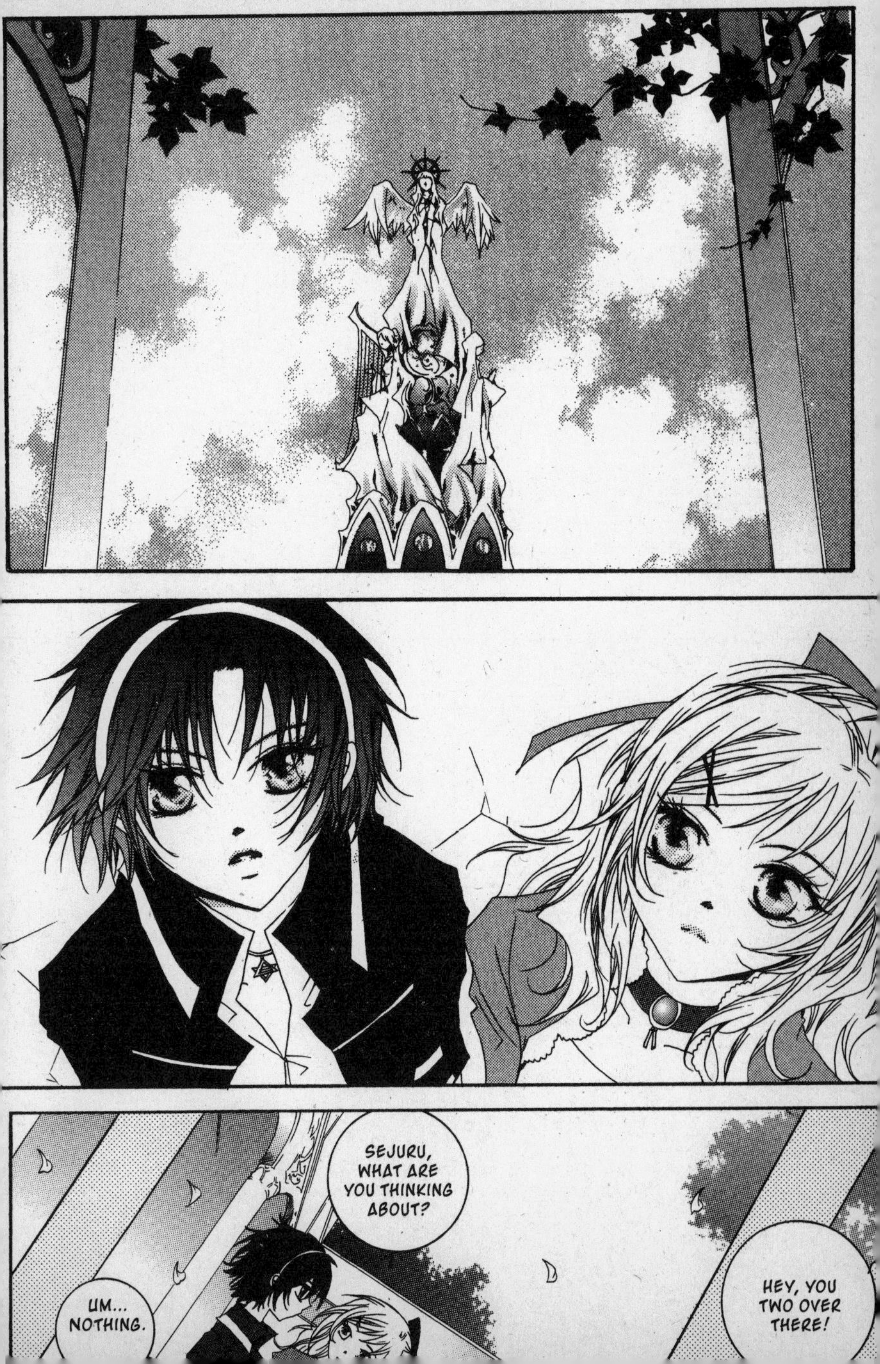
SEJURU, WHAT ARE YOU THINKING ABOUT?
UM... NOTHING.
HEY, YOU TWO OVER THERE!

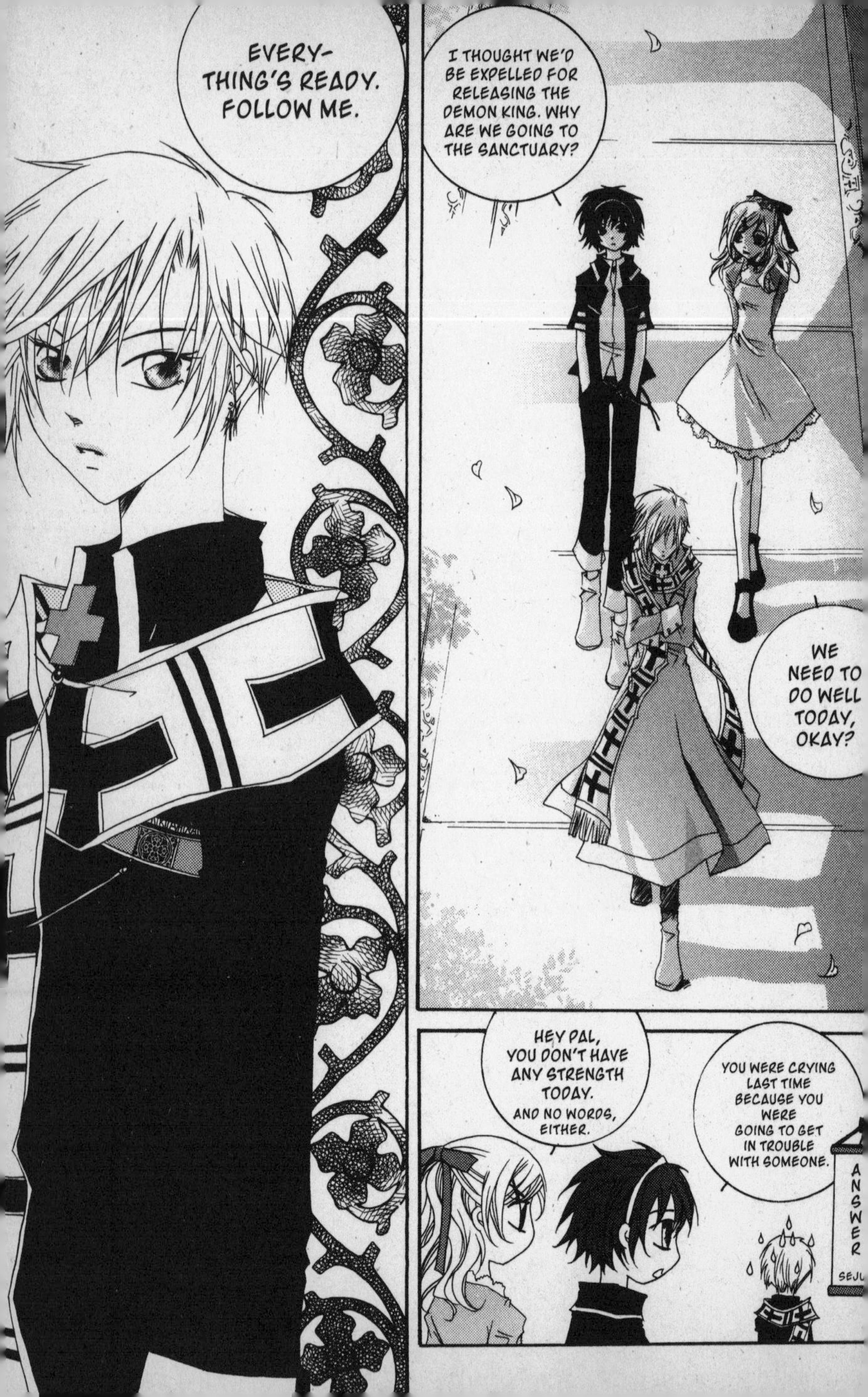
I THOUGHT WE'D BE EXPELLED FOR RELEASING THE DEMON KING. WHY ARE WE GOING TO THE SANCTUARY?
WE NEED TO DO WELL TODAY, OKAY?
HEY PAL, YOU DON'T HAVE ANY STRENGTH TODAY. AND NO WORDS, EITHER.
YOU WERE CRYING LAST TIME BECAUSE YOU WERE GOING TO GET IN TROUBLE WITH SOMEONE.
ANSWER
EVERY-THING'S READY. FOLLOW ME.

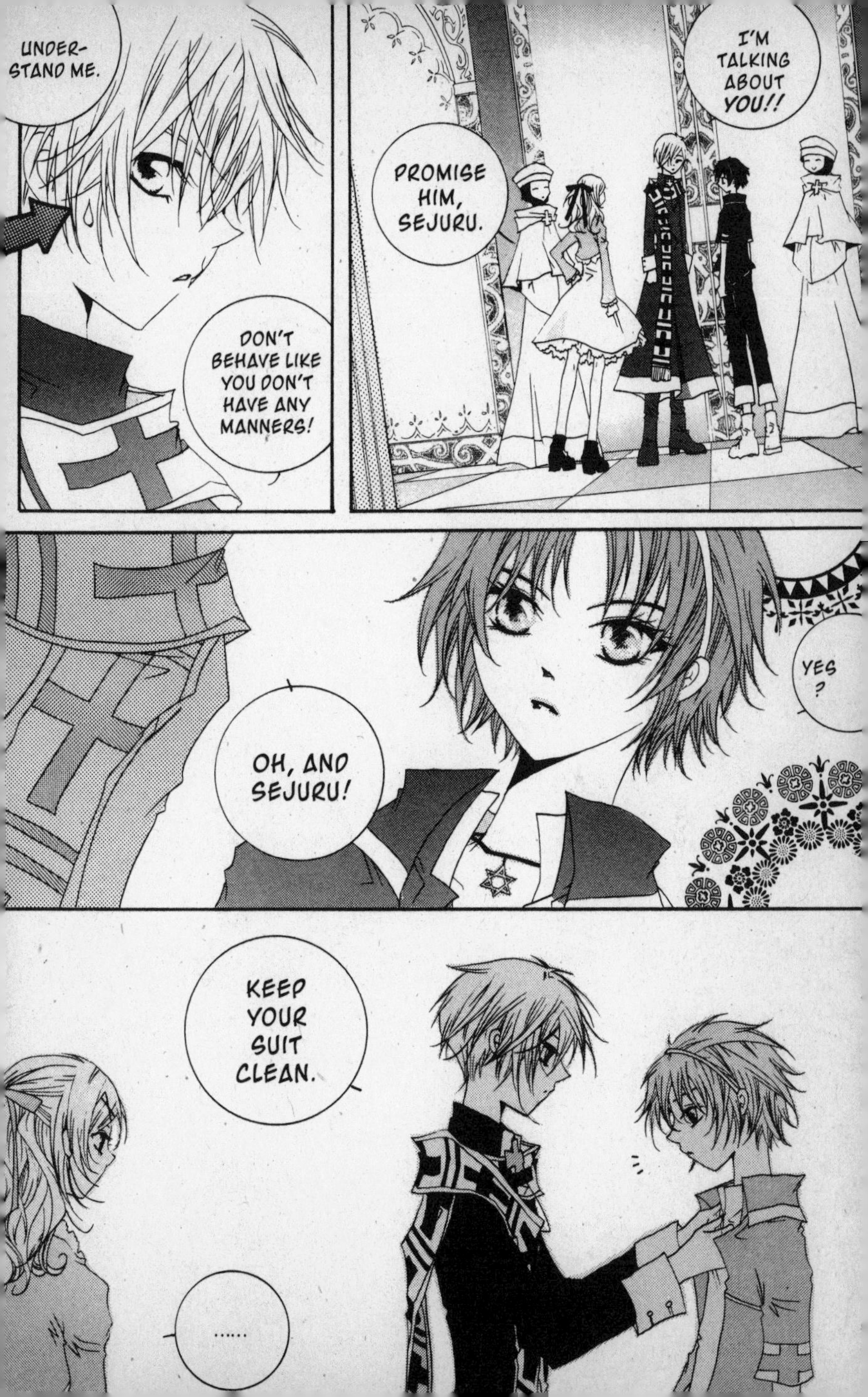
I'M TALKING ABOUT YOU!!
PROMISE HIM, SEJURU.
UNDER-STAND ME.
DON'T BEHAVE LIKE YOU DON'T HAVE ANY MANNERS!
YES?
OH, AND SEJURU!
KEEP YOUR SUIT CLEAN.
......

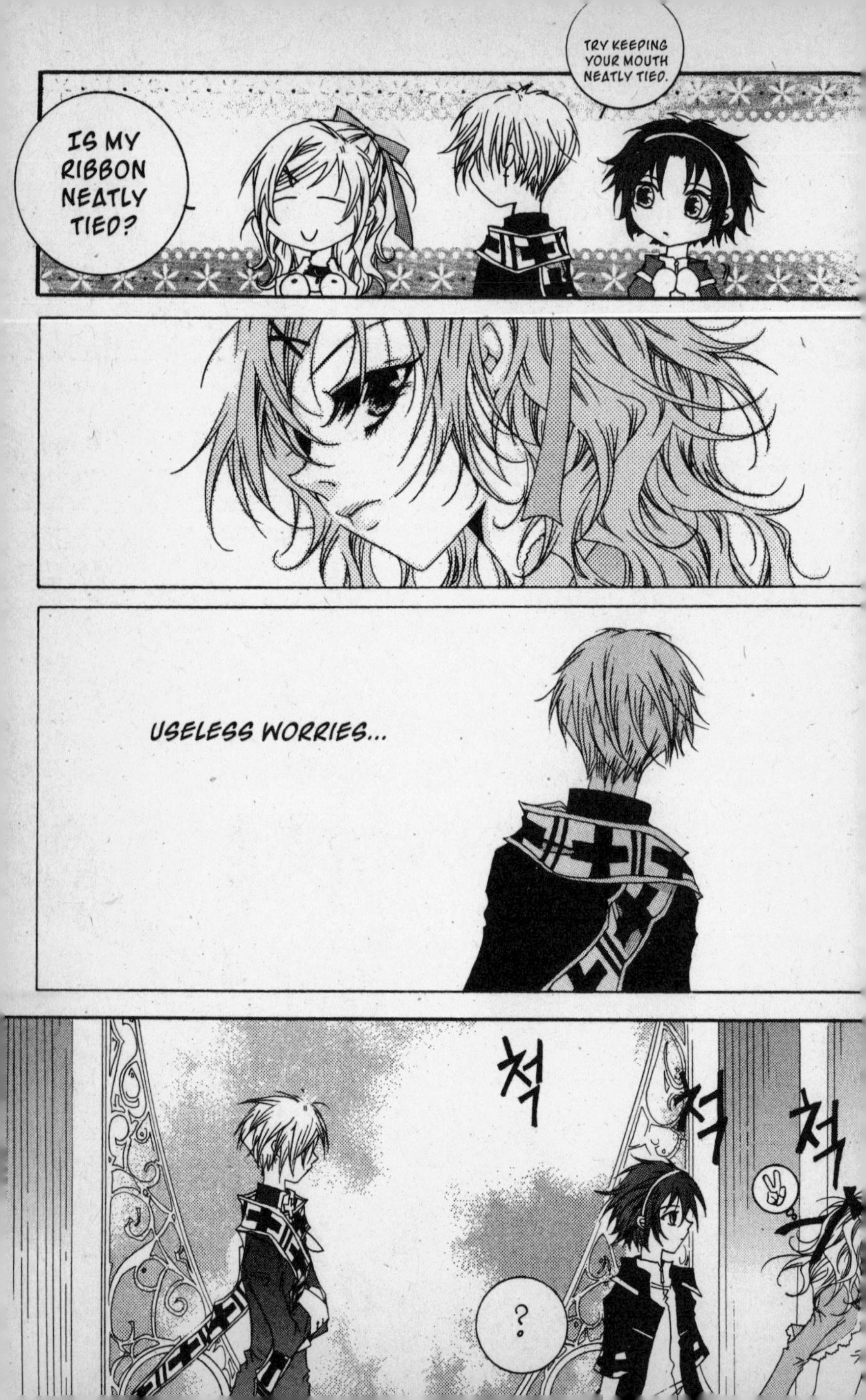
IS MY RIBBON NEATLY TIED?
TRY KEEPING YOUR MOUTH NEATLY TIED.
USELESS WORRIES...
척
척
척
?

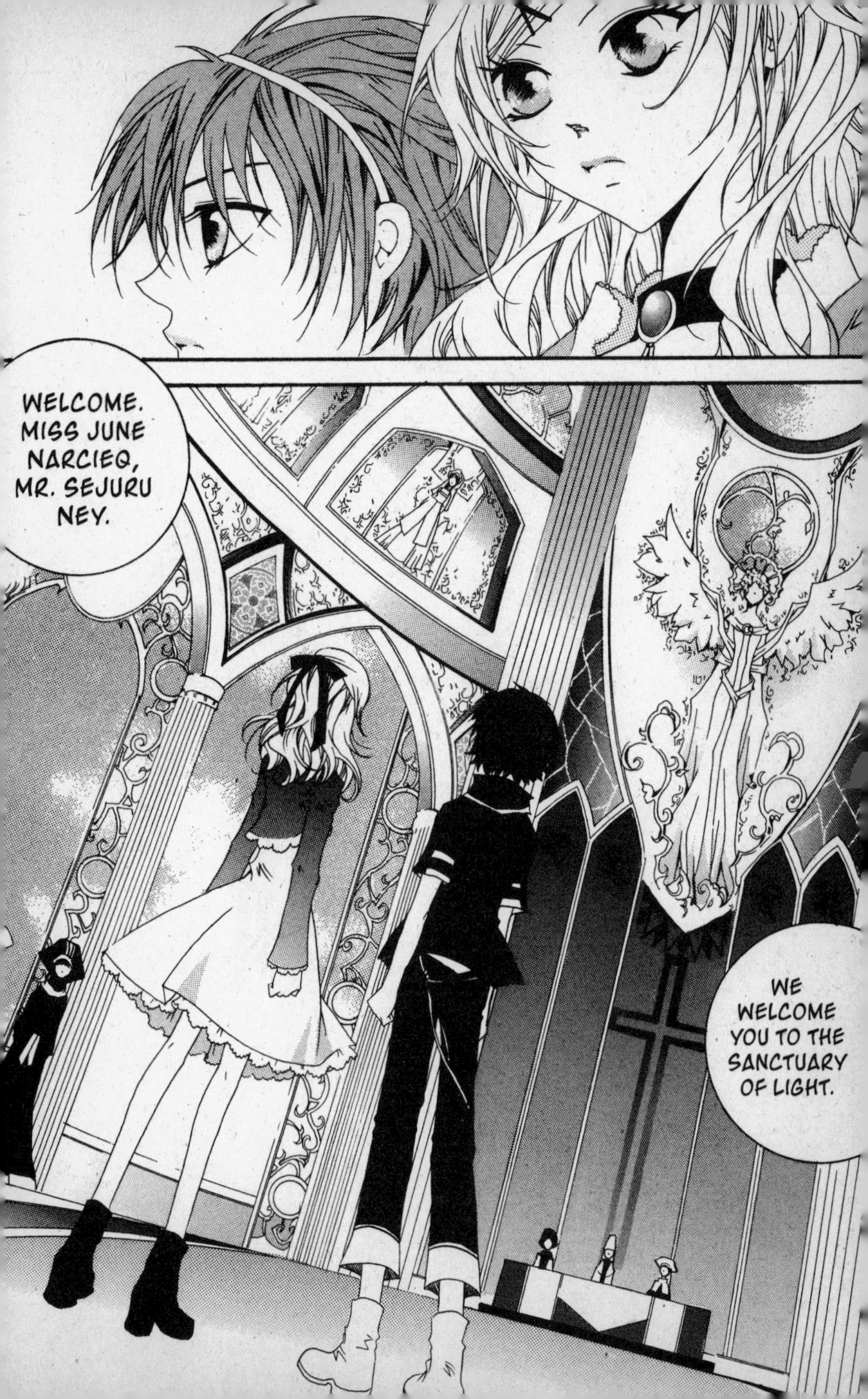
WELCOME. MISS JUNE NARCIEQ, MR. SEJURU NEY.
WE WELCOME YOU TO THE SANCTUARY OF LIGHT.

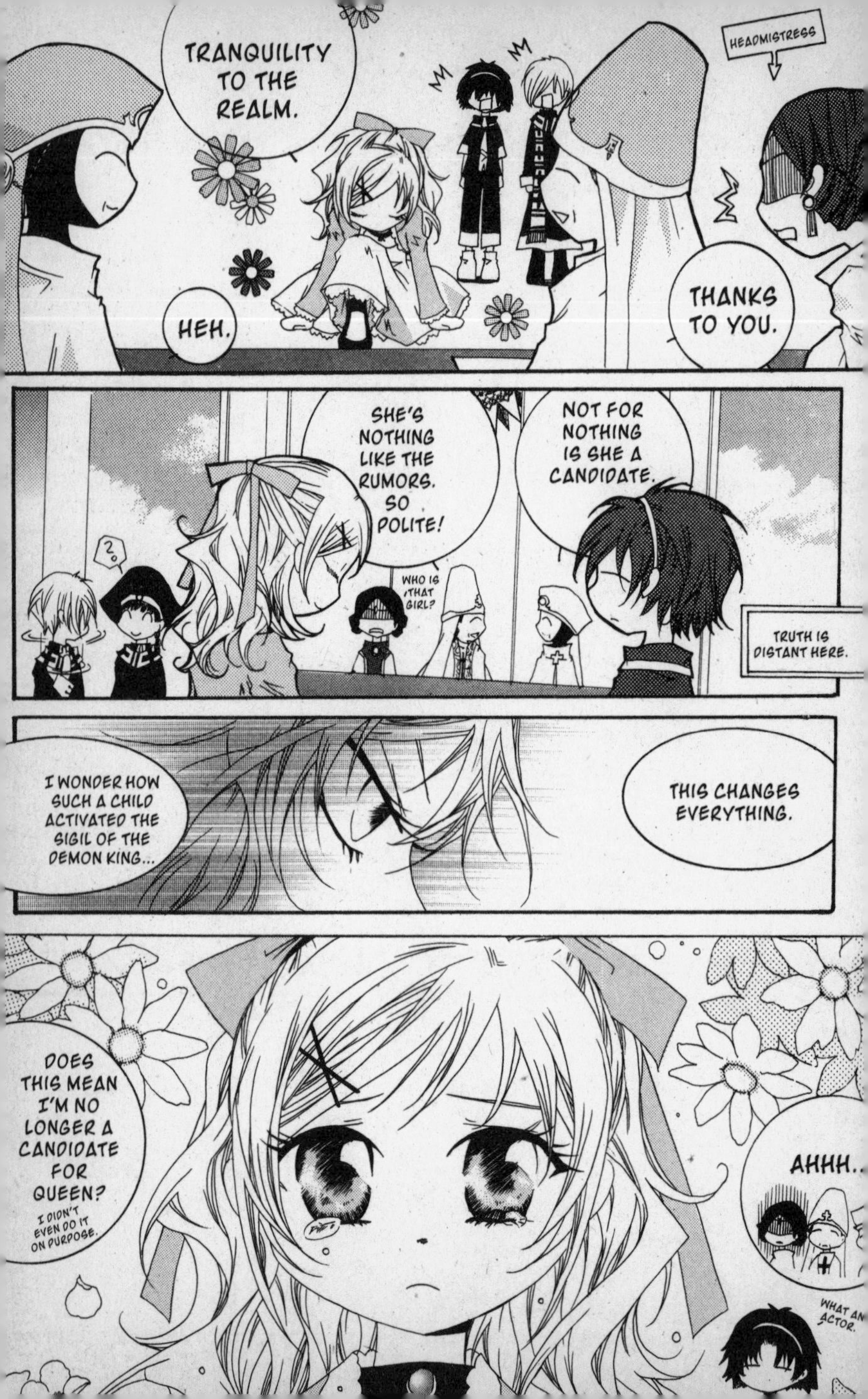
HEADMISTRESS
TRANQUILITY TO THE REALM.
THANKS TO YOU.
HEH.
TRUTH IS DISTANT HERE.
NOT FOR NOTHING IS SHE A CANDIDATE.
SHE'S NOTHING LIKE THE RUMORS. SO POLITE!
WHO IS THAT GIRL?
?
THIS CHANGES EVERYTHING.
I WONDER HOW SUCH A CHILD ACTIVATED THE SIGIL OF THE DEMON KING...
AHHH..
WHAT AN ACTOR.
DOES THIS MEAN I'M NO LONGER A CANDIDATE FOR QUEEN?
I DIDN'T EVEN DO IT ON PURPOSE.

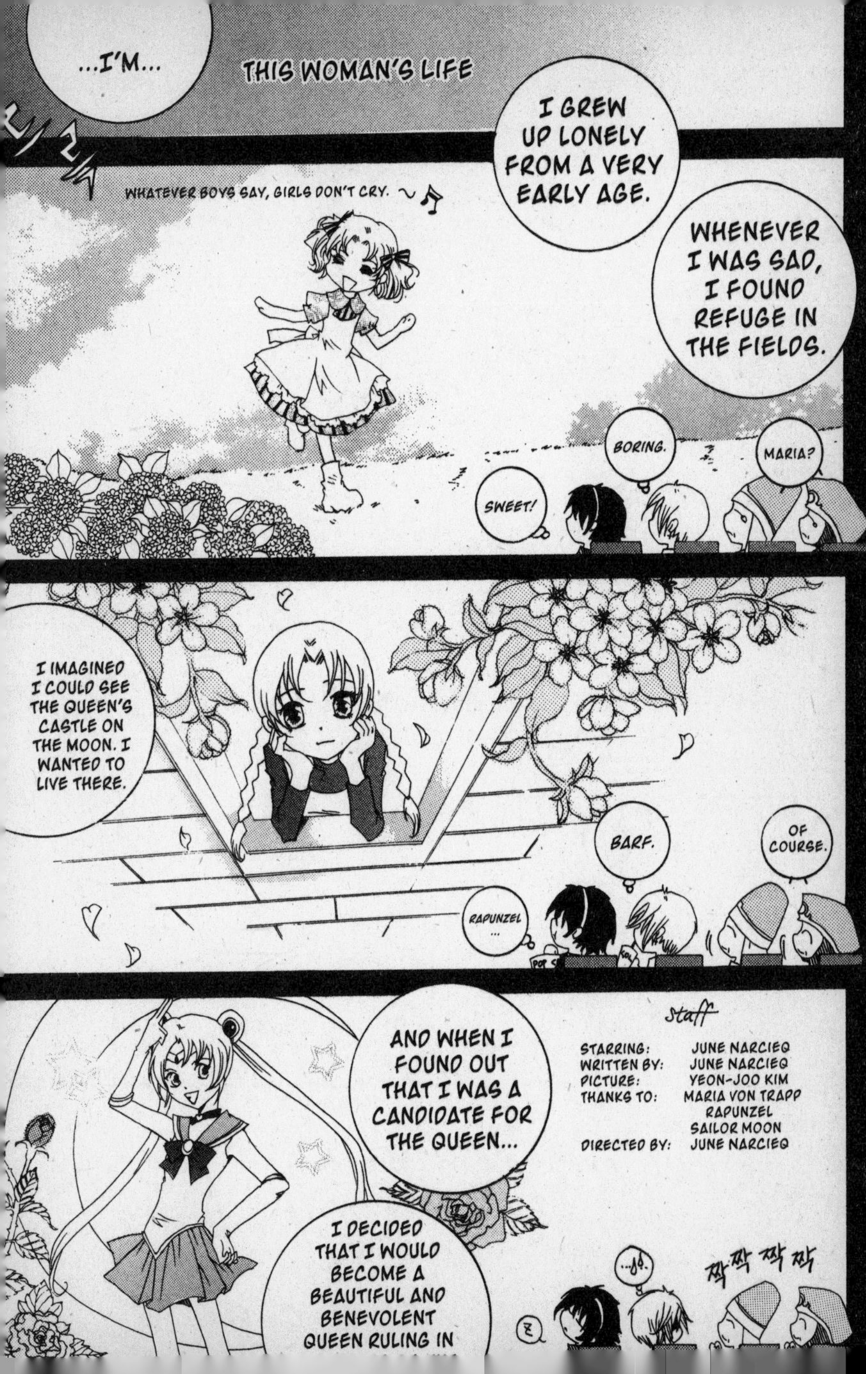
...I'M...
THIS WOMAN'S LIFE
I GREW UP LONELY FROM A VERY EARLY AGE.
WHATEVER BOYS SAY, GIRLS DON'T CRY. ~♪
WHENEVER I WAS SAD, I FOUND REFUGE IN THE FIELDS.
SWEET!
BORING.
MARIA?
I IMAGINED I COULD SEE THE QUEEN'S CASTLE ON THE MOON. I WANTED TO LIVE THERE.
RAPUNZEL ...
BARF.
OF COURSE.
AND WHEN I FOUND OUT THAT I WAS A CANDIDATE FOR THE QUEEN...
Staff
STARRING: JUNE NARCIEQ
WRITTEN BY: JUNE NARCIEQ
PICTURE: YEON-JOO KIM
THANKS TO: MARIA VON TRAPP
RAPUNZEL
SAILOR MOON
DIRECTED BY: JUNE NARCIEQ
I DECIDED THAT I WOULD BECOME A BEAUTIFUL AND BENEVOLENT QUEEN RULING IN
짝 짝 짝 짝

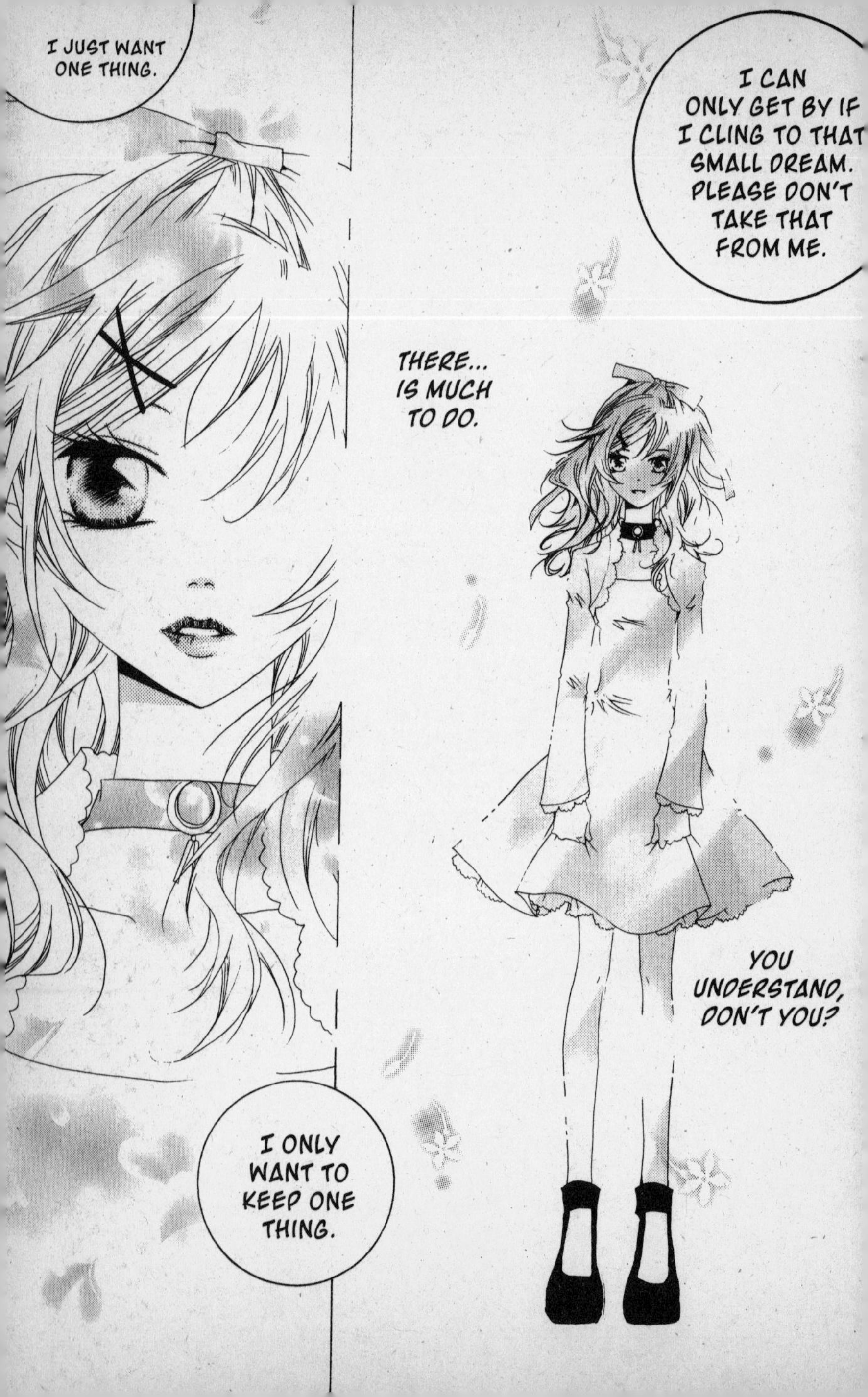
I CAN ONLY GET BY IF I CLING TO THAT SMALL DREAM. PLEASE DON'T TAKE THAT FROM ME.
THERE... IS MUCH TO DO.
YOU UNDERSTAND, DON'T YOU?
I JUST WANT ONE THING.
I ONLY WANT TO KEEP ONE THING.

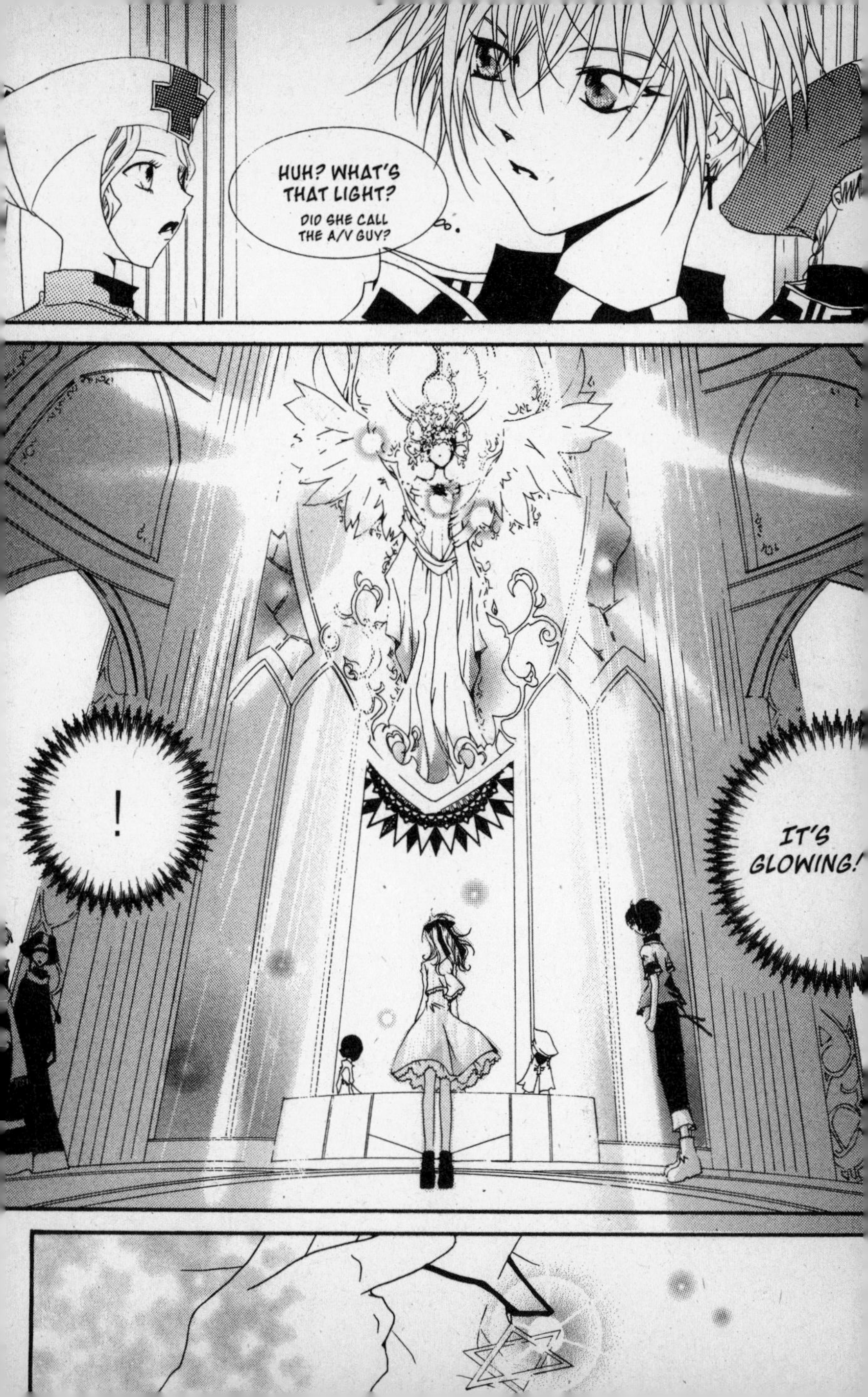
HUH? WHAT'S THAT LIGHT?
DID SHE CALL THE A/V GUY?
IT'S GLOWING!
!

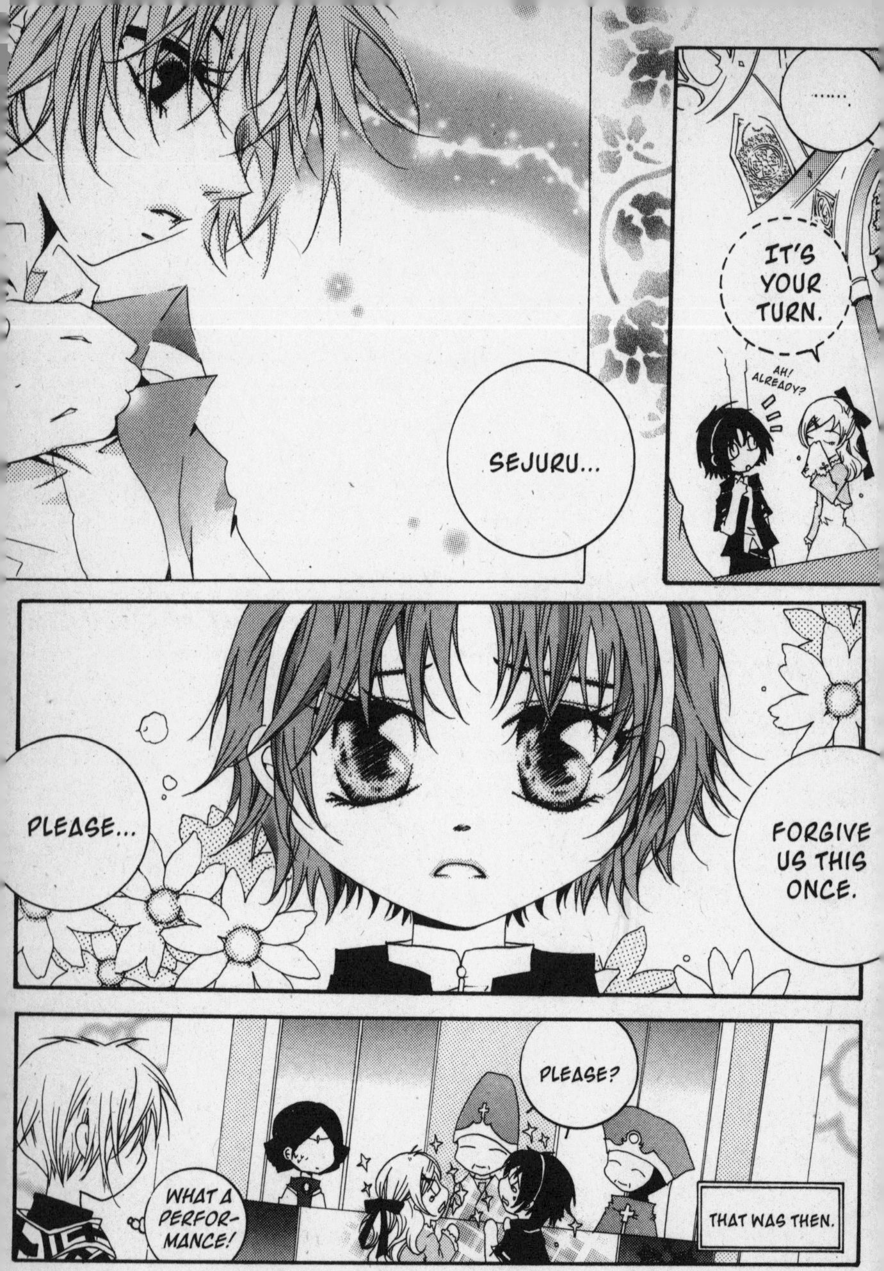
....
IT'S YOUR TURN.
AH! ALREADY?
SEJURU...
PLEASE...
FORGIVE US THIS ONCE.
PLEASE?
WHAT A PERFORMANCE!
THAT WAS THEN.

TEN MINUTES LATER...

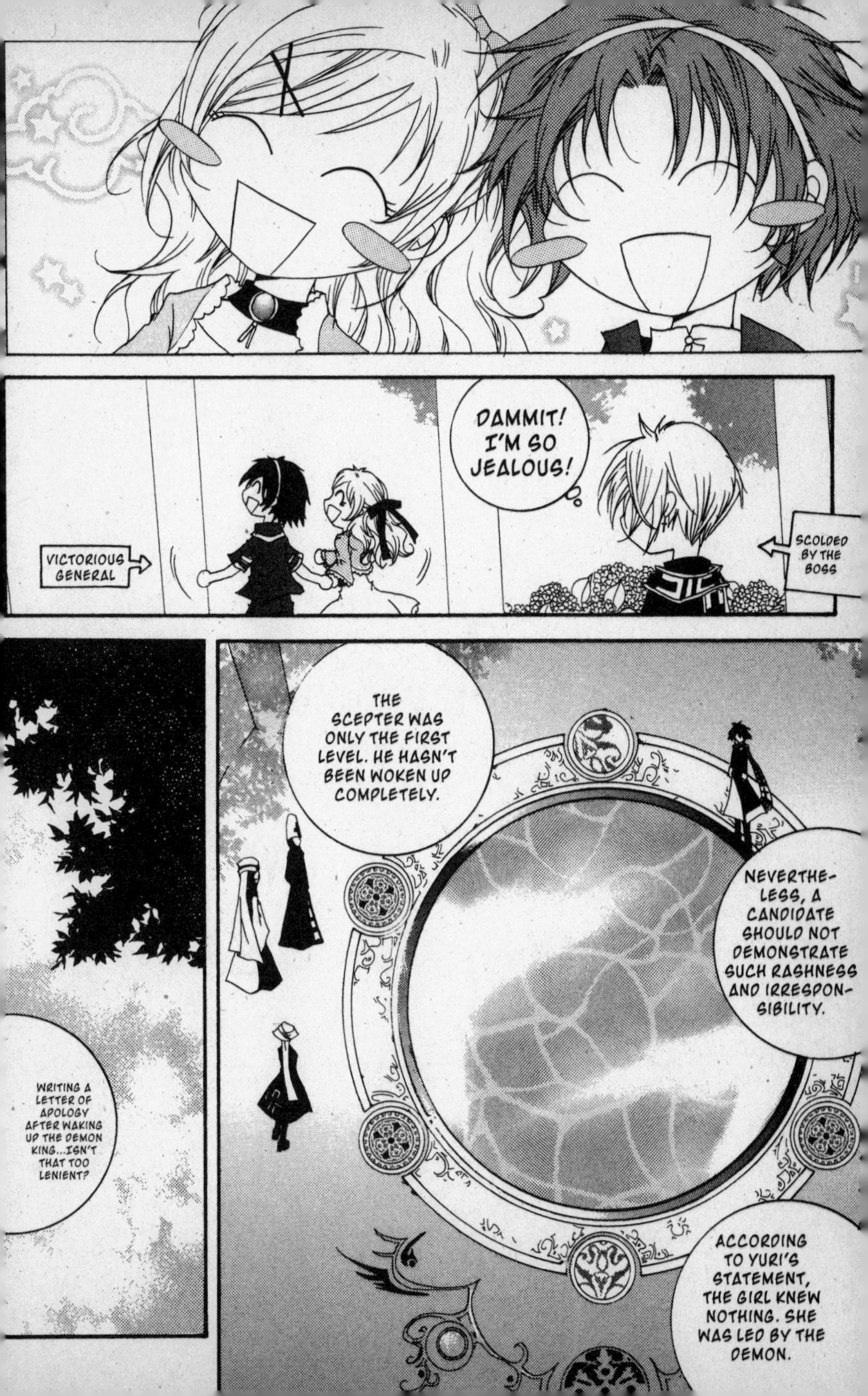
DAMMIT! I'M SO JEALOUS!
SCOLDED BY THE BOSS
VICTORIOUS GENERAL
THE SCEPTER WAS ONLY THE FIRST LEVEL. HE HASN'T BEEN WOKEN UP COMPLETELY.
NEVERTHE-LESS, A CANDIDATE SHOULD NOT DEMONSTRATE SUCH RASHNESS AND IRRESPON-SIBILITY.
ACCORDING TO YURI'S STATEMENT, THE GIRL KNEW NOTHING. SHE WAS LED BY THE DEMON.
WRITING A LETTER OF APOLOGY AFTER WAKING UP THE DEMON KING...ISN'T THAT TOO LENIENT?

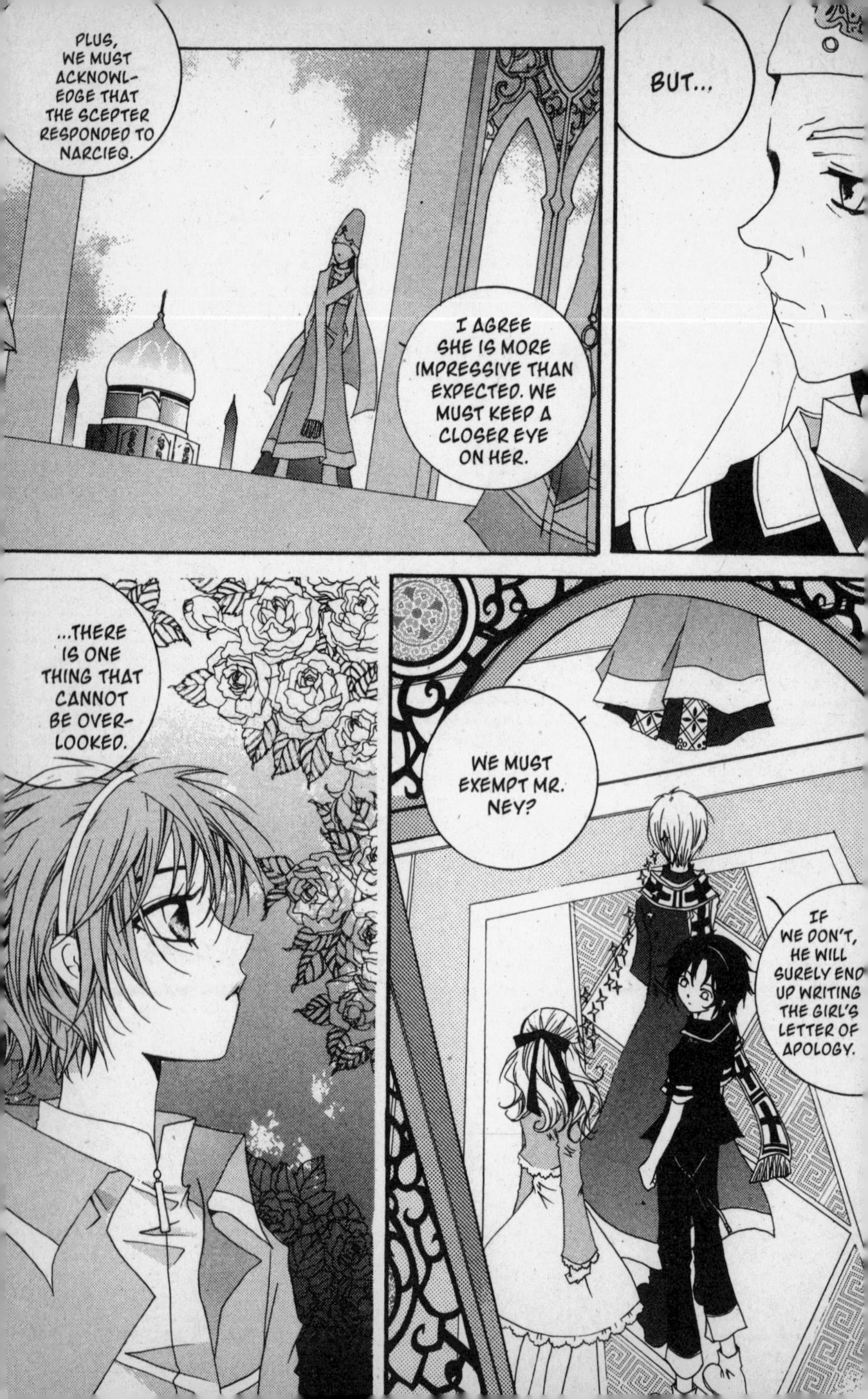
PLUS, WE MUST ACKNOWL-EDGE THAT THE SCEPTER RESPONDED TO NARCIEQ.
I AGREE SHE IS MORE IMPRESSIVE THAN EXPECTED. WE MUST KEEP A CLOSER EYE ON HER.
BUT...
...THERE IS ONE THING THAT CANNOT BE OVER-LOOKED.
WE MUST EXEMPT MR. NEY?
IF WE DON'T, HE WILL SURELY END UP WRITING THE GIRL'S LETTER OF APOLOGY.

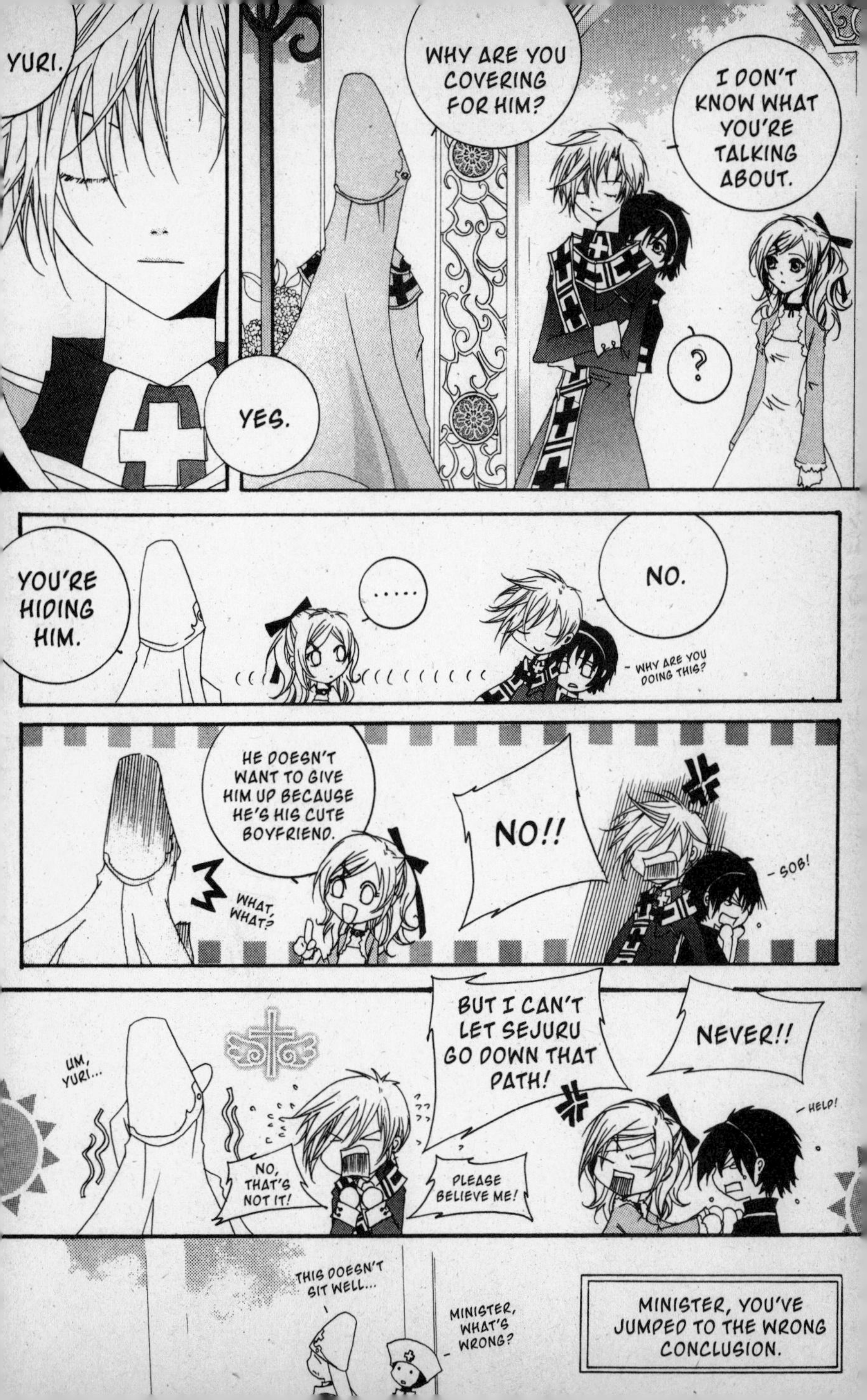
WHY ARE YOU COVERING FOR HIM?
I DON'T KNOW WHAT YOU'RE TALKING ABOUT.
?
YURI.
YES.
NO.
- WHY ARE YOU DOING THIS?
.....
YOU'RE HIDING HIM.
- SOB!
NO!!
HE DOESN'T WANT TO GIVE HIM UP BECAUSE HE'S HIS CUTE BOYFRIEND.
WHAT, WHAT?
NEVER!!
- HELP!
BUT I CAN'T LET SEJURU GO DOWN THAT PATH!
PLEASE BELIEVE ME!
NO, THAT'S NOT IT!
UM, YURI...
MINISTER, YOU'VE JUMPED TO THE WRONG CONCLUSION.
MINISTER, WHAT'S WRONG?
THIS DOESN'T SIT WELL...

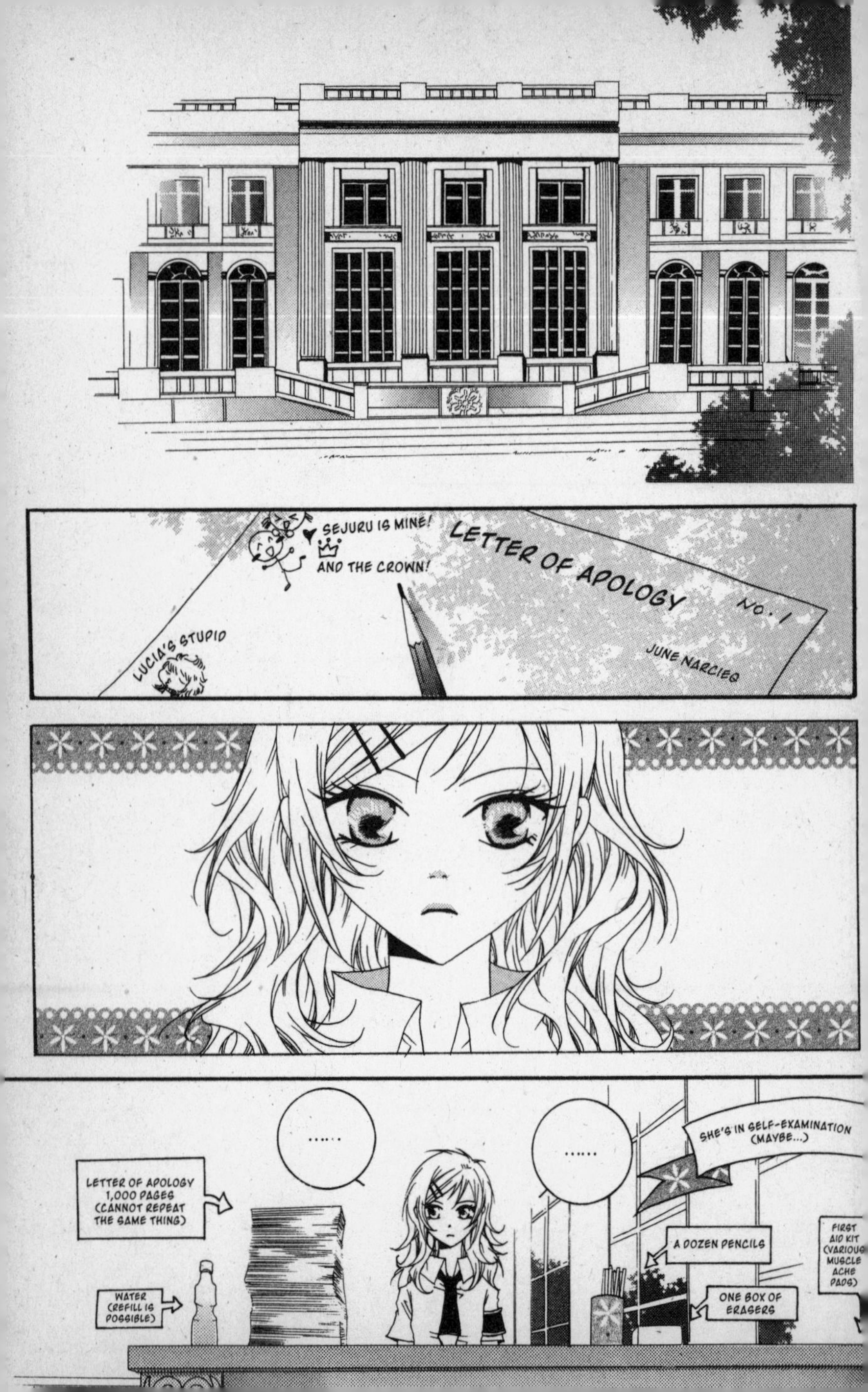
LETTER OF APOLOGY
NO. 1
JUNE NARCIEQ
SEJURU IS MINE!
AND THE CROWN!
LUCIA'S STUPID
......
......
SHE'S IN SELF-EXAMINATION (MAYBE...)
LETTER OF APOLOGY 1,000 PAGES (CANNOT REPEAT THE SAME THING)
FIRST AID KIT (VARIOUS MUSCLE ACHE PADS)
A DOZEN PENCILS
ONE BOX OF ERASERS
WATER (REFILL IS POSSIBLE)

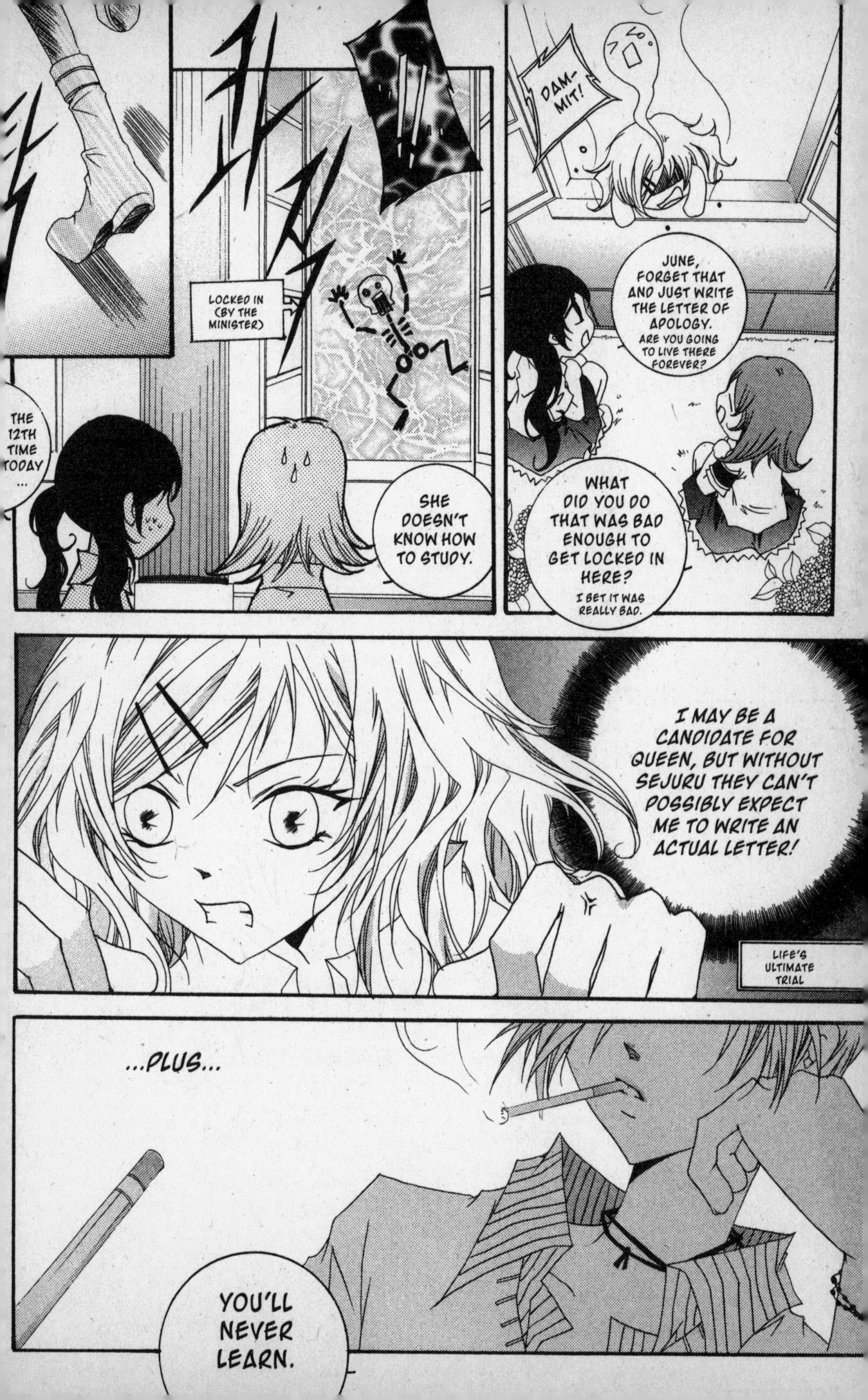
DAM-MIT!
JUNE, FORGET THAT AND JUST WRITE THE LETTER OF APOLOGY. ARE YOU GOING TO LIVE THERE FOREVER?
WHAT DID YOU DO THAT WAS BAD ENOUGH TO GET LOCKED IN HERE? I BET IT WAS REALLY BAD.
LOCKED IN (BY THE MINISTER)
SHE DOESN'T KNOW HOW TO STUDY.
THE 12TH TIME TODAY ...
I MAY BE A CANDIDATE FOR QUEEN, BUT WITHOUT SEJURU THEY CAN'T POSSIBLY EXPECT ME TO WRITE AN ACTUAL LETTER!
LIFE'S ULTIMATE TRIAL
...PLUS...
YOU'LL NEVER LEARN.

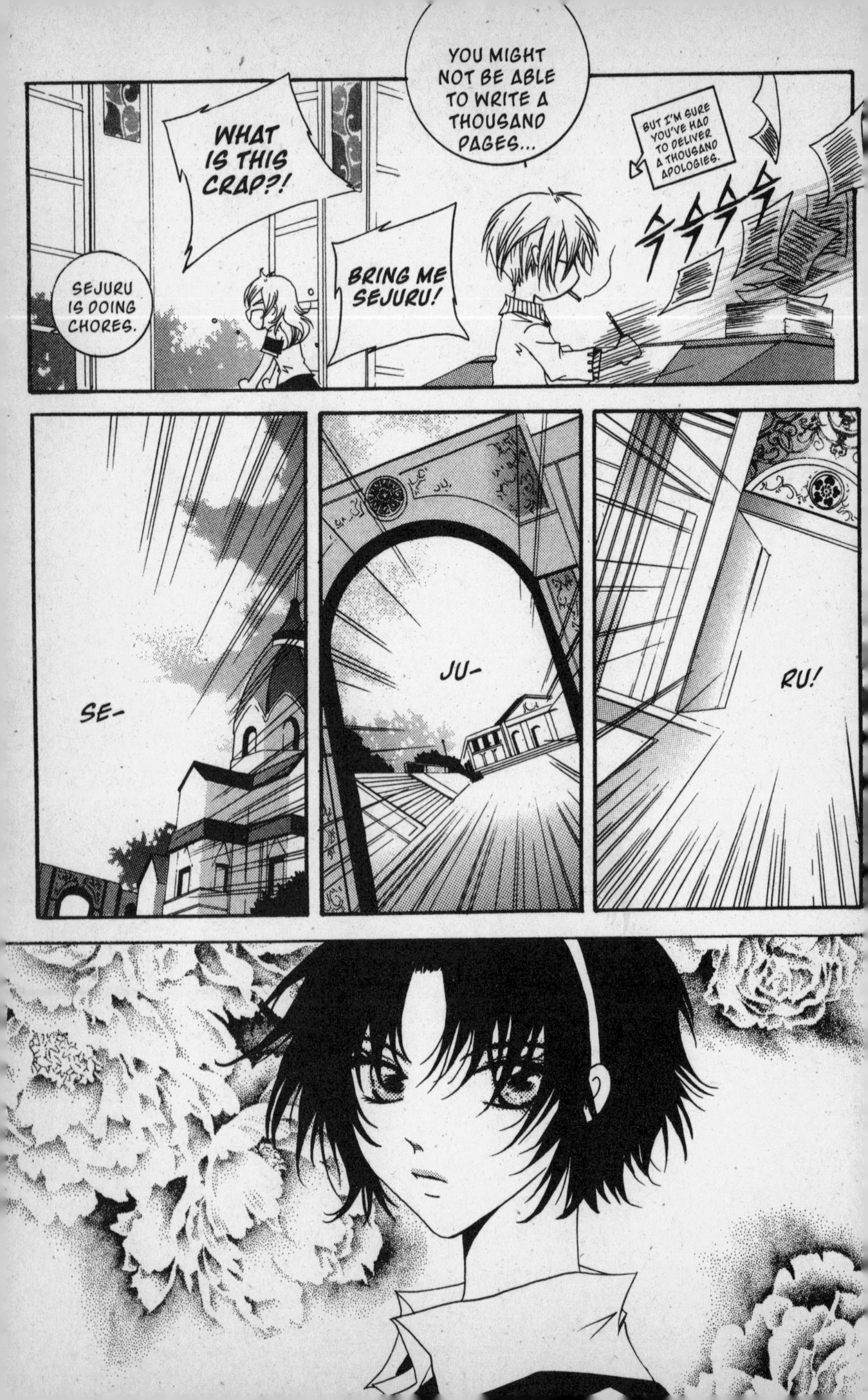
WHAT IS THIS CRAP?!
YOU MIGHT NOT BE ABLE TO WRITE A THOUSAND PAGES...
BUT I'M SURE YOU'VE HAD TO DELIVER A THOUSAND APOLOGIES.
BRING ME SEJURU!
SEJURU IS DOING CHORES.
SE-
JU-
RU!

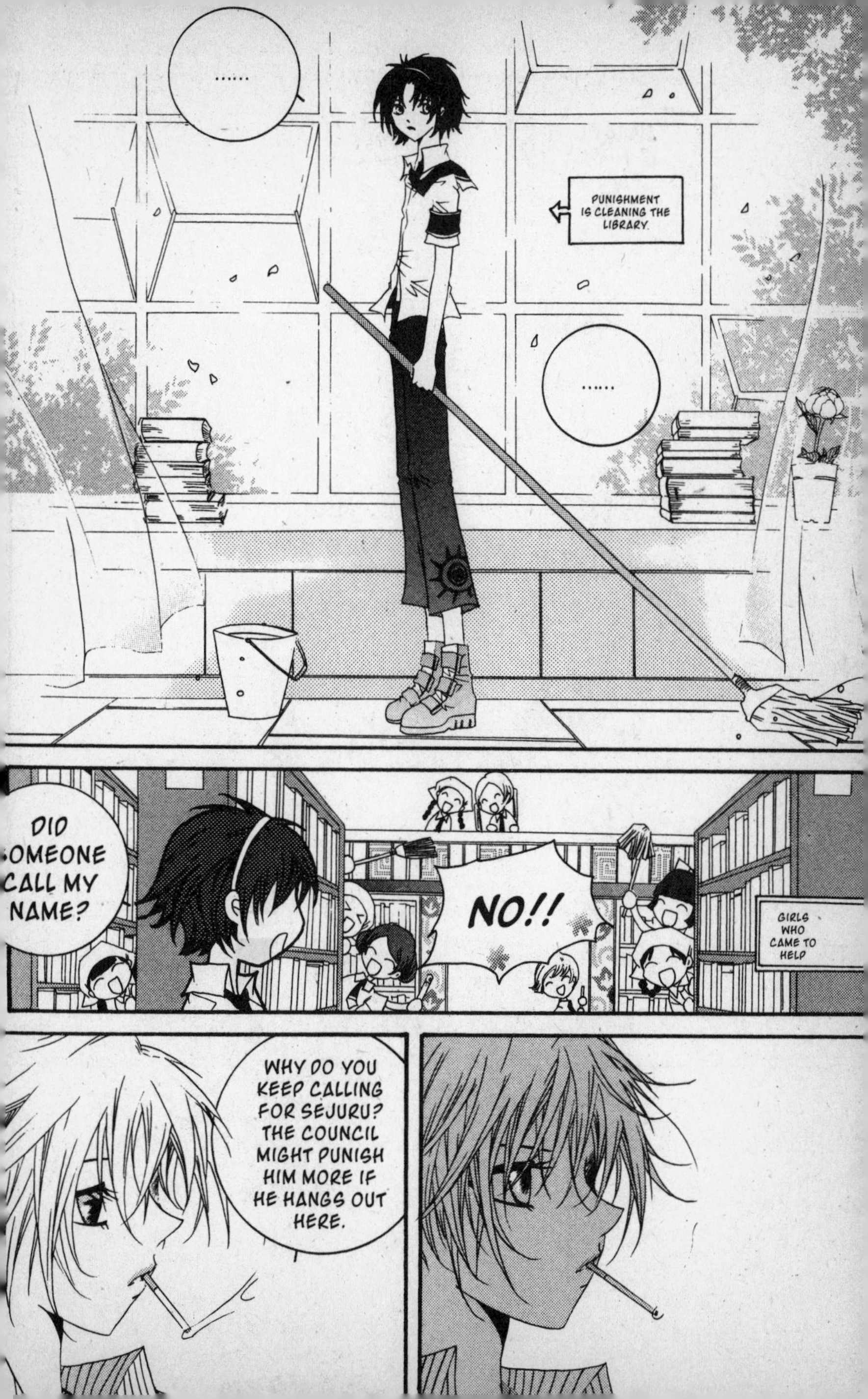
......
PUNISHMENT IS CLEANING THE LIBRARY.
......
GIRLS WHO CAME TO HELP
NO!!
DID SOMEONE CALL MY NAME?
WHY DO YOU KEEP CALLING FOR SEJURU? THE COUNCIL MIGHT PUNISH HIM MORE IF HE HANGS OUT HERE.

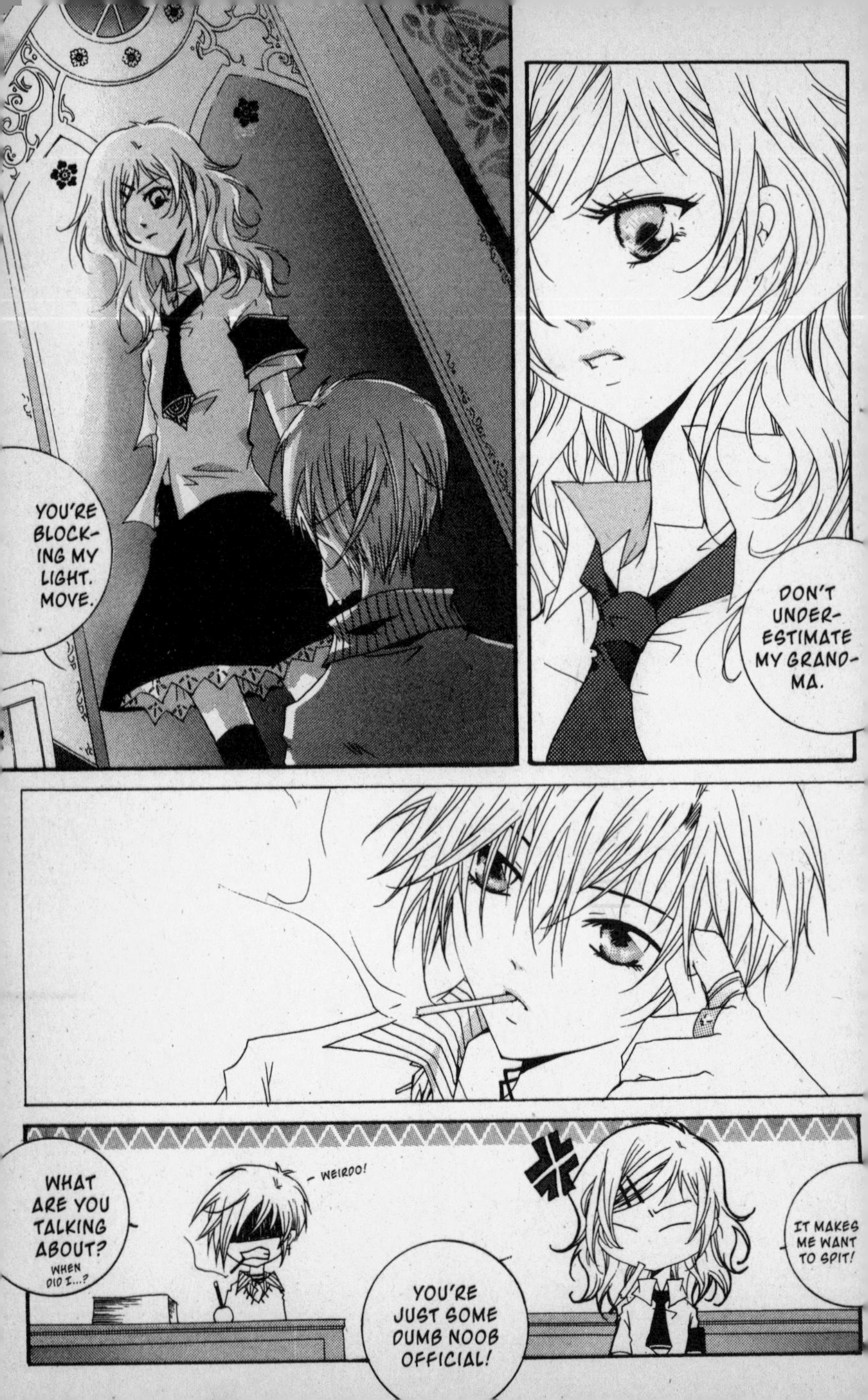
DON'T UNDER-ESTIMATE MY GRAND-MA.
YOU'RE BLOCK-ING MY LIGHT. MOVE.
IT MAKES ME WANT TO SPIT!
YOU'RE JUST SOME DUMB NOOB OFFICIAL!
- WEIRDO!
WHAT ARE YOU TALKING ABOUT?
WHEN DID I...?

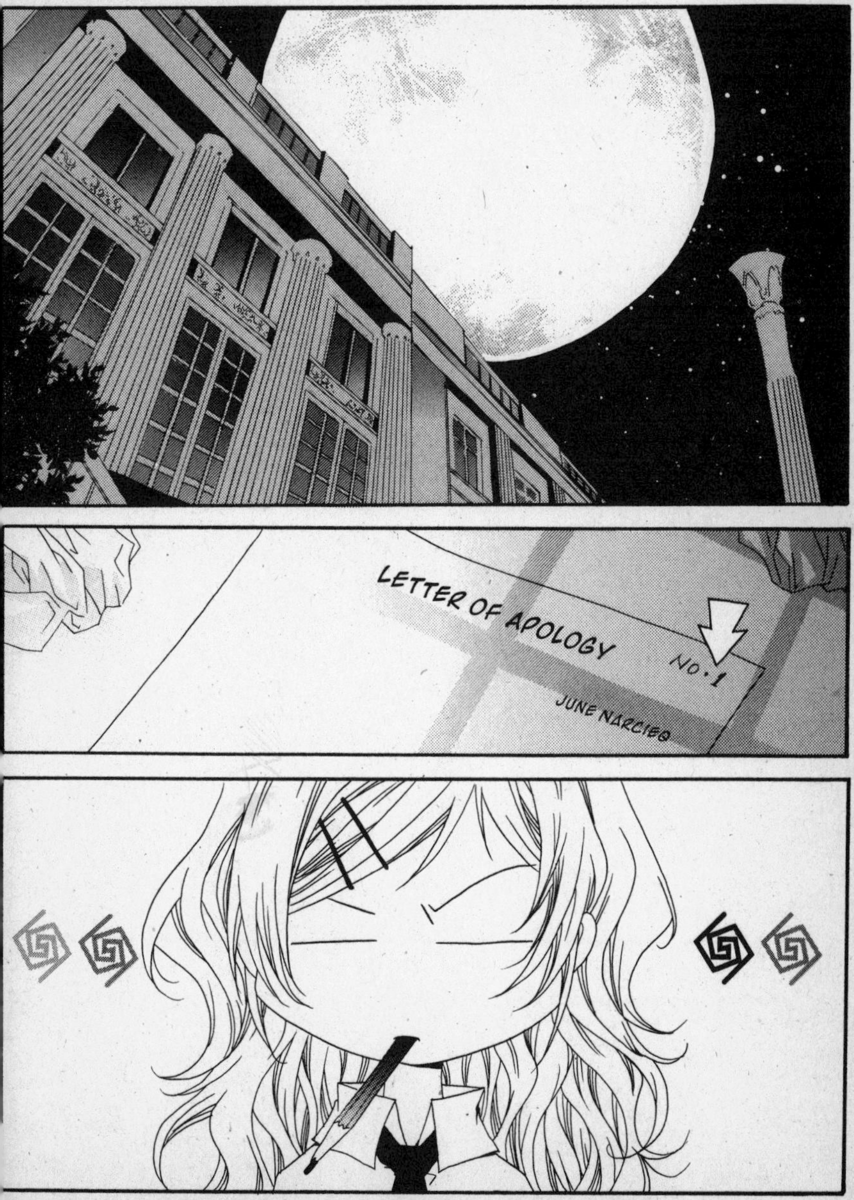
LETTER OF APOLOGY
NO. 1
JUNE NARCIEQ

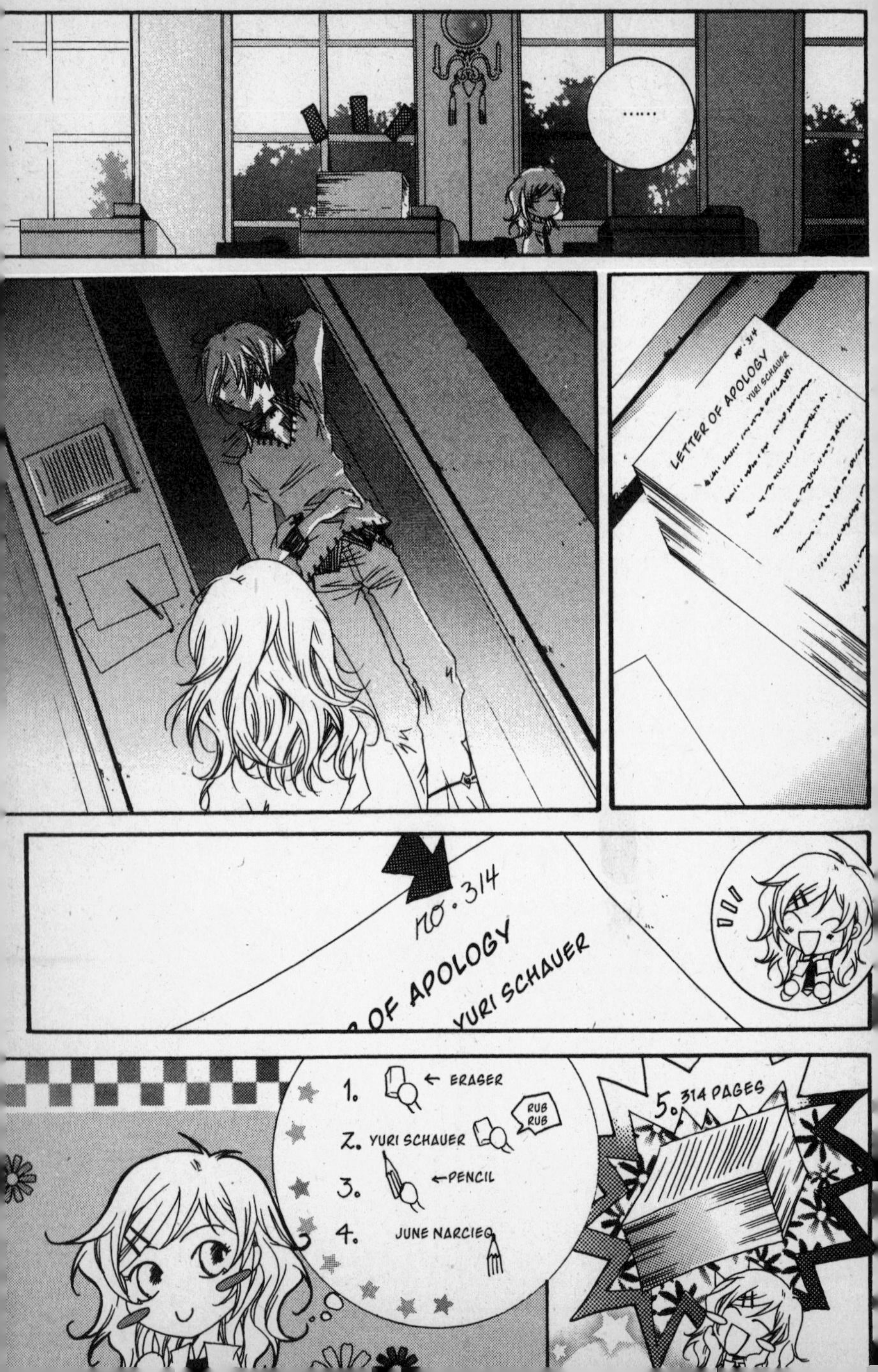
......
NO. 314
LETTER OF APOLOGY
YURI SCHAUER
NO. 314
OF APOLOGY
YURI SCHAUER
5. 314 PAGES
1. ← ERASER
RUB RUB
2. YURI SCHAUER
3. ←PENCIL
4. JUNE NARCIE

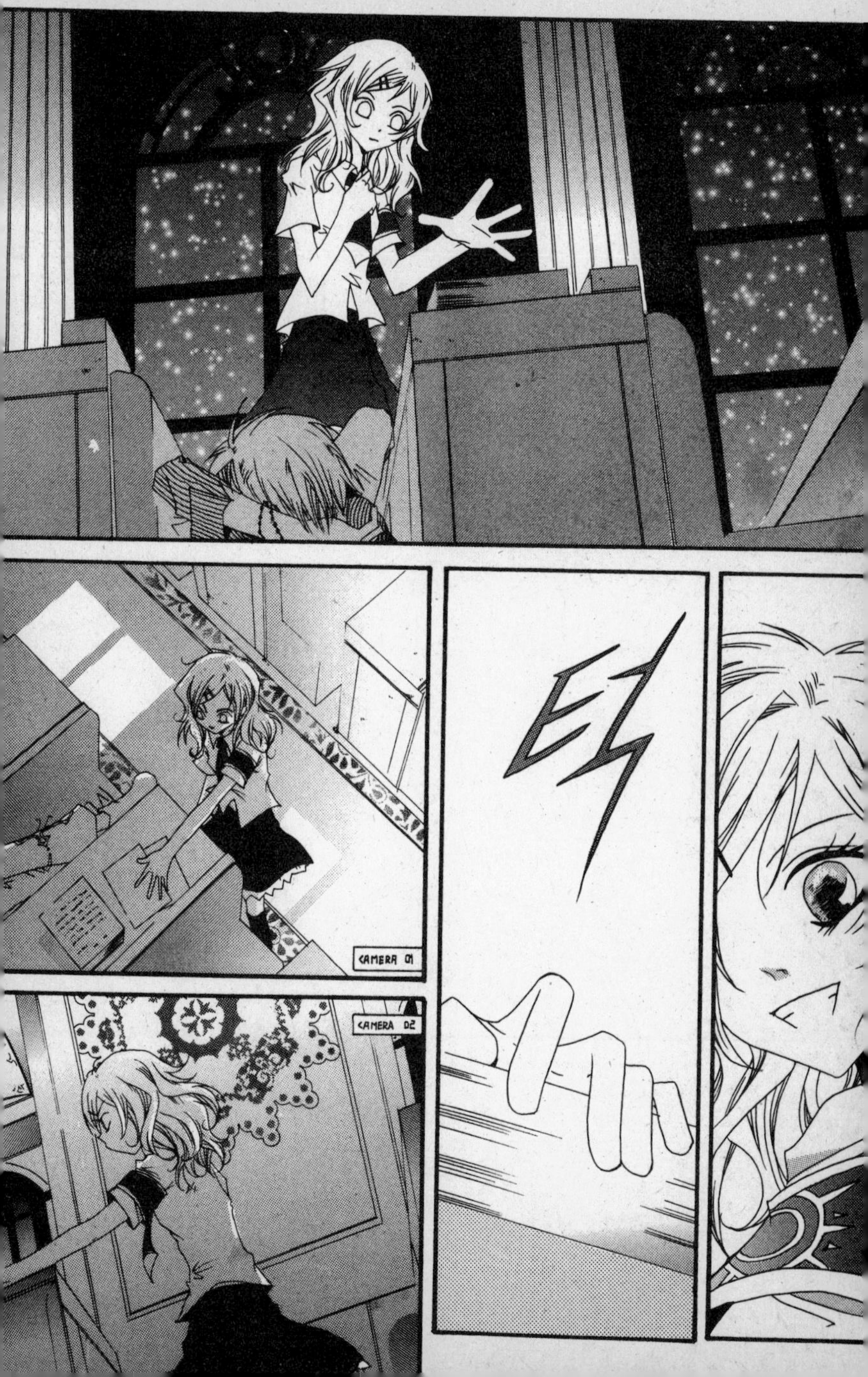
CAMERA 01
CAMERA 02

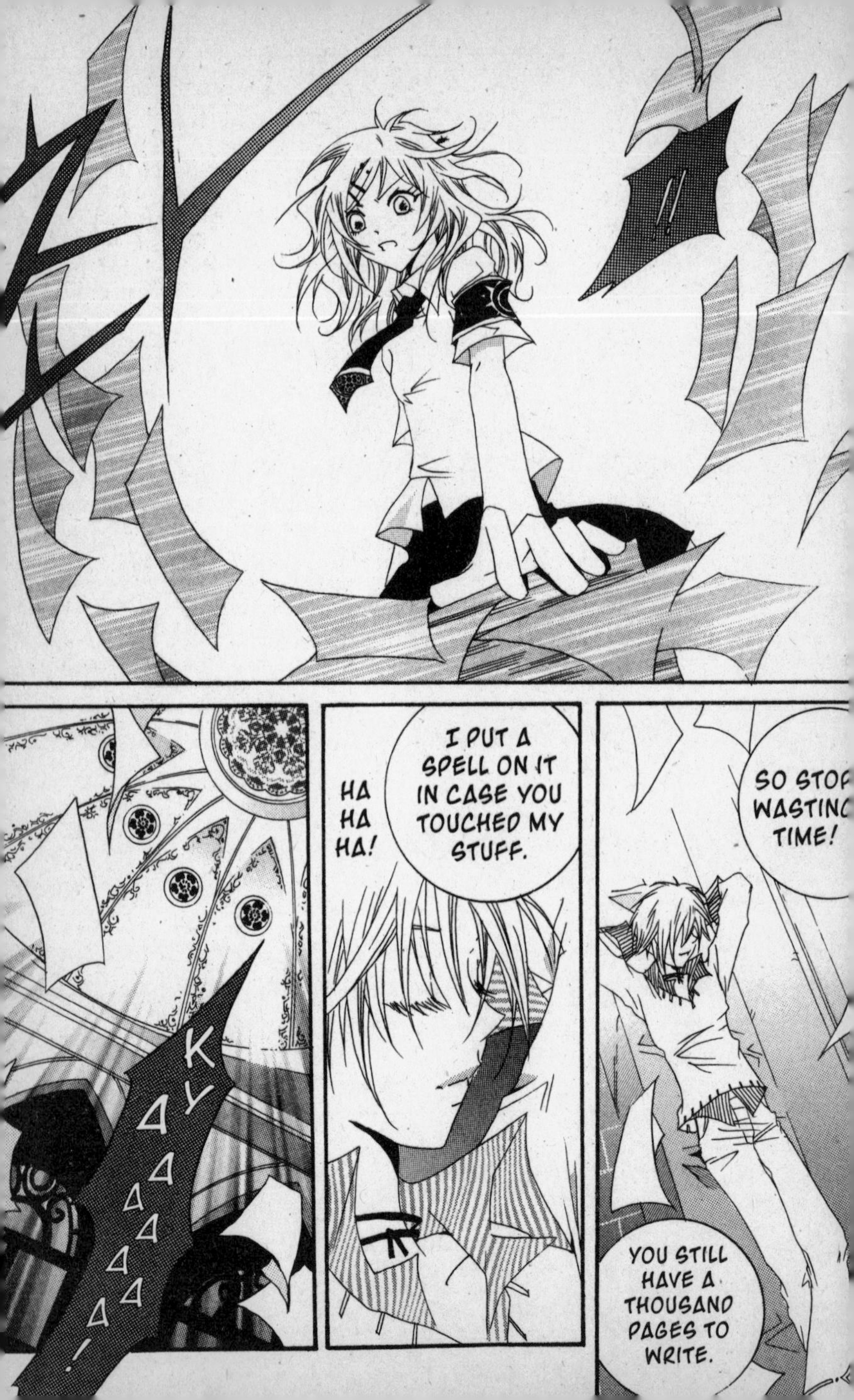
!!
KYAAAAAAAAA!
HA HA HA!
I PUT A SPELL ON IT IN CASE YOU TOUCHED MY STUFF.
YOU STILL HAVE A THOUSAND PAGES TO WRITE.
SO STOP WASTING TIME!

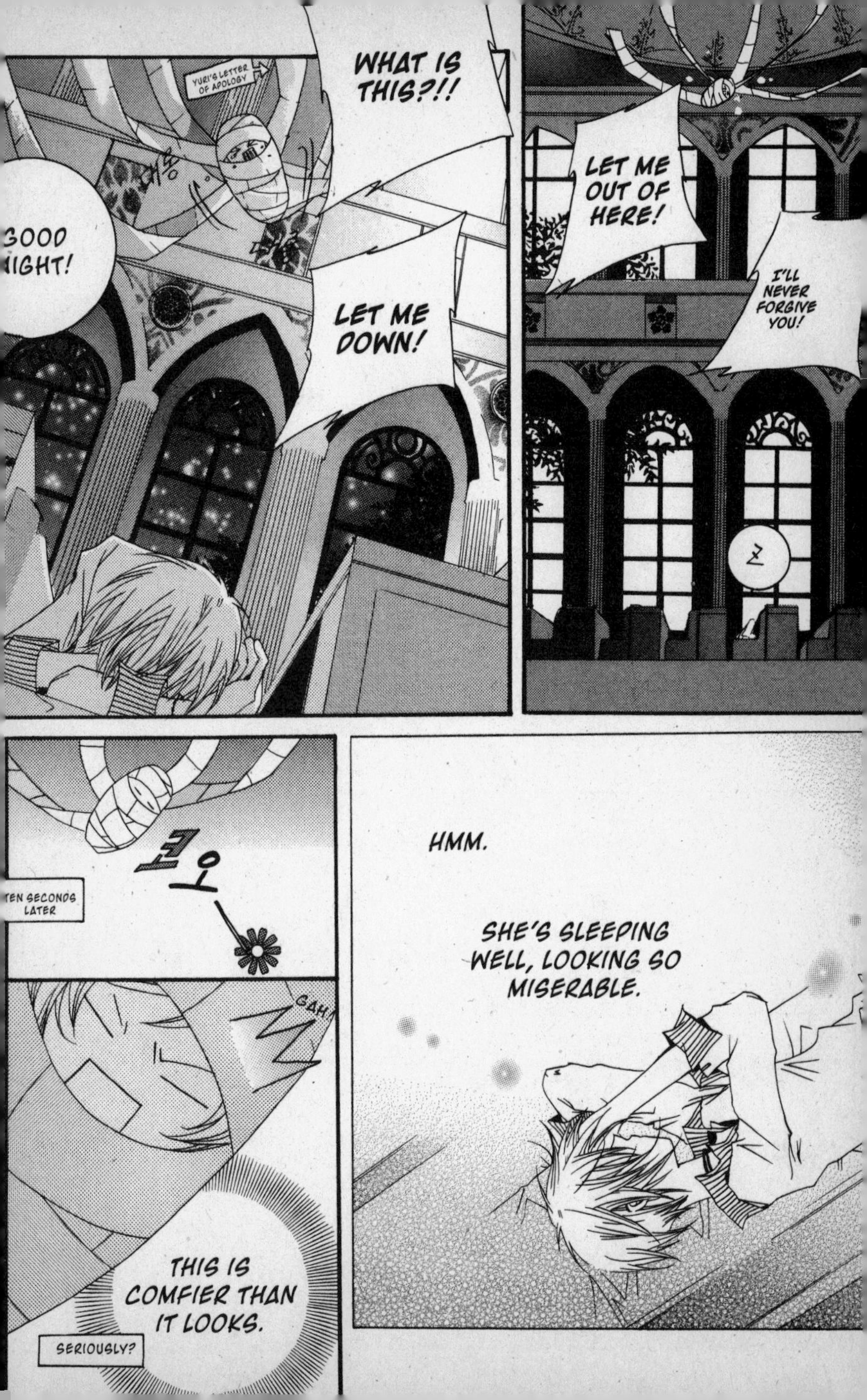
LET ME OUT OF HERE!
I'LL NEVER FORGIVE YOU!
Z
WHAT IS THIS?!!
YURI'S LETTER OF APOLOGY
GOOD NIGHT!
LET ME DOWN!
HMM.
SHE'S SLEEPING WELL, LOOKING SO MISERABLE.
TEN SECONDS LATER
GAH!
THIS IS COMFIER THAN IT LOOKS.
SERIOUSLY?

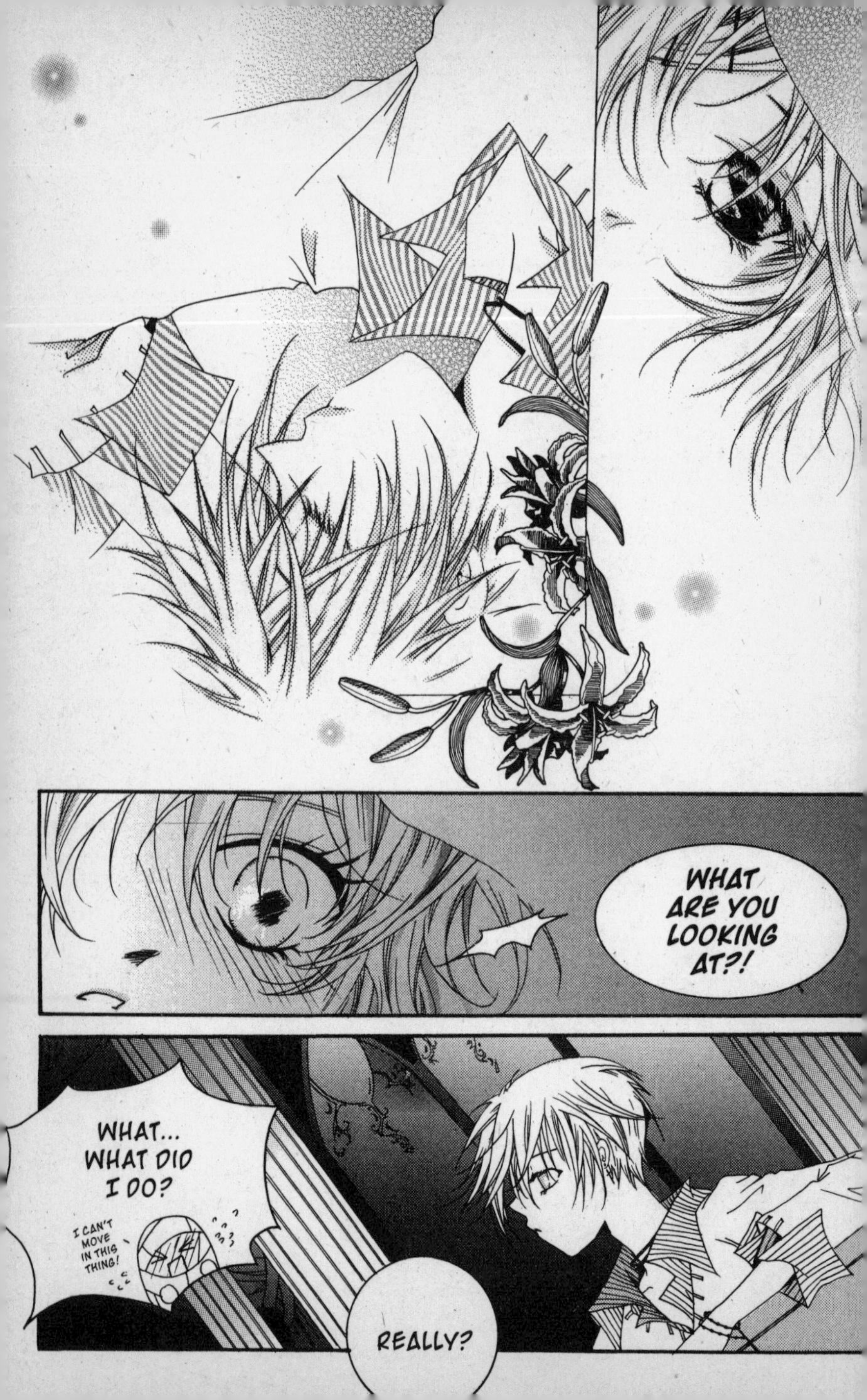
WHAT ARE YOU LOOKING AT?!
WHAT... WHAT DID I DO?
I CAN'T MOVE IN THIS THING!
REALLY?

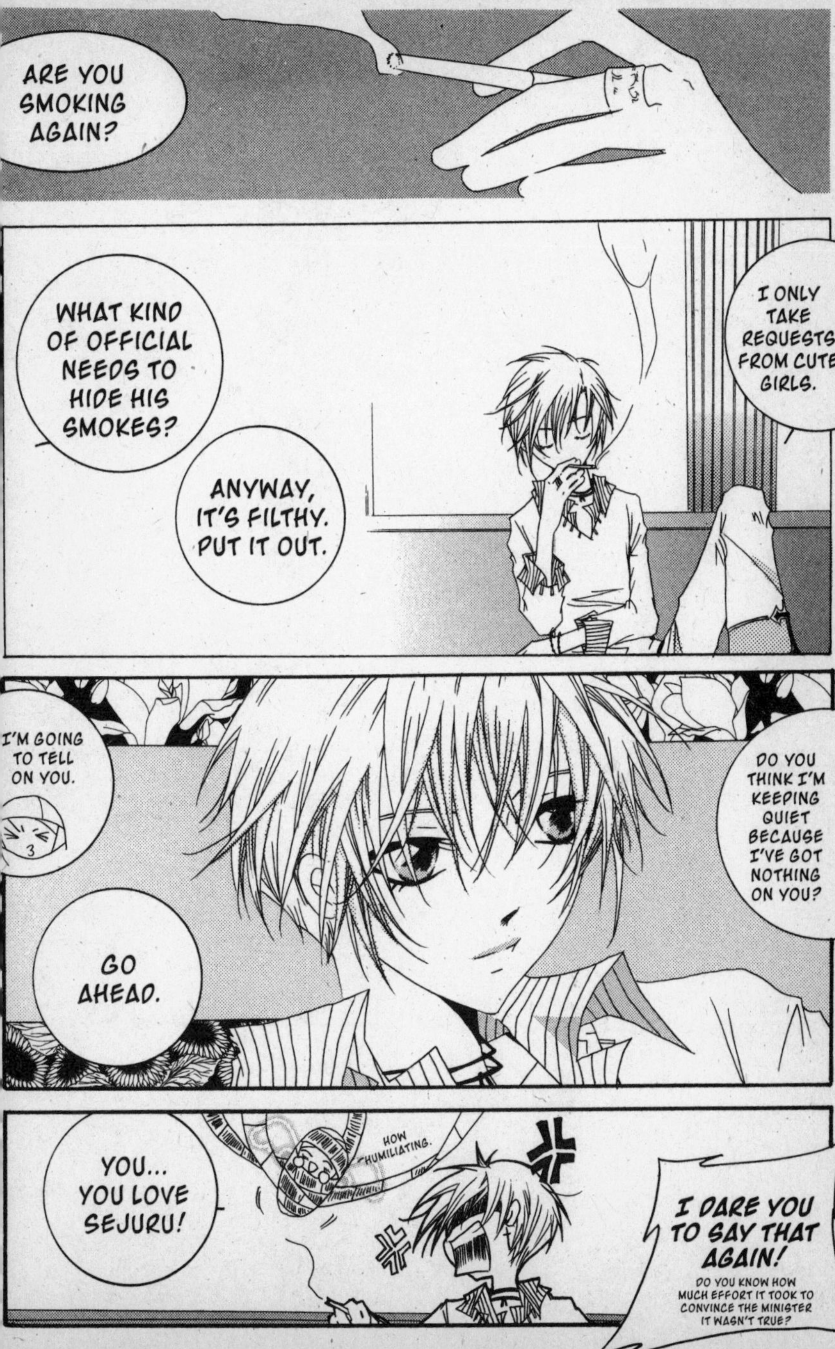
ARE YOU SMOKING AGAIN?
WHAT KIND OF OFFICIAL NEEDS TO HIDE HIS SMOKES?
ANYWAY, IT'S FILTHY. PUT IT OUT.
I ONLY TAKE REQUESTS FROM CUTE GIRLS.
I'M GOING TO TELL ON YOU.
GO AHEAD.
DO YOU THINK I'M KEEPING QUIET BECAUSE I'VE GOT NOTHING ON YOU?
YOU... YOU LOVE SEJURU!
HOW HUMILIATING.
I DARE YOU TO SAY THAT AGAIN!
DO YOU KNOW HOW MUCH EFFORT IT TOOK TO CONVINCE THE MINISTER IT WASN'T TRUE?

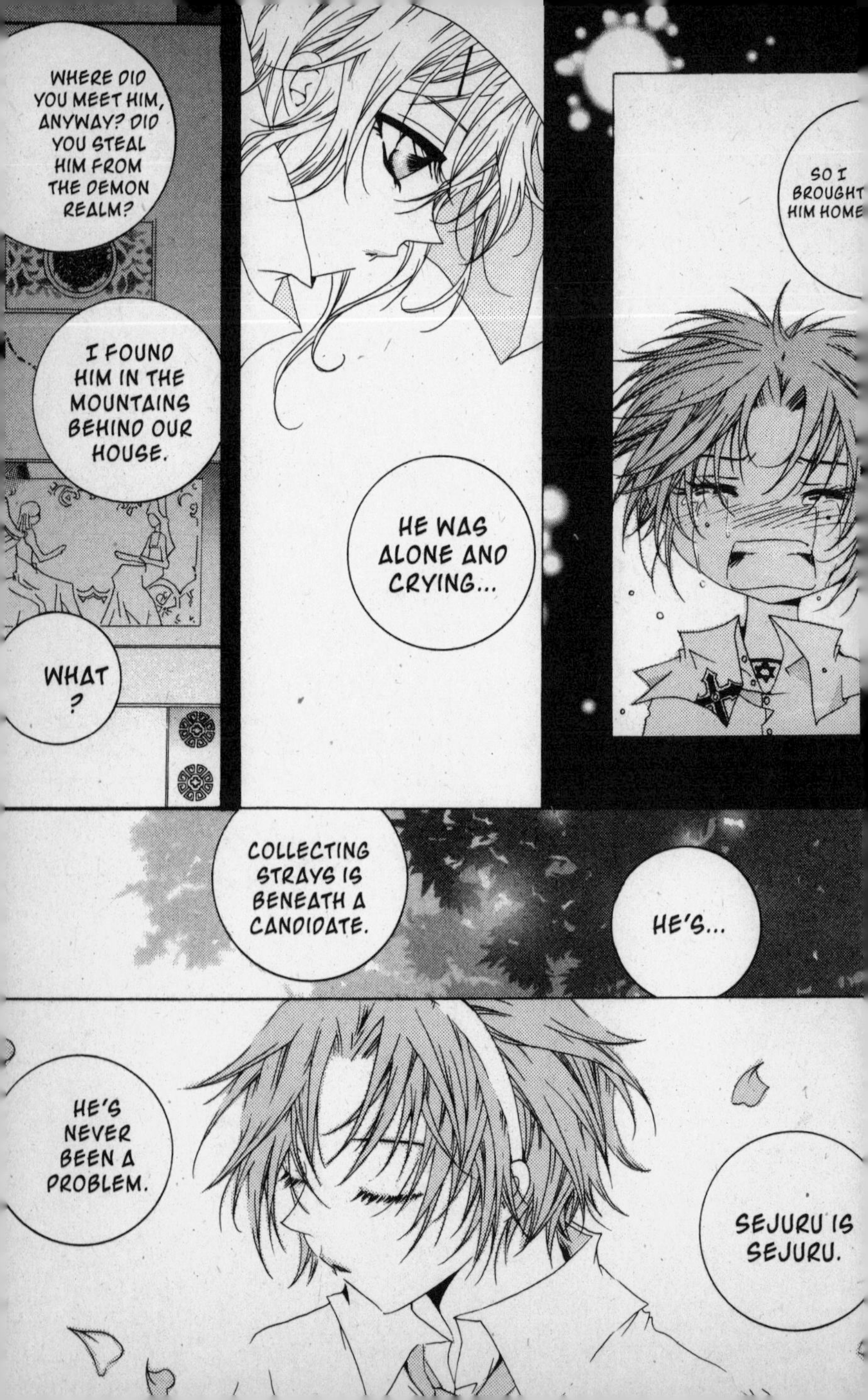
WHERE DID YOU MEET HIM, ANYWAY? DID YOU STEAL HIM FROM THE DEMON REALM?
I FOUND HIM IN THE MOUNTAINS BEHIND OUR HOUSE.
WHAT?
HE WAS ALONE AND CRYING...
SO I BROUGHT HIM HOME
COLLECTING STRAYS IS BENEATH A CANDIDATE.
HE'S...
HE'S NEVER BEEN A PROBLEM.
SEJURU IS SEJURU.

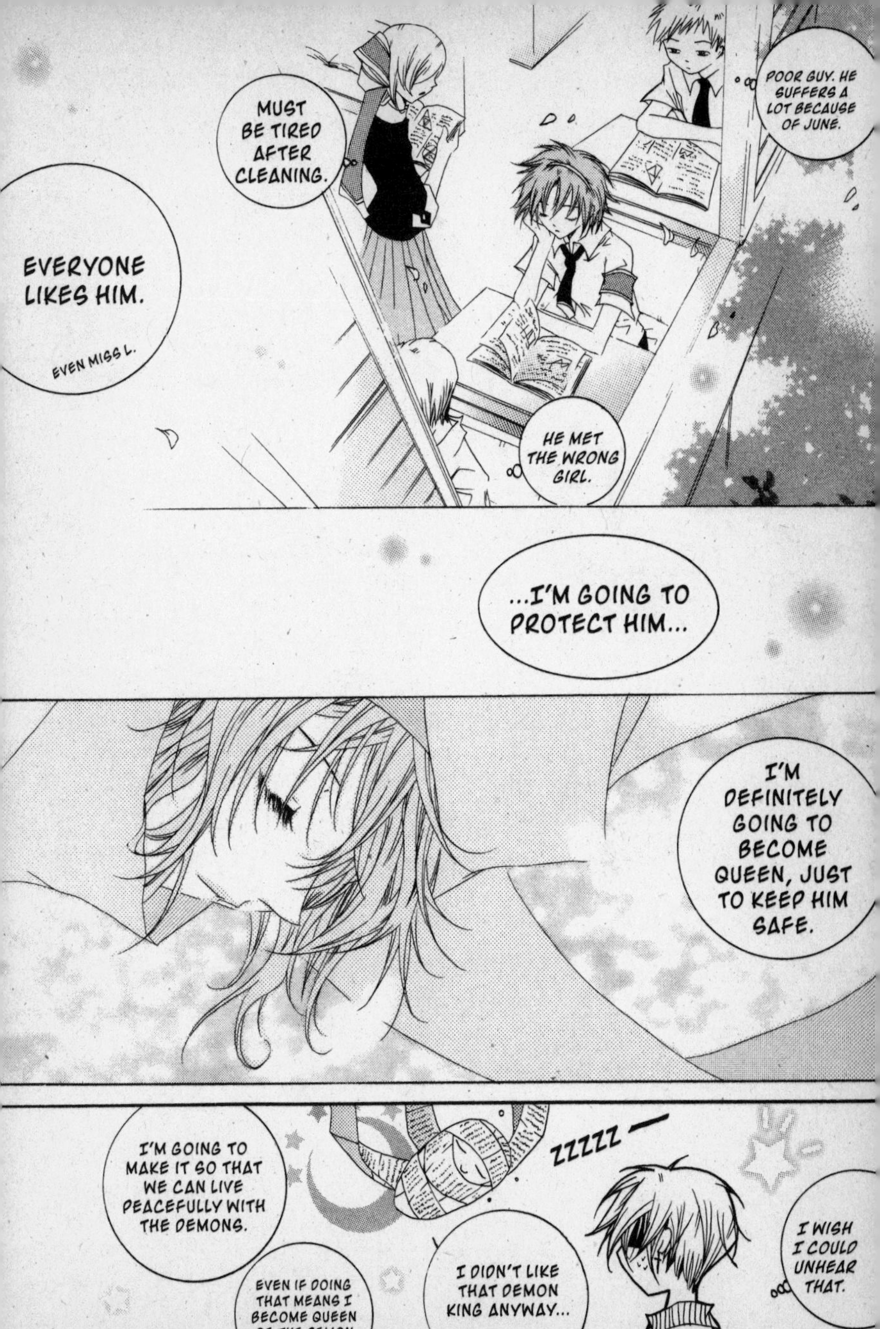
POOR GUY. HE SUFFERS A LOT BECAUSE OF JUNE.
MUST BE TIRED AFTER CLEANING.
HE MET THE WRONG GIRL.
EVERYONE LIKES HIM.
EVEN MISS L.
...I'M GOING TO PROTECT HIM...
I'M DEFINITELY GOING TO BECOME QUEEN, JUST TO KEEP HIM SAFE.
I'M GOING TO MAKE IT SO THAT WE CAN LIVE PEACEFULLY WITH THE DEMONS.
EVEN IF DOING THAT MEANS I BECOME QUEEN OF THE DEMON REALM AS WELL.
I DIDN'T LIKE THAT DEMON KING ANYWAY...
ZZZZZ —
I WISH I COULD UNHEAR THAT.

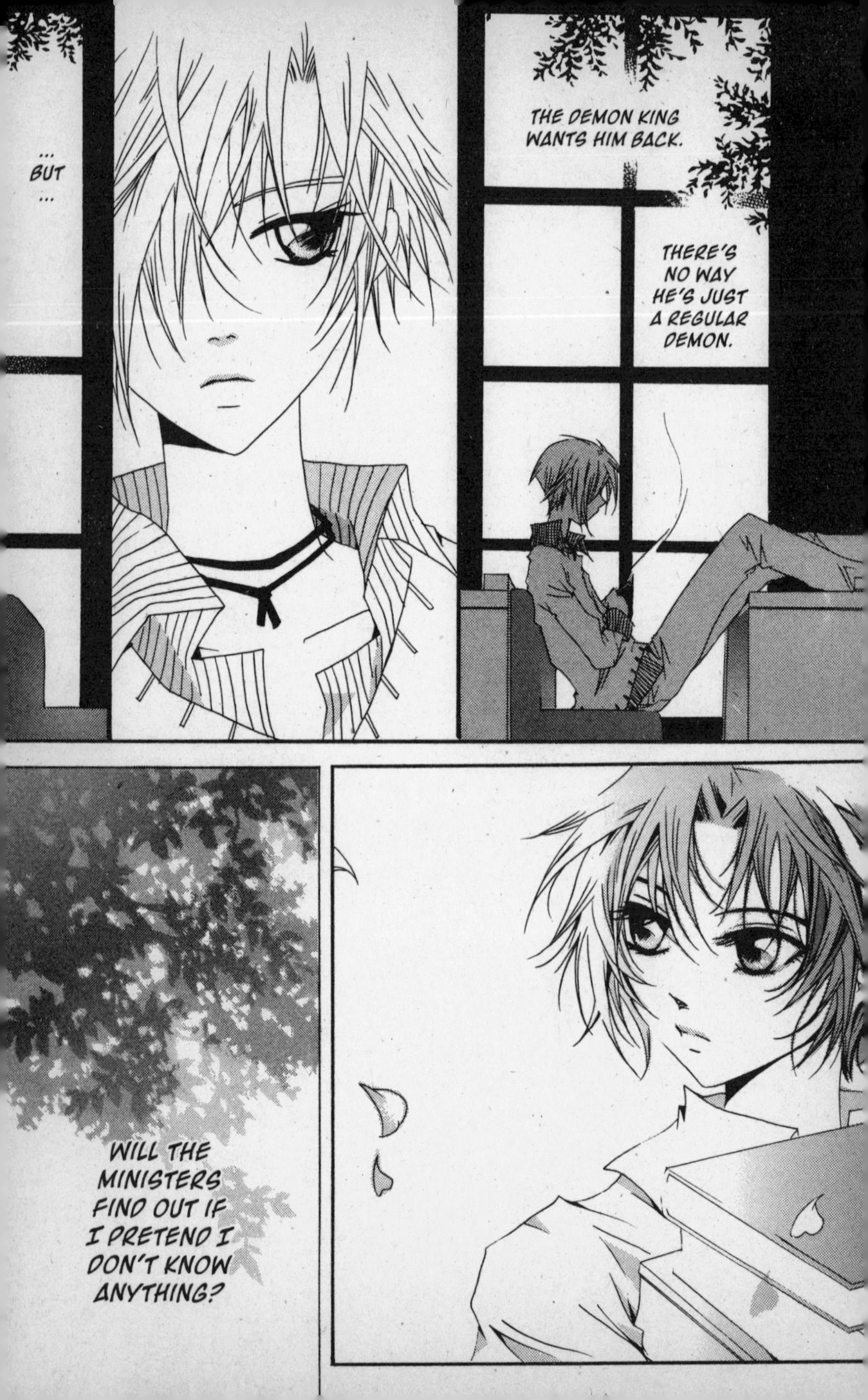
THE DEMON KING WANTS HIM BACK.
THERE'S NO WAY HE'S JUST A REGULAR DEMON.
... BUT ...
WILL THE MINISTERS FIND OUT IF I PRETEND I DON'T KNOW ANYTHING?

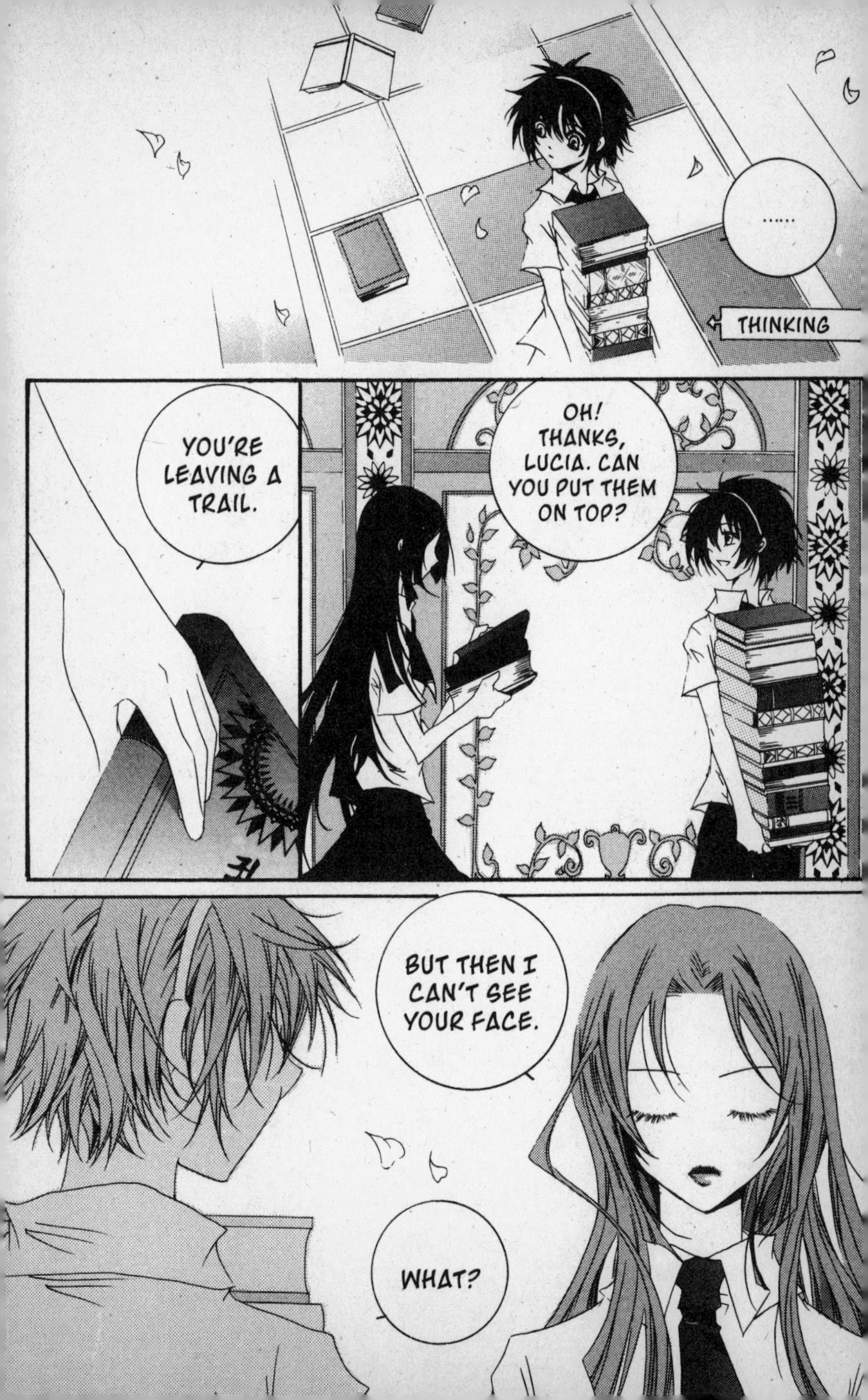
......
THINKING
OH! THANKS, LUCIA. CAN YOU PUT THEM ON TOP?
YOU'RE LEAVING A TRAIL.
BUT THEN I CAN'T SEE YOUR FACE.
WHAT?

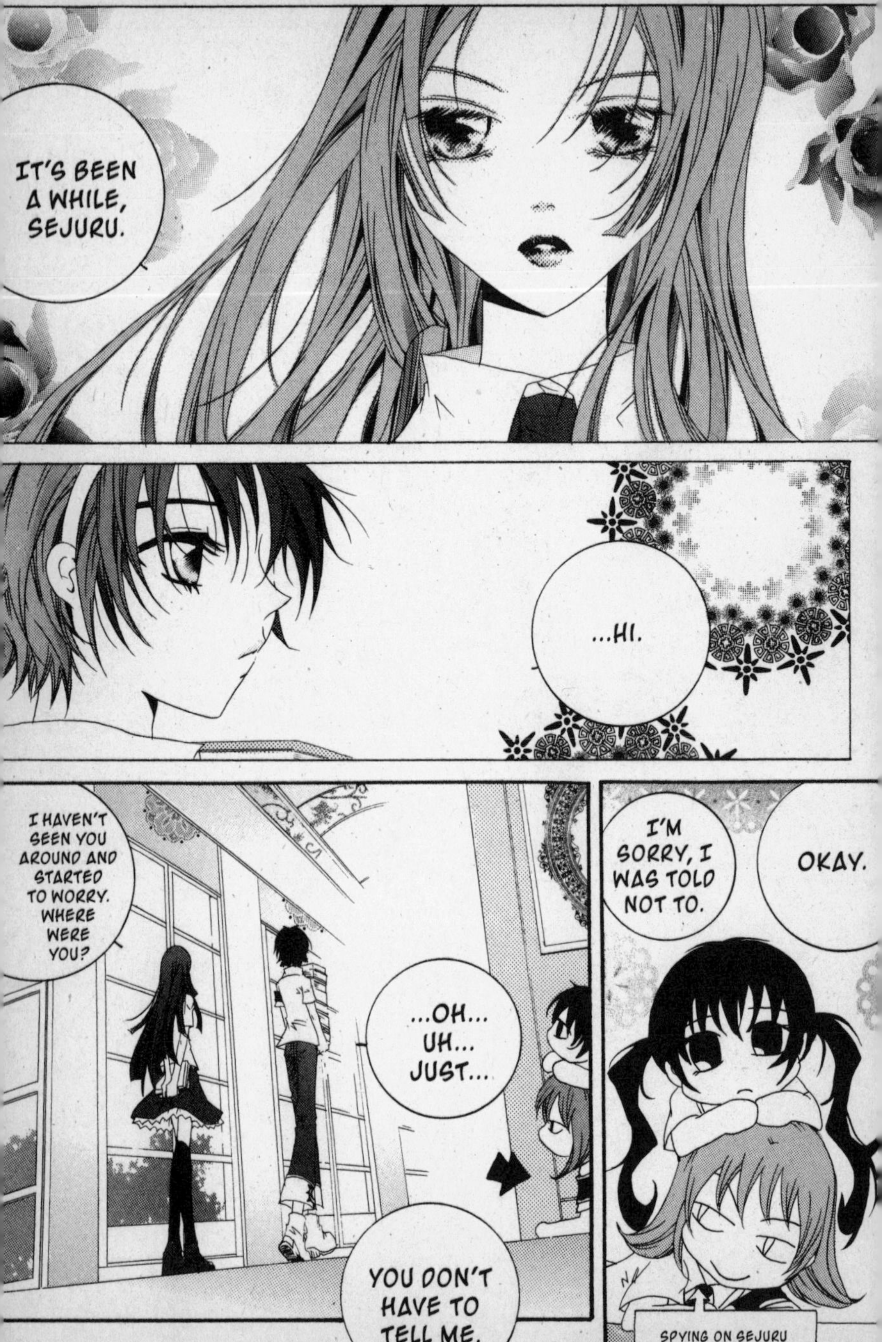
IT'S BEEN A WHILE, SEJURU.
...HI.
I HAVEN'T SEEN YOU AROUND AND STARTED TO WORRY. WHERE WERE YOU?
...OH... UH... JUST...
YOU DON'T HAVE TO TELL ME.
I'M SORRY, I WAS TOLD NOT TO.
OKAY.
SPYING ON SEJURU

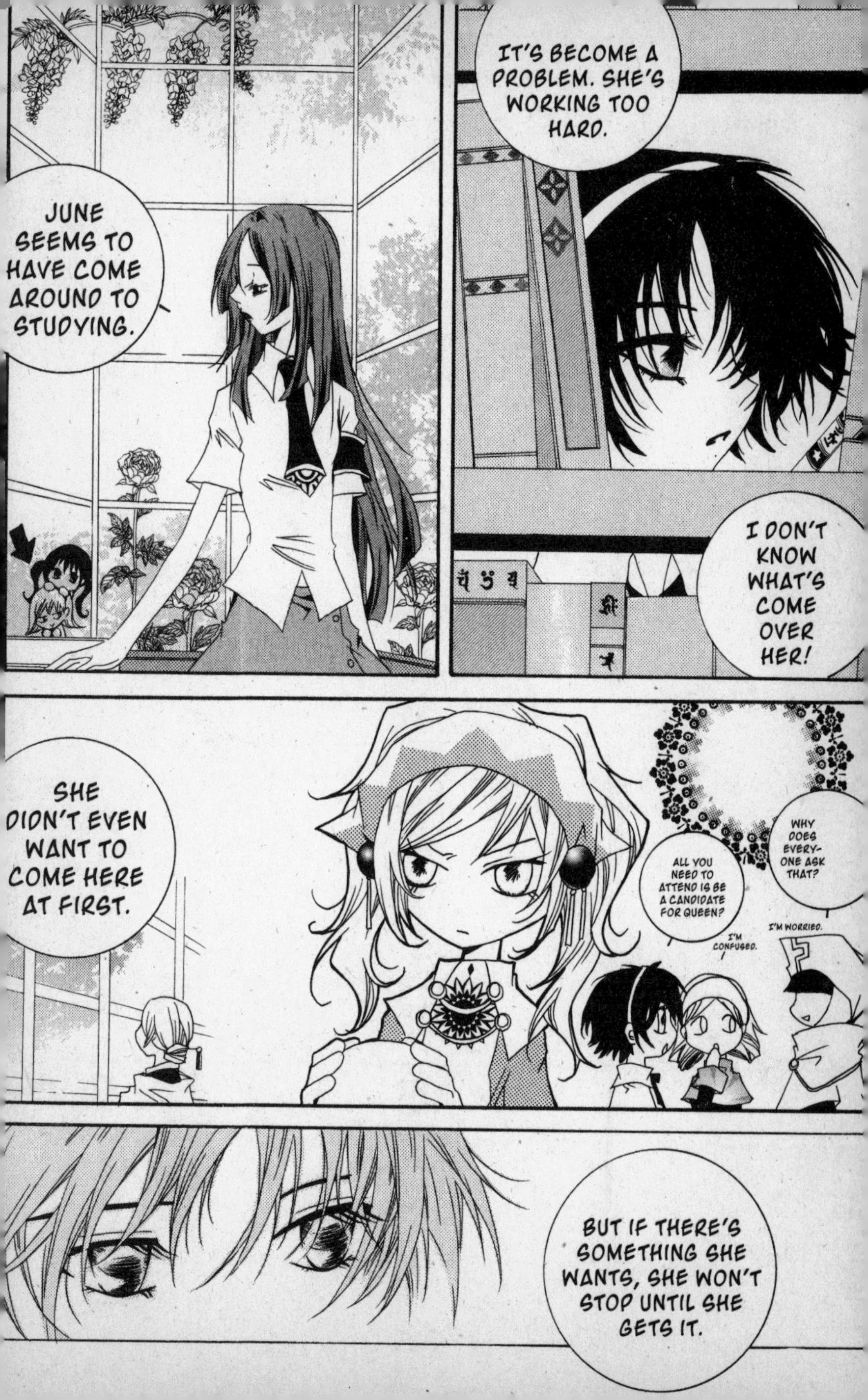
IT'S BECOME A PROBLEM. SHE'S WORKING TOO HARD.
I DON'T KNOW WHAT'S COME OVER HER!
JUNE SEEMS TO HAVE COME AROUND TO STUDYING.
SHE DIDN'T EVEN WANT TO COME HERE AT FIRST.
ALL YOU NEED TO ATTEND IS BE A CANDIDATE FOR QUEEN?
WHY DOES EVERY-ONE ASK THAT?
I'M WORRIED.
I'M CONFUSED.
BUT IF THERE'S SOMETHING SHE WANTS, SHE WON'T STOP UNTIL SHE GETS IT.

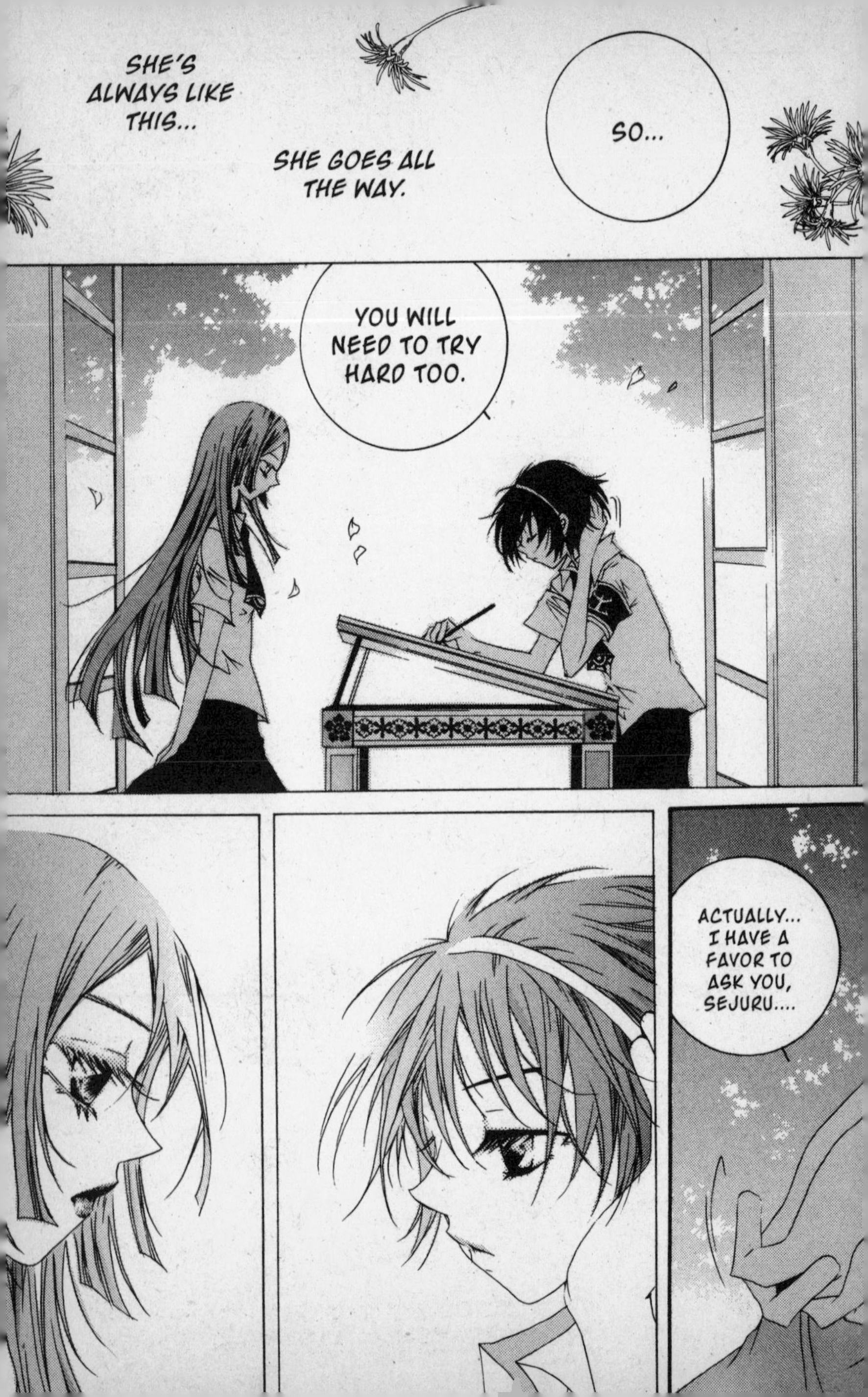
SO...
SHE GOES ALL THE WAY.
SHE'S ALWAYS LIKE THIS...
YOU WILL NEED TO TRY HARD TOO.
ACTUALLY... I HAVE A FAVOR TO ASK YOU, SEJURU....

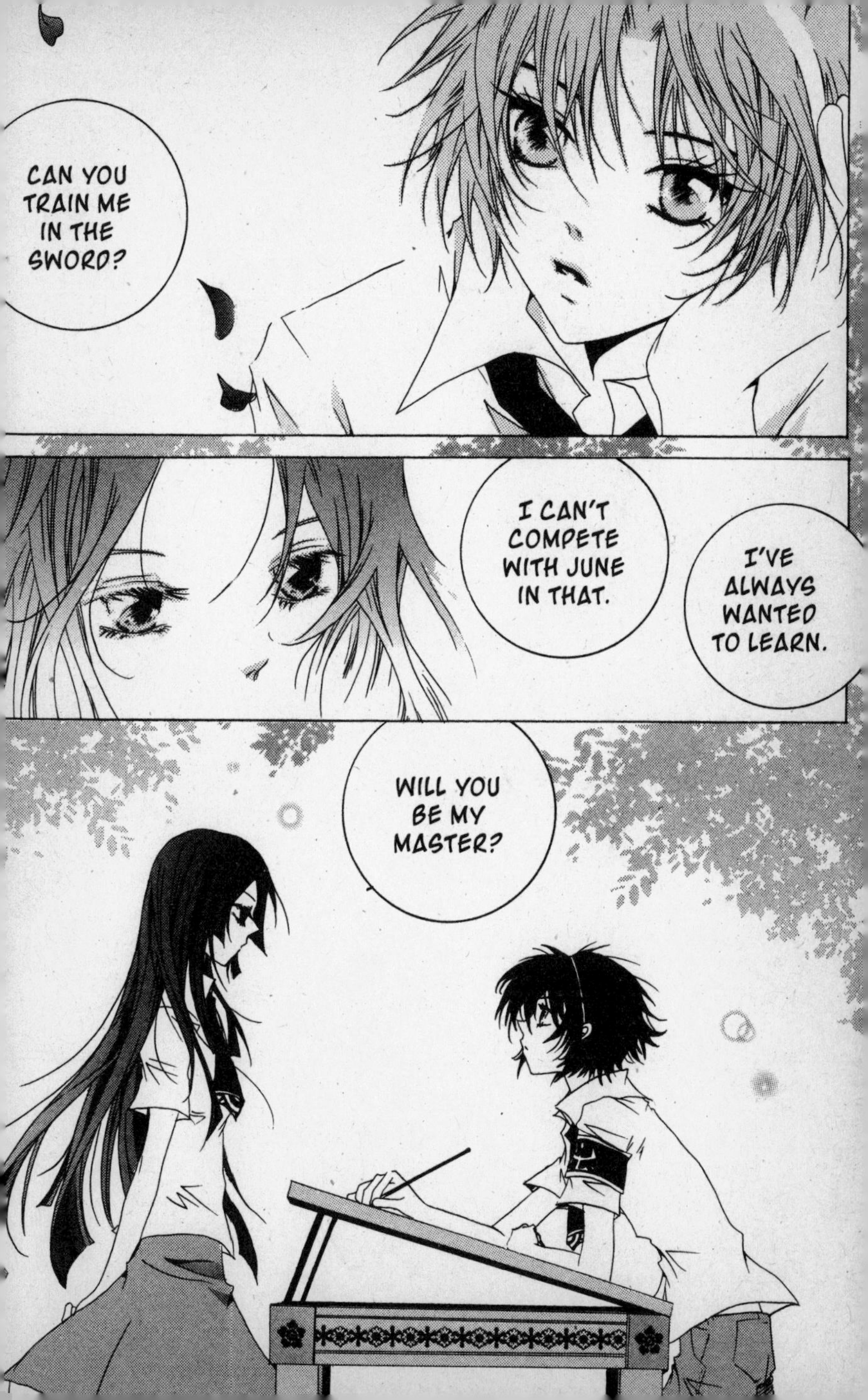
CAN YOU TRAIN ME IN THE SWORD?
I'VE ALWAYS WANTED TO LEARN.
I CAN'T COMPETE WITH JUNE IN THAT.
WILL YOU BE MY MASTER?

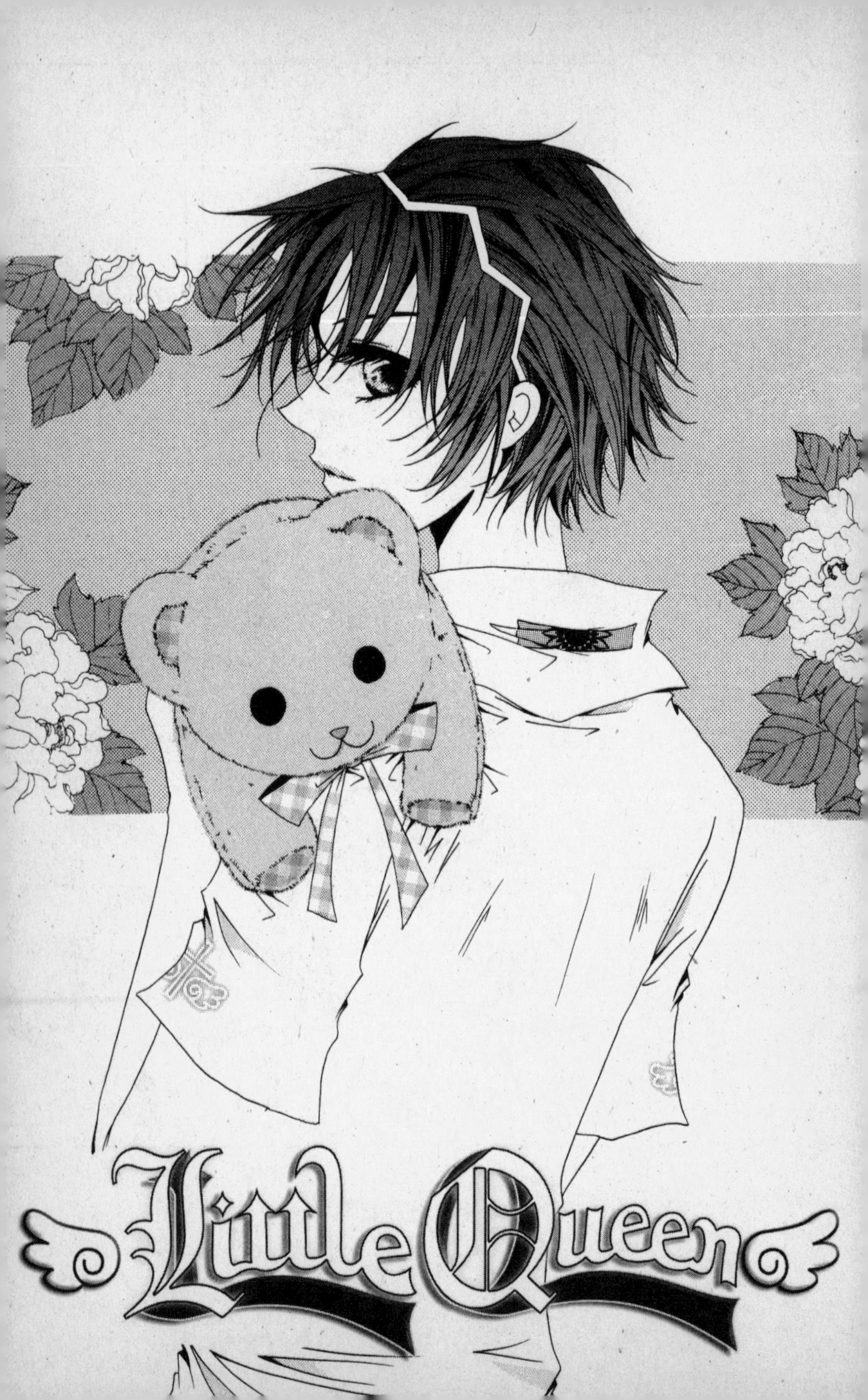
Little Queen

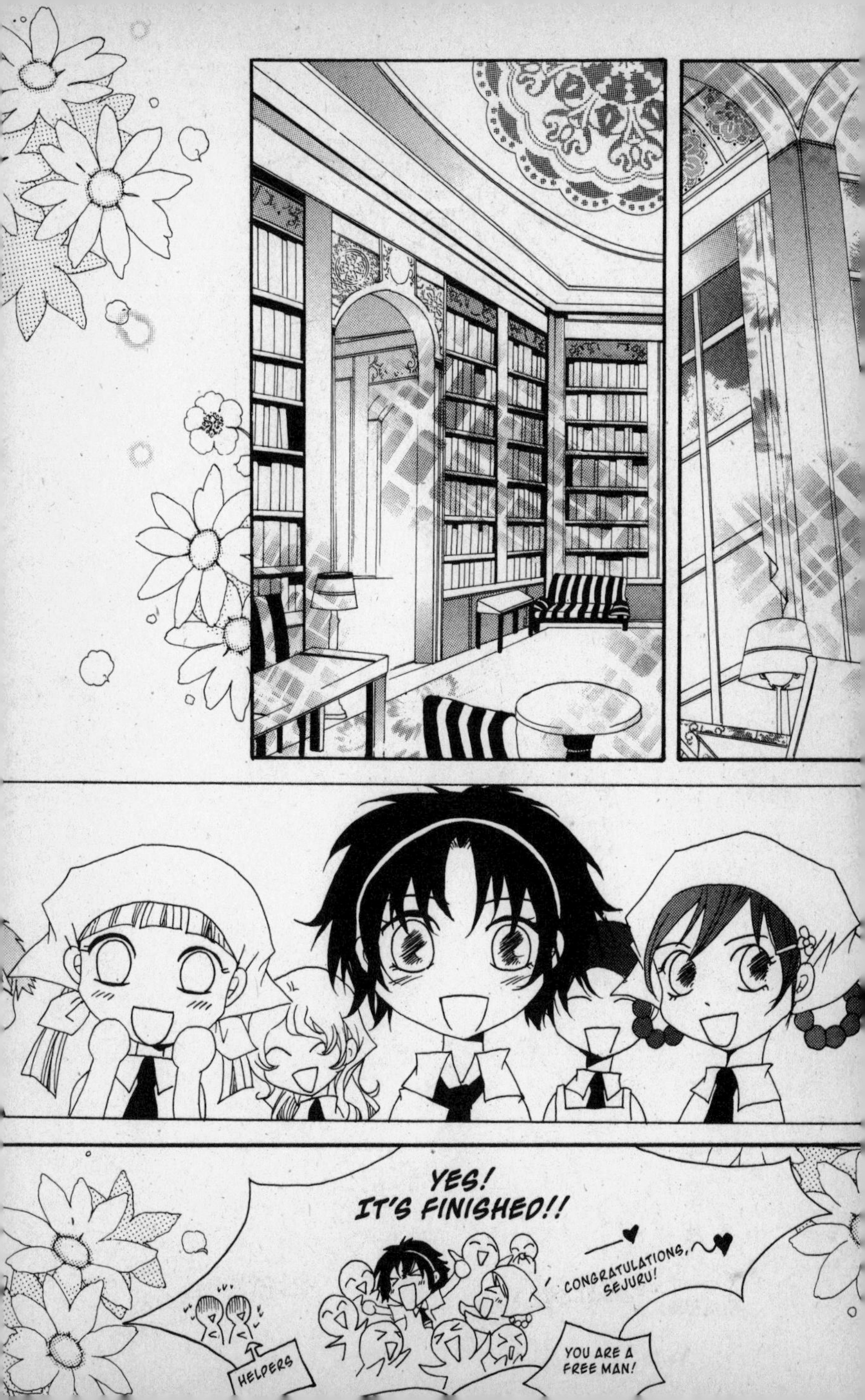
YES! IT'S FINISHED!!
CONGRATULATIONS, SEJURU!
YOU ARE A FREE MAN!
HELPERS

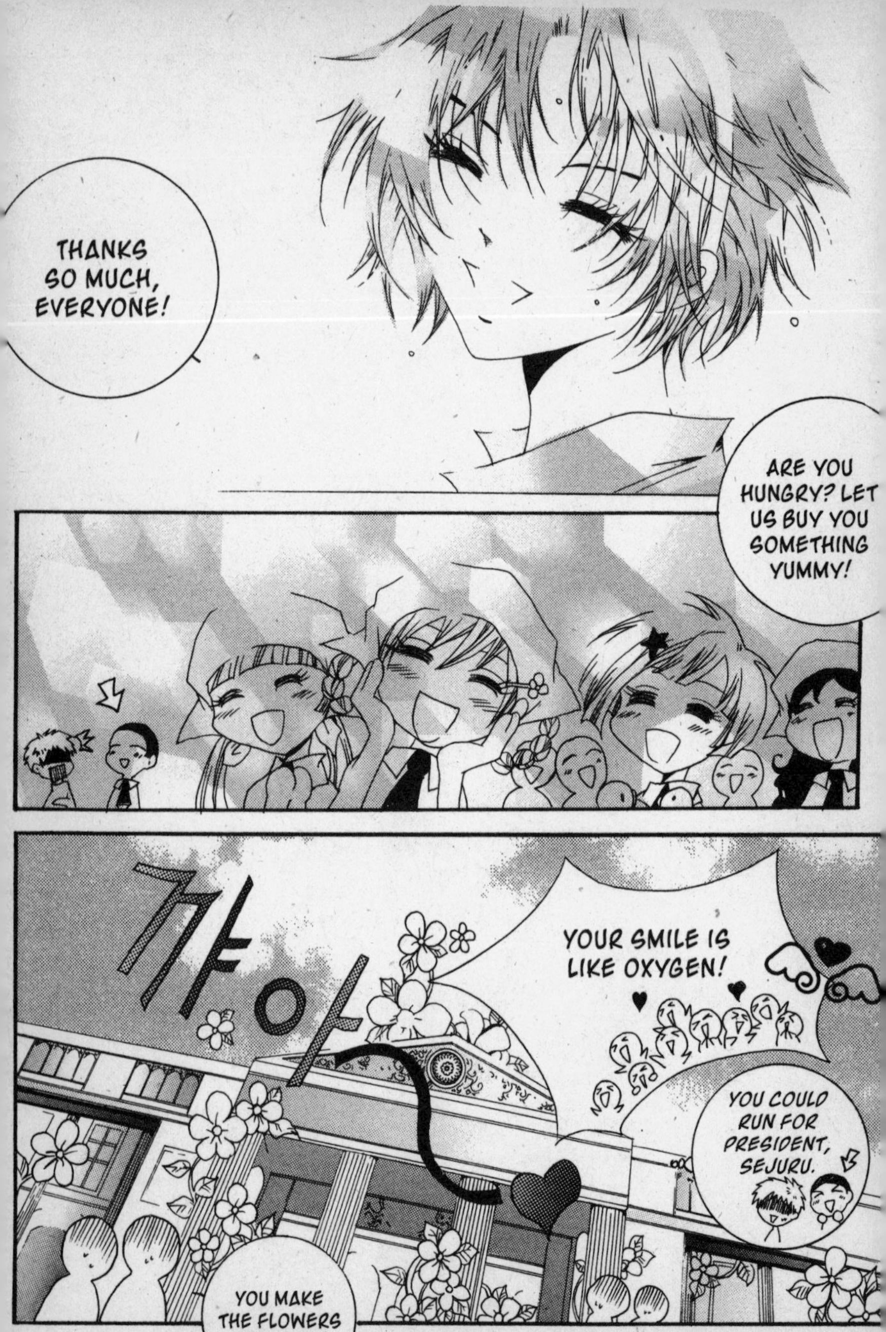
THANKS SO MUCH, EVERYONE!
ARE YOU HUNGRY? LET US BUY YOU SOMETHING YUMMY!
캬아~
YOUR SMILE IS LIKE OXYGEN!
YOU COULD RUN FOR PRESIDENT, SEJURU.
YOU MAKE THE FLOWERS BLOOM!

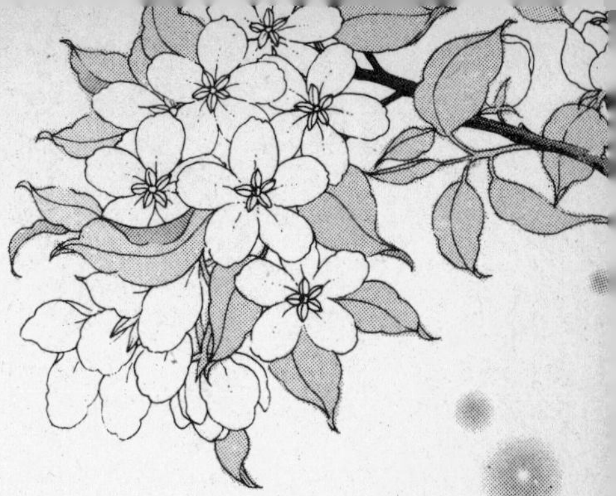

Piling Up Drop by Drop, Shining Twinkle by Twinkle

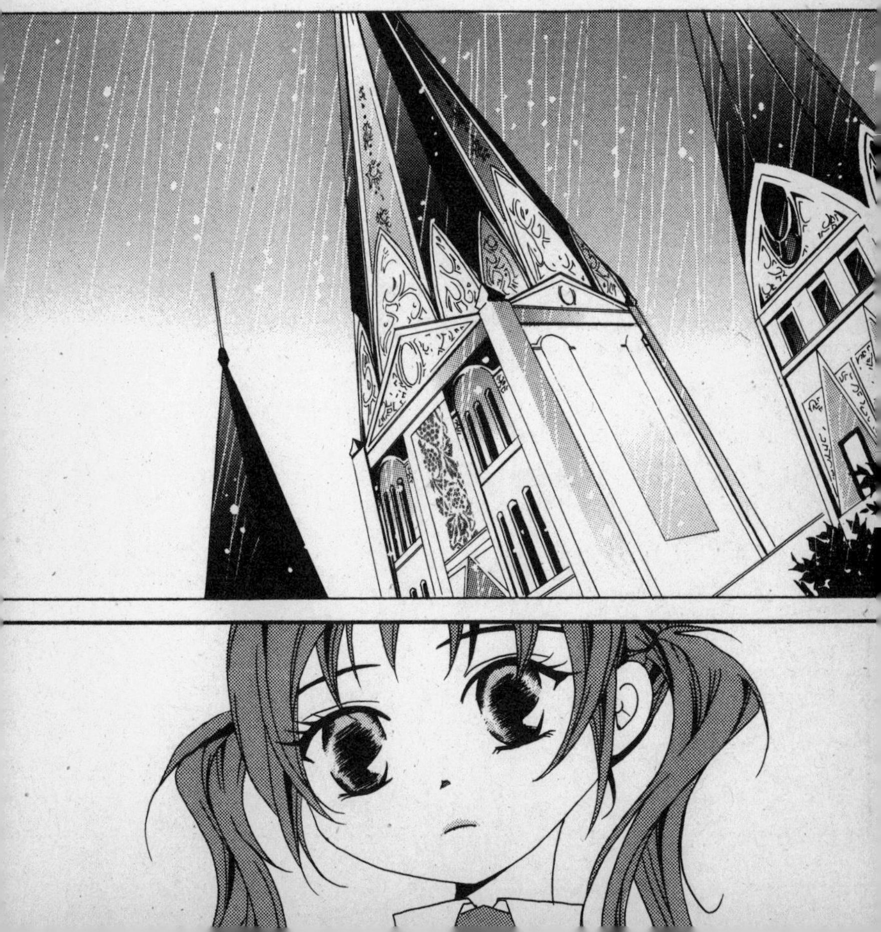

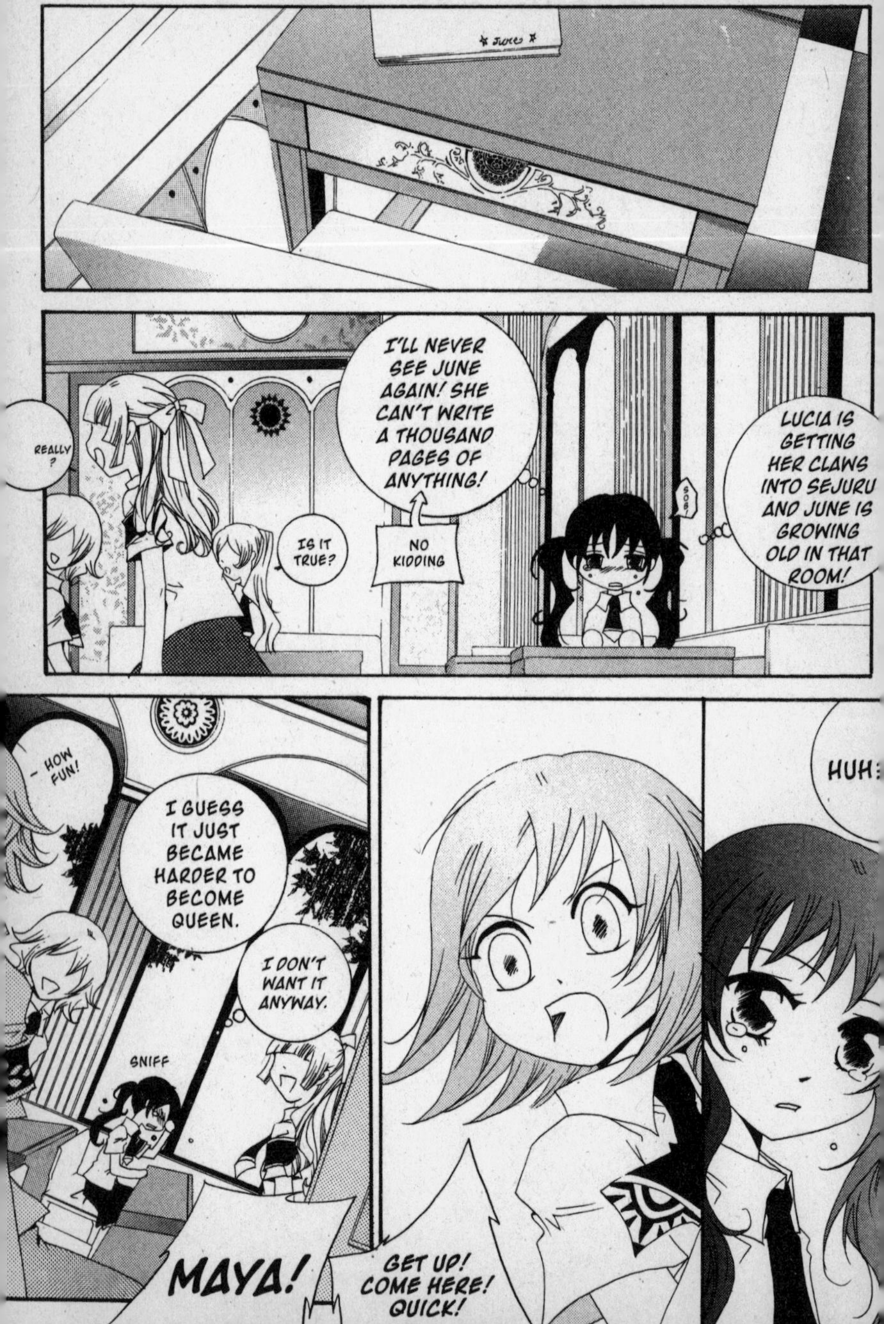
June
REALLY?
IS IT TRUE?
NO KIDDING
I'LL NEVER SEE JUNE AGAIN! SHE CAN'T WRITE A THOUSAND PAGES OF ANYTHING!
SOB!
LUCIA IS GETTING HER CLAWS INTO SEJURU AND JUNE IS GROWING OLD IN THAT ROOM!
- HOW FUN!
I GUESS IT JUST BECAME HARDER TO BECOME QUEEN.
I DON'T WANT IT ANYWAY.
SNIFF
MAYA!
GET UP! COME HERE! QUICK!
HUH

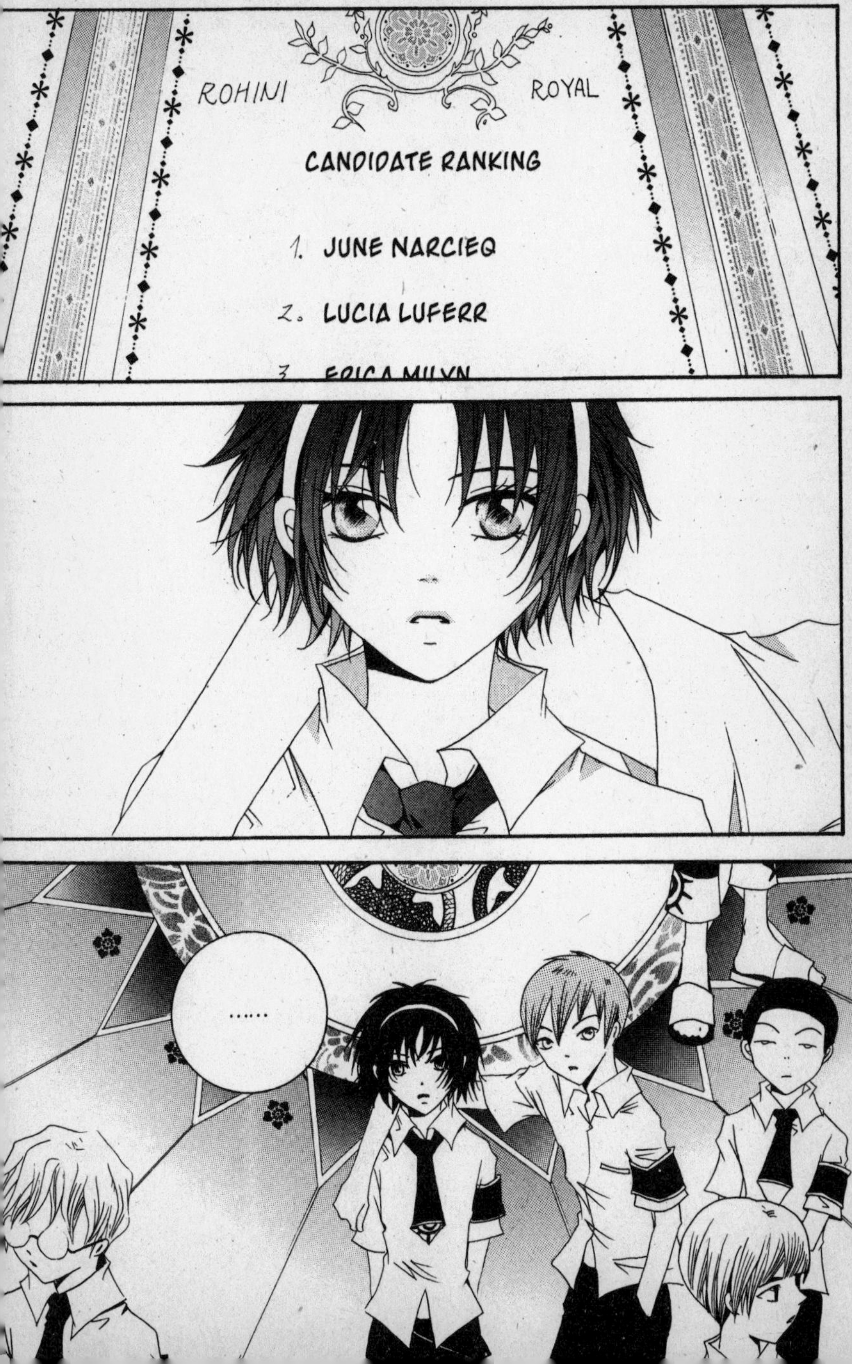
ROHINI ROYAL
CANDIDATE RANKING
1. JUNE NARCIEQ
2. LUCIA LUFERR
......

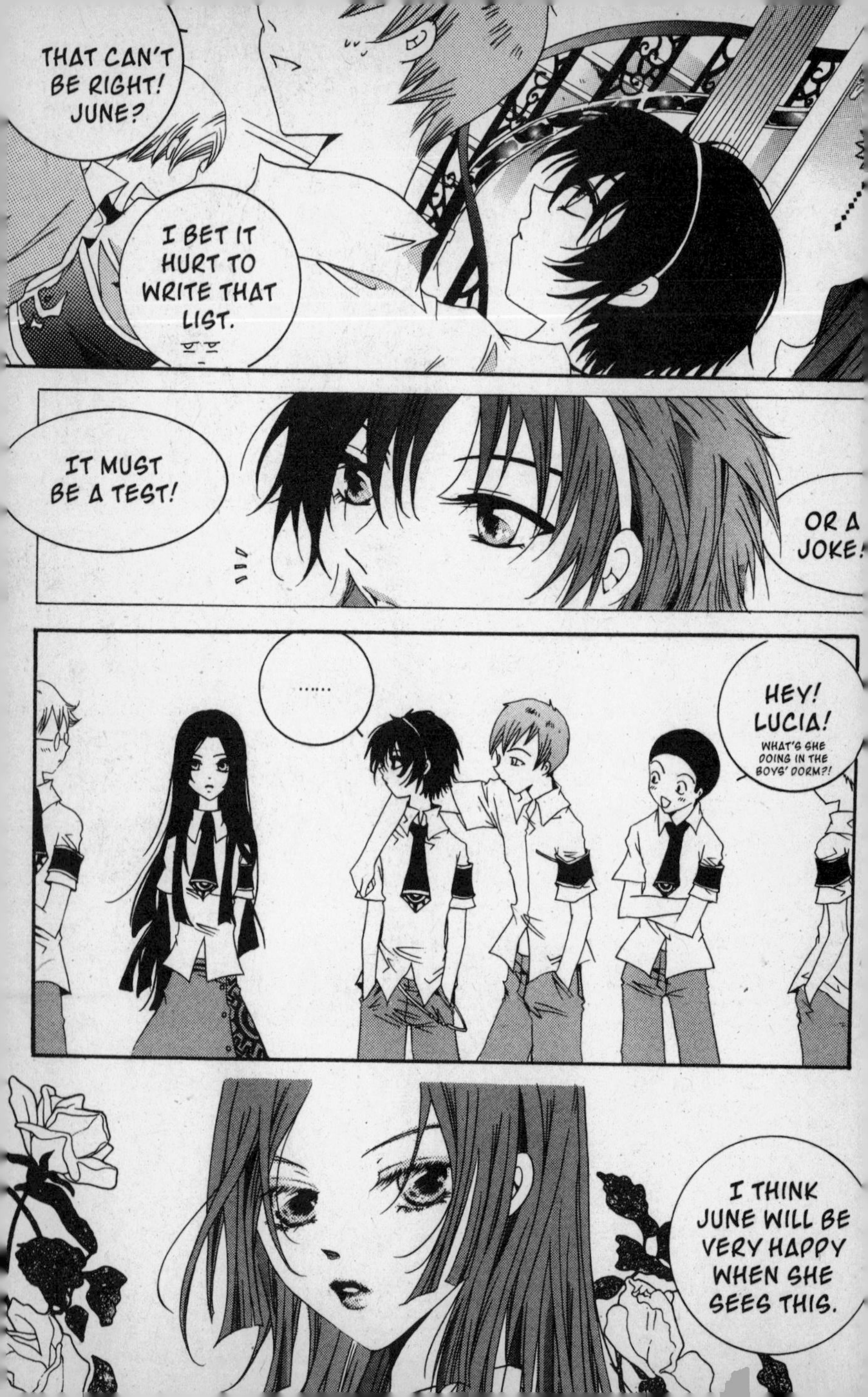
THAT CAN'T BE RIGHT! JUNE?
I BET IT HURT TO WRITE THAT LIST.
IT MUST BE A TEST!
OR A JOKE!
......
HEY! LUCIA!
WHAT'S SHE DOING IN THE BOYS' DORM?!
I THINK JUNE WILL BE VERY HAPPY WHEN SHE SEES THIS.

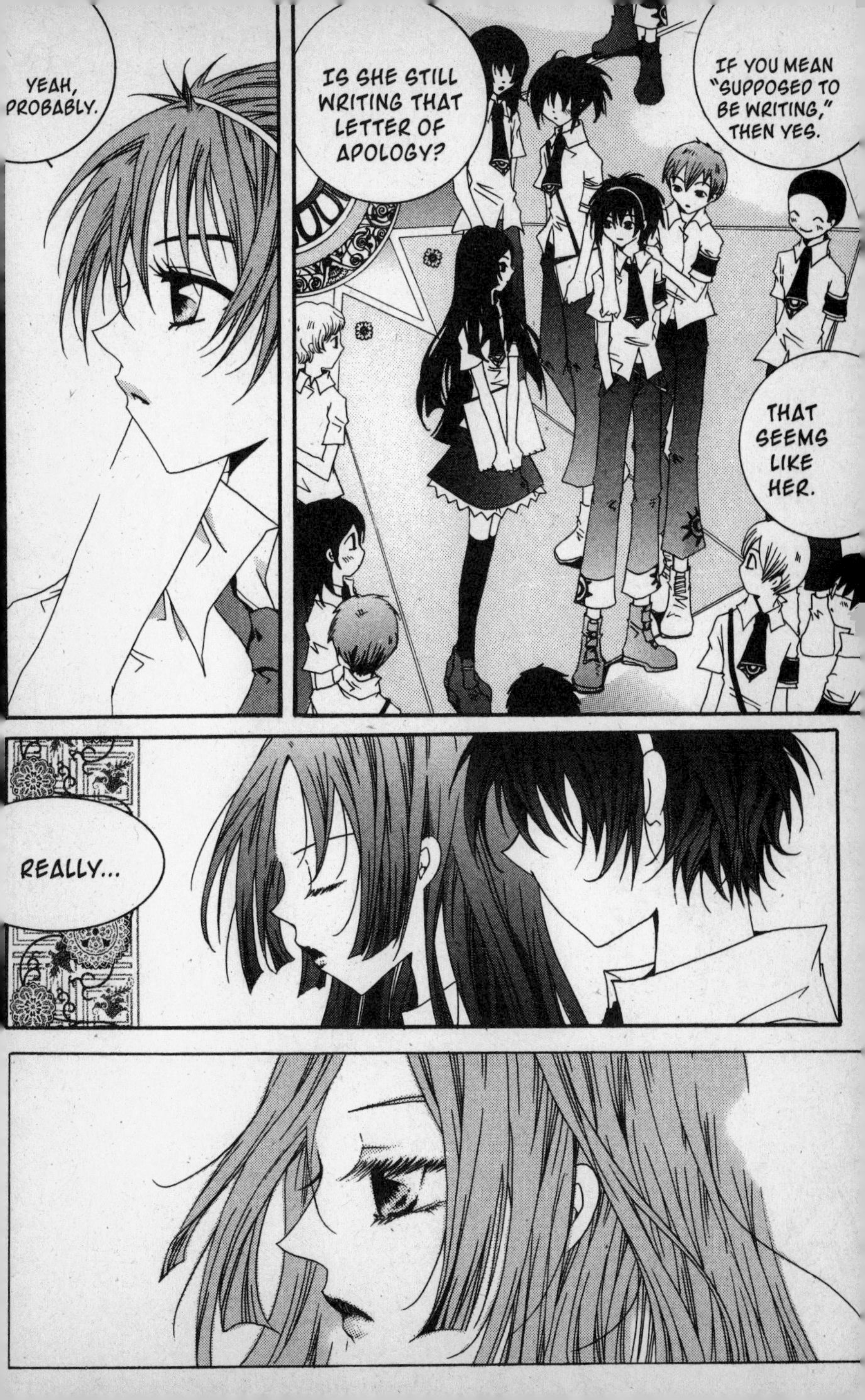
IS SHE STILL WRITING THAT LETTER OF APOLOGY?
IF YOU MEAN "SUPPOSED TO BE WRITING," THEN YES.
THAT SEEMS LIKE HER.
YEAH, PROBABLY.
REALLY...

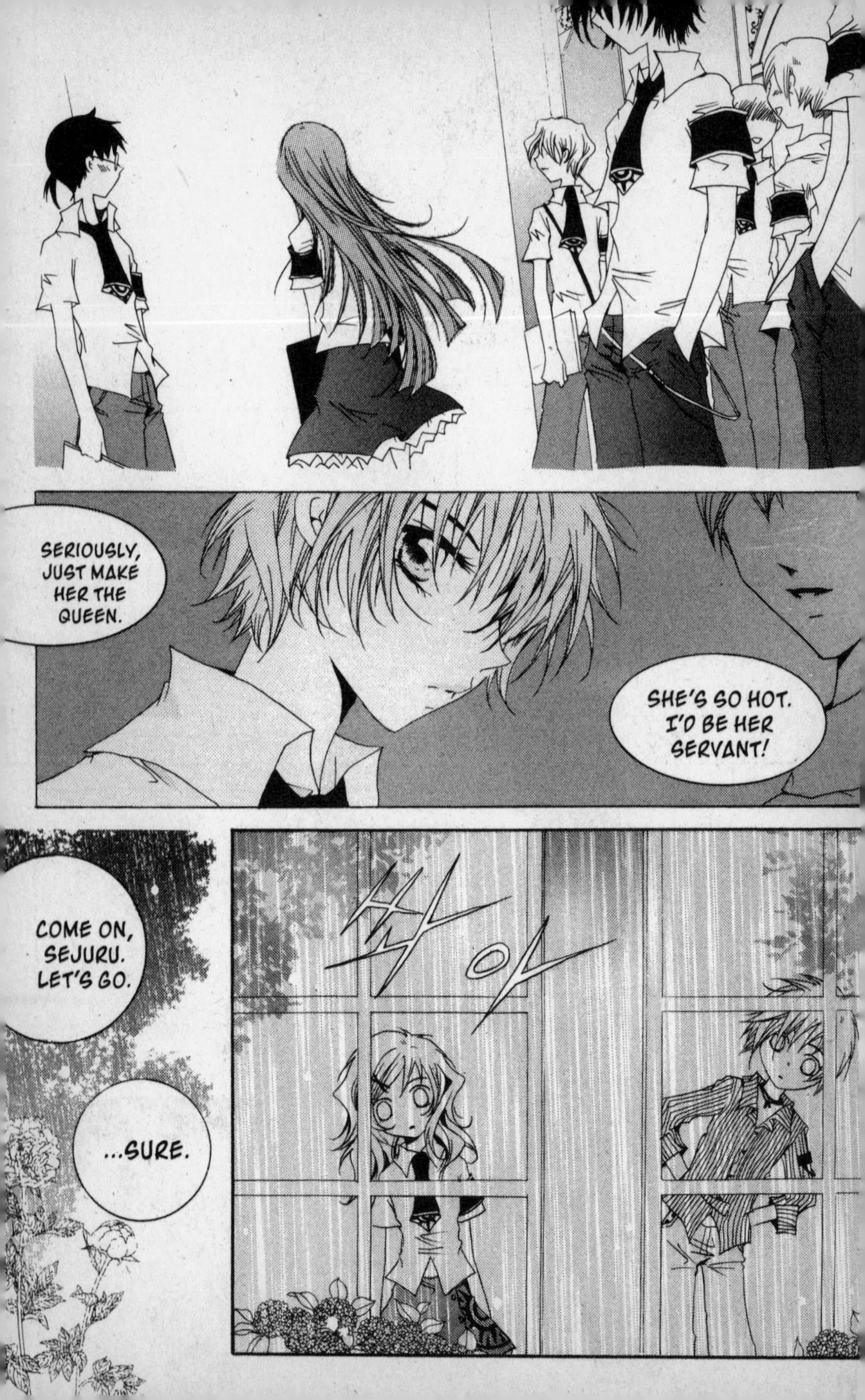
SERIOUSLY, JUST MAKE HER THE QUEEN.
SHE'S SO HOT. I'D BE HER SERVANT!
COME ON, SEJURU. LET'S GO.
...SURE.

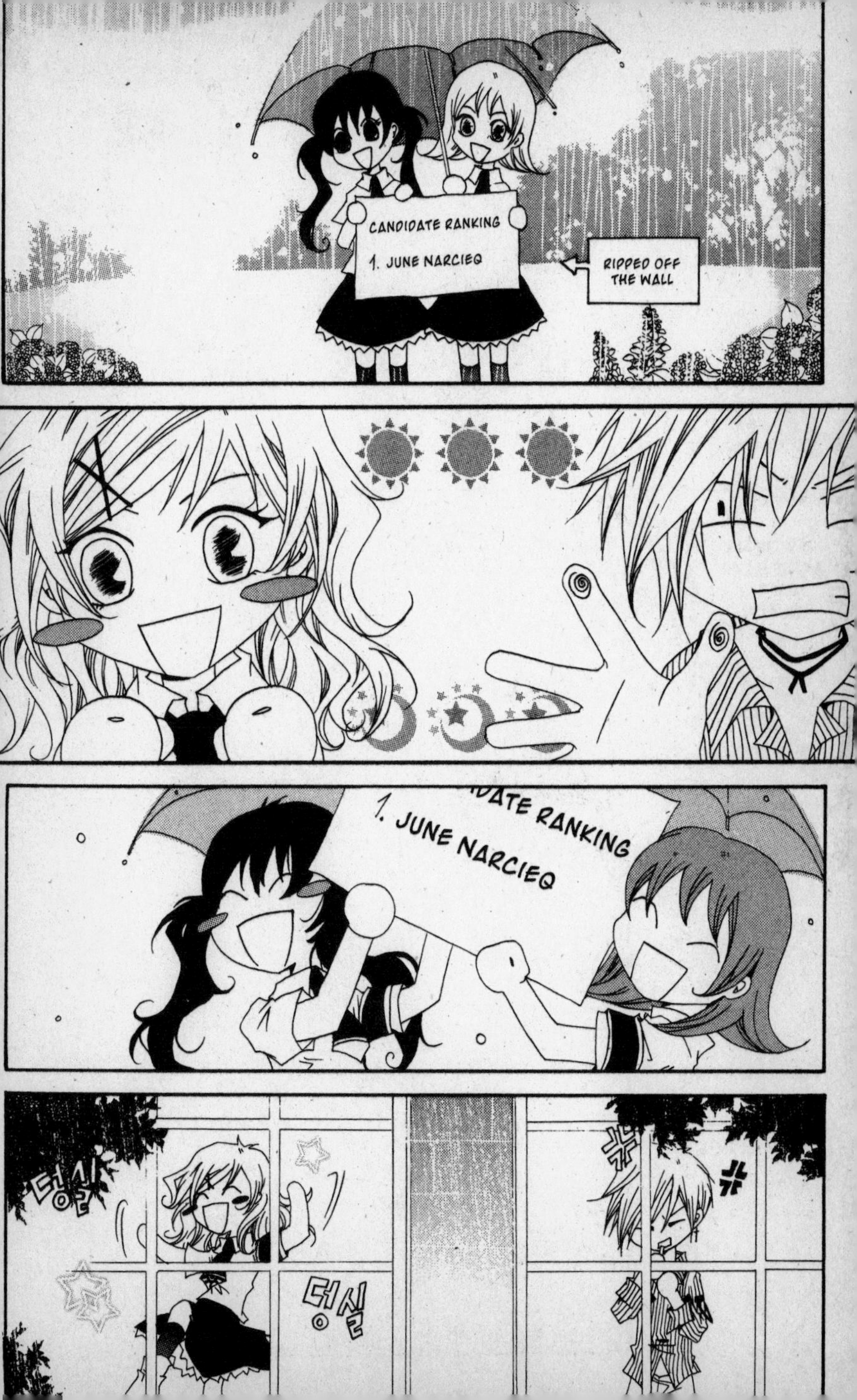
RIPPED OFF THE WALL
CANDIDATE RANKING
1. JUNE NARCIEQ
RANKING
1. JUNE NARCIEQ
덩실
덩실

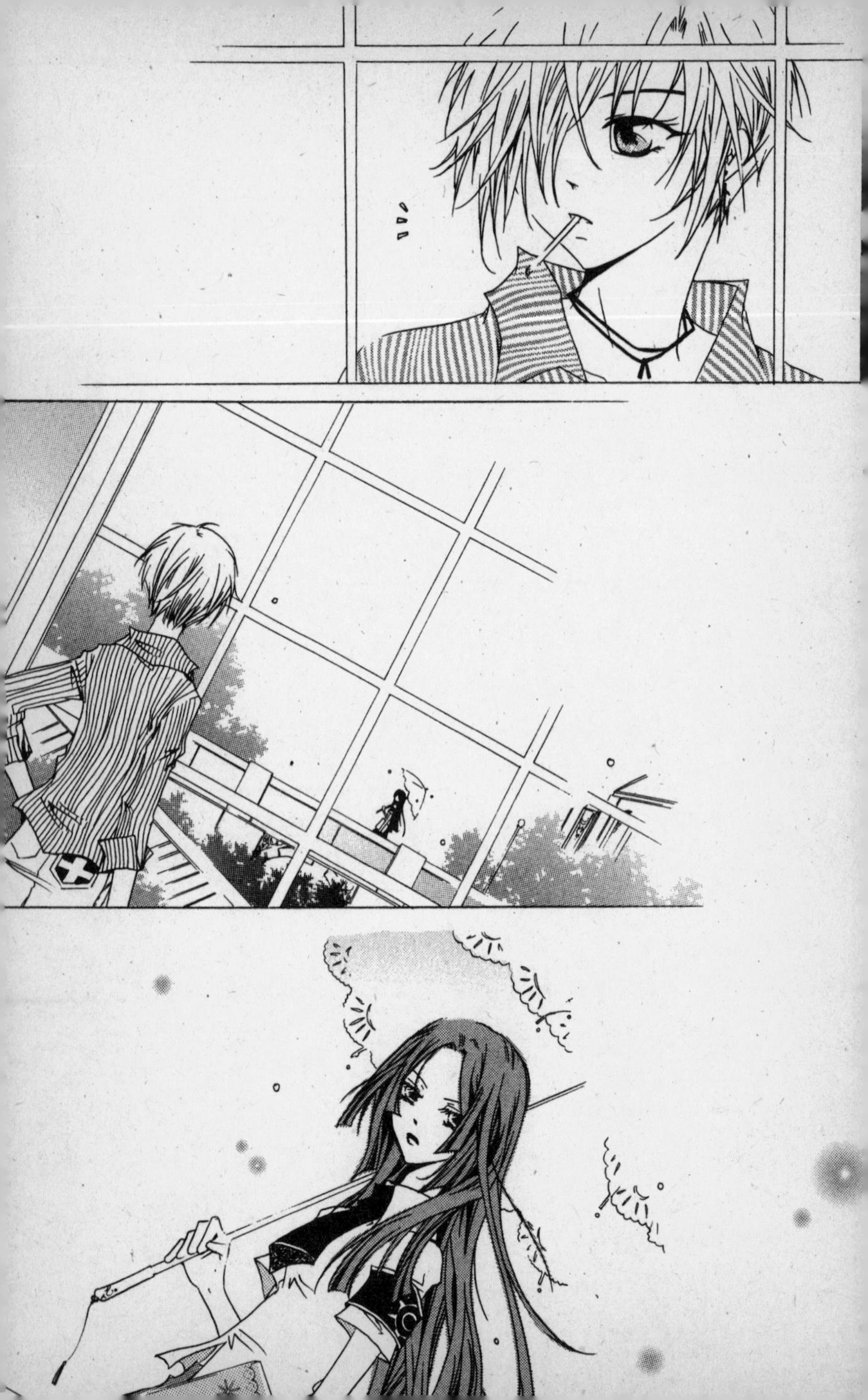

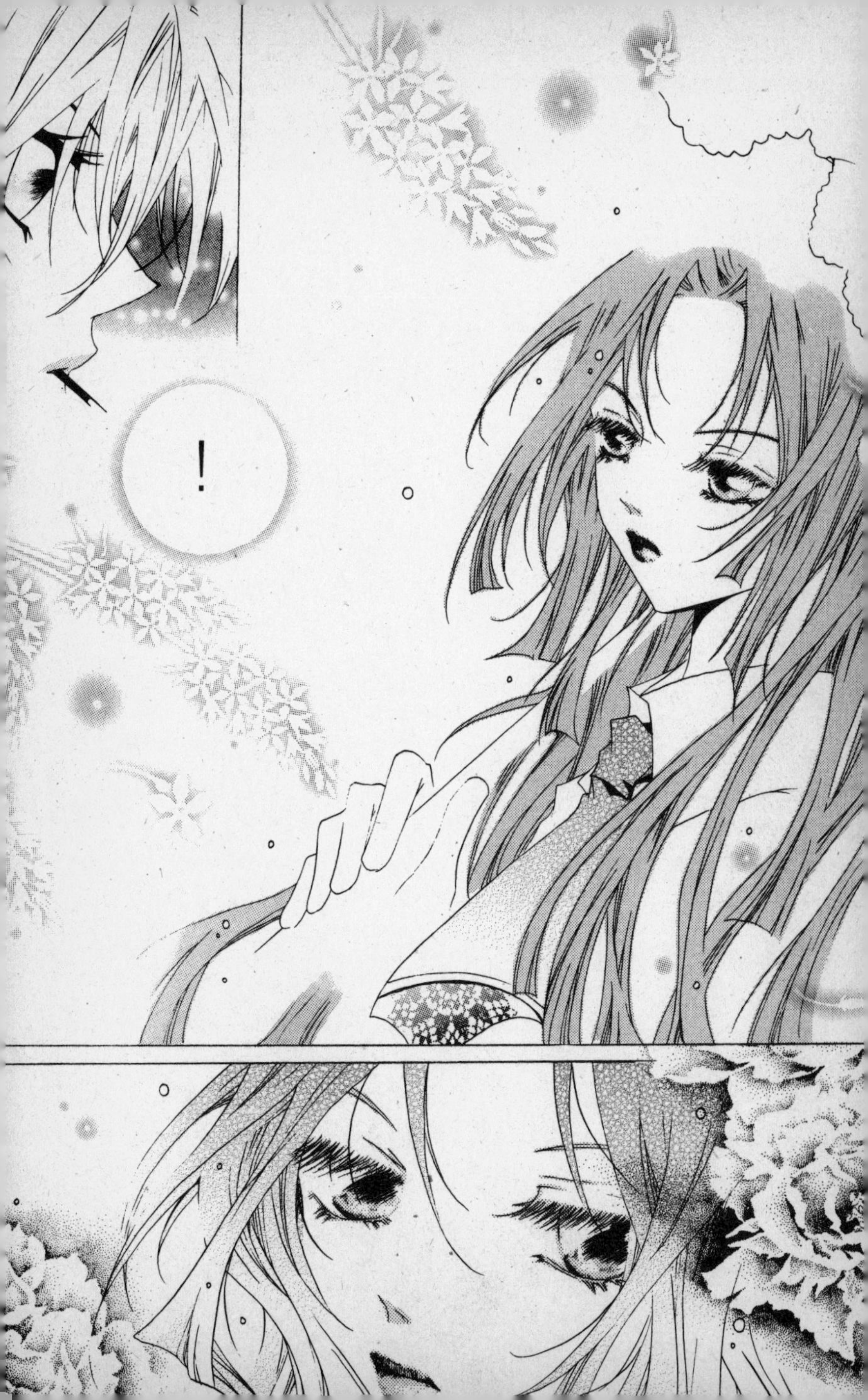
!

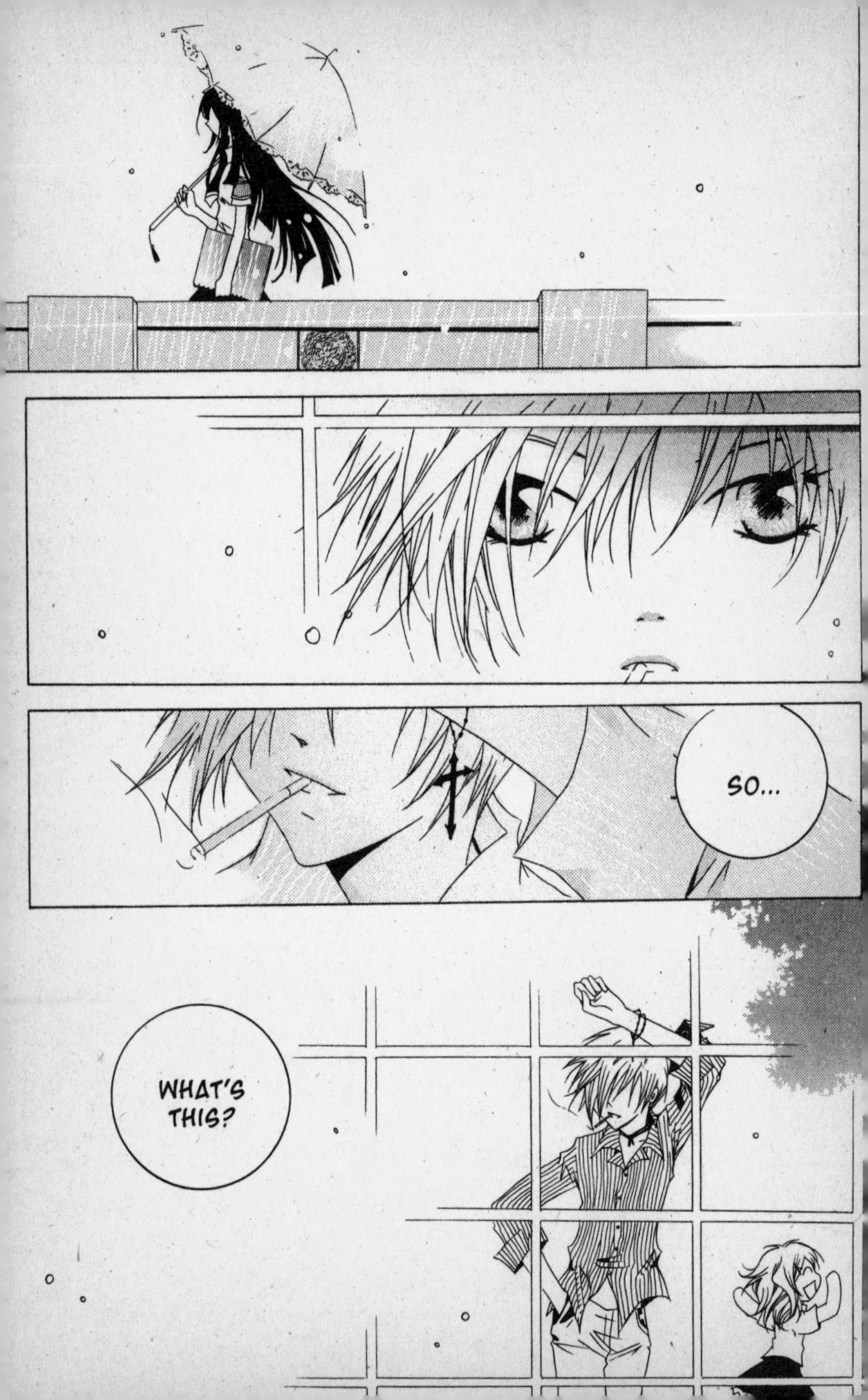
SO...
WHAT'S THIS?

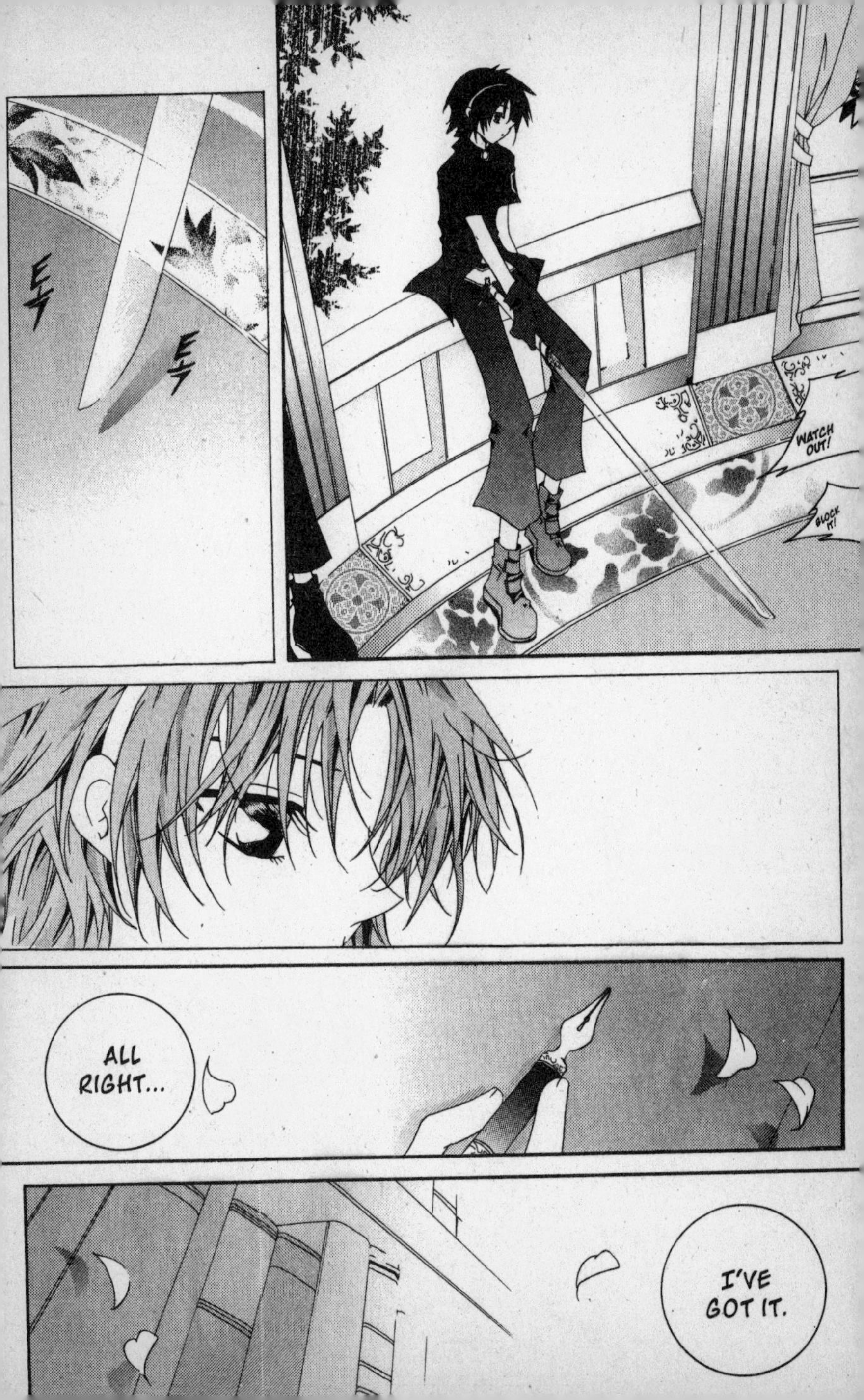
WATCH OUT!
BLOCK IT!
ALL RIGHT...
I'VE GOT IT.

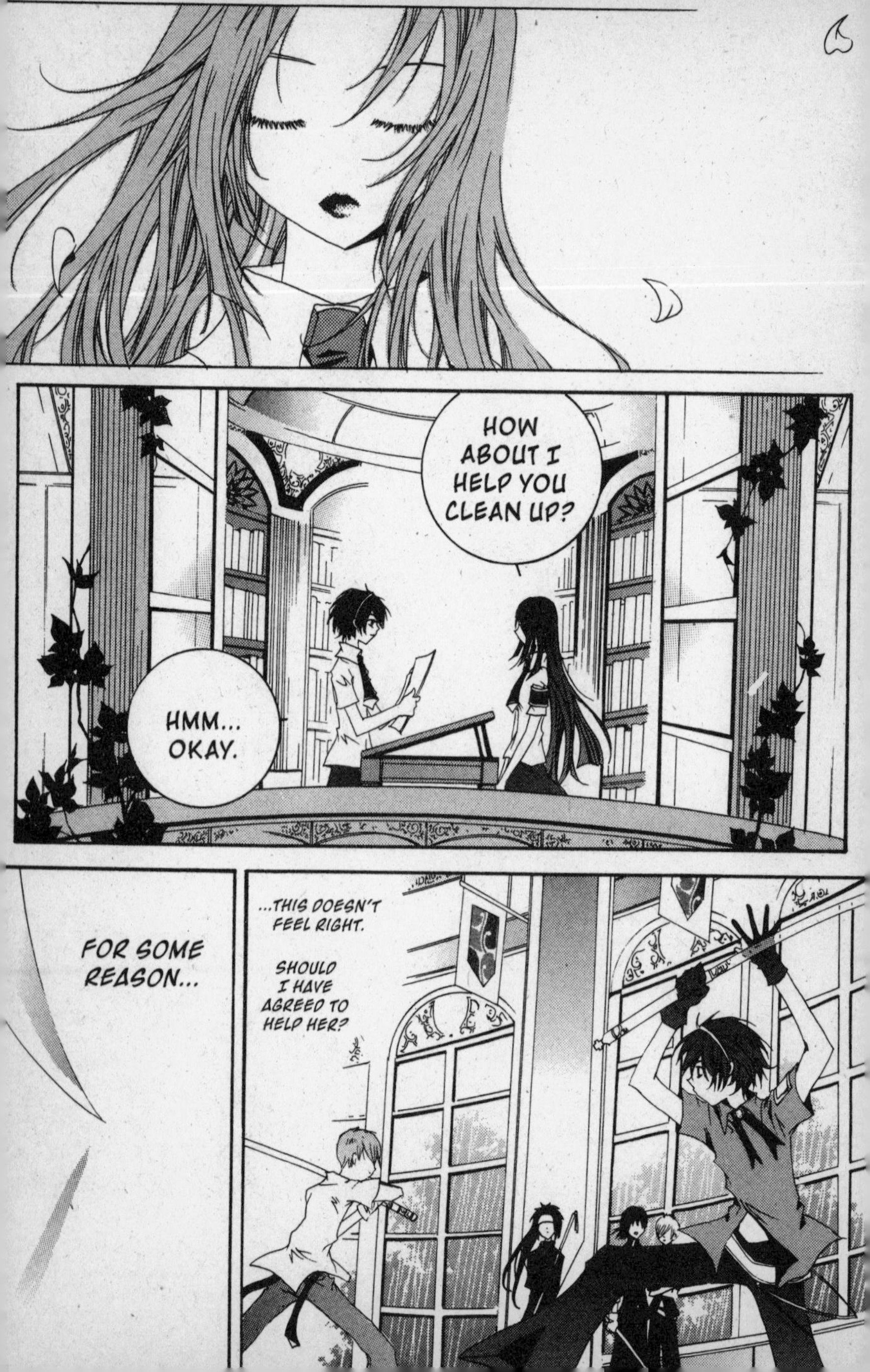
HOW ABOUT I HELP YOU CLEAN UP?
HMM... OKAY.
FOR SOME REASON...
...THIS DOESN'T FEEL RIGHT.
SHOULD I HAVE AGREED TO HELP HER?

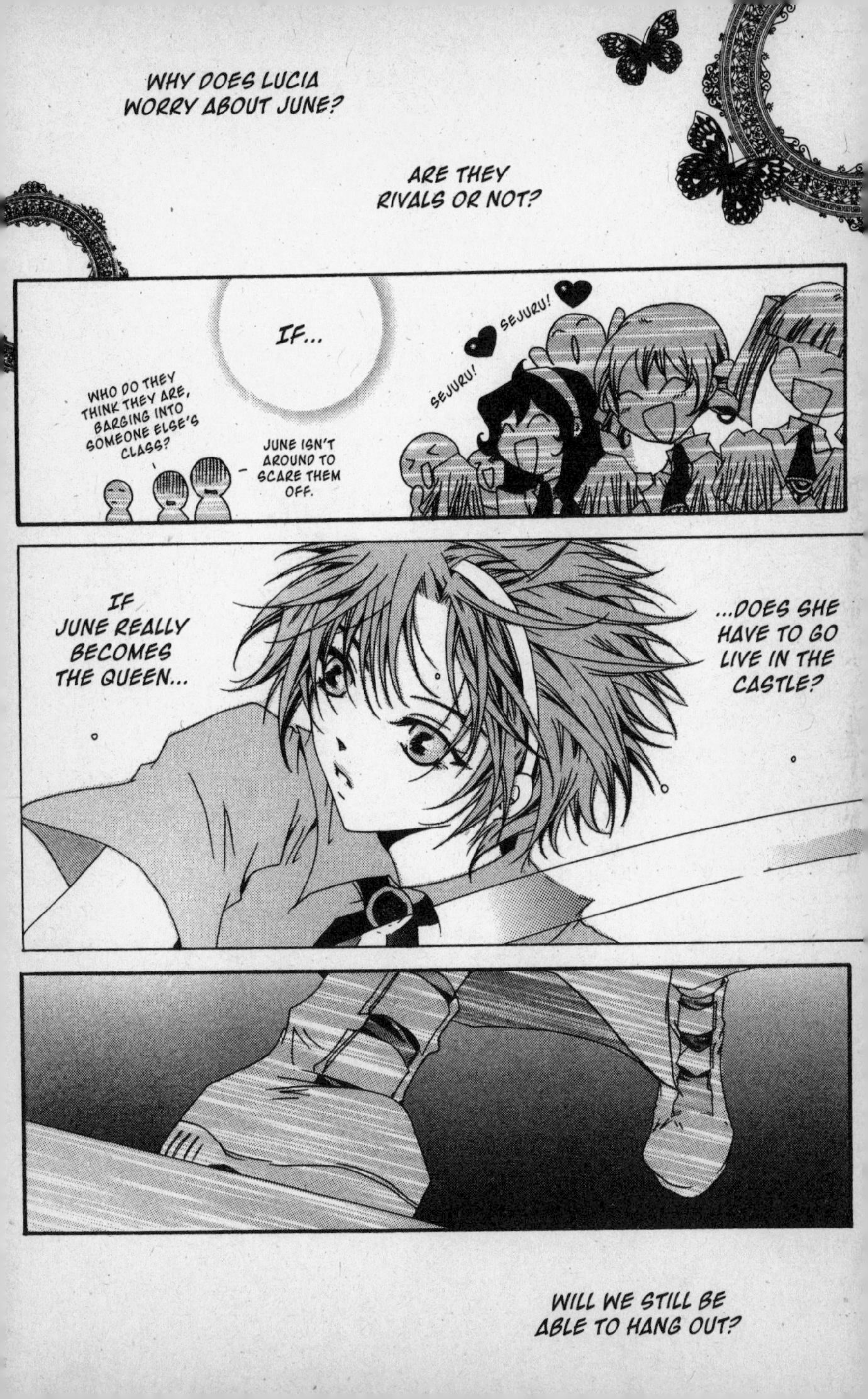
WHY DOES LUCIA WORRY ABOUT JUNE?
ARE THEY RIVALS OR NOT?
IF...
WHO DO THEY THINK THEY ARE, BARGING INTO SOMEONE ELSE'S CLASS?
JUNE ISN'T AROUND TO SCARE THEM OFF.
SEJURU!
SEJURU!
IF JUNE REALLY BECOMES THE QUEEN...
...DOES SHE HAVE TO GO LIVE IN THE CASTLE?
WILL WE STILL BE ABLE TO HANG OUT?

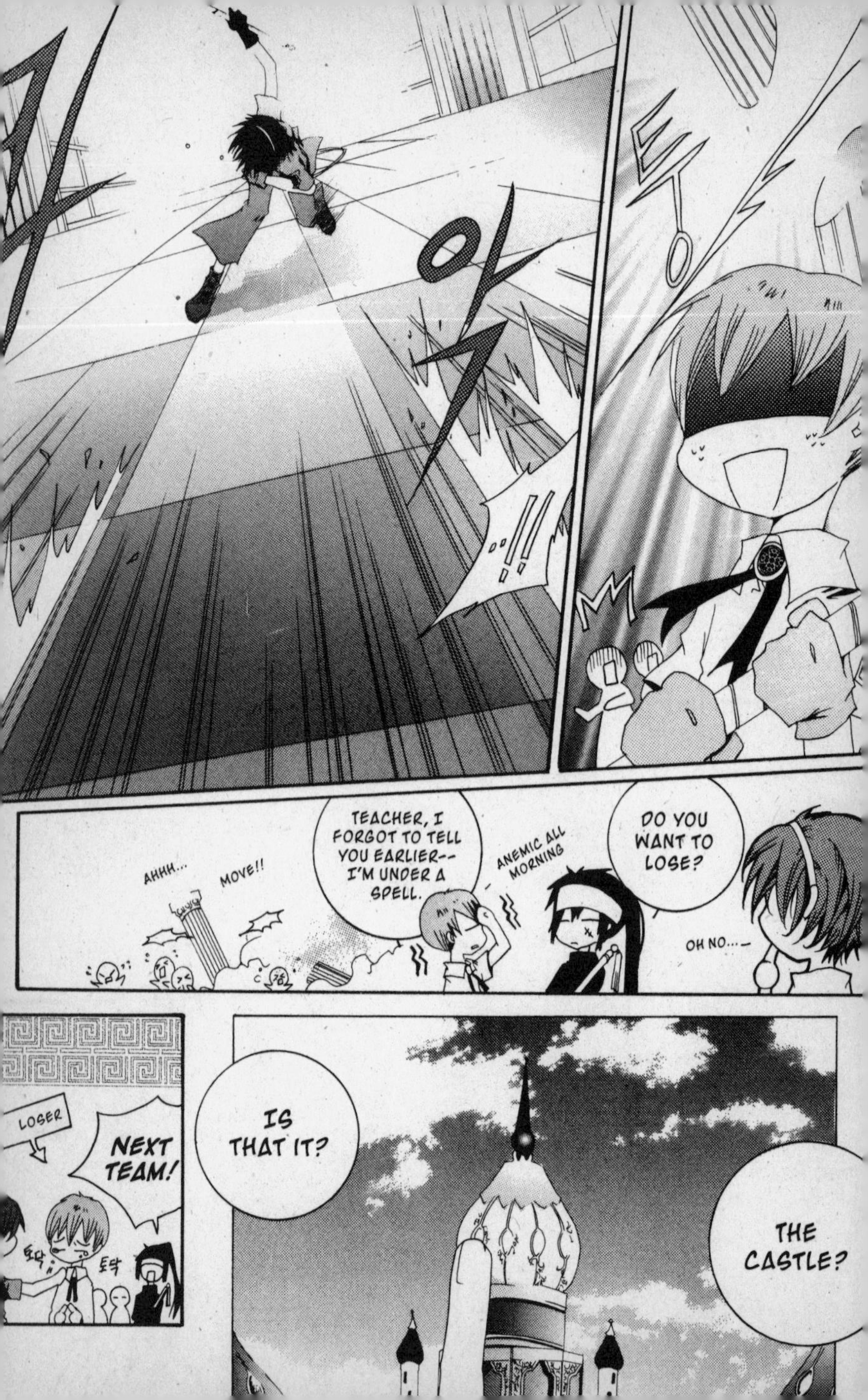

DO YOU WANT TO LOSE?
OH NO...
ANEMIC ALL MORNING
TEACHER, I FORGOT TO TELL YOU EARLIER-- I'M UNDER A SPELL.
MOVE!!
AHHH...
THE CASTLE?
IS THAT IT?
NEXT TEAM!
LOSER
토닥
토닥

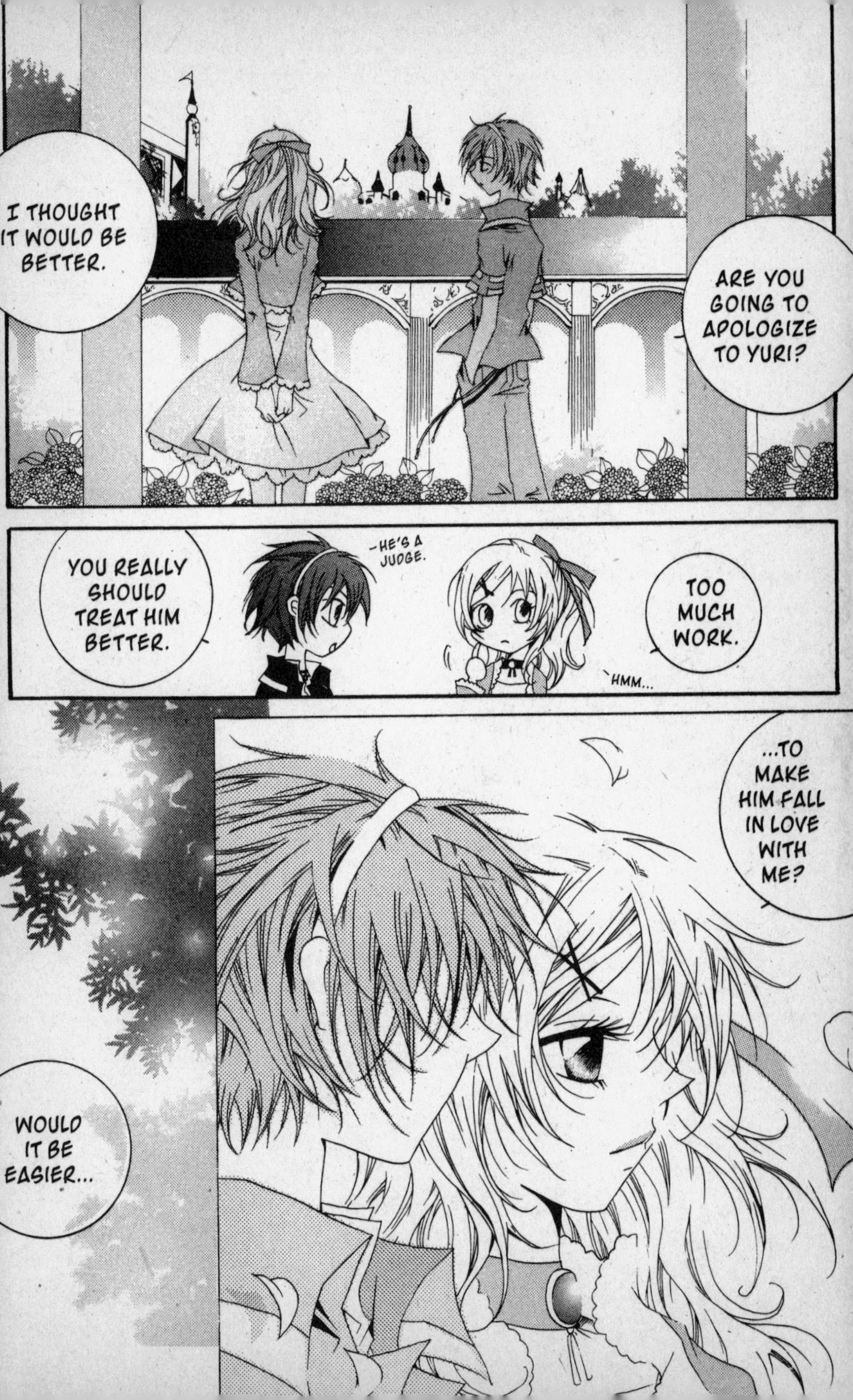
ARE YOU GOING TO APOLOGIZE TO YURI?
I THOUGHT IT WOULD BE BETTER.
TOO MUCH WORK.
HMM...
HE'S A JUDGE.
YOU REALLY SHOULD TREAT HIM BETTER.
WOULD IT BE EASIER...
...TO MAKE HIM FALL IN LOVE WITH ME?

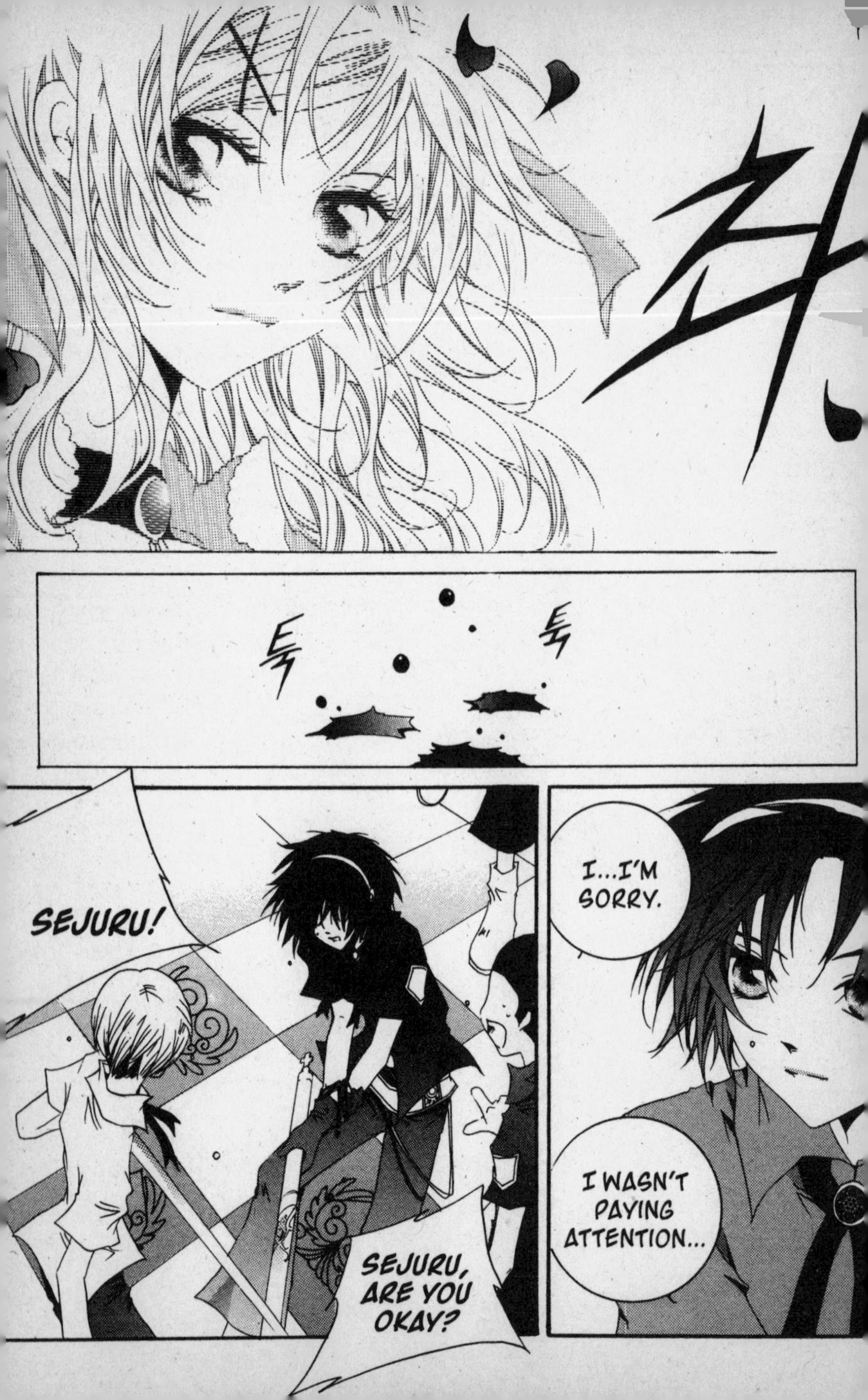
SEJURU!
SEJURU, ARE YOU OKAY?
I...I'M SORRY.
I WASN'T PAYING ATTENTION...

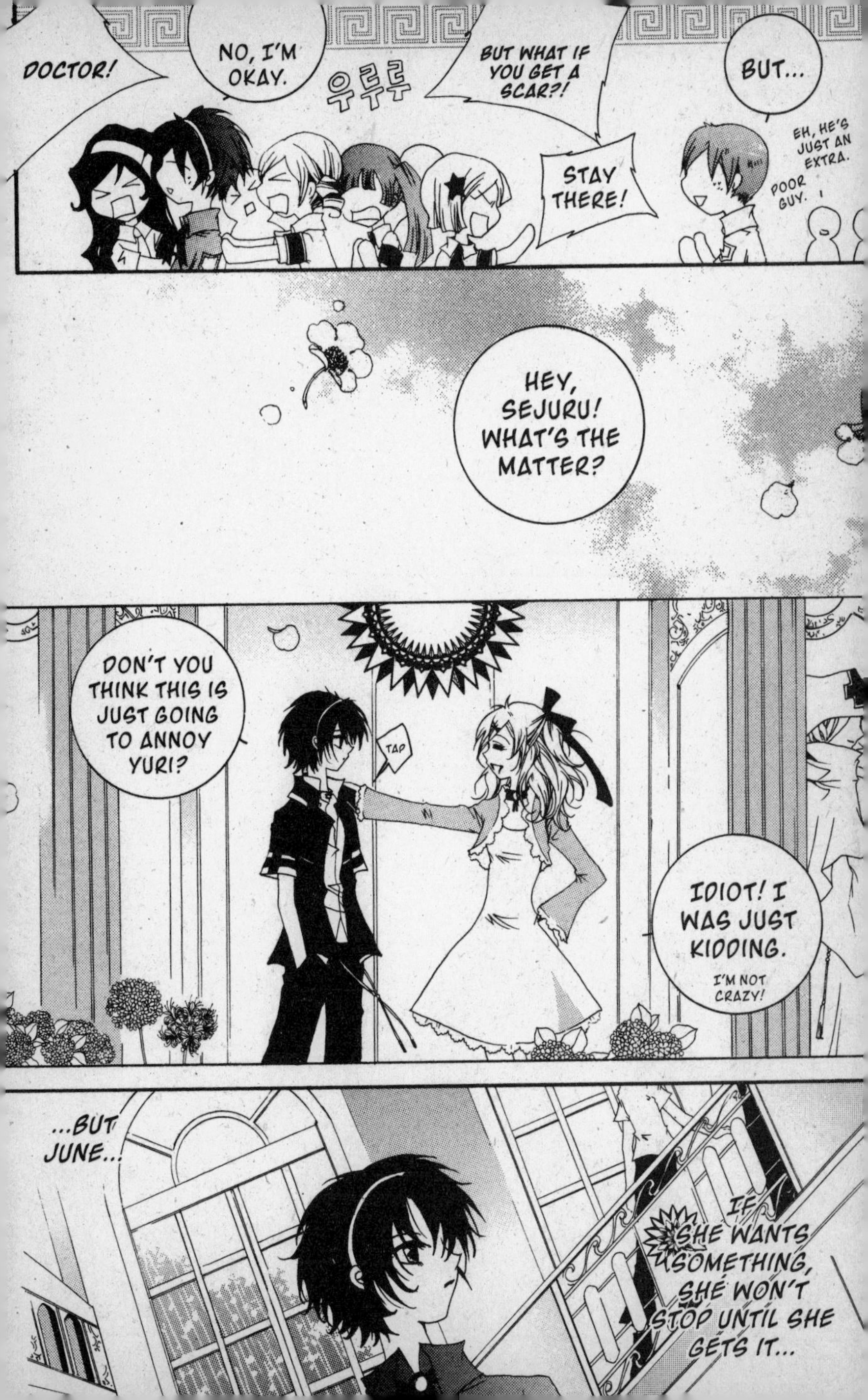
DOCTOR!
NO, I'M OKAY.
우르르
BUT WHAT IF YOU GET A SCAR?!
STAY THERE!
BUT...
EH, HE'S JUST AN EXTRA.
POOR GUY.
HEY, SEJURU! WHAT'S THE MATTER?
DON'T YOU THINK THIS IS JUST GOING TO ANNOY YURI?
TAP
IDIOT! I WAS JUST KIDDING.
I'M NOT CRAZY!
...BUT JUNE...
IF SHE WANTS SOMETHING, SHE WON'T STOP UNTIL SHE GETS IT...

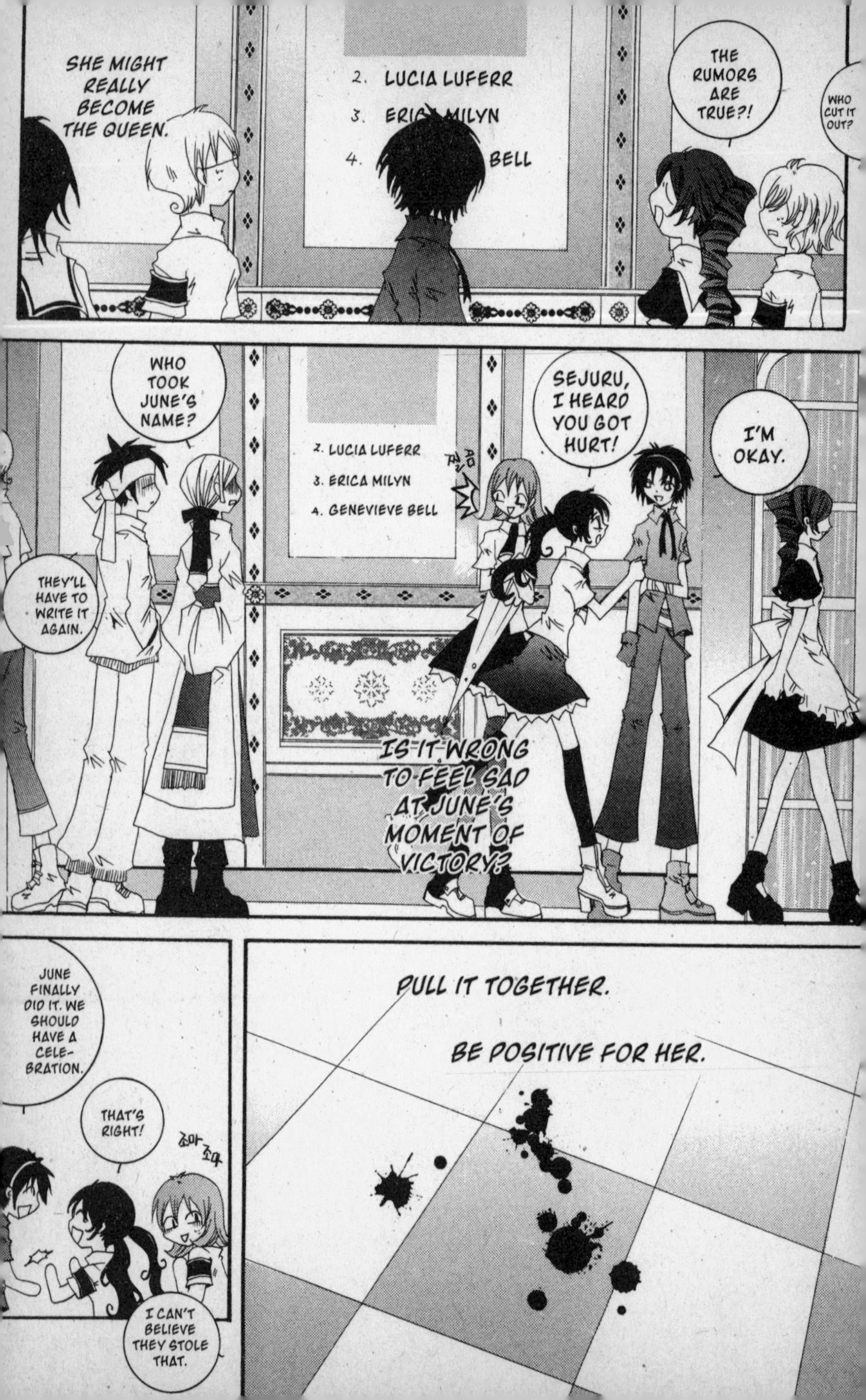
SHE MIGHT REALLY BECOME THE QUEEN.
2. LUCIA LUFERR
3. ERIC MILYN
4. BELL
THE RUMORS ARE TRUE?!
WHO CUT IT OUT?
WHO TOOK JUNE'S NAME?
THEY'LL HAVE TO WRITE IT AGAIN.
2. LUCIA LUFERR
3. ERICA MILYN
4. GENEVIEVE BELL
SEJURU, I HEARD YOU GOT HURT!
I'M OKAY.
IS IT WRONG TO FEEL SAD AT JUNE'S MOMENT OF VICTORY?
JUNE FINALLY DID IT. WE SHOULD HAVE A CELE-BRATION.
THAT'S RIGHT!
I CAN'T BELIEVE THEY STOLE THAT.
PULL IT TOGETHER.
BE POSITIVE FOR HER.

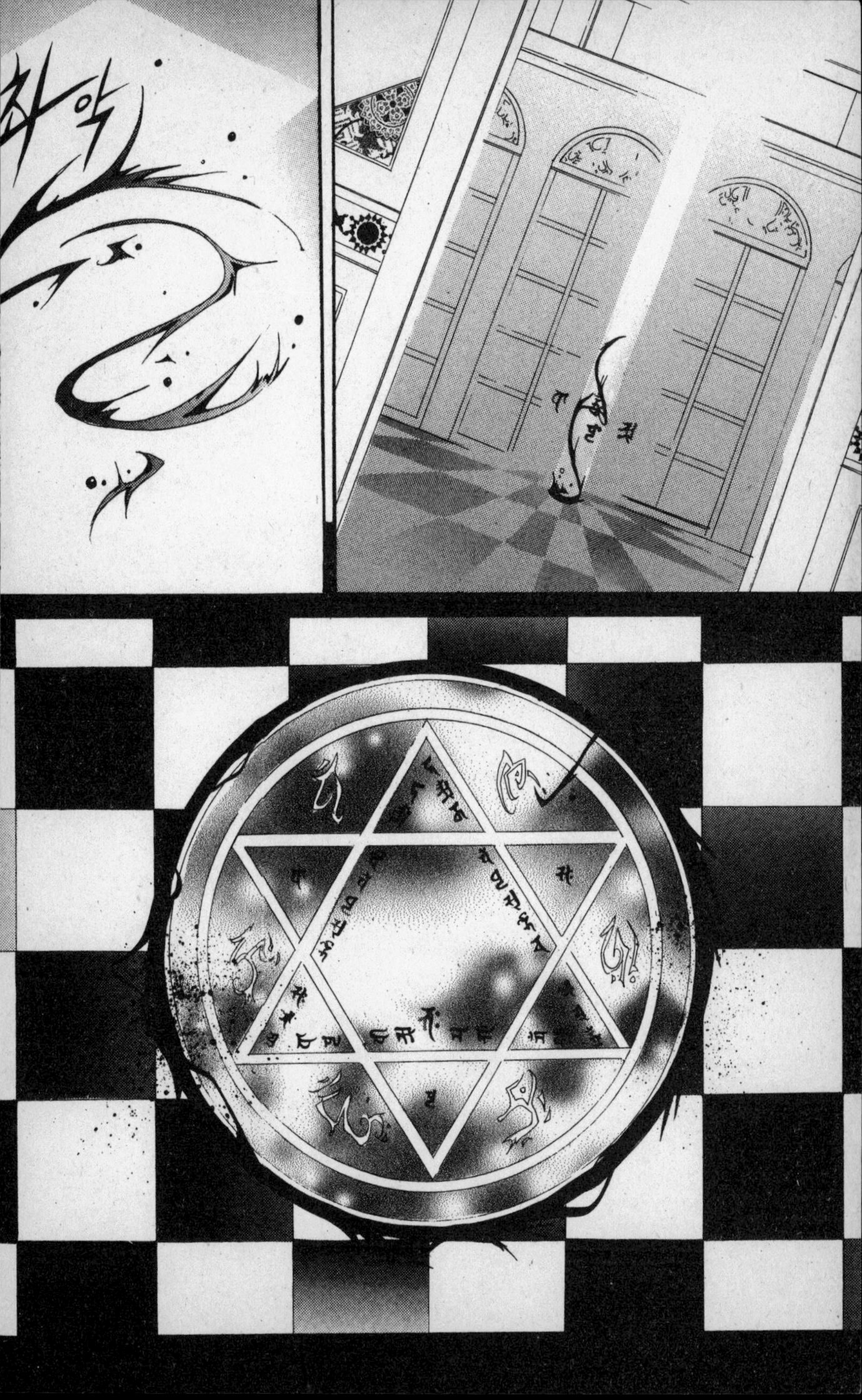

TO BE CONTINUED

Next, demons invade the Academy, intent on capturing
Sejuru! What is it about the mysterious young student
that they are so drawn to? Sejuru desperately tries to
fight them off, but is soon overcome. Sensing her friend
is in danger, June breaks free from the confines of the
Academy Library and comes to Sejuru's defense. In
a last-ditch effort June uses a power she doesn't fully
understand to protect both Sejuru and the Academy.
But will it be enough?

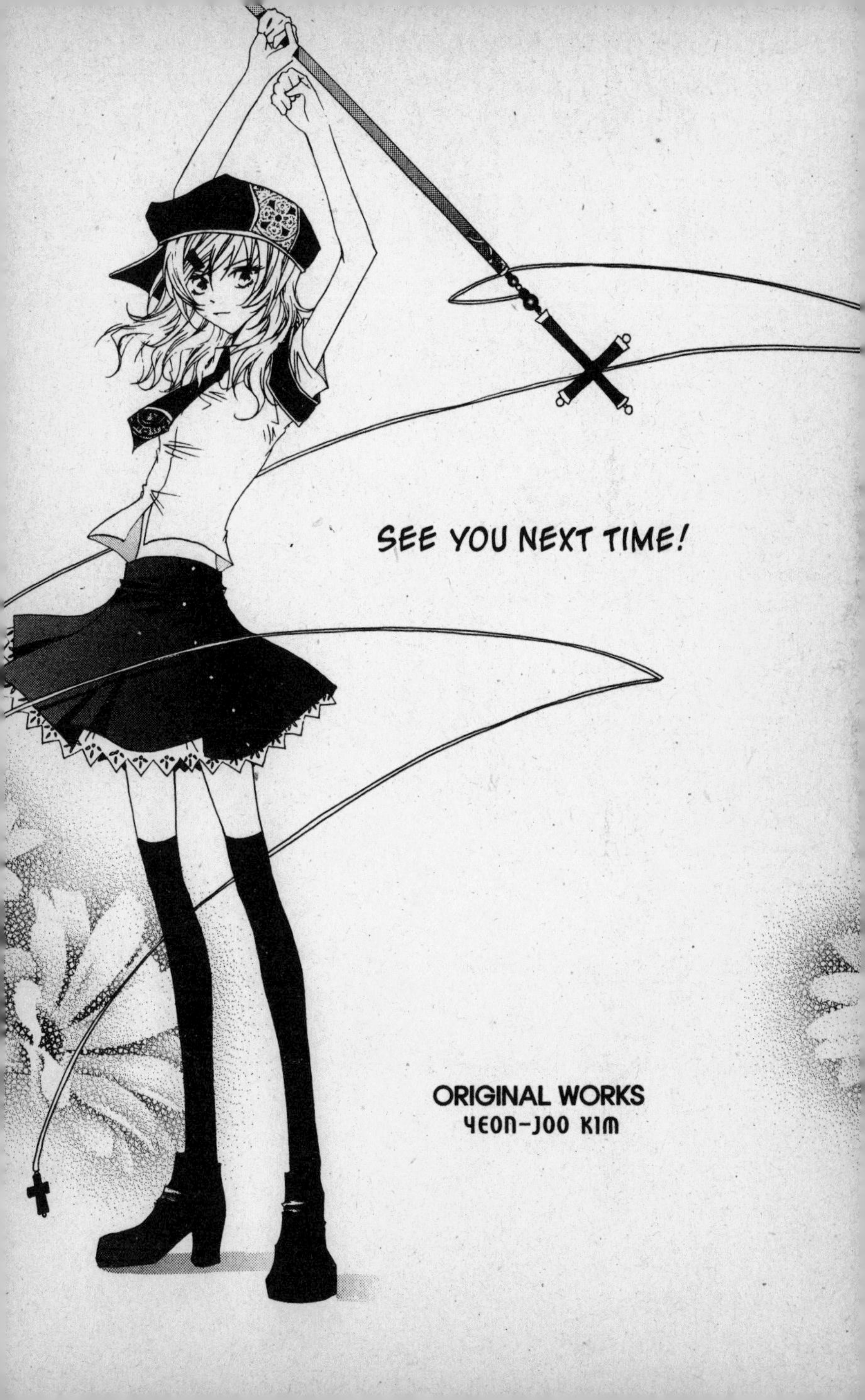
SEE YOU NEXT TIME!
ORIGINAL WORKS
YEON-JOO KIM

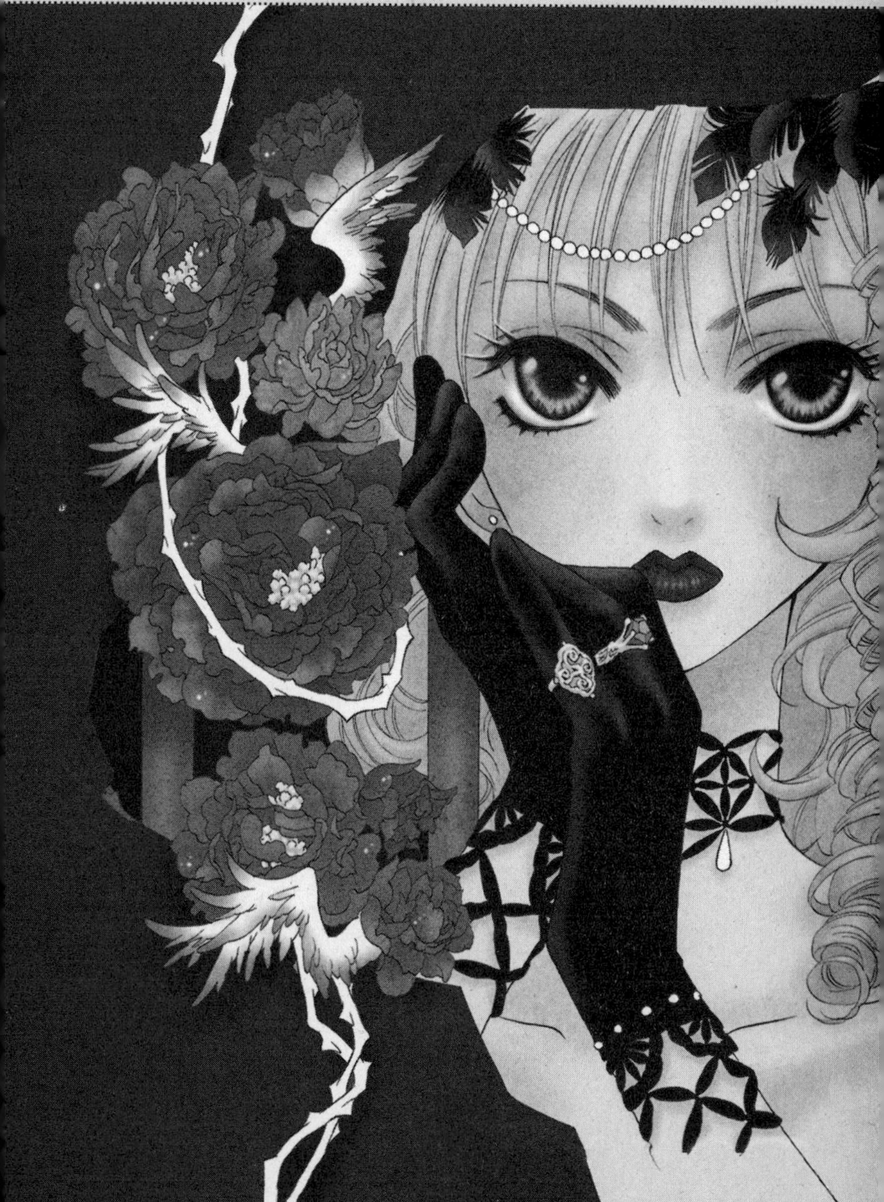

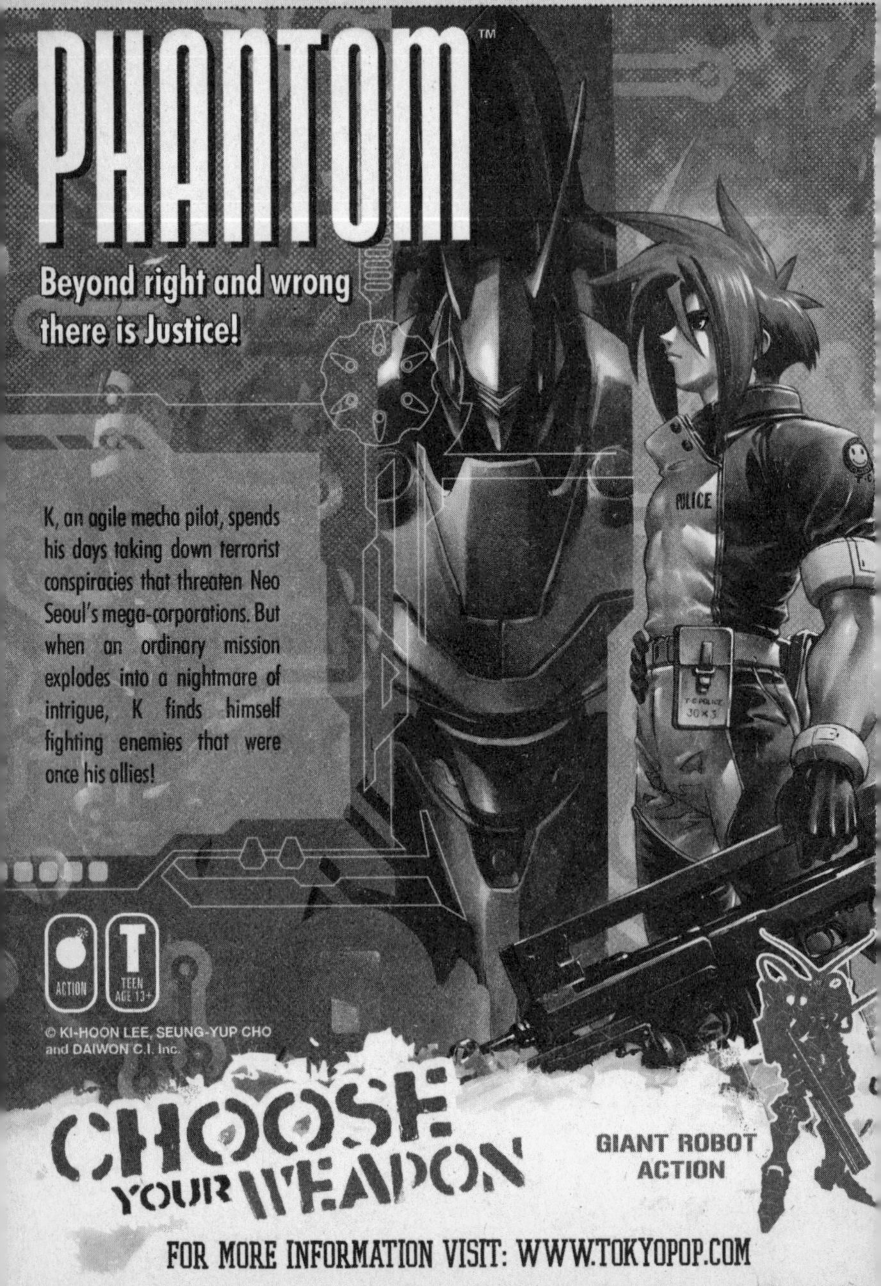
PHANTOM™
Beyond right and wrong there is Justice!
K, an agile mecha pilot, spends his days taking down terrorist conspiracies that threaten Neo Seoul's mega-corporations. But when an ordinary mission explodes into a nightmare of intrigue, K finds himself fighting enemies that were once his allies!
ACTION
T TEEN AGE 13+
© KI-HOON LEE, SEUNG-YUP CHO and DAIWON C.I. Inc.
CHOOSE YOUR WEAPON
GIANT ROBOT ACTION
FOR MORE INFORMATION VISIT: WWW.TOKYOPOP.COM